W9-ANF-111

FORT WORTH PUBLIC LIBRARY

3 1668 02078 0604

391.009 LISTER
Lister, Margot.
Costume : an illustrated
survey from ancient times
to the twentieth century /

JAN 1 0 1998

CENTRAL LIBRARY

Costume: An Illustrated Survey from Ancient Times
to the Twentieth Century

Costume: An Illustrated Survey from Ancient Times to the Twentieth Century

by Margot Lister

Publishers   PLAYS, INC.   *Boston*

© 1968 by Margot Lister

First American edition published by
PLAYS, INC. 1968

Reprinted 1993

All Rights Reserved
No part of this publication may be reproduced, stored
in a retrieval system, or transmitted in any form or by
any means, electronic, mechanical, photocopying or
otherwise, without prior permission of the copyright owner.

Library of Congress Catalog Card Number: 67–29412
ISBN: 0 8238 0096 2

Printed in the United States of America

CONTENTS

PREFACE

It has been my aim in this book to give a true over-all impression of the dress worn in the periods under consideration, and at the same time to provide as much detailed information as possible. I hope that the drawings and their captions, in conjunction with the text, will combine to achieve this.

The descriptions of colour and materials are intended to offer suggestions not only for the use of both in accordance with contemporary taste and resources, but also to complete the representation of individual costumes. As the dyes and stuffs existing today must obviously be utilized for practical purposes, I have written of them in modern terms. Colours known or believed to have been available have been ascribed to the dress of some early centuries in which the fading of old paintings has made the definition of colour uncertain.

I have adapted the conventionalized human figures in some of this ancient art to more realistic forms, and have been fortunate in finding references which explain the arrangement of many draperies, both conventionalized and naturalistic. Where I have not found the guidance of a previous investigator, I have made use of my own deductions.

My thanks are due to the publishers for their forbearance during the time it has taken to write and illustrate the book. I should like especially to thank Mr T. W. Eagle, of Herbert Jenkins, for his kindness and encouragement. I am also indebted to A. and C. Black for permission to quote from the works of Mary Houston and Lucy Barton, and to the museum authorities and librarians who have given me valuable help and facilities.

GLOSSARY

Aiguillettes: bobbin-shaped ornaments, often with a tab of silk or velvet, fastening open sleeves or fronts of dresses.

Alb: white linen full-length robe worn by priests.

Arbalest: cross-bow.

Arquebus: early firearm.

Bag-sleeves: bag-shaped sleeves, sewn into bands at wrists, sometimes with inner seam open, mid-14th–mid-15th centuries.

Baldrick: sword-belt, later an ammunition belt for soldiers, worn from shoulder to opposite hip, early times onward.

Barbette: band put under the chin and fastened on the top of the head, worn by women, 12th–14th centuries.

Bases: full, circular skirts of padded pleats worn by men, early 16th century.

Bertha: deep, round collar for women's dresses, usually worn below shoulders, 17th, mid-19th, early 20th centuries.

Bipennis: double-headed axe, Greece, Crete, known in Egypt.

Bliaut: 12th-century dress of fine material, largely pleated, worn by men and women.

Bolero: short open jacket ending above or at the waist.

Bollonais sleeves: sleeves made in many puffs, from shoulders to wrists, late 16th century.

Bongrâce beaddress: flat headdress with veil at back, worn by women, late 15th–early 17th centuries.

Bonnet-shaped cap: head-fitting cap, with frills framing face, 18th century.

Bootbose: lace- or embroidery-topped hose, usually white, worn inside boots and turned over to show at the top, 17th century.

Boss: metal ornament on shield, early times onward.

Braccae, Braes: loose trousers ending below knees or at ankles, and tied in there, Roman, early European.

Brandenburg: greatcoat, late 17th century.

Bucket-top boots: boots with wide tops, mid-17th century.

Butterfly spur leathers: large butterfly-shaped pieces of leather worn over front of instep and holding spurs at the back.

Byecocket: hat with long peak in front, upturned brim at back and long cone-shaped crown, 15th century.

Calasb: folding hood worn by women, latter half 18th century.

Calcei: military boots worn by Romans.

Canions: upper leg coverings worn usually over complete hose, late 16th century.

Canons: garters with deep lace frill turned downward, worn below knees and appearing like frills to the breeches.

Casque: helmet.

Cassock: name given to loose outer wrap or garment, 16th–17th centuries.

Caul: jewelled net worn as women's head-covering, 14th–15th centuries; small cylindrical ornamented cap worn on back of head by women, 16th century.

Chaperon: hat contrived from winding long 'liripipe' (*q.v.*) round cap, later made as complete headgear, mid-14th–15th centuries.

Chasuble: circular cape with aperture for head, Byzantine, 15th century.

Chemisette: insert of linen, lawn, lace, gauze or other delicate material to fill in décolletage, 19th–20th centuries.

Chignon: knot or coil of hair pinned up on the head.

Chiton: Greek tunic.

Chlamys: Greek rectangular cloak.

Circular cloak: see chasuble.

Clavi: strips of purple fabric, later embroidery in various colours, worn on Roman and Byzantine tunics.

Cloak-bag breeches: full breeches banded at the knee, usually bordered with rosettes or bows ending in 'points' (i.e. ends like those of bootlaces).

Coif: close-fitting cap of white linen later embroidered or made in black, 12th–17th centuries.

Copotain: tall crowned hat with moderate sized, often flexible brim, later 16th–early 17th centuries.

Cornet: small version of fontange (q.v.), late 17th century.

Cote: tunic or gown, 12th–15th centuries.

Cote-hardie: gown for men or women, 14th–15th centuries.

Courtepy: very short, hip-belted tunic, latter 14th century.

Crepidae: bootees worn by Romans.

Crinoline: petticoat stiffened by bands of cane, steel or whalebone, 1850s–'60s.

Cuirass: Roman military corselet.

Cyclas or *gardcorps*: outer gown, usually sleeveless, with side and front openings, 13th–14th centuries.

Dagged edges, dagges: edges of material cut in points, scallops or castellated shapes.

Dalmatic, dalmatica: late Roman and Byzantine gown, later a church vestment.

Darabookab: Egyptian barrel-shaped drum.

Dormeuse cap: woman's cap, late 18th century.

Doublet: man's garment ending at waist or hips, late 15th–early 17th centuries.

Dutch breeches: loose breeches not caught in at the knees, early 17th century.

Falchion: cutlass or curved sword.

Falling band: ruff or collar lying flat or turned down.

Farthingale: petticoat stiffened with bands of steel or cane, from early 16th century to early 17th; latterly in form of 'bolsters' tied on at waist.

Fasces: axe bound round with rods and carried as an emblem by Roman lictors.

Feuille morte: name given to material the colour of dead leaves.

Fillet: band tied round the head, Egypt, Greece, Rome, Byzantium, Western European dress to mid-15th century.

French hood: headdress with curved stiffened front and veil or cap at the back, late 15th, greater part of 16th centuries.

Frock: name given to 18th-century men's coat with flat, round collar and skirts neither widely flared nor sloped away.

Gable headdress: headdress with stiffened 'gable' in front, worn by women late 15th, early 16th centuries.

Galon: edging of gold, silver or colour.

Ganache: loose outer garment, 13th century.

Gilet: Inner waistcoat, 19th century.

Goblet cuffs: cuffs extending over the hands in goblet shape from tight-fitting sleeves.

Golilla: lace collar with square-cut base, early 17th century.

Gorget: linen neck-covering, 13th–15th centuries.

Grosgrain: finely ribbed taffetas.

Hanging sleeves: sleeves of over-gown left hanging or put on over other sleeves.

Hauberk: military corselet of mail or leather.

Head-rail: Saxon head-covering for women.

Hennin: cone-shaped or cylindrical headdress for women, 15th century.

Himation: rectangular outer robe worn by Greek men and women.

Houppeland: voluminous gown worn by men and women, late 14th century, greater part of 15th century.

Jerkin: outer garment, usually sleeveless, covering doublet, 16th–17th centuries.

Journade: very short, full, beltless tunic, mid-15th century.

Khat: striped linen headdress worn by the Pharaohs.

Kirtle: petticoat or underskirt, 16th–17th centuries.

Kolobos: Greek tunic.

Lappet: side or back appendage of cap.

Largesse: alms thrown to the poor.

Lettice cap: head-fitting cap of white fur, early 16th century.

Lictor: Roman civil functionary.

Liripipe: long 'tail' depending from hood or chaperon, 14th–15th centuries.

Lorica: Roman military corselet of leather or metal.

Lunette: crescent-shaped ornamentation with straight-lined base.

Lutestring: ribbed silk.

Mahoytered sleeves: sleeves puffed at the shoulders.

Mandillion: short tabard-shaped outer garment for men, side seams open from armpits, late 16th–early 17th centuries.

Maniple: strip of silk embroidery laid across the left wrist of a priest.

Mappa: large handkerchief used by the Romans.

Marie Stuart cap: cap fitting the head with downward curve or point in centre of forehead, mid-16th–early 17th centuries.

Melon hose: see round hose, trunk hose.

Mitre: headdress known in Assyria, Persia and Greece. Bishop's mitre.

Morion: helmet of late 16th–17th centuries.

Morse: fastening of cloak, 12th–14th centuries.

Mule: slipper with front of upper only.

Nebulae headdress: narrow halo-shaped headdress of gauze, 15th century.

Nether-stocks: stockings, as opposed to upper-stocks (q.v.).

Paenula: travelling cloak worn by the Romans.

Pallium (a), *Palla* (b): Roman name of himation worn (a) by men, (b) by women.

Paludamentum: rectangular cloak with corners rounded, worn in Rome and Byzantium.

Paning, panes, pane: material showing through 'slashings' in garments.

Partlet: guimpe or insert of lawn, linen or gauze to fill in the décolletage, late 15th–early 17th centuries.

Pattens: separate platform soles put on over shoes to raise the feet from the ground.

Peascod belly: padded, downward point protruding above doublet-belt, late 16th century.

Pectoral: jewelled decoration worn on the chest.

Pedule: Byzantine high boot of Frankish origin.

Petasos: Greek hat of felt or straw, worn by peasants and travellers.

Petticoat breeches: loose breeches cut to resemble a kilt, mid-17th century.

Phrygian cap: cap with bulging coxcomb peak in front. Persia, Greece, early European dress, 12th century.

Pickadil: see underpropper.

Pinner: flat cap of lawn, lace or embroidery, worn on the top of the head, first half of 18th century.

Plastron: strip of jewelled stuff sewn down the front of open-sided gown from neck to hips.

Points: device of laces and eyelet holes to fasten sleeves to shoulders, tights to under-doublet, etc.

Polonaise: overdress with back pleats and drapery, 18th and late 19th centuries.

Pomander: orange stuck with cloves to dispel odours, often put inside perforated sphere of goldsmith's work.

Pompon: small hair ornament of lace, flowers and ribbons, greater part of 18th century.

Poulaines: very long-toed shoes, 15th century.

Pourpoint: under-doublet, 15th–16th centuries.

Psaltery: ancient and mediaeval stringed instrument, played with a plectrum or with the fingers.

Purple: name given to several forms of red and actual purple, also including indigo blue. Ancient times.

Ramshorn headdress: cap with coiled earpieces, 13th century.

Rebato: large standing collar usually in three curved sections framing the head.

Rebeck: early form of fiddle.

Redingote: outer coat, late 18th–19th centuries.

Retiarius: gladiator bearing a net.

Rhinegrave breeches: see petticoat breeches.

Robe: name given in the present day to a type of draped Egyptian or Persian gown.

Rondel: crescent-shaped, circular or halo-shaped head-dress, 14th–15th centuries.

Round-eared cap: head-fitting cap, first half 18th century.

Round hose: short padded breeches, usually paned to show lining or other material, 16th century.

Samnite: armoured gladiator of particular corps.

Sari: name given in the present day to woman's draped gown, Egyptian New Kingdom.

Secutor: gladiator appointed to follow net-bearer in arena. See retiarius.

Shadow: woman's cap with downward point over brow and extended sides, late 16th–early 17th centuries.

Shift: woman's chemise.

Shoe roses: rosettes decorating the fronts of shoes, late 16th–early 17th centuries.

Shoulder rolls, wings: shoulder decoration covering seam, 16th–early 17th centuries.

Sideless gown: woman's gown open at the sides to the hips, 14th–15th centuries.

Sistrum: form of rattle used in Egyptian religious ceremonies.

Slashes: cuts in garments showing panes (q.v.), late 15th–early 17th centuries.

Spanish hose: long breeches, not fastened at the knees, ending at calves, usually put on at a high waist-level, mid-17th century.

Spoon bonnet: bonnet with crown sloped away towards the back and short flounce hanging there, 1860s.

Standing band, ruff: collar or ruff stiffened to stand upright.

Steinkirk: neckcloth put through buttonholes of coat, 18th century.

Stephane: Greek diadem worn by women.

Stola: gown worn by Roman married women.

Stole: strip of embroidered stuff shaped to put round the neck and hang down in front, worn by priests. Scarf of silk, feathers, velvet or gauze, worn by women, late 18th, early 19th centuries.

Stomacher: panel of trimmed or jewelled stuff, in form of inverted triangle, superimposed on front of bodice, 16th–18th centuries.

Surcote: outer garment, 12th–15th centuries.

Sword-carriage: straps and loops of leather depending from belt to accommodate sword.

Tabard: sleeveless outer garment with open side-seams, worn by men, mid-15th century, and always by heralds.

Tablion: square, oblong or circular appliqué ornament on Byzantine tunics and cloaks.

Tippet: white linen bands with strip hanging down worn tied on above elbows, 14th century. Small fur necklet, 17th–19th centuries.

Toga: Roman outer garment.

Tonsure: name given to the ecclesiastical haircut involving a fringe of hair left round the head with a shaved crown.

Tricorne: three-cornered hat.

Trunk hose: see round hose.

Trunk sleeves: full sleeves from shoulder to wrist, diminishing towards wrist.

Tunica: Roman tunic.—*Talaris:* Late Roman and Byzantine form.

Underpropper: device worn at the back of the neck to make a ruff stand upright.

Upper-stocks: name for early form of breeches, late 15th–early 16th centuries.

Uraeus: royal cobra emblem used as decoration on head-dress and 'aprons'. Egypt.

Venetians: breeches fastening below the knee, late 16th, early 17th centuries.

Vestal virgin: member of an order of Roman priestesses.

Virago sleeves: open puffed sleeves from elbow to wrist, banded by ribbons above the elbow.

Vulture headdress: cap in the form of a vulture worn by Egyptian queens.

Wimple: head and neck covering, 12th–15th centuries.

I ANCIENT EGYPTIAN DRESS

From the examples of Egyptian art that are known to us it is assumed that the dress worn in Egypt 5,000 years ago remained as a foundation of Egyptian costume until the Roman conquest was completed in the 1st century B.C. After this time Greek influence in costume as well as in general culture was increased. Before this time, however, Egyptians wore more varied garments introduced from time to time by foreign nations and adapted to their own taste, as well as their simple traditional dress. Assyrian and early Persian elements intruded as did those of other lands further east. Many of these persisted, so that Asian trends are still found in the later dynasties when Greek and further Persian influences were also established.

In the second millennium before Christ, Egypt gradually became a prosperous Empire. In this period, called the New Kingdom or New Empire, the highest pinnacle of its culture was reached. It is at this time that the beauty and sophistication of Egyptian dress, with its foreign embellishments, are seen at their finest. It is therefore the time in which a knowledge of Egyptian costume finds its most fruitful sources. In the wall paintings and sculpture of the New Empire that remain to us the Pharaohs and their families, the soldiers, priests, courtiers, officials and people are portrayed in the activities of their daily lives. It must be remembered, however, that Egyptian kings and queens are often represented in ceremonial dress attributed only to immortals and not to living human beings, so that there may be doubt in some instances whether a costume could in fact have been worn in life.

DRESS OF THE OLD KINGDOM (3407–2111 B.C.)

Hair—Men: The practice of shaving the head or cropping the hair originated in very early times. Occasionally the natural hair was seen grown to a 'bobbed' length. Boys had their heads shaved but wore one lock of hair at the side of the head to show their youthful status. Men were clean shaven but artificial ceremonial beards were worn by kings and priests.

Hair—Women: Women's hair is seen in Egyptian art grown to a moderate length or 'bobbed', cropped or shaved. It was allowed to grow long in time of mourning. Dancers are seen with the natural hair braided or loose and women servants sometimes had long hair.

Wigs and Headdress: Wigs were worn by the upper classes and by officials and some workers. The wig took the place of headdress to a great extent among Egyptians and was probably a protection from the heat, being woven in such a way as to allow air to reach the head. Priests and some servants are often represented in Egyptian art with shaven heads and without wigs. Circlets and fillets were worn by the upper classes of both sexes.

Garments—Men: Men of the Old Kingdom wore the wrap-over kilt or skirt, reaching from the waist to the thighs, knees, calves or ankles.

Garments—Women: Female dancers, acrobats and many workers wore short kilts like men, but women were more frequently seen in skirts to the ankles. Both types of garment

FORT WORTH PUBLIC LIBRARY

02078 0604

left the upper part of the body bare. Another type of women's dress was a close-fitting tunic with or without wide shoulder-straps from beneath the breasts to the ankles.

Royal Dress: A corselet, held up by two broad shoulder-straps or a single one, is seen in the paintings of the Egyptian kings of the period. They wore a knee-length kilt with an animal's tail, later artificial and conventionalized, hung from the back of the belt as a ceremonial accompaniment of the costume. They are usually represented as wearing the Red Crown of Lower Egypt or the bottle-shaped White Crown of Upper Egypt, or a combination of both, and are often armed with a club or curved sword. Queens appear at this time in the close-fitting tunic already described.

a   b   c

I.1. Old Kingdom Onwards

Hair: (a) The hair is unseen, possibly shaved. (b) The hair is parted in the centre and hangs in a straight, even line at the bottom. (c) Unseen beneath the headdress.

Headdress: (a) The Pharaoh of the Old Kingdom wears the White Crown of Lower Egypt, probably made of stiffened linen or leather. (c) The Pharaoh, in a dress seen in Egyptian art throughout its history, wears the khat or linen headdress, in blue and white stripes. An uraeus or cobra of gold, jewels and enamel is fastened to a gold band which encircles the head beneath the folds of the headdress.

Garments: (a) The Pharaoh wears a single garment of natural-coloured linen, fastened on the left shoulder and leaving the right shoulder bare. (b) The man is wrapped in a large rectangle of natural-coloured wool. It is first hung in shawl-fashion over both shoulders, leaving a good part of the length in the right hand and with the left shoulder-covering placed diagonally across the body. The length in the right hand is wound round the body, passing round the back beneath the left shoulder-covering but over that on the right, so that the right arm is covered, and supported, across the body again and round the back and tucked in under the right arm. (c) The kilt is of white linen, the front of it bearing a Royal apron of stiffened linen, appliquéd in many colours and wider at the base than at the waist. Its central panel of ornament is of green, blue and red enamel set in gold and adorned with gold beads, also a gold uraeus, bearing the sacred disc on its head, at each of the lower corners.

Footwear: (b) The man wears simple sandals of natural leather, with a strap round the ankle just above the heel meeting another from the sole on either side.

Jewellery and Accessories: (a) The Pharaoh wears a broad belt with a real or artificial animal's tail hanging from it. This was a royal emblem. He has a club in his right hand. (b) The man carries a staff, of the type often used by Egyptians when walking. (c) The Pharaoh wears a wide collar of gold, green enamel and lapis lazuli and gold armlets set with green enamel.

Footwear: Feet were generally bare during this epoch.

Materials and Colours: Linen of varying thickness, some of it spun to gossamer fineness, was the most favoured material of Egyptian dress. Wool was used mainly as a protection against cold. From very early times the art of stiffening, pleating and goffering linen garments was practised, though more lavishly in the later periods than in the dress of the Old Kingdom. Shades of wine-red, terracotta, vermilion, yellow, green, indigo and a lighter blue with the use of a good deal of white, and of black as contrast, were among the colours employed. Designs were appliqués or set into material by needlework and were geometrical in pattern or had conventionalized flowers as their motifs.

Jewellery: The beaded collar which is so distinctive of Egyptian dress was in use at the time of the Old Kingdom. It was worn by the wealthier classes but does not appear in the dress of the workers.

Bracelets and necklaces were often composed of beads strung together in different combinations of colours and geometrical designs. The goldsmiths' work in more elaborate jewellery was already of great beauty. The circlets of delicately wrought flowers, usually conventionalized lotus or papyrus blossoms, alternating with jewels or rosettes of gold are as exquisite as much of the later work.

DRESS OF THE MIDDLE KINGDOM (2111–1576 B.C.)

There were few alterations in the costume of this epoch from that of the Old Kingdom. A short rectangular cape, with two corners fastened together over the chest, was worn by both sexes. The same applied to a large rectangular shawl or blanket of thick woollen stuff, often striped, and variously draped, sometimes put on round the shoulders as a simple wrap, at others enclosing one arm and hand in a swathe of the material. This seems to have been merely a casual addition to the dress as a protection against cold.

The Uraeus, or cobra, had now become a royal emblem and appeared at the front of circlets for the head and as a decoration of royal bracelets, necklets and Pharaonic aprons, while the hawk also appeared as a symbol of protection for royalty.

Hair and Headdress: There was little change from the preceding period in the wigs or arrangement of the natural hair of men or women.

Garments—Men: A skirt or tunic of transparent linen over a short kilt was an innovation in men's dress of this period.

Garments—Women: No change is to be noted in women's dress at this time.

Footwear: Plain leather or hempen sandals, with a thong between the big and second toes, leading to one round the ankle and another over the instep, were now occasionally seen.

Royal Dress: This remained much as it had been formerly.

Materials and Colours: These were identical with those of the Old Kingdom.

Jewellery: It is in jewellery that greater elaboration and variety of design are seen. The pectoral, with a counterweight worn at the back, is an addition to the beaded collar, worn by royalty and high officials.

DRESS OF THE NEW KINGDOM (1596–525 B.C.)

In the profusion of art produced during this period more diversity and elegance in dress are represented than in previous epochs.

Innovations are the introduction from Assyria and Asiatic sources of military corselets and hauberks of a different type from those already known in Egypt; the 'T-shaped tunic', which

I.2. Egyptian Priests, Workers, Dancers

Hair: (a), (b), (c) and (d) The four priests have shaven heads. (e), (f) and (h) The three male workers have their hair cut in a 'bob', the front hair being brought forward in a short fringe. (g) The female gleaner has her hair over her forehead in a fringe and long at the back. (i) and (j) The male dancer and flute-player have their hair cut similarly to that of (e), (f) and (h). (k) and (l) The female harpist and dancer have hair only a little longer than that of the men, fringed in front like theirs.

Headdress: (k) and (l) The harpist and dancer have white fillets binding their hair, put on near the top of the head.

Garments: The garments of the four priests are of white linen. (a) has narrow shoulder-straps to hold up his plain, close-fitting gown. (b) has a 'skirt' arranged in folds or pleats, with a band at the waist and strips and loops of its own material at the sides. A pleated band is worn diagonally from left shoulder

may have reached Egypt from any one of a number of neighbouring or near eastern countries; the 'robe', a Persian garment of ancient origin which had been adopted in Egypt at this time; and the shawl or 'sari', draped in various ways to form the graceful gowns worn by Egyptian women of position in the paintings and sculpture of this period. It probably reached Egypt from across the Persian Gulf if not actually from India.

Hair and Headdress—Men and Women: The shaven heads and the wigs for both sexes continue to appear. It is thought that women in some cases had their heads shaved to accommodate a headdress.

A fashion of the New Kingdom was to wear a painted cone of perfumed fat on the top of the head. This melted in a warm atmosphere and ran down over the wig or hair. Circlets and fillets still decorated the heads of the well-to-do.

For crowns see Royal Dress.

Garments—Men: The kilts and skirts already mentioned continued to be worn. They were usually rectangular or possibly made in segments to form a semicircle and might be wrapped round the waist, two corners being tied together to form a fastening, or pulled tightly round the body from the back and the ends crossed to hang down in front forming a sort of apron. One form of wrap-round kilt had a triangular piece which hung down beneath the over-wrap. This might be either base-upwards or apex-upwards and it is uncertain whether it was an added piece or part of the garment which had been folded inwards. It is also shown in a larger form as a definite added piece, padded and stiffened and worn outside the over-wrap. Some kilts appear to have had a band at the waist whose ends could be tied as a girdle. Workers who sat at their trade often had a leather patch to reinforce the seat of the kilt.

Men had jerkins of padded linen, often embroidered, on similar lines to the hauberks of the soldiers, which were worn with a 'skirt' or over a robe, probably for warmth.

The robe was a long voluminous garment formed of two rectangles of stuff joined to form a gown usually about 5 feet long by 45 inches wide, which could hang loose from shoulder to hem or be girdled, in these two instances the side seams being joined. It could also be worn with the side seams open. The front length of the garment was in this case drawn to the back and its sides fastened there; the back length was brought round to the front and tied or fastened at waist level. For active pursuits the fullness of the front length could be drawn to one side and fastened under one arm to give greater freedom. The circular opening for the head had a vertical slit in front, the edges of which were tied. The garment could be embroidered at the edges, with an all-over pattern as well.

The T-shaped tunic was in use from ancient times in many Mediterranean or near eastern countries, but seems to have been most worn in Egypt from the time of the New Kingdom onwards. It had a circular opening for the head, with ties, and short sleeves cut in one with the garment. It could vary in length from above the knee to the ankle and fitted the body closely.

Garments—Women: The long, close-fitting sheath gown, now sometimes seen to cover the breasts, with wide shoulder straps, continued to be worn, as did the wrap-round 'skirts' and rectangular shoulder-capes. Female dancers and acrobats and women workers still often

---

to right hip. (c) wears an enveloping cloak, which covers the arms entirely. (d) has on a wrap-round kilt from the waist to the ankles. (e) is a scribe, and wears a transparent white linen 'T'-shaped tunic of calf-length over a short, plain white linen kilt. (f) wears a wrap-round kilt of natural linen. (g) wears a wrapped skirt of natural-coloured linen. (h) wears a loin-cloth of natural linen. (i) and (j) are naked except for a narrow belt of red-and-white stuff diagonally striped and with its ends hanging in front. (k) and (l) are naked.

Jewellery and Accessories: (a) carries a vessel from which he is pouring a libation. (e) is seated on a three-legged stool at a low table. He is writing on his tablets with a reed-pen and has another behind his ear. (f) is a sower and carries a basket of grain as he scatters the seed with his right hand. (g) has a basket on her shoulder, the strap of which she holds in her right hand, while she picks up the fragments of wheat-stalks with her left. (h) is a potter and holds the bowl that he has formed on the mould before him. (j) has a flute and (k) a harp. (l) wears circular gold earrings.

I.3. New Kingdom. Entertainers

Hair: (a) This youth wears his own hair cut to bobbed length and fringed in front. (b) Another has his straight hair similarly cut. (c) The hair is hidden by the headdress. (d) There is one tuft of hair on the crown of the head. The line across the forehead may represent not a cap but the edge of shaved or closely cut hair. (e) The head is shaved, with three tufts left standing. (f) This girl has her hair cut to bobbed length. (g) The drummer wears either her own longish hair, with a fringe in front, or a wig.

Headdress: (b) The upstanding feathers in the fillet denote that the youth is a foreigner. (c) The bottle-shaped headdress, possibly of straw, was worn by 'Mou-Mou' dancers, performers in a religious ceremony. (d) Probably no headdress is worn (see 'Hair'). (f) A round, shallow, ornamented cap of various colours is worn.

Garments: These are all of white or natural linen. (a) wears the straight, close-fitting tunic leaving

wore short kilts. 'Mou-Mou' dancers who took part in religious ceremonies and whose tall headdresses may have been of straw, wore knee-length kilts or sometimes, in the case of women, the sheath gown.

The T-shaped tunic, reaching to the ankles, is seen in paintings of women attendants and musicians.

The 'robe' was worn a great deal by women. They wore the open-sided type, fastened at the back and front as already described, or with the front length left loose and only the back length fastened when brought round to the front. All fastenings of the robe in front for women were at a high-waisted level. They also wore it hanging loose, with sides seamed.

The 'sari', or shawl, was a long, delicately woven scarf, wide enough to reach from the waist to the ground and capable of being draped in various ways.

The author is indebted to Mary Houston and to A. & C. Black Ltd, the publishers of her book, *Ancient Egyptian, Mesopotamian and Persian Costume*, for permission to quote from it the descriptions of four methods of draping the sari. These are as follows, with the lettering as on the rectangular diagram on page 19.

1. 'Take the garment (which should measure about 162 inches by 45 inches) and first tie a cord round the waist and tuck into it corner B at the left-hand side of the waist, pass edge B around the back and round the right side to the front again, then gather up some of the material into pleats and tuck them into the centre front of the waist-cord; now pass it round the back again to the right side; catch up the whole drapery and throw it upwards from the right-hand side of the waist under the left armpit, pass it on round the back and over the right shoulder towards the front, then throw the remaining portion of the garment across the chest and backwards over the left shoulder; take corner A and bring it round under the right armpit, release corner B which was first tucked into the waist-cord and tie it to corner A. The corner C will hang down at the back and the corner D will appear at the bottom hem beside the left ankle.'

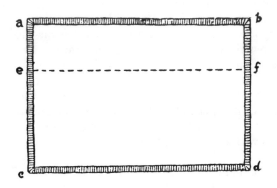

2. 'Take the corner A and hold it at the right side of the waist in front, pass the edge A–B round the back and round the left side to the front again, tuck in some pleats in the centre front and pass the remainder round the back to the left side of the waist under the left arm towards the front; catch up the entire drapery and throw it over the right shoulder, pass the upper edge of the garment round the back of the neck and over the left shoulder

arms and shoulders bare, with one diagonal shoulder-strap. (b) wears a similar tunic, with a strap passing round the back of the neck. (c), (d) and (e) are probably naked to the waist, the Mou-Mou dancer and perhaps the other two wearing a knee-length kilt. Mou-Mou dancers could be men or women and usually wore this kilt, but female dancers of this and other types are sometimes seen in the 'sheath' dress. (f) wears a semi-transparent 'sheath' gown exposing one shoulder. (g) wears the same traditional close-fitting gown, in this case covering the bosom and having two shoulder-straps incorporated.

Jewellery: (d) and (e) have heavy circular earrings of gold or baser metal. (c), (d), (e) and (f) have ornamental collars or necklets in various colours.

Accessories: (a) plays a double flute. (b) a drum resembling an elongated barrel. (f) the long-stemmed, narrow Egyptian guitar. (g) a small drum known as a 'darabookah'.

and downwards across the breast to the right, where the corner B should be tied to the corner A. Corner D hangs down in a point at the back and corner C hangs down near the right ankle.'

3. 'Tie a waist-cord and hold the corner A at the left side of the waist in front, then throw the whole garment upwards over the right shoulder to the back; take the corner C, bring it round under the right arm and hold it together with the corner A; draw the edge A–B (which still hangs over the right shoulder) downwards across the back to the left side of the waist. Bring it round to the front of the waist and pin it to the corners A and C at the left side of the waist in front, passing the garment on round the front; form a few pleats in the centre front and tuck them into the waist-cord, then pass it round the right side of the waist and upwards across the back, over the left shoulder, downwards across the breast to the right side of the waist; here pass a loop of material over the left wrist; now pass a girdle round the waist over the entire drapery and knot it at the right side of the waist, so confining the drapery. The corners A and C are hidden under superimposed drapery at the left side of the waist. The corner B appears near the left hand and the corner D hangs down near the left ankle.'

4. 'Take the corner A and hold it at the right side of the waist in front, pass the edge A–B round the back of the waist to the left side and across the front of the waist, pass it round to the right side again under the right arm and towards the back, now upwards over the left shoulder; tie the corner A to the corner B in front. Here A and B are knotted together, D hangs down "over the left arm" and C is near the right ankle.'

Royal Dress: The Pharaoh was now frequently portrayed wearing the robe, in one or other of its drapings. He usually wore a royal apron of gold and jewels, pendant from a wide jewelled belt, over a kilt which may be covered by a transparent robe hanging loose, or put on over it. It is difficult to determine, because of the conventions of Egyptian painting, just how this combination of garments was worn by the Pharaoh, but the robe was probably left open in front, fastened at a high-waisted level, as with women, and the apron put on over the front length of the robe, which was fastened at the back.

The Pharaoh was sometimes dressed for warfare in a kilt and a cross-over corselet or in a short-sleeved hauberk of mail or of leather sewn with small pieces of bone or metal.

In addition to the Crowns of Upper and Lower Egypt and their combination as one, the Pharaoh now wore the War Crown and the 'khat', or striped linen headdress which was gathered into a queue of the material at the back. The tall Crown of Osiris was given to him in his immortal character as the god. It is a moot point to what extent the high, intricately wrought crowns seen in so much New Kingdom painting were ever actually worn in life.

Queens wore the robe and the sari, as well as the sheath gown. They are seen in sculpture and paintings wearing the vulture headdress, the Crowns of Upper and Lower Egypt, or tall symbolic crowns which may or may not have been actual. Queen Nefertiti in the famous bust wears a high close-fitting flat-topped cap over an apparently shaven head.

Princes and princesses, also wearing robes, saris and kilts or skirts, had a circlet or fillet to keep in place the conventionalized lock of youth attached to the wig.

Footwear: Egyptians went barefoot most of the time, but people of position wore sandals of the various kinds shown in the illustrations to this chapter and women also had shoes of soft stuff or kid in pale colours.

Materials and Colours: Materials were still headed by the miraculously fine linen, stiffened, goffered or pleated. By the time of the New Empire some silk was used by the well-to-do. Cotton was always in use and warm garments were often padded with it.

Colours remained much the same through the centuries until the Persian, Greek and Roman conquests brought greater variety, particularly the clear sea-green, rose-colour and saffron of the Greeks.

Jewellery: The beaded or jewelled collars, pectorals, necklets, earrings and bracelets

I.4. New Kingdom. Egyptian Royal Headdress

Hair: (b) The Pharaoh has his hair or wig cut to a moderate length, with a fringe over the forehead. (c) The Princess has her hair or wig in the usual 'bobbed' cut, with a short fringe in front.

Headdress: (a) This headdress, similar to that worn by Queen Nefertiti in the well-known bust, is of red leather or linen stretched on a stiffened foundation, probably of linen. The bands of decoration are in blue, red, fawn-colour and white. An uraeus of gold, enamel and jewels ornaments the front. (b) The Pharaoh wears a tall, elaborate crown of gold, jewels and enamel. It is uncertain whether crowns of this type were worn in actuality or whether their presence in the wall-paintings is symbolic. As many of these paintings are limited in tones, it is not possible to give a definite suggestion of the colour of the decoration. (c) The Princess also wears a possibly symbolic headdress above a fillet of gold. The plumes of Isis which surmount it are supported on a miniature plinth decorated with small cobra-emblems and transfixed by a lotus blossom. A gold-bound artificial 'youth-lock', denoting her youthful status, is attached to the fillet.

were well in evidence in this epoch. All jewels were of course unfaceted and most were semi-precious, such as turquoise, lapis lazuli, cornelian and amethyst.

Military Dress: Many soldiers of the Egyptian army were mercenaries from other lands. They wore a version of Egyptian dress or sometimes a kilt or hauberk of their own country, e.g. the Cretan kilt, and a distinctive helmet or cap that indicated their foreign nationality. Feathers in the headdress were an indication of foreign origin and some bands of mercenaries are represented as wearing a single upright feather on the top of the head.

The Egyptian soldiers were bare-headed or wore striped headdresses of linen or yarn or a cap with tassels on the crown. They were naked to the waist as a rule, wearing kilts of varying designs, but sometimes hauberks of mail, leather or stout yarn by the time of the New Empire. They had oblong shields, some very large, and fought with spears, curved swords, slings, javelins, hatchets and bows and arrows. Their shields were arched or pointed at the top and rectangular or slightly spreading at the base.

I.5. Egyptian Girl. Old, Middle and New Kingdoms

Hair: This is covered entirely by the wig, which is dressed across the forehead without parting and arranged in curled segments closely stitched together.

Garments: The dress is the closely fitting sheath-gown, put on below the breasts. In this case it has one diagonal shoulder-strap attached to the top of the gown. It is of pale green linen, patterned in blue.

Jewellery and Accessories: The girl wears heavy circular gold earrings and carries a basket of grapes.

I.6. Boy Pharaoh. Middle or New Kingdom

Hair: The hair, or shaved head, is covered by the head-dress.

Headdress: This is the Red Crown of Lower Egypt. It has a thin antenna-like ornament in front, of gold wire or feathers.

Garments: The Pharaoh wears a pleated white linen 'skirt', drawn upward and wrapped over in front and covered by a royal apron enamelled and jewelled in many colours, depending from a belt. The upper part of his body is bare except for collar and bracelets.

Footwear: The gilded leather sandals are of the kind worn by Egyptian royalty, with soles protruding beyond the toes and curved upward, a broad instep-band raised in a curve and a thong meeting it from between the first two toes.

Jewellery and Accessories: The ornamental collar extends to cover the points of the shoulders and is decorated with green and gold beads. The armlets are of gold, green enamel and cornelian and are rigid or segmented. The Pharaoh carries the short stick used in play or for minor punishments.

I.7. Pharaoh. New Kingdom

Hair: This is hidden by the headdress.

Headdress: The khat, or royal head covering of blue and white striped linen, is formed into a bag-shape, fastened into a kind of queue at the back. A gold uraeus or royal cobra-emblem is attached to a gold band over the forehead. The artificial, conventionalized ceremonial beard is kept in place by a band attached to the forehead-band.

Garments: The white linen wrap-over kilt is covered by the Royal apron, probably of leather, decorated with enamel, jewels and glass of various colours. The lowest row of ornament consists of small cobra-emblems. The belt is ornamented and the Pharaoh's 'cartouche' (name-plate) is on the front of it. The shoulder-cape of stiffened and pleated white linen is supported by bands of the same stuff, crossing the upper part of the body.

Footwear: The Pharaoh wears royal sandals, extended into a turned-up point beyond the toes.

Jewellery and Accessories: The collar and armlets are of beads, gold, glass, jewels and enamel. The Pharaoh carries a royal emblem, the symbol of life, in his right hand and a sceptre-like staff in his left.

I.8. Pharaoh with Flail and Crook

Hair: The hair is unseen beneath the headdress.

Headdress: The Pharaoh wears the Red Crown of Upper Egypt, with a gold jewelled and enamelled uraeus in front.

Garments: The Pharaoh's garment is the robe, made in transparent white linen. The front length of the un-seamed garment is fastened together at the back of the waist, while the back length is brought together at the breast in front and the remainder allowed to hang loose. The belt and royal apron, decorated with gold, cornelian, lapis and red and green enamel, are put on over the front length of the robe but under the back length. The apron is ornamented with a lion's head in gold and eight small golden cobra-emblems bearing the sacred disc on their heads. The Pharaoh's cartouche, or name-plate, appears in the centre of the belt and hieroglyphic writing in the middle of the apron.

Footwear: The Pharaoh has on the long pointed sandals with upturned toes worn by royalty. These are of gilded leather.

Jewellery and Accessories: The beaded collar, armlets and bracelets are in the same colours and jewels as the belt and apron. The Pharaoh carries royal emblems, the flail and crook.

I.9. Pharaoh. New Kingdom

Hair: This is covered by the headdress.

Headdress: The Pharaoh wears a blue war crown, probably of stiffened linen or leather, with an uraeus decorating the front and streamers hanging at the back.

Garments: The corselet, which leaves a good deal of the midriff bare, and the belt are probably of linen or leather. The device of hawks, with wings spread over the Pharaoh's chest, was believed to give him special protection. The white linen wrap-over kilt has a central strip hanging in front and laid in pleats. The animal's tail is an appurtenance dating from the Old Kingdom, and is artificial and conventionalized.

Footwear: The gilt sandals have an instep band and central thong, the former being broad in the middle. The soles turn upward beyond the toes.

Jewellery and Accessories: The Pharaoh wears an ornamental collar of many colours. He carries a pole-axe and club.

I.10. Egyptian Prince. New Kingdom

Hair: The hair is hidden by the wig, which is curled in closely formed segments and has no parting.

Headdress: Attached to the white fillet, which ties at the back, is a conventionalized 'youth lock', in various colours, probably made of leather and stiffened linen. This was worn by the sons of the Pharaoh to show their youthful status during his lifetime.

Garments: The prince wears the Robe in white linen, with a separate folded girdle or sash wound round the waist and hips.

Footwear: The sandals of white leather have a band over the top of the instep and a thong meeting this, coming from between the big and second toes.

Jewellery and Accessories: The prince wears a collar in red and green enamel and gold beads and carries the special single-feather fan bestowed on the Friends of the Pharaoh.

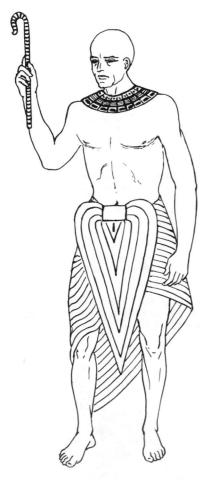

I.11. Pharaoh in Military Kilt. New Kingdom

Hair: The head is closely shaven.

Garments: The military kilt of pleated white linen has the additional front of stiffened linen worn by soldiers. The kilt is draped in such a way that one corner of its rectangular shape hangs down at the back of the right leg, while the three other corners are wrapped in at the waist.

Jewellery and Accessories: He wears an ornamented collar of gold beads and lapis lazuli and carries the crook, a royal emblem.

I.12. Egyptian Priest. New Kingdom

Hair: This is hidden by the wig. The small chin-beard is artificial and worn for ceremony. The wig has no parting, hangs down all round from the crown of the head and is formed into ringlets, touching the shoulders.

Garments: The priest wears a white linen pleated 'kilt', wrapped round the body and tied so that the ends fall to ankle-level down the front. There is a wide diagonal band of pleated linen from the right hip over the left shoulder, to keep the kilt in place. A conventionalized leopard skin is worn over the left shoulder, with one front paw laid over the left arm and the other apparently used as a fastening at the back, passed under the right arm. The rest of the 'body' of the 'skin' is brought forward over the right side and part of the front of the kilt. The gold artificial head of the leopard holds in its mouth the royal ceremonial apron, which is beaded, enamelled and jewelled in many colours.

Footwear: The sandals have a band round the top of the instep and a thong between the two first toes.

Jewellery and Accessories: The priest wears a double collar of thick gold segments, and an armlet of gold and enamel. He carries an incense burner.

I.13. Egyptian Queen. New Kingdom

Hair: The wig is arranged at the back in curled or plaited segments. The front is hidden by the headdress. The traditional 'vulture' headdress, dating from the Old Kingdom, is made of linen or leather, gilded and coloured, with the vulture's head in front made of gold and jewels.

Garments: The pale yellow 'sari' dress is draped in Style 1, described in Chapter I.

Footwear: The slippers of gilded linen or kid are decorated in a criss-cross design and have a strap or band over the instep threaded through a thong coming from above the toes.

Jewellery and Accessories: The queen wears a jewelled, green-enamelled collar and drop earrings of unfaceted green jewels and goldsmith's work. She carries a metal looking-glass.

I.14. Queen or Royal Lady

Hair: The natural hair is worn flowing down the back, with a short fringe in front.

Headdress: A broad fillet of striped linen, in blue, yellow and white, is tied at the back with strips of yellow linen.

Garments: Over a plain, close-fitting 'skirt' from beneath the breasts to the ankles is the Robe, unseamed, with the front length hanging loose and that at the back brought round to be tied together beneath the breasts, and then to hang loose. Both are of parchment-yellow linen. A diagonal shoulder-strap, striped in blue and yellow, holds the skirt in place.

Footwear: The sandals are those worn by royalty, with upturned toes, and made of gilded leather.

Jewellery and Accessories: The bracelets and beaded collar have ornaments of gold, lapis and green enamel. An ivory sistrum, or rattle, used in religious observances, is carried in the right hand and an incense burner in the left.

I.15. Egyptian Queen. New Kingdom

Hair: The queen's hair or wig is entirely covered by her headdress.

Headdress: The headdress of gilded leather has a fillet with a jewelled gold uraeus or cobra-emblem in front worn over it.

Garments: The gown is a sheath in violet linen, put on below the breasts, and flowing out in a flare on either side below the knees. Its two shoulder-straps are joined between the breasts. A vertical strip of gilded material ornamented in blue and gold decorates the front of the dress. The lines could represent stripes or pleats.

Footwear: The slippers are of gilded kid, with criss-cross decoration, and have a central thong meeting a narrow band across the top of the instep.

Jewellery and Accessories: The beaded collar is ornamented in gold and blue lapis lazuli. The queen carries three papyrus flowers.

I.16. Egyptian Woman. New Kingdom

Hair: The hair is hidden by the wig. The thick, rather unwieldy wig is made in closely curled, plaited or crimped formations and is unusually wide.

Headdress: The round, ornamented cap of stiffened linen or leather is of a size to accommodate the wig. It is ornamented in red and black on a yellow ground.

Garments: The white linen 'sari' gown is draped in style 2, described in Chapter I.

Footwear: The red slippers have a central thong through which the ankle-strap is passed.

Jewellery and Accessories: The bracelet is rigid or hinged in segments and is of gold, ornamented in black and red. The collar is of black, red and yellow beads and enamel. Two lotus buds are carried.

I.17. Egyptian Woman with Stoppered Jar. New Kingdom

Hair: The wig is dressed in small segments and has a centre parting with a circular ornament at the level of the cheekbones on either side. A circlet or fillet is worn high on the forehead.

Garments: The 'sari' type of gown of orange linen sewn all over in gold thread is draped in style 3, described in Chapter I, 'Garments—Women'.

Footwear: The slippers, of fine natural-coloured basket-work, have ankle and instep bands and a thong, meeting these, from above the toes, arched over the foot.

Jewellery and Accessories: The ornamental collar is of gold beads and green enamel and the matching bracelets are rigid or segmented and jointed. The pottery, glass or metal jar held in the left hand could hold unguent or perfume.

I.18. Egyptian Woman. New Kingdom

Hair: The wig is dressed with a centre parting and each of its tightly curled or plaited segments ends in a small corkscrew curl.

Headdress: The two fillets are of pink woven stuff; one binds the head at the level of the forehead and the other keeps back the thick hair of the wig. Both are tied at the back. The perfume cone has lotus-flowers thrust through it by the stems.

Garments: The semi-transparent 'sari' type of gown of parchment-coloured linen is draped in style 4, described in Chapter I.

Footwear: The soft slippers are of pink kid or linen, orna-mented with stripes and with a central thong over the front of the foot through which the ankle-strap is threaded.

Jewellery: The beaded collar is of chalcedony and black enamel. The earrings are gold.

I.19. Egyptian Soldier with Falchion. New Kingdom

Hair: The headdress covers the hair or shaved head.

Headdress: A striped linen head-cloth in red and white, binds the brow, with the remainder of the fullness covering the head.

Garments: A wrap-round kilt in white pleated linen has an extra piece depending at the back and seen between the legs. The upper part of the body is naked.

Footwear: The leather sandals have bands round the ankles and under the arch of the foot, and a thong from between the big and second toes meeting in the front of the instep.

Accessories: The soldier carries a falchion, or curved sword, and a spear, also a shield of wood and leather. This is held to the upper part of his left arm by a leather band at the back and is supported by a strap encircling his waist.

I.20. Egyptian Soldier with Bow and Arrow. New Kingdom

Headdress: The tasselled military cap, of which the front view is seen in the 'Soldier with Sword and Shield' is boldly striped in red and white, probably of coarse linen, and may have been padded to protect the head. It fits closely, showing the ears and covering all the hair and is fringed along the back of the neck.

Garments: The soldier wears a white linen kilt, wrapped over in front and ending a little above the knees. His corselet is of leather or horsehair.

Footwear: The leather sandals are of the same type as those worn by the 'Soldier with Falchion'.

Accessories: The quiver is slung from the right shoulder to left hip and hangs at the left front of the body. The bow is slung on the left shoulder and held by the left hand. The soldier also carries a double-headed axe.

I.21. Egyptian Soldier with Sword and Shield. New Kingdom

Hair: The cap entirely covers the hair.

Headdress: The military cap, probably of striped, coarse linen in red and white may have been padded and has two tassels attached at the top of the head.

Garments: The kilt is of white pleated linen, with the military adjunct of a separate front of stiffened, possibly padded linen. The corselet is probabiy of leather or horsehair.

Accessories: The soldier carries a short sword and a shield of leather stretched on wood, with a leather band inside through which his left hand is thrust. The arched shape of the top of the shield has a point.

I.22. Egyptian Man with Scroll and Reed Pen. New Kingdom

Hair: The man is wearing his own hair, grown fairly long at the back and cut in a fringe across the forehead.

Garments: The white linen waist-to-ankle 'skirt' appears to be seamed so that the wearer steps into it and to be tied at the front of the waist either by separate ties or twists of its own material. The semi-transparent rectangular cape is also of fine white linen thrown over the left shoulder and tied by the two corners of one end under the right arm.

Footwear: The sandals have the usual instep-band and central thong.

Accessories: The man holds a papyrus scroll and reed-pen.

I.23. Egyptian Man with Wine-jar. New Kingdom

Hair: The segments of the front part of the wig are laid across the head from side to side in three parallel rows, without a parting. At the back the segments are horizontal.

Garments: The man wears a thigh-length wrap-over kilt in white linen with a broad belt and tie in front. Over it he has a transparent white 'T'-shaped tunic, in this case longer at the back than the front. His tunic dates probably from the Old Kingdom, but was worn throughout the periods of the Middle and New Kingdoms.

Accessories: He is holding the cord handles of a large wine- or water-jar.

I.24. Priest-Harpist. New Kingdom

Hair: The head is shaven.

Garments: The priest wears the Robe, seamed down the sides and allowed to hang loosely. It is of white linen.

Footwear: The sandals are woven of fine basket-work.

Jewellery and Accessories: The beaded collar is ornamented with red and gold beads and black enamel. The large harp has ornamentation of gold, blue, green and white and bears a replica of the Pharaoh's head, wearing the Red Crown.

I.25. Foreign Female Attendant. New Kingdom

Hair: This is covered by the wig.

Headdress: The thick, curled wig is surmounted by a round, decorative cap, a perfume cone and two lotus blossoms.

Garments: The dress of multi-coloured beads, jewels and black net, with a gold clasp between the breasts, is not Egyptian but is taken from the costume of a group of dancing girls of foreign origin.

Jewellery and Accessories: The beaded collar has a higher neck-band than is usual. The girl carries a fan of parchment, feathers or slivers of leather mounted on wood and metal or ivory. The bracelets and armlet are probably of gold or ivory and set with jewels or enamel.

I.26. Girl Musician with Tambourine. New Kingdom

Hair: The thick, curled wig has a decorative band in red and green round the head at the top of the forehead with massed ringlets falling over it from a centre parting.

Garments: The girl is wearing the Robe in pale green linen, with the two edges of the front breadth pinned together at the back and the edges of the back breadth brought to the front and fastened at a high-waisted level.

Footwear: The slippers of pale green decorated with red, with a central thong meeting the instep band have rather thicker soles than usual.

Jewellery and Accessories: A collar of beads, enamel and unfaceted jewels in green and red is worn. The instrument is a tambourine. A variant of this shape could have the two short sides made straight instead of curved inward and a piece of framework parallel with these, in the centre, forming a partition down the middle of the instrument. It could also be made in the more familiar circular shape.

I.27. Egyptian Girl with Lyre. New Kingdom

Hair: The natural hair is fringed in front and drawn back behind the ears, where it forms thin, separate ringlets reaching the shoulders.

Headdress: The round, ornamented cap in blue, green and black leather is set on the top of the head. It has a perfume cone on the top.

Garments: The gown is the 'T'-shaped tunic, in white linen, fitting closely to the figure.

Footwear: The sandals of green leather have a band over the instep, met by one from between the two first toes. Another comes upwards from the heel and all three meet at the ankle strap.

Jewellery and Accessories: The girl wears a collar of gold, lapis lazuli and green enamel with a high neck-band and large hoop earrings of gold. She carries a seven-stringed lyre. This instrument could have five, seven, ten or eighteen strings. In this instance the two 'limbs' are of different lengths, enabling the player to push the strings along the transverse bar to tune them. When the two limbs were of equal length, the strings were tightened by being rolled round the transverse bar. The lyre could be played by means of a plectrum or with the two hands.

I.28. Egyptian Female Attendant. New Kingdom

Hair: The hair is cut to a moderate length and has a fringe in front.

Headdress: The fillet is placed high on the head and tied at the back. The perfume cone on top of the head is probably of soft, painted wax and would gradually melt in a warm atmosphere, sending a sweet-smelling grease over the hair and forehead.

Garments: The girl wears a transparent, ungirdled version of the Robe in sea-blue as her sole garment, with a beaded collar.

Accessories: The beaded collar is of lapis, gold and pearl. She carries a small bowl containing perfume or unguent.

I.29. Egyptian Female Attendant. New Kingdom

Hair: The wig is arranged from a centre parting in plaited or crimped formations attached to each other at the sides.

Headdress: The fillet of gold thread is placed high on the head and a perfume cone set on the top.

Garments: The shoulder-cape of parchment-yellow is transparent and the high-waisted, matching skirt, with one diagonal shoulder-strap, could also be so.

Jewellery and Accessories: The beaded collar is put on over the shoulder-cape and is of gold, amber and cornelian. The girl carries a tall fan of parchment or linen 'leaves'.

I.30. Egyptian Girl Attendant with Wine-jar and Wine-skin. New Kingdom

Hair: The girl's own shoulder-length hair is parted in the centre.

Headdress: The hair is held back by a green ribbon which passes round the back of the hair and is tied there, then brought round and secured underneath it in front, on each side of the face, presumably by combs or prongs attached to the band.

Garments: The 'sheath' gown is of pale sea-green linen, with one shoulder-strap incorporated.

Jewellery and Accessories: The necklace of deep blue stones or beads has pendant drops all round. The girl holds a Greek wine-skin of dressed and ornamented leather in her left hand and an Egyptian wine- or water-jar on her right shoulder.

II BIBLICAL DRESS

The people of the Old Testament derived their costume from the many different nations and tribes with whom they lived under protection or in captivity or whom they conquered. In their wanderings and sojournings and their eventual life in Palestine the Hebrews absorbed the culture and copied the dress first of the inhabitants of Chaldean cities 2000 years B.C., and later of the Egyptians, Assyrians, Babylonians, Persians, Greeks and Romans.

At some time in the early stages of Chaldean civilization the main garments of the Ancient World appeared: the rectangular shawl or cloak and the kilt or skirt. The forebears of Abraham would have worn such clothing, made of sheepskin or other animal hide or coarsely woven stuff. More urban populations evolved the close-fitting tunic, the kilt of linen or woollen stuff, and the finely woven shawls, with jewellery of beads, gold wire, thin plates of gold and delicate inlay.

At the outset of their wanderings under the guidance of Abraham, the Hebrews are thought to have worn the tunic or the kilt, ornamented in many colours, with the shawl to form a cloak. At some unknown date, probably about 1000 B.C., the change was made to the nomad's headdress of a square of cloth folded cornerwise and bound on with a cord, the loose open coat with wide sleeves and the gown with a broad girdle such as desert dwellers have worn through the ages. Similar dress, with a veil for the head, is thought to have been worn by women. These garments have been assumed to form the basis of traditional Hebrew dress, and although it is impossible to assign definite dates or to be sure when the costume obtained its footing, it seems reasonable to suppose that it existed, along with other types of dress, in New Testament times.

There are, however, no pictorial records of the dress of the Hebrews except in those of the nations who held them captive. We assume, therefore, that when their journeying brought them to Egypt, their dress followed the trend of traditional Egyptian costume. The Canaanites in the Promised Land provided an Assyrian culture, which also influenced the Phoenicians and the Philistines. The Court of Solomon may have displayed mixed Assyrian and Egyptian influences of the New Empire, and the Assyrian ascendancy from the 9th to the 6th century B.C. must have resulted in continued adherence to Assyrian styles. The Persian rule that followed must in its turn have influenced the costume of the Hebrews. Greek dress entered the situation after the conquest of Persia and its provinces by Alexander the Great and remained in Graeco-Roman form to lend its character to representations of Christ and His followers. Some characteristics of the dress worn in Palestine before and during the Christian development, however, are definitely connected with the eventual independent Hebrew culture. At a later stage Byzantine dress influenced the painters of Christian religious subjects in their choice of costume.

CHALDEAN DRESS

Hair—Men: In the third millennium B.C. shaved heads and a small fringe of beard round the chin distinguished the men of early Chaldea. There is evidence that men in approximately 2800 B.C. had long hair put up in a chignon and bound with a fillet (see 'Babylonian Dress').

a   b   c   d

II.1. Chaldean–Babylonian. About 2000 B.C. Four Figures

Hair: (a) Man of ancient Semitic tribe. The hair is cut in Egyptian fashion, in a straight 'bob' with a thick uncurled fringe over the forehead. (b) Babylonian ruler. The short curled hair is almost hidden by his headdress. The curled beard is probably artificial. (c) Babylonian woman. The hair is arranged in the fashion that obtained for many centuries in various countries of the Ancient World, including Crete and Greece. It is parted in the centre and formed into a figure-of-eight chignon, set vertically at the back of the head. (d) Babylonian-Assyrian female attendant. The hair is in short thick curls all over the head.

Headdress: (b) The cap of the Babylonian ruler has a crown of red felt. Its deep, upturned, close-fitting brim is encrusted with uncut jewels and small gold ornaments. (c) A gold riband is bound round the head from the forehead and twisted to enclose the centre of the chignon.

Garments—Men: (a) The man is wearing a rectangular wrap or shawl of woollen stuff, with embroidered or appliquéd chevrons in red and blue and fawn-coloured circles. One corner of the rectangle is longer than the others and is drawn backwards over the left shoulder to be fastened to another corner. The right arm is left free, the drapery passing beneath it round the back. The garment is probably open down the left side and worn over a knee-length kilt, also ornamented in colours. (b) The king wears a large draped rectangular shawl of vermilion-dyed woollen stuff bordered with gold. The method of draping it is to be found in Chapter II, page 38.

(c) The woman's draped shawl is of silky material woven from camel's hair and bleached to an ivory colour with a green and gold border. It is draped as follows: It is twice as long as its own width, which covers the wearer from the chest to the feet. The middle of one of the long sides is held against the chest and the rest of the drapery taken under the arms on both sides and crossed at the back. The two corners are then brought forward again over the shoulders and hang down on either side of the chest. The crossing-over at the back, the right side going over the left, results in a close, diagonal draping over the front and back of the body, the garment being deep enough in width to touch the ground at the back. (d) The Babylonian-Assyrian attendant wears a 'T'-shaped tunic with a close, round neckline and sleeves ending above the elbows. It is long enough to touch the ground and is of white linen with a blue fringe and a wide stiffened belt of blue material ornamented in yellow.

Footwear: (a) The man wears sandals of dark brown leather. (b) The king wears slippers of fine leather in bands of white, gold and red. (c) The woman has slippers of white kid, fastening with small jewels over the insteps and encrusted with jewels in various colours on the fronts. (d) The female attendant is bare-footed.

Jewellery and Accessories: (a) The man carries a wooden club. (b) The king wears a necklace of gold. (d) The attendant carries a rigid flag-shaped fan, probably of palm-strands framed in wood or ivory.

Hair—Women: Women's hair, worn long, was piled on the head in braids, twists and curls, or coiled into a lock at the back of the neck. Wigs were worn, as in Egypt, dressed in accordance with the fashion in hairdressing.

Headdress—Men: Hoods, coming well down on the brow, and probably made of two rectangles of felt or wool fastened together and tied under the chin, appear in early Sumerian mosaics. At this time men wore headbands of gold chains and beads of gold and lapis lazuli. They are thought to have held a headcloth in place.

Headdress—Women: Elaborate headdresses, with a foundation of gold wire, or of beads sewn on to a cap of soft leather, carried flowers, leaves, rosettes and tiny models of birds and animals all wrought in gold, with thin strips and plates of gold and gold rings over the forehead. Lapis lazuli, cornelian, chalcedony, agate and various inlays were used in the decoration, which included combs with inlaid gold flowers raised on 'stems' of gold.

Garments—Men: In early times in Sumer kilts ending below the knee or at the calf, probably made of sheepskin or other leather, or of wool or felt, formed the main garments, with cloaks of the same materials.

Padded belts, similar to those worn in Crete (see Chapter III), seem to have been worn in Sumer. At some time between 3000 and 2000 B.C. it would appear that there was wider use of woven material which could be draped, largely superseding sheepskin, leather and the coarser woollen weaves (see drapery described under 'Babylonian Dress', this Chapter).

Garments—Women: Women are represented in practically the same costume as that worn by men, though part of the wrap-over of the kilt could be drawn over one shoulder from the back. Their kilts ended a little above the ankle. Between 3000 and 2000 B.C. there has been evidence that women had woven gowns or coats with long sleeves. Rectangular shawls probably formed outer wraps, worn tied at the neck as capes or draped on the body. A method of draping the shawl was to 'hold one corner under the left armpit, draw it across the back, under the right armpit, across the chest, under the left armpit, across the back, under the right armpit again, throw it across the chest over the left shoulder, bring the rest around the back and tuck it in just in front of the right arm'. This drapery is given in Lucy Barton's book, *Historic Costume for the Stage* (A. & C. Black Ltd).

Footwear: Feet are represented as bare in mosaics and reliefs.

Materials, Colours and Ornament: Wool, felt, sheepskin, soft leather and linen were the materials chiefly used. Vegetable and mineral dyes gave green, brown, blue, yellow ochre, terracotta and, it is thought, a brilliant red.

Beads of lapis, cornelian and chalcedony were used for ornament on dress. The scalloped edge shown in the kilts may have been actual and shawls were edged with fringe.

Jewellery: Gold was used a great deal for rings, pins, necklaces, bracelets, large crescent-shaped earrings and 'dog-collars'. Shell inlay was a favourite form of decoration. For the semi-precious stones used, see 'Materials, Colours and Ornament'. Many strings of beads were worn together and all jewellery was worn by men as well as women. It is thought that the wearing of a single earring may have been a masculine custom.

Military Dress: Soldiers wore the kilts, capes and hoods seen in the mosaics, though their hoods may have been metal helmets.

BABYLONIAN DRESS

Hair—Men: Short, very curly or bushy hair appears under the hats or helmets of men in later Sumerian times and in Chaldea–Babylon. It was also known for men to wear their hair long and to put it up in a chignon at the back of the head, bound by a fillet, as already described in 'Chaldean Dress'.

Hair—Women: Women's hair was put up in the chignon as described in 'Hair—Men', now a usual mode of hairdressing, or was left loose, bound in both cases by a fillet. The elaborate early Sumerian mode of hairdressing seems to have disappeared in the early part of this period, but returned by 1000 B.C. when it was also the fashion to dress the hair in a short mass of curls all over the head.

Headdress—Men: Men wore a round cap with a broad band for a brim, and a war helmet with pointed crown was worn by soldiers. The mitre began to make its appearance and lasted throughout the period of Assyrian and Persian costume. Men wore fillets of ribbon or swathed material (see 'Jewellery').

Headdress—Women: Women are thought to have worn fillets like those of men.

Garments—Men: A wrap-round kilt of woven stuff, trimmed with fringe along at least one edge, could be accompanied by a small rectangular shawl, probably also fringed, worn over the left shoulder with two ends tied together on the right hip.

A drapery which covered the body and left arm, leaving the right arm and shoulder free, is given by Mary Houston in *Ancient Egyptian, Mesopotamian and Persian Costume* as being the civilian state costume from about 2370 until 2100 B.C. Her directions for putting it on are as follows:

'Taking the rectangle as being numbered A, B, C and D at each corner, place the corner B under the left armpit, and draw the edge B–A round the back of the shoulders under the right armpit, across the front of the chest and round the back again and under the right armpit once more; then throw the edge B–A upwards across the chest and over the left shoulder; the corner A will then hang down the back. Take this corner A and tuck it in at the right side of the breast.'

Men's dress began to approximate to Assyrian styles before the end of the Babylonian period, particularly in royal dress of the third millennium B.C. The T-shaped tunic is found in Babylonian costume by 2000 B.C.

Garments—Women: A garment that appears to be a long-sleeved tunic with a close, round neck-line is thought to have been made of stuff with small loops all over the surface in imitation fleece. Its date is approximately 3500 B.C.

Women also wore shawl draperies, one being draped in the way described in 'Garments—Men'. Another has been illustrated and described in the accompanying caption.

Footwear: Leather sandals are occasionally seen in Babylonian art, and decorative slippers both for men and women.

Materials, Colours and Ornament: In order to drape the shawls used as garments, the people of this time must have had soft, finely woven fabrics that would hang well. Fringe was the trimming most in favour, with tassels at some edges, embroidered borders and belts and often woven patterns on the dresses themselves. Black, green, white and the varieties of 'purple', that is, from a dark indigo blue through wine and violet to crimson and vermilion, were probably the colours in use.

Jewellery: 'Dog-collars' and bracelets are the main items of jewellery. Necklets with amulets are another feature of the period. Fillets among people of important position often consisted of a thin strip of gold across the brow and ribbons to go round the head and tie at the back.

ASSYRIAN DRESS

There was little change in the dress of the Assyrians during the whole period of their ascendancy, from about 1100 to 490 B.C.

Hair—Men: The hair of the Assyrians was black and bushy and was allowed to grow long, often past the shoulders. It is possible that bulky wigs were worn. All men wore thick, curling beards and moustaches, with the exception of eunuchs. The beards were large and luxuriant and in many cases probably artificial.

Hair—Women: Women's hair was like that of men and was worn about the same length.

Headdress—Men: Men usually wore a fillet or swathed band to confine the hair, but are sometimes represented as being bare-headed. Eunuchs as a rule did not wear headdress. The tiara, a tall-crowned cap, probably of felt, tapering slightly towards the crown, was a head-covering very frequently worn. It had a small conical 'tag' on the top. Kings are often seen in Assyrian reliefs wearing this form of hat, but the mitre, a taller and more ornate version of the tiara, was their headdress on ceremonial occasions. Both the mitre and the tiara usually had pendant ties at the back, and the mitre often had a swathe of material round the base. A soft-crowned pointed cap was also finished in this way.

Headdress—Women: Women wore fillets or coronets, according to rank, and folds of their shawls were drawn over their heads if needed.

Garments—Men: Tunic and shawl were the main garments, the tunic being T-shaped and close-fitting, with sleeves ending above the elbow and a close, round, ornamented neckline. The garment ended at the knee or instep. The long tunic was worn by many grades of people, and the tunic to the knee was worn by kings as well as commoners. Men's waist-belts were very wide, with narrow over-belts. The shawl could be draped in several ways and varied very much in size. Two versions of the same draping given in Mary Houston's *Ancient Egyptian, Mesopotamian and Persian Costume* have been combined and simplified and are partially quoted here (see diagram, page 19):

1. Tie a waist-cord over the tunic. 'Take the garment and fold it over on the line E–F, so that E–F–A–B hangs down outside'; then pin the point E to the waist-cord of the tunic at the right front; throw 'the shawl backwards over the right shoulder. Draw the edge E–F round the back of the neck and form a sling over the left arm'. Roll 'the edge E–F round the waist towards the right, passing under the right arm at waist-level, then on round the back and left side', continuing to roll, until it reaches the left front of the waist; 'now fold the remainder of the drapery underneath' the roll and fasten it to the tunic at the point where E is already fastened.

2. Fasten a folded shawl, at a point mid-way in its width, to the tunic on the left shoulder; take the drapery round the back, across the front of the body, and over the left shoulder to hang down the back.

3. A similar effect to (2) is achieved by tucking the shawl into the belt of the tunic at the right front, passing it across the front of the body, round the back, under the right arm and over the left shoulder.

4. A shawl about 20 inches square may be tucked under the broad waist-belt to hang down over the buttocks, or a wider one may encircle the waist and hips after the same fashion.

Garments—Women: Women wore the long tunic, in some cases with three-quarter length sleeves. Representations of women's costumes are rare, even in the case of captives. It can probably be accepted, however, that they wore narrow waist-belts, if any, and that the close round neckline, usually with a 'dog-collar', was the rule.

The following method of draping is given by Mary Houston in describing the dress of a captive woman, and she states later that an example of an Assyrian queen's shawl was similarly draped, but going the opposite way:

'To drape this shawl, place one corner under the left armpit and draw it across the back, under the right armpit, wrapping it once round the body; draw it then across the back and over the right shoulder. A corner of the fringed end will hang down in front of the right shoulder.'

Footwear—Men: Sandals and shoes as shown in the illustrations to this section were worn in Assyria. Boots ending at the calf or just below the knee, of soft leather, with lacing down the front, were a feature of later Assyrian costume, possibly an introduction from some other country. Men were often barefooted, especially peasants and workers.

Footwear—Women: Women's shoes were made of fabric or soft leather, but they are shown, when at all, as bare-footed in the case of captives.

Materials, Colours and Ornament: Pliable leather, wool, linen and tapestry were the materials chiefly in use, with silk for the very wealthy and important. Approximately the same colours as those used by the Babylonians were worn in Assyria. Gold thread, coloured embroidery and borders of fringe or tassels were used as decoration. The motifs of tapestry and embroidery were used repetitively, without change. They included the palmette, the lotus and bud, the rosette, and some geometrical formations.

Jewellery and Accessories: Men as well as women wore heavy, barbaric gold bracelets, arm-bands, earrings and jewelled 'dog-collars' and circlets. A vessel of bronze or basket-work, presumably for small personal possessions, is often seen in Assyrian art, carried by men. Fans and parasols were held by slaves.

Military Dress: Assyrian infantry wore a long tunic of mail shaped like the civilian tunic. It had a broad belt, with a narrow over-belt. The Assyrian helmet was round, with a tall, conical top. Shields were in the form of an ellipse pointed at both ends and in some cases were large enough to protect the whole body. Cavalrymen wore a wrap-round kilt and a waist-length corselet of mail. They wore boots to the calf or just below the knee and mail over the knees. Arms were swords, javelins, bows and arrows, clubs, spears, slings, and falchions with a curved and sometimes toothed blade.

PERSIAN DRESS

From approximately 600 B.C. the main Persian garments were the robe, tunic, coat and trousers.

The robe of the New Kingdom in Egypt was derived from Persian influence and the Persians themselves took it from the Medes.

The long-sleeved tunic with close neckline may have been the forerunner of the tunica talaris worn later by the Romans, but the coat and trousers of the Persians had no relationship with the civilizations of Egypt, Chaldea–Babylon, Assyria or Rome. It originated in Central Asia and the development of 'braccae', the leggings worn in North-Western Europe and copied by Roman invaders, seems to have been contemporaneous and independent.

In these early times the Persians were Zoroastrians, sun-worshippers. With the rise of Mohammedanism Persian dress took on a more distinctly Oriental aspect and is a matter for separate study.

Hair—Men: The hair of Persian men was curly and thick but worn shorter than that of the Assyrians. Moustaches are almost always present in ancient Persian art, but beards are not necessarily worn and some men are seen as clean-shaven.

Hair—Women: There are very few examples of Persian women's dress to give us any information, but one that has come down to us from the 5th century B.C. shows hair in small curls on the forehead. The rest is hidden by the veil and what may be a fillet or a cap, worn behind the row of curls.

Headdress—Men: A high, domed cap, with pendant lappets at the back, and a tiara made of ribbed material are often found in Persian art. A plain or twisted fillet could bind the hair. The Phrygian cap, with long lappets of which the two in front could be fastened under the chin, was an important form of headdress. It differed from the hood, made in one piece to fit over the neck and collar-bones, with an opening for the face. The crown of this was made in various shapes, which rather resembled the Phrygian cap. Part of the neck-fold was often pulled up to cover the chin.

Headdress—Women: The instance of Persian women's dress referred to previously shows a simple, long veil worn over the head and hanging down over the shoulders and back.

Garments—Men: The 'robe' of the Medes was not restricted to the use of royalty but seems to have been worn by many different kinds of people, including ambassadors and members of the King's Bodyguard. It was basically the same garment as the 'robe' in Egypt.

a b c

II.2. Hebrew. About 1000 B.C. Onwards. Three Figures

Hair: (a) Man in tasselled outer gown. The hair is hidden by the cap. A short beard is worn on the chin and round the jaws. (b) Man in traditional desert-dweller's dress. The hair is not seen. A moustache and full beard are worn. (c) A Levite. The hair is long and thick, and he wears a beard and moustache.

Headdress: (a) The pointed cap, with a tassel at its peak, is of buff-yellow woollen stuff. (b) The folded headcloth is of white linen, bound with a red cord. (c) The conical cap is of wine-red felt and has a scarf of soft finely-woven white linen wound round its base.

Garments: (a) The instep-length 'T'-shaped tunic is in stripes of yellow, black and gold. The tabard-shaped garment worn over it is of brilliant red wool, with thick gold fringe. It has tassels at the four corners. (b) The gown ends at the insteps and has long, wide sleeves. It is of purple linen, with stripes of gold and deep blue. The open loosely-hanging coat is of white woollen stuff striped in crimson. The folded sash-girdle is striped in purple and red on a white ground. (c) The Levite's gown is of white linen, and the ribbons ornamenting it are in the wine-red variant of purple, decorated with small silver ornaments. The sleeves are long and close-fitting, and the neckline rounded, fitting the neck closely. The earliest date of this dress is uncertain, as with other Hebraic costume, but it may have developed from Persian or Far-Eastern influences.

Footwear: (a), (b) and (c) wear sandals of brown or natural leather.

Accessories: (a) He carries a scroll. (b) A staff is held in the left hand. (c) The Levite carries a ram's horn trumpet for use in Temple ceremonies.

Trousers were a distinctive feature of Persian dress. Close-fitting or baggy, they were worn with tunics, sleeved coats and under the robe. In the mosaic of the Battle of Issus the close-fitting trousers of the Persians are patterned, either with embroidery or designs woven into the material.

The tunic ended at the knee and had long sleeves, a close round neckline and a narrow belt. Like the trousers, it could be ornamented.

The coat ended at the ankle, sometimes the instep, and had long, inset sleeves. It could be ornamented with patterned borders or all over and had tie fastenings over the chest. It was often worn slung over the shoulders, open, with the sleeves hanging loose.

From the 4th to the 2nd century B.C. the rectangular cloak, fastened in the centre or on the right shoulder, was worn, perhaps as a result of Greek influence, but it did not supersede the coat.

Garments—Women: The long, close-fitting T-shaped tunic and the long veil, which formed a covering garment as well as a headdress, were, as far as is known, the standard dress for women in the early part of the period. An over-dress ending below the knee appears in an early representation. Later, long sleeves are worn and the over-dress is replaced by a swathe of the veil wound round the waist, by a separate rectangular wrap drawn over the left shoulder and round the waist, or by the same type of wrap draped round the waist and falling to the instep or a little below.

A draping for a shawl over the simple tunic for Persian women is as follows: 'Take a scarf about twelve inches wide and three yards long, fringed on one side and both ends. Hold it with one end falling from the right shoulder to a little above the knee. Pass the rest of the scarf over the right shoulder, across the back, over the left shoulder and diagonally across the back to the right hip. Now bring the scarf across the back to the left armpit and, with fringe turned inward, forward and up to the left shoulder, letting the last end hang down the back. Pin the folds together on the left shoulder' (*Historic Costume for the Stage*, by Lucy Barton).

Footwear—Men: Men's shoes in ancient Persia were tied just below the ankle-bone, or had three button-like fastenings over the insteps.

Footwear—Women: Women in all probability had shoes like the ornamented Assyrian shoes worn by women, or were barefooted.

Materials, Colours and Ornament: Materials and colours in ancient Persia were much the same as in late Egyptian dress. Silk was known and was sometimes made with woven patterns.

Jewellery and Accessories: Jewellery among the Persians followed Assyrian models, but was more delicate in design. It is shown mainly in crowns, necklets, earrings and girdles, the long sleeves making bracelets or arm-bands unusual, and, in the final part of the period under consideration, jewelled garments, crowns, quivers, belts, sword-hilts and scabbards, baldricks, collars and the 'brace' used to gird the tunic under the arms for freedom of movement.

Military Dress: The hood, tunic and trousers were worn by warriors. Weapons were swords, bows and arrows, spears and javelins. Bowmen are sometimes shown wearing the robe and ribbed tiara. Shields were round and convex.

II.3. Assyrian King Wearing a Mitre

Hair: The hair or wig falls to the shoulders in thick curls. The beard is in rows of small curls from the level of the cheek-bones, meeting the moustache, with ringlets at the lower edge.

Headdress: A royal mitre of 'purple', ornamented in gold, has two streamers hanging at the back and a small knob on the top.

Garments: The 'T'-shaped tunic has a 'rosette' pattern of wool embroidery, of dull green and buff-yellow. The decorative border is repeated at the hem with two additional borders in dull green and red. The bordered and gold-fringed 'purple' shawl is draped according to method 2 in Assyrian Dress, Chapter II, 'Garments—Men'.

Footwear: The king's leather sandals have an ornamented heel-piece sloping upward from the arch of the foot to the back of the ankle. There are thongs round the big toe and two on either side tying over the instep.

Jewellery and Accessories: The gold drop earrings are heavy and ornate. The gold and jewelled armlets and wrist-bracelets are rigid. The king carries a hatchet in his right hand and a short sceptre in his left.

II.4. Assyrian King

Hair: The hair (possibly a wig) hangs down on to the shoulders in a mass of close curls from behind the ears, which are exposed, with thick, ridged curls covering the head from front to back. The moustache meets the bulky, probably artificial beard, which is arranged in small tight curls and two rows of vertical sausage-curls.

Garments: The usual 'T'-shaped tunic ends at the ankles with a heavy border of tasselled fringe. Its all-over design in red and dull blue suggests that it is made of tapestry. The red shawl is draped according to method I in Assyrian Dress, Chapter II, 'Garments—Men'. It has a fringed and ornamented border.

Footwear: The sandals differ a little from those in 'Assyrian King Wearing a Mitre', an extra thong round the big toe being added.

Jewellery and Accessories: The king wears gold bracelets and carries a sceptre with a thick tassel at the end, probably gilded.

II.5. Assyrian King or Nobleman

Hair: The hair or wig is set in thick, ridged waves and hangs in curls from a centre parting to the shoulders. The thick, curled beard and moustaches may also be artificial.

Headdress: The diadem-shaped head-band is ornamented in various colours.

Garments: The 'T'-shaped tunic of white woollen stuff is ornamented with embroidery, either of tapestry or of wool on linen in terra-cotta and dull green and is bordered with gold tasselled fringe. The narrow belt is probably of leather.

Footwear: The sandals have thick leather soles and narrow thongs, two coming from between the two first toes, and two crossing the instep and joined to a fifth which is part of the sole and forms a heel-band.

Jewellery and Accessories: The nobleman wears large, ornate drop earrings, gold armlets and gold bracelets on his wrists. He carries a spear and wears a sword on a baldrick.

II.6. Assyrian Queen

Hair: This is bushy like that of the men and worn at shoulder length. It may be real or a wig. It is drawn back to expose the ears and has a fringe of short curls on the forehead.

Headdress: The castellated gold circlet, probably jewelled, denotes the queen's royal rank.

Garments: The white linen tunic, like that of the men except for its three-quarter-length sleeves, has six bands of ornamentation in blue and red in two different designs, to border the hem and sleeves, also a single band at the neck, forming a close-fitting high collar. The pinkish-red shawl is draped in the fashion described in Assyrian Dress, Chapter II, 'Garments—Women', but in the opposite direction.

Footwear: The flat leather slippers are of red leather. The fronts are differently ornamented from the backs and join them over the instep.

Jewellery and Accessories: The large circular gold earrings and the rigid, gold bracelets are decorated in a rosette pattern.

II.7. Assyrian Bowman

Hair: The hair is arranged in closely grouped ringlets and the beard in rows of tight curls. Both may be artificial.

Headdress: The metal helmet comes down over the forehead and rises in a point over the crown of the head.

Garments: The soldier wears a wrap-round kilt, ornamented and fringed. It could be of painted leather, of wool-embroidered linen or of tapestry. Suggested colours are red, purple and white. He wears a wide belt with a narrow over-belt. A metal or leather collar and gorget protect the base of his throat. His legs are encased in mail, with leather bands fastened round them just below the knees.

Footwear: The leather boots have tongues projecting at the tops, come up to the lower part of the calves and are fastened with thongs in front.

Accessories: The bowman carries a sword on a baldrick from right shoulder to left hip, a club in his right hand and a bow in his left. His quiver of arrows is supported by a second baldrick from left shoulder to right hip.

II.8. Assyrian Fish-seller

Hair: Although it is very bushy, it seems likely that this is the natural hair, grown thick and long, and that the beard and moustache are also real.

Headdress: The head-band is plain, probably white and identical with that most commonly worn by Assyrians engaged in their ordinary pursuits and sometimes by warriors or hunters.

Garments: The 'T'-shaped tunic of natural-coloured wool, ending a little above the knees, is the one most usually worn for practical purposes, with a neck-band and wide, swathed belt. In this case it is unadorned, the garment of a tradesman, peasant or ordinary citizen.

Accessories: The basket in which the fish-seller carries his fish is probably an elliptically shaped tray, without handles, woven of cane and rushes.

II.9. Persian King

Hair: The hair is arranged in bushy curls that suggest a wig. The beard, also possibly artificial, meets the moustaches. It is pointed and has small vertical ringlets below two rows of tight curls.

Headdress: The tall crown, or mitre, is ornamented and could be jewelled. It is probably of gold.

Garments: The gown, in pale terra-cotta colour, is a version of the 'Robe' worn in Egypt, with the sides seamed and an opening made for the head. A jewelled belt is worn at waist-level and a large amount of fullness pulled upward and outward to form the sleeves, which have a decorative border, repeated on the collar and round the hem. It is possible that the cut of the garment is rather different from that of the Egyptian version, and that the sleeve-borders are cut on the cross and the sleeves themselves shaped to give the flowing effect. The Robe is decorated by an all-over rosette pattern in red. Narrow red pantaloons, tapering at the ankles, are worn beneath the Robe.

Footwear: The shoes are of soft leather, with three fastenings across the insteps.

Jewellery and Accessories: The king carries a tall staff with a gold and ivory knob.

II.10. Persian Man with Walking Stick

Hair: The hair is of moderate length, thick and tightly curled. The beard is also curly and thick and is joined by the moustache.

Headdress: The Persian 'Mitre' cap is of white felt and has two white streamers at the back.

Garments: Close-fitting black woollen trousers, slightly wrinkled, end just below the ankles. The tunic, red with a pattern of small brown squares, and ending at mid-thigh, has long tight sleeves and a round, close neckline of dark red dots on a white ground, repeated in the borders round the hem and wrists. The long straight coat, worn over the shoulders with the arms not in the sleeves, is of purple wool with a border all round of blue, white and black, repeated at the ends of the sleeves. It is tied in the centre of the chest.

Footwear: The shoes are of white leather coming up to the ankle-bones and tied in front with matching thongs of leather.

Accessories: The man carries a tall walking-stick, with an ivory top. At his waist a sword in a light-coloured leather scabbard is slung from a black leather belt.

III ANCIENT GREEK DRESS

CRETAN DRESS (2100–1100 B.C.)

The ancient civilization in the island of Crete evolved much of its costume on different lines from those of Assyria and Egypt. In the first instance, about 2000 B.C., the simple tunic from the shoulder to just above the ankle worn by Cretan women had some resemblance to the tunic worn in Chaldea. The same stuff, woven with loops all over the surface, which resembled flounces, was in use and is supposed to have been made in imitation of fleece, as in Chaldea. Men in Crete, however, in these early times, were naked except for a belt with dagger attached, and at hardly any time during the thousand years of Cretan civilization did men wear more than a kilt, an apron back and front depending from a belt, or a short tunic such as was worn on the Greek mainland. The exception to this was the long Greek tunic, worn for ceremonial occasions. Women, on the other hand, wore dresses from an early date with full, almost crinoline-shaped skirts, leaving the breasts exposed. The strange, exotic beauty of these costumes and their contrast to classical Greek dress makes them of unusual interest.

This early civilization is known as Minoan, Early, Middle and Late, these epochs coinciding roughly with the three main periods of Egyptian history. The Homeric legends and plays based on them are often costumed in Late Minoan dress, which was also worn in Mycenae on the Greek mainland.

Hair—Men: Cretan men are thought to have worn their hair short in the earliest centuries of this epoch, but let it grow to waist-length in the final period from 1580 to 1100 B.C. Beards, neatly trimmed, were worn by some men in this period, when examples of short hair are also found, especially when Greek 'mainland' dress is worn. Long hair was sometimes twisted into a tightly bound lock at the back of the neck.

Hair—Women: Women's hair was worn long, flowing loose in very early times with the simple tunic, or bound up in a tall pointed hat worn with an early wrap-round dress. In the Minoan periods the hair is done in a chignon high at the back of the head, reminiscent of Greek fashion, with curls over the forehead and tresses hanging over the back and shoulders, worn loose with a fillet or put up in a fillet-bound chignon in the manner described in Chaldean dress.

Headdress—Men: In very early times men are thought to have worn a close-fitting round cap, but some authorities believe this to have been long hair wound round the head. Fillets or diadems were worn at the hairline or higher, sometimes pushed backward with curls over the forehead showing below them. A round cap, with up-turned brim a little wider at the top than at the brow, and with plumes springing from a central ornament on the crown, was a notable headdress, probably worn on ceremonial occasions.

Headdress—Women: Women wore the round cap with plumed crown described in 'Headdress—Men'. The famous statuette of the Snake Goddess wears it with a small figure of a leopard on the crown. Her priestess, in another well-known statuette, wears a tall mitre-like hat tapering to a flat top, with spiral decoration. Apart from these head-dresses, of which the last two described obviously have state or religious significance, women are usually seen wearing diadems or fillets, sometimes with strings of pearls wound in the hair.

Garments—Men: The first representations of men's dress in Crete show a nude figure with a belt and dagger or with a short leather apron or sheath depending from the belt. The next examples show a kilt from waist to mid-thigh in front and rather shorter at the back. A long tassel finishes the downward-pointing centre front of the garment. It is patterned and bordered and the belt is extremely tight. These belts, made of metal or leather, were an important feature of Cretan dress and were worn throughout the epoch.

While the kilt is thought to have been in fashion only for a short time, disappearing near the beginning of the final period (1580–1100 B.C.), the apron remained throughout. In the Late Minoan period it was shorter in front than at the back, where it ended about a third or half-way down the thigh. The dagger was thrust through the belt.

The Greek Ionic chiton, ending just below the ankle, was a part of Cretan dress in the latest period, and is believed to have been worn on important ceremonial occasions.

A shorter version, ending well above the knee, was worn in Mycenae and may also have been worn in Crete, as there was some interchange of styles in the latest part of the period before 1100 B.C. Mycenaean men, however, wore short drawers, often with decorative borders, in place of the apron, sometimes leaving the upper part of the body bare or wearing a short-sleeved 'vest'.

For the dress of 'bull-leaping' athletes, see 'Garments—Women'.

Garments—Women: The straight tunic of woven stuff imitating fleece was followed about 2000 B.C. by a semicircular wrap-round garment cut with two holes a short distance from the straight edge through which to put the arms and bound with a padded girdle.

A little before 1580 B.C. bodices closely moulded to the figure, exposing the breasts and laced corset-fashion below them, and skirts fitting over the hips, flaring slightly towards the ground-length hem and made in several tiers or flounces, possibly over a form of hoop or bustle, introduced a fashion peculiar to Crete. An apron was sometimes worn over the skirt and is thought to have had a religious significance. Seams in the bodices show how accurately they were fitted and suggest that the material was leather. Sleeves ended above the elbow and some were slightly raised at the shoulders. The belt, as in men's dress, was very tight, made either of metal or padded leather. Dresses were decorated with various geometrical designs, probably in leather appliqué.

At the beginning of the Late Minoan period (1580–1100 B.C.) the bodice could be worn open, like a short jacket, with a transparent under-bodice. The tight belt in this case is worn under the jacket.

A calf-length skirt is worn by a female huntress, with a 'vest' top like those of the Mycenaean men, and a priestess is seen in the short close-fitting bodice but with a long wrapped 'apron' of some animal's hide in place of a skirt.

The long Ionic Greek tunic, identical with that of men, was worn by women for ceremonial occasions.

The girl athletes who took part in the extraordinary 'bull-leaping' activities in Crete were dressed like their male counterparts in aprons, tight belts, boots with 'puttees' and wrist-bands.

Footwear—Men: From earliest times Cretan men seem to have worn calf-high leather boots out of doors, though it is thought that they went bare-foot in their houses. In the latest period they are shown wearing sandals and 'puttees' of leather as an alternative to boots. Leggings ending just below the knee were worn over bootees for hunting and other active pursuits.

Footwear—Women: Women are usually represented as bare-footed, though an example showing a huntress has short boots ending just below the swell of the calf.

Materials, Colours and Ornament: Leather, wool and linen, with rare use of silk in the Late Minoan period, were probably the materials used.

Colours included a clear sea-blue, orange, red, terracotta, maroon, brown, grey, green and black, with a good deal of white used in the 'mainland' dress. The leather appliqué, embroidery and tapestry which decorated gowns, kilts and aprons in a variety of geometrical formations was probably supplemented by metal tags sewn on as ornamentation (see 'Jewellery').

Jewellery and Accessories: Gold diadems which were tied on over the forehead, carved seals of sardonyx or other semi-precious stones, gold ornaments to be sewn on the dress in the form of tassels or buttons, necklets and bracelets of gold, chains, beads, strings of pearls to wind in the hair, and dagger-sheaths inlaid in gold were items of jewellery known in Crete.

Military Dress: Cretan warriors in the latest part of the period wore civil dress, except that the upper part of their bodies was usually bare. Helmets were of four kinds: (1) tall and pointed; (2) similar in shape but with a blunt top to the crown; (3) made of rings of stout, padded leather in a round shape, decreasing towards the top, where a plume was set; (4) basin-shaped, with the suggestion of a brim back and front and sometimes having cheek- and nose-pieces as well. Arms were spears, bows and arrows, short swords and daggers, and large double-headed axes. Iron and bronze were the metals used. Shields were of three kinds: rectangular, fairly large; figure-of-eight shaped, very large, protecting the whole body; and rectangular with a 'fire-screen' shape to the top. The two last were probably made of wood, covered in bull's hide.

GREEK DRESS

After the fall of the Minoan civilization, when the Greeks are thought to have invaded and destroyed it about 1100 B.C., little is known of Aegean history for about 500 years. It is believed that the dress of the Late Minoan period was still worn for a time in Greece during the intervening centuries, while characteristic Greek dress was also in use.

From about 600 B.C. examples of sculpture and painting have existed to show in detail the clothes worn for the remainder of the Grecian epoch, with the changes and developments that occurred.

The two main types of Greek dress, the Doric and the Ionic chiton or tunic, also the rectangular wrap and the close-fitting tunic with short or three-quarter sleeves, are the chief subjects for consideration.

The Doric chiton, the more ancient type, was made of a wide rectangle of wool or heavy linen folded double and joined at the shoulder, with a deep, bordered over-fold of the material hanging loosely at front and back to waist or hip level. It was a feminine garment, rarely worn by men.

The Ionic chiton, also made of a large rectangle of stuff, had no over-fold and was joined at the shoulders by a series of brooches or later by seams. This was worn in its various forms both by men and women.

The himation, the large rectangular outer wrap of the Greeks, could be draped in several ways. The chlamys was a smaller version of this, usually fastened on the right shoulder.

The close-fitting tunic or gown for men and women seen in Archaic vase-painting had Greek features such as the shoulder fastenings of the Ionic chiton for both sexes and sometimes the over-fold of the Doric both for men and women, but it seems otherwise to have been much like the T-shaped tunic, apart from sometimes having three-quarter length sleeves for women. It co-existed with the softly falling, hardly sewn draperies of typical Greek dress from the earliest times now under review.

It was a habit of the Greeks throughout their civilization sometimes to cover one garment with another, so that a thin Ionic chiton might show the graceful drapery of its 'sleeves' from under the over-fold of a heavier and naturally sleeveless Doric chiton. In this way a

III.1. Greek. Three Figures

Hair: (a) (6th century B.C.) A little of the soldier's hair is seen, covering his ear below the helmet. (b) (5th century B.C.) Only the curled fringe over the forehead is seen. (c) (6th century B.C.) A front of small curls (possibly false) forms an arc over the forehead. The chignon (unseen) would be half-way up the back of the head.

Headdress: (a) The bronze Corinthian helmet is pushed back so that the metal mask is lying flat. It would be pulled down over the face for battle. The crest is of metal and horsehair. (b) A fold of the himation covers the head. (c) A white fillet is bound round the head behind the front curls and tied at the base of the skull. Its ends are seen on the shoulders.

Garments: (a) The soldier has a chlamys of deep coral-red woollen stuff, bordered in Greek key-pattern in black on a white ground. It is his sole garment and is fastened on the right shoulder. (b) The green chiton is of soft pleated or crinkled linen. Over it is a himation of pale orange-coloured wool, draped as follows: One corner is dropped down over the body on the left side of the front to calf-level. The remainder of the drapery is taken over the head and shoulders and brought across the chest to the left shoulder. Draped over this arm and shoulder, leaving the hand free, it is taken round the back and brought over the right shoulder, enfolding the bent right arm and covering the hand. The folds are loosened a little so that the drapery descends in a diagonal over the left hip. It is taken round the back again and folds are once more loosened so that the top edge may be tucked into the girdle at the right side of the waist and the remainder may be dropped down on the right side, one end being lifted to the left side of the waist and tucked in there. The left hand is in a position to hold two portions of the drapery together at the waist. (c) The Doric chiton is of white wool, ornamented on the overfold in wool embroidery of indigo blue. The ends of the overfold are long and narrow, coming down to knee level. There are four visible in front and four unseen at the back. The neckline is gathered into a band and the sleeves formed out of the two meeting lengths of drapery, fastened from shoulder to elbow with brooches at intervals. The left side may be open or seamed.

Footwear: (b) The woman wears white leather sandals. (c) This is hardly seen, but could consist of soft white kid slippers.

Accessories: (a) The soldier carries a spear. (c) The large parasol is of the type known to the Ancient World.

short chiton might be put on over a longer one and a woollen one over one of fine or transparent linen.

The influences of surrounding nations notably contributed tunics of narrow cut, some decoration and fairly thick material. In a vase-painting, the goddess Athene wears a narrow, heavily patterned T-shaped tunic of calf-length over her pleated chiton and with her crested helmet.

Hair—Men: Archaic Period (600–480 B.C.): Men's hair was worn long during this period and dressed in the ways described below:

(*a*) Bound with a fillet, the hair being combed forward all round the head and tucked in over the fillet, leaving the ears exposed and a few curls hanging loose over the neck.

(*b*) Combed in the same way, but with a small fringe of curls in front of the fillet, a twist of hair at the back turned up under it, with the ears exposed and some curled locks hanging loose behind them.

(*c*) The fillet put on behind a fairly thick cluster of curls over the forehead and the hair at the back bound up in the fillet and allowed to spring out over it in a short 'pony-tail'.

(*d*) The hair combed forward in a turned-in fringe low on the forehead and the back hair, twisted or plaited, fastened across the back of the head just above the level of the ears, with a ringlet on each side in front of them.

(*e*) Bound with a fillet, the back hair twisted into a tightly bound lock.

Men of dignity and age could have curled beards, worn with or without moustaches.

Hair—Men: The Golden Age (480–400 B.C.): Men's hair was short at this time and as a rule combed downward round the head and curled lightly or closely.

Young men were generally clean-shaven, but during this century there was a fashion for wearing slightly curled side-whiskers ending below the level of the ear-lobe.

Older men of position and dignity might wear well-tended beards.

Peasants and mendicants at any time in the Greek civilization wore ragged hair and unkempt beards.

Hair—Men: The Alexandrian and Hellenistic Periods (338–146 B.C.): Men's hair was allowed to grow longer than in the preceding epoch and was now worn in curls all over the head. By 200 B.C. it was cut short again and remained so while Greek independence lasted.

Most men were clean-shaven, though orators, philosophers and scholars wore beards as before.

Hair—Women: Archaic Period (600–480 B.C.): Waved and curled hair, hanging in ringlets down the back and over the shoulders, with waves or curls arranged above the forehead without parting and sometimes swathes or plaits round the head as well, was the fashion for women at this time. Sometimes a ringlet hung at each side in front of the exposed ears.

The method of dressing the hair with a chignon at the back bound up in a fillet, which existed in Chaldea and Babylon and later in Crete, is also found in Archaic Greece.

Hair—Women: The Golden Age (480–400 B.C.): The hair was done in a chignon, fairly high at the back of the head, during this time, still with the ears uncovered and often with a 'pony-tail' of hair coming from the middle of the chignon. There could be a centre parting, with short curled or semi-curled strands in front of the ears or taken back towards the chignon with short curled hair arranged over the forehead. Ringlets did not now hang down the back, except in the case of young girls.

Hair—Women: The Alexandrian and Hellenistic Periods (338–146 B.C.): A simpler form of hairdressing was usual in this period, the hair being taken back, with or without a centre parting, to a chignon lower down at the back of the head than formerly.

The hairdressing of the former epoch could still be worn, however, in a modified form.

Women throughout the centuries of Greek civilization cut their hair short in time of mourning.

Headdress—Men: The use of the fillet which almost always bound the hair in Archaic Greece has been described under 'Hair—Men' in this chapter, as it was found difficult otherwise to describe the hairdressing. It was worn less often throughout the Golden Age and the Alexandrian and Hellenistic Periods, as the hair was then considerably shorter.

The round cap, probably of felt, and the large round straw or felt hat, the petasos, were the chief items of headgear. In Archaic times the latter could be turned up at the back, not unlike the byecocket of the 15th century in England and France. A close-fitting decorated skull-cap was a feature of the Archaic Period for men. In Archaic times also a garland of leaves or flowers might be worn, or the fillet could be worn in diminished form round the crown of the head. A fold of the himation could be drawn over the head (see 'Garments—Men'). The Phrygian cap, a fashion borrowed from Persian adversaries, was worn with the other Persian adjuncts of long sleeves and leggings after the Persian Wars.

Headdress—Women: The fillet was worn by women encircling the loose hair in Archaic times, often in smaller form on the crown of the head as described in 'Headdress—Men'. It bound the chignon to the head in the ancient mode of hairdressing already mentioned. The diadem or stephane developed from the fillet in these early times and was worn throughout the Grecian epoch, as were garlands of flowers or leaves.

In the Golden Age, with the elongation of the coiffure, many varieties of headdress were evolved in addition to the fillet and wreath. The diadem became larger and higher and was occasionally worn back to front, with the broadest part enclosing the chignon. Sometimes it had attached to it a long pointed cap which enclosed the chignon, the ornamented point hanging at the back. Another addition to the diadem was a support, in metal or stiffened linen, holding up the chignon, with an ornamented band round the base of the 'pony-tail'. Again, two bands of embroidered material might bind the hair, one across the top of the head, narrowing to a point just above and behind the ears, the other crossing the back of the head beneath the chignon, meeting the first band at the point above the ears where it joined the diadem.

Narrow strands of ribbon or material, usually three, might bind the hair in the same way. Scarves or veils were folded over the head and chignon together in a sort of 'dust-cap' formation, sometimes with a wreath of flowers added. A round, loose-fitting cap with a tag on the top, looking remarkably like a tam-o'-shanter, was another covering for the whole head, enveloping the hair.

The fillet in the Golden Age was worn as before, though not in the small form at the top of the head. It was sometimes tied low on the forehead so that the chignon and the hair at the sides of the head could be turned up over it.

A fold of the himation (see 'Garments—Women') could be pulled over the head as a wrap and this was done especially in time of mourning. Oblong veils were worn as an alternative.

In the Alexandrian and Hellenistic Periods the diadem was the most frequent form of headdress. It was a frequent practice for women to pin up their hair without headdress.

In this latest period of Greek history women are occasionally seen wearing the conical cap over the chignon and back of the head.

The Phrygian cap, with lappets, worn by Amazons came into use through Persian influence.

Garments—Men: The Ionic chiton, or tunic, was the usual wear for men. It was made of a rectangle of fine linen or thin wool, folded double, with two of the unjoined edges seamed together and the two at the top of the garment at right angles to these, joined at intervals by brooch-fastenings, leaving openings for the head in the middle and for the arms at either side. The garment was very voluminous, being usually fashioned from a rectangle of material seven feet long. A tunic to the instep was usual for elderly men and for important and ceremonial occasions, but for all ordinary purposes it ended well above the knee. A depth of at least three feet six inches was generally a minimum, as the garment was shortened by the girdle and often considerably pouched over it. As the Greeks wove material for tunics or cloaks with a selvedge all round, hems were never necessary. The shoulder-fastening on a short tunic was often left unclasped to give greater freedom of movement.

By the 5th century B.C. the part covering the upper arms was gathered a little in order to form sleeves.

In the Alexandrian and Hellenistic Periods, the openings for the arms were often left in the side of the garment below the shoulder level. There is a theory that the Greeks wove this later type of chiton all in one piece, with openings for head and arms already made in the process of weaving. Alternatively, the garment was contrived from two separate rectangles seamed together at the sides.

For a time in the Alexandrian Period long, close sleeves in imitation of the Persians were worn with this chiton.

Charioteers in this period of Greek history wore the long chiton, bound on with cords crossed over the chest, looped together at the back.

It was unusual for men to wear the Doric chiton, though examples of this exist in the vase-paintings.

The cloaks of the Greeks, the large himation and the smaller chlamys, were both rectangular. There were various methods of draping the himation for men: it could be worn quite simply over the shoulders, like a shawl; folded into a smaller compass and worn in the same way; put on over the left shoulder, hanging towards the left foot, the rest of the garment being brought round the back, under the right arm and thrown over the left shoulder or laid across the left arm; or, when the garment was very large, put on as before with the drapery thrown over the left shoulder or laid across the left arm; or, when the garment was very large, put on as before with the drapery thrown over the left shoulder, drawn across the back and over the right shoulder enclosing the bent right arm and twisted before being again thrown over the left shoulder, arm and hand. The right hand held the cross-over together at the chest. With this drapery part of the top fold could also be pulled up over the head.

A small himation worn over the shoulders was often the only male garment in Archaic times. A wrap-round kilt was worn by slaves and by other men for active pursuits throughout the epoch.

The chlamys was worn covering the left arm and shoulder and fastened at the two ends of the top edge on the right shoulder.

Garments—Women: The draped garments of women in the Greek civilization were in some cases put on over a foundation of kid or other soft leather to which its folds could be pinned if necessary.

They wore the Ionic chiton to the ankle or instep. It was girdled at the waist or hips and could be considerably shortened by pouching it over one or more girdles to give freedom of movement, especially to female athletes. It might also be made shorter in the first place for athletic purposes and was often worn unclasped on one shoulder, particularly in the case of Amazons.

The Doric chiton was constructed in the same way as the Ionic, but with a deep over-fold in the original rectangle of stuff, which, when the garment was put on, hung over the chest and back. The over-fold varied in depth and could extend below the hips, with a girdle worn over it. This chiton was usually of wool, often thick enough to make any outer garment unnecessary. In its original draped form, the open side was left unsewn, exposing one side of the body, and when it was seamed the zig-zag effect of the edges falling together was sometimes preserved in the sewn version. The chiton was joined on each shoulder by a pin or brooch, the back edge being brought a little over the front. It could be worn ungirdled or with one or more girdles.

Women wore the himation draped in the same ways as those worn by men, with some additions. The cloak could be fastened on the right shoulder, having been brought loosely under the left arm; and in Archaic times this fastening could be continued along the right arm with a series of brooches, while the upper edge, which crossed the body back and front before being fastened on the shoulder, could be gathered on a draw-string.

Another method, belonging to the Golden Age, was to hang the garment over the left shoulder descending towards the left foot in front, bringing the rest of it across the back, allowing some of its fullness to hang there and drawing the remainder across the front of the body and the length hanging in front, tucking some of its fullness into the girdle at the left side of the waist.

The chlamys was worn by Amazons and by huntresses and ordinarily an oblong veil could be used as a wrap for the shoulders and, if needed, for the head.

A form of Phrygian dress was also worn by Amazons. It consisted of a complete close-fitting covering for the body, arms and legs in soft leather, woven stuff that would stretch, or possibly knitted wool, resembling tights, and sometimes with a short kilt worn over it.

Footwear—Men: Sandals and boots were worn from early times and were finely made. Boots fitted the leg and foot snugly, in some cases exposing the toes, were laced up the front or without fastenings (suggesting the use of some stretching material) and ended at the top of the calf. Sandals had thin thongs arranged in various ways and could retain the natural colour of the leather or be gilded or coloured red, white or black.

Footwear—Women: Women had delicately made sandals in pale or brilliant colours. Amazons wore boots very similar to those of men. Both sexes were often barefooted indoors.

Materials, Colours and Ornament: Wool of all weights and qualities, including felt, linen of various textures, some of it woven in oil so that it shone, a 'crinkled' type of fine linen, worn mostly by women, some cotton and gauze and, more rarely, silk, were the materials used.

Colours were the varieties of 'purple', which ranged through violet, indigo, wine-colour, dark red, crimson, scarlet and vermilion to terra-cotta and, one assumes, in dilute dye-mixtures to rose madder and pink, saffron, sulphur and ochre shades of yellow, sea-blue (since it was known in Crete it was presumably known in Greece), emerald, dark green, clear green, variants of brown, grey and dun colour and of course black and white.

Greek 'key' pattern, palmette, egg-and-dart, 'wave', rosette, and acanthus leaves and flowers, conventionalized and always conforming to a formal border or diapered all-over pattern, or arranged in wide strips of ornament, were some of those known throughout the epoch. In the Archaic period deep embroidered or tapestry bands might decorate a whole dress, one below the other. Figures of men and women, chariots, horses, birds, fish and other animals made up the designs, interspersed perhaps with more conventional patterns.

Designs painted on with dye were sometimes used, but in general they were woven into the stuff, both sides being perfect, or embroidered.

Jewellery and Accessories: The taste of the Greeks was restrained, and their jewellery was delicate in its designs, but fairly large. Long pins with ornamented heads, rings, bracelets, pendant earrings, brooches and necklets (the last usually with ornaments hanging downwards from a circular neck-chain) were nearly always of gold, and not often set with stones (unfaceted) until the Hellenistic Period. Cameos and intaglios were of great beauty. The bronze or golden stephane or diadem was embossed with patterns in gold.

Military Dress: Three of the main types of Greek helmet are to be found in the illustrations and are described in the captions. In Archaic times the crest of the helmet was raised on a metal rod above the top of the head and the Greek soldier wore only this and the chlamys when he went into battle, but later a short chiton, also a cuirass of leather, horsehair or bronze and bronze greaves were added. A baldrick carried the short sword or a quiver for arrows when a bow was used. Spears, javelins, slings and axes (often double-headed) were other weapons.

Shields were oval in early times, but later they were made in a circular shape.

Some Greek Borders

III.2. Ancient Greek Dress. Cretan Man

Hair: The long hair is cut in a fringe in front and drawn behind the ears to flow loosely down the back. A short lock hangs in front of each ear.

Garments: The ornamented kilt of leather or linen comes down to a point in front, where a tassel on a strip of ornamented stuff, is hung, descending from the belt, to which it is attached. The back of the kilt is shorter than the front, coming only a short distance down the back of the thighs. The decoration is in a multiplicity of colours, covering the surface of the kilt.

Footwear: The leather bootees with thick soles have three borders of woven stuff in red, white and yellow.

Jewellery and Accessories: The man wears a necklace, armlets and bracelets of leaves in gold and green enamel. He carries a wine-skin in the right hand and a drinking-cup with a pointed base, intended to be set down on a deeply sanded floor, in the left.

III.3. Cretan Woman

Hair: The hair is dressed in several rolled curls on the head and there is a short curled fringe in front. A lock hangs over the diadem in front and one in front of the right ear. The hair at the back is divided into two or more ringlets which hang down the back or over one shoulder.

Headdress: A gold diadem is worn on the forehead and rows of pearls are wound between the rolls of hair and among the ringlets.

Garments: The 'blouse' or short tunic is of transparent white linen and has a round, flat collar of red beads. The jacket, possibly of leather, is ornamented all over in red and blue and is worn open in front. Its sleeves end above the elbows and have slightly raised, probably padded shoulders. The skirt, thought to be of leather stretched over a 'crinoline' of cane, is flounced and ornamented in many different colours in geometric forms and a design of leaves.

Footwear: The feet are bare, as was usual with women in Crete.

Jewellery and Accessories: The woman carries a pottery jar.

III.4. Mycenaean Man

Hair: The natural hair is long enough to hang a short way down the back in a plait or twist. A lock of hair hangs in front of each ear and the front is cut in a short fringe.

Headdress: A fillet of white linen is worn high on the head and a strip of some woven stuff is wound round the queue of hair at the back.

Garments: The 'T'-shaped garment of natural linen or leather, covering the upper part of the body, may be made in one with the drawers. The all-over decoration could be appliqué, possibly of wool or felt, or may be intended to imitate tufts of wool on a garment of sheepskin. Short streamers are added to the sleeves and drawers.

Footwear: The calf-high boots of pliable leather have the same decoration as the garments.

Accessories: A long spear is carried.

III.5. Greek Woman of the Archaic Period

Hair: The hair, some of which may be false, is dressed in long ringlets, with a short, curled fringe on the forehead and a broad plait wound round the head.

Garments: The yellow ankle-length tunic, ornamented in green, is Ionic, with ornamentation round the neck and along the shoulder line that covers the upper arm. Over it is worn a short himation of orange-coloured wool ornamented in gold, fastened by two of its corners on the right shoulder, with the other two hanging down on the right side. It is fastened at intervals to cover the right upper arm and has an ornamental border. One of its long sides crosses the body diagonally at front and back passing under the left breast and arm. This fold of the garment is gathered on a draw-string at the top to keep it in place.

Footwear: Thongs fastened to the sole of the sandal just behind the arch of the foot pass between the two first toes and are fastened to the sole again at that point.

III.6. Greek Girl of Archaic Period.
6th Century B.C.

Hair: The hair hangs loose and is brought forward in a fringe.

Headdress: A garland of leaves is worn.

Garments: The close-fitting gown of dark green linen dotted with a white pattern is fastened along the upper arms in the manner of the Ionic chiton. The belt and flat, round neckline have identical ornamentation in white and yellow while the border at the hem is different though the colours are the same.

Accessories: The large amphora, or wine-jar, has the pointed base that enables it to be implanted in a floor of sand.

III.7. Greek girl, Archaic Period.
6th Century B.C.

Hair: The hair is brought forward into a thick fringe and hangs in a swathe down the back.

Headdress: The diadem-shaped fillet of white linen is tied at the back.

Garments: The chiton is close-fitting in the archaic manner and has a Doric overfold. This is embroidered with a small all-over design and the skirt with tapestry patterns including representations of dolphins, birds and chariot-drawing horses. Several borders also decorate it and the wide belt is of tapestry. Predominating colours are red, violet, gold and blue.

Footwear: The girl's feet are bare.

Accessories: The basket holds bobbins and balls of wool.

III.8. Athenian Soldier. Archaic Period

Hair: The thick hair at the front of the head is brought forward in a curled fringe, with a short lock in front of each ear. The hair at the sides and back is grown long and dressed in ringlets.

Headdress: The soldier wears the round, segmented cap known in Greece from very early times. It is of red and white leather.

Garments: The corselet may be of metal or leather and has metal studs forming the fastening of its shoulder-pieces and ornamenting the neck and body of the garment. The star-shaped ornament on the shoulder-piece is probably of metal. A fastening or perhaps an amulet is slung across the chest from one shoulder-piece to the other. The short kilt of white linen has an ornamented border of green and red and appears to be made in joined segments. The long, narrow chlamys of red wool is thrown over his left shoulder, the front folds held in his left hand.

Accessories: The sword-scabbard is slung on a baldrick from right shoulder to left hip. A spear is held in the right hand.

III.9. Greek Youth in 'Petasos'

Hair: The hair is unparted, brought forward on to the forehead and hanging to a moderate length at sides and back.

Headdress: The youth wears the 'petasos', the Greek countryman's or traveller's hat, in this case of dried woven grass.

Garments: The only garment is a small rectangular wrap of natural-coloured wool, put on to form a kilt or loin-cloth.

Accessories: A basket of a type made to stand on weighing scales, and containing stalks of corn, is held in the left hand, while in the right is a scythe of a kind commonly used in the Ancient World.

III.10. Greek Seaman, Peasant or Artisan

Hair: The hair is cut moderately short, in the manner of the Golden Age or later, and brought forward to form a fringe over the forehead. The beard and moustache are fairly neatly trimmed.

Headdress: The conical cap, in this case of red felt, was frequently adopted by seafaring men and others engaged in active pursuits.

Garments: The man wears a short, unadorned Ionic chiton or tunic of dun-colour, dropped below the left shoulder and girdled at the hips with the fullness concealing the girdle. His red chlamys, or rectangular cloak, is fastened by two of its corners on the left shoulder.

III.11. Greek Warrior. Golden Age

Hair: The hair is visible only at the back of the helmet and is rather long.

Headdress: The bronze helmet has a forehead-piece, cheek-guards and a tall crest with a horse-hair tail pendant from beneath it.

Garments: The short chiton of white linen can be seen below the leather strips hanging from the cuirass, which is of metal, or possibly leather, ornamented on the breast, neck and arm openings. The leg-guards, or greaves, are of embossed metal.

Accessories: The warrior carries a short sword and a large circular Greek shield. In very early times the figure-of-eight shield known in Crete was carried by Greek soldiers.

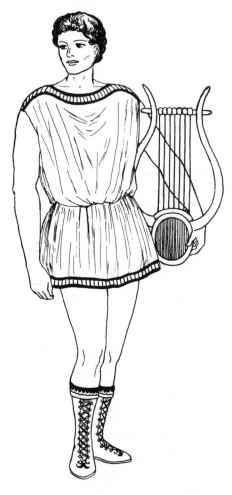

III.12. Greek Youth with Lyre. 5th Century B.C.

Hair: The youth has lightly curled hair, cut moderately short but with some thickness at the back and brought forward from the crown on to the forehead.

Garments: He wears a short Ionic chiton of white linen with a narrow girdle hidden by the blousing of the tunic and a decorative border of blue tapestry running across the boat-shaped neckline to the top of the upper arms, with another round the hem.

Footwear: The boots of white stretching material are pulled up to the top of the calf and have decorative turned-over tops in blue and green, also a small decoration on the toes.

Accessories: The seven-stringed lyre has limbs made of the horns of an animal or a conventionalized imitation.

III.13. Greek Man in Large Himation. Golden Age (5th Century B.C.)

Hair: The hair is moderately short and brought forward towards the forehead.

Garments: The large himation of natural or 'off-white' wool appears to be the only garment. It is put on with one edge hanging forward over the left shoulder towards the left foot. The garment is then brought round the back of the neck, enveloping the bent right arm, and turned over at the top edge into a deep overfold at the centre of the chest to support the right elbow and forearm. It is then thrown over the left shoulder, enclosing the left arm and hand. This hand, hidden in the drapery, keeps the fold taut across the body at the left hip. The right hand holds on to the top of the over-fold in the centre of the chest. This large himation, worn without a chiton, was favoured by scholars, orators and philosophers.

Footwear: The natural leather sandals have a strap over the instep. A wide thong from between the two first toes meets this and another crosses the foot at the base of the toes.

III.14. Greek Girl with Dove. Golden Age

Hair: The hair is drawn back in a 'pony-tail' and has a curled fringe on the forehead and a ringlet hanging in front of each ear, leaving the ears exposed.

Headdress: A broad, decorative band in gold and green leather or linen is worn across the top of the head and another across the back, beneath the pony-tail. These diminish to a point on either side of the head above and a little behind the ears and are joined together there. Another narrower band, also ornamented, encircles the hair at the base of the pony-tail.

Garments: The girl wears a simple Doric chiton of sea-green linen, left unseamed down the open side and arranged to form an attractive drapery.

Jewellery and Accessories: The earrings are long gold drops set with unfaceted jewels and the gold shoulder-fastenings are also jewelled.

III.15. Greek Girl with Pitcher. 5th Century B.C.

Hair: The hair is curled over the forehead and the rest drawn back, to end in a half-uncoiled chignon at the level of the top of the head.

Headdress: A decorative stephane (diadem) of gold is put on behind the forehead-curls. A curved and ornamented support crosses the back of the head, attached to the diadem and is joined to a strip of blue embroidered material which is twined round the chignon to hold it in place.

Garments: The azure blue Ionic chiton has crossed straps over the bosom, shoulder-fastenings and a girdle at waist-level. A himation of cream-coloured wool is folded and caught together on the left shoulder. It has a deep, decorative border in pale green.

Footwear: The white leather sandals have a band across the foot at the base of the toes. Ankle and heel straps join a narrow thong attached to the sole at the arch of the foot. Ornamental heart-shaped pieces of leather cover the insteps.

Jewellery and Accessories: The girl wears drop earrings, an elaborately wrought necklace with pendant drops, a snake armlet on her right upper arm and brooches on her shoulders, all of gold and ivory. She carries an ornamental pitcher of metal or earthenware.

III.16. Greek Woman with Pitcher. 5th Century B.C.

Hair: The hair is lightly curled into a fringe in front, with the ears exposed, and is dressed at the back in a 'pony-tail'.

Headdress: Three narrow bands of white linen are arranged across the head at intervals and the pony-tail is tied at the base by another.

Garments: The Ionic chiton of pale yellow crinkled linen is dropped from the right shoulder and girdled at the waist. The himation of ivory-coloured wool is draped by dropping one end of the rectangle, with folds close together, down the left front of the body from the left shoulder. Part of the remainder of the drapery is brought round the back under the right arm, left to hang down in a fold below the right hip and then brought across to the left side of the waist, where its top edge is tucked up the girdle. The rest of the wide drapery, taken across the back, hangs down behind the left shoulder.

Jewellery and Accessories: Long gold earrings are worn. The pitcher in the right hand has a design of ducks.

III.17. Greek Girl with Fan. 5th Century B.C.

Hair: The thick fringe and some hair on the temple are visible under the scarf covering the head, but the shape of the chignon can be seen.

Headdress: A scarf of thin rose-pink stuff is wound over the hair and fastened behind and above the right ear. A garland of leaves is worn over the scarf.

Garments: The Ionic chiton of slate blue linen has a crinkled top, fastened at intervals along the upper arms. The skirt has pleats in vertical rows, with plain material between. The shaping of the pleats gives a pointed effect so that the skirt has an uneven hem. The girdle is invisible under the blousing at the waist.

Footwear: The white linen sandals have two thongs attached to the sole between the two first toes. These go round the foot at the back, forming a heel-band.

Jewellery and Accessories: The girl wears large earrings and plain bangles of gold, also a delicately wrought necklace. She carries a painted fan.

III.18. Greek Girl with Tasselled Cap.
5th Century B.C.

Hair: The hair is brought forward in a curled fringe over the forehead and put up in a chignon fairly high at the back of the head.

Headdress: The ornamented gold stephane is attached to a cap that encloses all the hair except that over the forehead and ends in a tasselled point at the back. It is embroidered in a border design behind the stephane and diagonally round the point at the back, in azure blue, grape-purple and gold.

Garments: The Doric chiton of pale green linen has a decorated border of dark green and gold at the edge of the over-fold and round the hem. It is girdled at the hips, where the fullness of the garment hides the girdle, and the back edges are brought over the front edges to form the shoulder-fastenings. A himation of fine violet-coloured wool with a black key-pattern border is held in the hands.

Footwear: Only the toes of the left foot can be seen under the long skirt, but the sandals would be one of the types illustrated elsewhere.

Jewellery: The girl wears hooped earrings of gold.

III.19. Greek Slave Girl and Child.
5th Century B.C.

Hair: The girl's hair is cut short since she is a slave. The child has her hair dressed in ringlets, with a centre parting.

Headdress: The slave girl is bare-headed but carries a circular peasant's hat of straw. The child has a ribbon band round her head.

Garments: The slave girl wears a long-sleeved Thracian tunic in grey linen bordered with orange, over a pleated Ionic chiton in pale green. The child's dress is embroidered over white with dark blue decoration and she wears a short white Ionic chiton beneath it.

Footwear: Both are barefooted as was usual with slaves and children.

Accessories: The child carries a bunch of flowers.

III.20. Amazon in Phrygian Dress. 5th Century B.C.

Hair: Only the fringe and a little hair on the temple can be seen.

Headdress: The red Phrygian cap of leather, with a thick overhanging peak and long lappets at sides and back, has a band of ornamented red and white woollen stuff round the head.

Garments: Tights in some stretching material cover the arms and legs as well as the body and are ornamented with 'dog's tooth' in red and white stripes. Over them the Amazon wears a short, full, white linen kilt with a wide belt. Her rectangular cloak, or chlamys, of black wool, is fastened on the right shoulder.

Footwear: Soft shoes or bootees of dressed natural-coloured leather fasten with ties over the insteps.

Accessories: A short sword is worn on a baldrick and a bow carried in the left hand with an arrow in the right.

III.21. Amazon. 4th Century B.C.

Hair: The hair is drawn back into a low chignon, in the fashion of the Hellenistic period.

Garments: The Ionic tunic of white linen is dropped from the right shoulder to give greater freedom of movement and is bloused over a girdle at waist-level. The left side-seam is open, also to give free movement.

Footwear: The white boots, resembling stockings, of some pliable material, are drawn up to mid-calf, where they have an ornamental border in yellow and white. The toes are exposed and a similar border edges the end of the 'upper' which is fastened down to the sole between the two first toes.

Accessories: The Amazon carries a curiously shaped shield and a double-headed axe.

III.22. Greek Man. Alexandrian Age
(400–320 B.C.)

Hair: The hair is short and combed forward from the crown of the head towards the forehead.

Headdress: The white fillet, tied at the back, is placed lower at the back of the head than in earlier times.

Garments: The long Ionic chiton in heavy yellow linen bordered in orange and black, has sleeve-openings below the shoulder-line, a feature of this later Greek period. A short sleeve is formed by the deep ornamental border. This garment, given the name of kolobos, is believed to have been made in a wide tubular form without side-seams and to have been the 'coat without seam' described in the New Testament. The decorative border is repeated at the hem. The himation is simply draped in the second method described in 'Garments—Men', and is of cream-coloured wool (Chapter III).

Footwear: The sandals have a piece of leather meeting an ankle-strap and fastened to the sole at the base of the heel; a thong, wide at the top and diminishing towards the toes, also meeting this ankle-strap and fastened to the sole between the two first toes; and thongs fastened to the sole on either side of the arch of the foot and meeting the ankle-strap over the instep. They are of white leather.

IV ANCIENT ROMAN DRESS

I. REPUBLICAN ROME

A Note on Pre-Republican Rome

Some, at any rate, of the peoples living from the 9th century B.C. onwards in what is now Italy are believed to have been emigrants from the civilizations of Greece and Asia Minor. The T-shaped tunic worn by men and the similar gown, ending at the instep, by women, are reminiscent of the clothes worn in many near-Eastern and Mediterranean countries, including Assyria and Crete. The Greek influence is the most important in the development of Roman costume, and many examples of Greek dress occur in the art of the Etruscans in the centuries that preceded the foundation of Rome in 753 B.C.

The toga seems to have originated independently of Greek or Asiatic cultures. Smaller in size than its later Republican form, it was in use as a garment, often the only one for men, from the 7th century B.C. onwards.

DRESS OF THE REPUBLIC (500–51 B.C.)

Hair—Men: The men of the Republic wore their hair short, combed forward from the crown of the head towards the brow and above the ears.

Hair: (a) (About 300 B.C.) The Etruscan man has his hair comparatively long and brought forward in a fringe over his forehead. (b) (Late 4th century B.C.) The soldier's hair is hardly visible under his helmet. He has a moustache and short, trimmed beard. (c) (About 500 B.C.) The man's hair is thick and fairly long over the back of the neck. It is brought forward in a fringe over the forehead. (d) (About 550 B.C.) The hair is parted in the centre and probably formed into a low chignon at the back, though this is not seen. (e) (About 300 B.C.) The peasant has straggling hair with a fringe in front. (f) (Early 5th century B.C.) The girl dancer has a fringe in front and three ringlets over each ear. The back hair is pinned up into a low chignon.

Headdress: (b) The soldier wears a Greek helmet of bronze with a red horsehair plume. (c) The man has a wreath of leaves on his head. (d) A fold of the rectangular wrap is brought over the head. (e) The peasant's natural-coloured felt hat is a small-brimmed petasos. (f) The dancer wears a wreath of green leaves and a covering of green woven stuff is put on over her chignon.

Garments: (a) The tunic of yellow wool is 'T'-shaped, rather loosely fitting in the upper part. The Etruscan toga worn over it is green, bordered in terracotta and black on the curved edge. It is hung forward from the left shoulder, taken round the back, under the right arm and thrown over the left shoulder, the straight edge being rolled. (b) The soldier's short tunic is of white linen, bordered in red. His leather cuirass is white, with decoration in red. The figure is taken from one of the representations of Greek dress found in Etruscan wall-paintings. (c) The toga is of deep blue wool, bordered along the curved edge in yellow on a pale green ground. It is put on across the body, with the two ends hanging down behind the shoulders, and is presumably caught together at the level of the shoulder-blades. (d) The woman's dress is a grey-violet 'T'-shaped tunic resembling that worn in Crete, banded with blue. Her rectangular wrap is of black woollen stuff, bordered in white and brilliant red. (e) The peasant's tunic and cloak are of animals' skins, with a hempen girdle. (f) The dancer wears a full-skirted transparent gown of finely woven linen in saffron yellow embroidered in two patterns, of green and brown respectively. Its sleeves are seen below the shoulders of the close-fitting, basqued bodice in brown, bordered in yellow, that is worn over it. Garlands of yellow flowers decorate the shoulders. Her dress is reminiscent of that worn in Crete.

Footwear: (a) The Etruscan man wears long boots of brown leather, ending at the calf and laced across

IV.1. Etruscans

the front. (d) The woman wears black leather bootees with upturned toes. (e) The peasant has on boots of natural leather, laced up the front. (f) The dancer has leather sandals with a strap round the ankle, and two others joining it from the arch of the foot and from between the first and second toes.

Accessories: (b) The soldier carries a wide-bladed Greek sword. (c) The young Etruscan carries a lamp, used in ceremonies, with oil placed in the base of the bowl. (d) The woman carries a sprig of leaves and small flowers. (e) The peasant has a staff in his right hand and a leather pouch attached to his belt.

Hair—Women: During the years of the Republic, women's hair was simply dressed, waved back from a centre parting or modest row of curls above the brow to a knot low on the neck, or followed Greek patterns, with a chignon on the level of the top of the head.

Headdress—Men: Roman men went bare-headed, except for the frequent practice of using a fold of the toga as a wrap. A hood made of two rectangles of stuff sewn together, with long ends for wrapping round the neck, was worn by workers, peasants and travellers, with the paenula or semi-circular cloak.

Headdress—Women: Women drew a fold of the palla over the head or wore an oblong veil.

Garments—Men: The toga of the Republic was made of segments of stuff forming together a segment of a circle, about eighteen feet long and six to eleven feet deep at its widest point.

The edging of 'purple' in the toga praetexta was along the straight edge and was about three inches wide. In the toga picta and the toga trabea (see 'Materials, Colour and Ornament') there may have been a coloured border on the curved edge as well.

The toga praetexta, the usual wear of senators, magistrates and children, was put on as follows: the straight edge was hung from the left shoulder to the left foot, the remainder being taken across the back, under the right arm, loosely draped, leaving enough 'slack' to turn the material over, so that an over-fold hung down over the right thigh and the upper part of the over-fold could be rolled and tucked into the belt of the tunic beneath. The remainder of the toga was thrown over the left shoulder and arm and hung down the back. The straight edge, which had hung down the front of the body in the first place, was now pulled up a little and turned over, creating a second and smaller over-fold at waist level. The sinus, or larger over-fold, could be drawn over the head as a covering or used to cover the right arm, while the left hand might be covered by the smaller over-fold, called the umbo.

For about three centuries after the founding of Rome in 753 B.C. the toga was still worn without additional dress. By the 5th century, however, owing to Greek influences on Roman costume, the Ionic chiton, or tunic, was added beneath the toga. The arms were put through openings below the shoulder-fastenings, in the position of armholes. The T-shaped tunic, made fairly full, was also worn, and became the recognized wear, with or without a rectangular or semicircular cloak, of plebeians, that is peasants, workers and minor officials such as lictors. Three stripes of wool tapestry in one of the variants of 'purple' (see 'Materials, Colour and Ornament') decorated the tunic of patricians or upper classes. One from the centre of the neck to the hem was called the angustus latus, or wide stripe; the other two on either side of it angusti clavi or narrow stripes. These stripes were a badge of rank in Republican times.

The tunica palmata, a ceremonial garment for generals at their triumph, was worn with the toga picta (see 'Materials, Colour and Ornament') and was of fine purple wool, or silk after the 1st century B.C., embroidered all over in gold. An example of the toga picta in its much later form is illustrated in Chapter V.

A wrap-round kilt from waist to knee, comparable to the similar garment in Egypt and Greece, was worn for active pursuits such as hunting and as ordinary wear by slaves, gladiators, peasants and manual labourers.

The cloaks worn by the Romans were chiefly rectangular, notably the abolla, a military cloak, the paludamentum, worn by soldiers as well as civilians, a rectangle with the two short sides cut in a slope; and other rectangular wraps, enumerated in 'Materials, Colours and Ornament'. The rectangular himation of the Greeks became the pallium of the Romans. The paenula was semicircular and could be fastened down the front by the two straight edges. A semicircle cut out at the centre point of the straight side allowed it to fit round the neck.

Garments—Women: Roman women wore the 'camisia' (a short, close-fitting body-covering or soft corselet, usually made of kid) as a foundation garment.

Young girls wore the Ionic chiton (see Chapter III) to the instep with the toga praetexta as an outer garment, until they reached adolescence. Only prostitutes wore the toga after this stage of life and in this way the appellation 'togata' became one of disgrace.

Married women wore the Ionic, or sometimes the Doric, tunic to the instep. The chiton was known as the stola in this feminine form in Rome. Over it was worn the rectangular palla the women's version of the pallium, in a variety of drapings (see Chapter III, himation).

Footwear—Men: Various types of sandals and boots, reaching to mid-calf, were worn, also bootees (calcei) or sandals with thongs coming above the ankle. Red leather was used for the boots of senators and magistrates. Crepidae were made like bootees at the back and had low sides of leather, fastening with criss-cross thongs across the foot and tied round the ankle, leaving the toes exposed.

Footwear—Women: Women wore sandals or soft slippers and the bootees of leather or material with a stretch to it seen on their Greek counterparts, in white and various colours.

Materials, Colours and Ornament: The toga was made of wool, the toga virilis assumed by boys on reaching manhood in natural colour, the praetexta in white with a 'purple' border along the straight edge which could vary in colour according to the dye used, many shades being known by the collective name of 'purple', from wine-red through crimson and magenta to scarlet, and including violet and dark indigo. The toga pulla, worn as mourning, was made in black or a dull colour; the toga candida, worn by candidates for office, in pure white; the toga trabea, worn by augurs, in white with a 'purple' hem and scarlet stripes; and the toga picta in 'purple' wool and, from the 1st century B.C., in silk, with decoration in gold embroidery. This was worn by victorious generals and by magistrates and provincial governors on ceremonial occasions.

Wool, linen, with a small amount of cotton and silk, very costly at this time and not known in Rome before the first century B.C., were the materials used for Roman dress. Felt was also used for boots, hoods and heavy cloaks. Linen or wool was used for the tunic and for the stola worn by women, which was made in different weights and thicknesses, including the marvellously fine and soft linen of whose weaving the Ancient World held the secret.

Wool was used a good deal in its natural colour or in white. The military cloak worn by officers, known as the abolla, was usually made in terracotta red or in one of the red variants of 'purple'. The paludamentum was made in one or other of these colours, of wool or heavy linen, and occasionally after the 1st century B.C. in silk. The rectangular cloak called the laena was meant for cold-weather wear and was made of thick wool in a rough weave or of felt. The lacerna and birrus were also made of rectangles of wool, as was the semicircular cape known as the paenula. The wrap-round kilt could be made of wool or linen.

Colours in use for the tunic and stola were, in addition to white and the range of 'purple', yellow ochre, saffron and sulphur yellow, orange, terracotta, green varying from pale apple-green to emerald and a deep sea-green or green-blue, and cerulean blue, black, brown, grey and dun-colour. These last more neutral colours were mainly worn by workers and peasants in their tunics and cloaks. The most usual wear for senators, magistrates and patricians generally was white or off-white with the clavi and borders in purple.

Jewellery and Accessories: The Romans followed Greek taste in jewellery, with the addition of the gold crowns given as military awards. These included the garland of gold leaves set with jewels worn by triumphant generals, the gold band ornamented with ship's prows in gold for naval victors and another with gold palisades or turrets for military leaders who successfully assaulted an enemy's camp or besieged his city. Gold rings were also awarded as military honours. In early times Roman seal-rings, worn by men, were of iron, and iron wedding rings for men and women were worn throughout Republican times.

Military Dress: The Roman officer wore a cuirass of bronze or leather moulded to the body or composed of overlapping scales. Leather strips covered his shoulders and hung from the lower edge of the cuirass, which ended at the hips. Under this he wore the T-shaped

IV.2. Etruscan and Roman Figures

tunic. His helmet was of bronze, with a crest or plume. He wore boots ending below the knee. (For cloaks see 'Garments—Men', and 'Materials, Colours and Ornament'). Legionaries also wore the T-shaped tunic. Examples of their helmets and cuirasses will be found among the illustrations.

II. IMPERIAL ROME

Hair—Men: Men wore their hair short and brushed forward from the crown of the head as under the Republic, but a fashion arose from time to time of allowing it to grow a little longer, into short waves and curls. Curling and waving the hair with tongs, also dyeing it, was known to men who wished to appear in the extreme of fashion. In the first two centuries A.D. some 'exquisites' put gold dust on their hair.

The circular cut, with hair turned inwards all round the head, favoured later in Byzantium, was a feature of the 4th century A.D.

The fashion for patches of hair on the cheeks seen on some Greek men in the Golden Age was revived during the 3rd century A.D. Roman men in the 1st century A.D. were generally clean shaven, except for some plebeians and elderly men. Beards came into favour in the 2nd century A.D. and could be worn during the following two centuries.

IV.2. Etruscan and Roman Figures

Hair: (a) (About 500 B.C.) The man's hair hangs in long ringlets down to his shoulders and a short fringe shows on his forehead. He has a moustache and small trimmed beard. (c) The Etruscan woman has her hair done in a chignon (unseen) on top of her head. The front hair shows a little at the sides and has a short fringe.

Headdress: (a) The Etruscan man wears a diadem of gold. (b) (Early Etruscan period.) The warrior has a cap-shaped helmet of brown leather that comes down a little over the back of the neck and has cheek-pieces. (c) (Early Etruscan period.) The woman wears a tall conical cap of dark red leather, with a border of narrow vertical pleats.

Garments: (a) The man wears as his sole garment a small toga in green woollen stuff, bordered in terracotta and light blue. It has the two corners of its straight edge fastened behind the left shoulder, with some drapery hanging at the back. (b) The soldier has a close-fitting brown leather tunic, with shoulder-straps. It has a narrow belt of black leather. He wears a short breastplate of bronze, with a circular metal ornamentation, and greaves of bronze on his legs. (c) The woman wears a dress like those in Archaic Greece, with fastenings down the outside of the sleeves, which end at the elbow. It is of dark rose-coloured wool, patterned in white, and is longer than the Greek dress of the same type. The broad collar is of dark red, pink and dark green glass and enamel. The rectangular wrap, folded and hung over the right shoulder, is of dark green wool, with a border of dark red and pink.

Footwear: (a) The man wears long-toed, open-fronted boots of black leather, ornamented with gilt metal studs along the opening. They come up to the lower end of the calf at the back. (c) The woman wears bootees of green leather, laced across the front, with pointed, upturned toes.

Accessories: (a) The man has a lyre slung over his right shoulder and carries the staff often seen in Etruscan paintings. (b) The soldier carries a spear of iron.

Hair: (d) (About A.D. 113.) The soldier has a short trimmed beard and a moustache.

Headdress: (d) (About A.D. 113.) The soldier wears a metal helmet with metal crest, a forehead-piece and cheek-pieces. (e) (About A.D. 113.) The legate or tribune (senior officer) wears a bronze helmet, with forehead and cheek-pieces, and a long plume of red-brown horse hair. (f) (About A.D. 113.) The bowman, probably a foreign mercenary, has a plain iron helmet with a knob on the top and with forehead and cheek-pieces.

Garments: (d) The soldier has on a tunic of light brick-red wool and a cuirass of overlapping metal scales. His military cloak is of dark red wool, fastened on the right shoulder. (e) The officer wears a tunic of saffron-yellow wool and a cuirass of gilded leather, with pendent strips of dark red leather, ornamented in gold. The overlapping leather scales at the base of the cuirass match them. The military cloak, with rounded corners, is of terracotta wool, fastened on the right shoulder. (f) The bowman wears a short tunic or corselet and breeches of brown leather. The longer tunic also worn is of natural linen.

Footwear: (d) The soldier has sandals with leather soles, bound on over his feet and ankles with straps of webbing in buff colour. (e) The officer wears bootees of white leather, with a scalloped decoration at the top. (f) The bowman wears sandals resembling those of (d), but with broader webbing.

Accessories: (d) The soldier carries a circular bronze shield and a spear. His cloak is fastened with a brooch. (e) The officer holds the hilt of his sheathed sword, which is attached to his leather belt, in his left hand and a scroll in the right. (f) The bowman carries his bow and has his left hand on his sheathed sword, which is slung on a baldrick from right shoulder to left hip.

Hair—Women: Various modes of hairdressing obtained during the Empire period. In the 1st century A.D. it could be waved or done in stiff curls on either side of a centre parting, with the ends curled on the neck or wound into a chignon fairly high at the back of the head, either twisted or in plaits. An alternative dressing was to bring the hair on the front of the head forward in a mass of close curls, with a high chignon at the back. These fashions were in force, with modifications, throughout the epoch. Artificial curls, on a tall framework, were often added over the forehead. In the 4th century the beginning of the Byzantine fashion for veiling the head resulted in the hair being wound in a roll on the top of the head or across it.

IV.3. 1st–2nd Centuries A.D. Roman Headdress

Hair: (a) The Roman boy has his hair cut short and brought forward over the forehead, in the manner worn during the Republic and early Empire. (b) This is a vestal virgin. Her hair is parted in the centre and rolled back on either side. The chignon is probably high on the head, covered by the headdress. (c) The young girl's hair is also parted in the centre and lifted in front to the top of the head, where a tress is bound round it and fastened. The rest of her hair falls on to her shoulders, but in the complete version of this coiffure the back hair is parted and brought up closely to join the hair on the top of the head.

Headdress: The vestal virgin has a headdress of linen arranged in small horizontal folds on a stiffened foundation, with a white veil thrown over it.

Garments: (a) The boy wears a white woollen 'T'-shaped tunic with the top arranged in funnel-shaped folds, and a toga virilis in off-white wool. A small fold of this covers his right shoulder. (b) The vestal virgin wears an Ionic chiton of white linen, with a folded collar fastened in front by a brooch and a narrow belt at a high-waisted level. (c) The young girl wears an Ionic chiton of pale orange linen, girdled at the waist.

Jewellery and Accessories: (a) The boy wears the bulla (a gold or leather-enclosed amulet) customarily worn by boys.

Headdress—Men: A fold of the toga was drawn over the head. The hood worn in the time of the Republic was worn by travellers, peasants and some workers.

Headdress—Women: The Greek stephane, sometimes in a diminished form, could be worn during this period, and a fold of the palla drawn over the head out of doors. When the Byzantine form of hairdressing came into fashion in the 4th century A.D., the veil thrown over the head could vary in length between one that ended just below the bosom, forming a cover merely for the head and shoulders, and one that fell almost to the hem of the dress. Pagan Roman brides wore a flame-coloured veil, the flamma. Christian brides wore a veil of white or violet colour.

Garments—Men: The cloaks described in Republican Rome continued in use, the paludamentum becoming gradually the most important. The toga remained an important feature of men's dress in the 1st century A.D. and its gradual decline and diminution in size took place during this period until, with the rise of the Byzantine Empire and the fall of Rome, it was altogether superseded by the paludamentum. The purple toga picta was now often made of silk and was heavily ornamented in gold, while the toga praetexta, little seen beyond the confines of Rome after the first hundred and fifty years or so of the Empire, could be put on in a different way during its remaining centuries. This form of the garment was known as the toga umbo. It was draped from the left shoulder to the left foot, as

a   b   c

IV.4. Roman Headdress. Republic and Empire

Hair: (a) (1st century A.D.) The Roman lady wears a front of false curls arranged in three rows on a framework. Her own hair is drawn back into a chignon fairly high at the back of the head and bound with four narrow plaits of false hair. (b) (1st century A.D.) The Empress wears a gold band round her head with two rows of curls mounted on a framework in the front of it. (c) (2nd century A.D.) The hair is parted in the centre and drawn down over the ears, with a short lock coming forward over the cheekbone on each side. The rest of the hair is formed into rolls and curls that cover the back of the head from the crown to the nape of the neck.

Headdress: (b) The Empress wears a veil of violet silk over her head behind the false front, leaving the ears exposed.

Garments: (a) and (c) wear the Ionic chiton in azure blue and parchment coloured linen respectively, fastened with brooches on the shoulders. (b) wears a 'T'-shaped tunic with folds arranged vertically across the front, in finely woven white linen.

originally, in the first place, but with the straight edge folded outward throughout to a depth of about one foot. The drapery was then brought across the back to the right side, twisted twice, drawn across the breast with its upper edge turned over, and over the left shoulder again and allowed to hang down the back. The Emperor was now added to the number of persons who wore the toga picta on triumphal occasions.

The tunic was now rather longer, ending just above or below the knee or at knee-level. The angustus clavus had purely a decorative significance from the end of the 1st century, and by the 3rd century often had embroidered designs on it, appliquéd or woven into the stuff. From the 2nd century the tunic could end at the instep and was made in a variety of rich stuffs.

The dalmatic, foundation of an important outer garment for men and women for some centuries to come, was a tunic with long, loose sleeves and a boat-shaped neckline, reaching the base of the neck in front and at the back. It came into fashion in the Roman Empire in the 3rd century A.D As worn by men it ended at the calf or ankle. It was ornamented with the angustus clavus and often with bands of colour at the ends of the sleeves as well. It was ungirdled.

IV.5. 2nd Century A.D. Onwards. Romans. Six Figures

Hair: (a) (4th century A.D.) The Emperor has hair combed downwards all round his head. He wears a moustache and small trimmed beard. (b) (4th century A.D.) The Empress has a centre parting with rows of ringlets set horizontally on either side. The back hair, unseen, is pinned up in a chignon level with the back of the head. (c) The charioteer has hair arranged in a forehead fringe and fairly long on the nape of the neck. (e) The gladiator's hair is without a parting combed forward all round his head.

Headdress: (a) The Emperor wears a thick circlet of gold set with precious stones in front and embossed with a gold laurel wreath. (b) The Empress wears a gold and jewelled ornament above her forehead. It keeps in place the fold of her palla draped over her head. (d) The gladiator, one of a corps named Samnites, has on a visored metal helmet with a neckpiece and with holes pierced for seeing and hearing. (f) This gladiator also has a visored helmet with a neckpiece and eye-slits.

The tunica talaris, a tunic reaching the calf which dated from about A.D. 250, had long sleeves tapering at the wrists and a slightly gathered effect at the boat-shaped neckline, with a narrow band to finish it. It was decorated with circles and curved oblongs of appliqué embroidery, the circles being placed on each shoulder and on the side-fronts of the garment, well above the knee, and the oblongs at the wrists. Often a border was added, which outlined the lower edge of the tunic and the edges of the slits at either side which were a feature of the garment. The motifs of embroidery did not necessarily match each other and might all carry different designs. It was usually ungirdled. Towards the end of the 3rd century it might end at the instep and was more narrowly cut.

By the 3rd century deep and vivid colours were used for the dalmatic and for tunics, any of which might be embroidered or stencilled all over in conventional designs. More than one tunic might be worn as a protection against cold, and braccae served the same purpose.

The pallium was the equivalent of the Greek himation and was worn chiefly by philosophers, orators and learned men, generally draped in similar ways to those used by the Greeks (see Chapter III). In the 4th century A.D. the method of wearing it was altered. It was folded several times until its width was only about eighteen inches and was then draped on the body in the same manner as when it was unfolded. Its width decreased in time, so that the thickness of the drapery also decreased, until the pallium was merely a long stole, from fifteen to eighteen feet in length by twelve to fifteen inches in width.

Garments—Women: The Ionic chiton was still the principal garment of Roman women during the 1st and 2nd centuries A.D. The Doric type, with an overfold in the upper half (cf. Chapter III, 'Ancient Greek Dress') was sometimes worn. The palla, in its varied drapings, continued as an outer garment (see Republican Rome, also Chapter III, 'Ancient Greek Dress'). The dalmatic was adopted as a feminine dress and by the 4th century could be the main visible garment, with the talaris worn beneath it. It resembled that of men except in its length, which varied from a short distance above the ankles to one that flowed on to the ground. It was made in various colours and decorated with the angustus clavus and with bands of colour as borders to the sleeves, all of which by the 3rd century were ornamented with embroidery.

From the 4th century A.D. onwards the dalmatic was more elegantly cut and widened gradually towards the hem. The sleeves were cut in a slanting shape, losing the square effect they had had hitherto. A belt was added at about this time, put on at the natural waist-line or a little above it. This ensemble, of talaris, dalmatic and veil, formed the foundation of Eastern and Western European women's dress until the end of the 13th century.

At about the same time the palla was revived in the folded form which the pallium worn by men had now taken on (see 'Garments—Men', this section). Its drapery for women was as follows: having been folded it was hung over the left shoulder, with the belt fastened over it and the end coming just below mid-calf, brought across the back, under the

---

Garments: (a) The Emperor wears a tunic of ivory silk, decorated in crimson and gold, with a gilt cord girdle at hip-level. The skirt of the tunic, which ends below the knees, is slit at the sides. The border round the hem decorates these slits, and there are wrist-bands to match it, also square emblems to right and left on the skirt, on the outside of the arms and forming short clavi above the belt. His cloak is of dark purple silk, with tablions (large oblong motifs) of flame-colour and gold. (b) The Empress wears a stola of yellow silk over a long-sleeved, ivory silk tunica talaris. Her palla is of violet silk, bordered with gold. It is attached to a waist-cord, wrapped twice round the body, at the first time letting the drapery dip towards the right and at the second raising it diagonally over the bust, then twisting the folds from the lower edge and bringing them over the head, behind the right arm, to hang forward over the left shoulder. (c) The charioteer wears a white woollen Ionic tunic, ending at mid-thigh. Cords are bound round his body from chest to waist, and round his thighs, as a protection. (d) The Samnite gladiator wears a scanty, aproned kilt of red wool or linen, with a leather belt. His left thigh and right arm are covered in narrow strips of armour. He wears greaves on his legs. (e) The retiarius (net-bearer) wears a short white woollen or linen tunic put on below the breasts, held up by a shoulder-strap and girdled with a narrow belt. His left shoulder and arm are encased in strip-armour. (f) This gladiator, known as the secutor or follower, because his duty was to chase the retiarius in the arena, wears a kilt fashioned into an apron in front. Bands of leather are fastened round the upper part of his body, which is otherwise naked, and round his left thigh and knee. A legging of leather, laced in front and ending in thongs bound round the ankle, protects his left leg from below the knee. Another from calf to instep is round the right leg.

Footwear: (a) The Emperor wears shoes of purple leather with gilded straps.

right arm and, with the folds dropped to cover the thigh and part of the calf of the right leg, thrown over the left shoulder again to hang down the back and trail a little, if desired, on the ground.

Footwear—Men: The same types of footwear were worn under the Empire as in the Republic.

Footwear—Women: As above.

Materials, Colours and Ornament: The dress of both sexes became progressively more ornate as time went on, with more colour and decoration, particularly the use of gold embroidery.

Jewellery and Accessories: Jewellery continued to follow Greek models, but with a trend towards extravagant ornamentation and coarsened taste.

Ecclesiastical Dress: Early in the 4th century A.D. it was decreed that deacons serving at the altar should wear the tunica talaris. This is the first known vestment of the Christian Church. Bishops and deacons in the 6th century wore the talaris (usually in white) and dalmatic, bishops adding the paenula, which became the chasuble when worn as a circular garment and the cope when open down the front.

Bearded Roman. 1st–2nd Century A.D.

IV.6. Roman Officer in Crested Helmet. Republic and Empire

Hair: This is cut short and is unseen beneath the helmet.

Headdress: The soldier wears a helmet of bronze with forehead and cheek-pieces. It is surmounted by a crest of brown horse-hair. Helmets of this type were worn by members of the Praetorian Guard, the bodyguard first of the ruler of the Republic and later of the emperor.

Garments: The tunic is of red woollen stuff. The cuirass is of gilded overlapping metal scales, with strips of gilded leather, ornamented in red, at the shoulders and in two rows over the hips.

Footwear: The boots are of white leather, laced in front over white woven hose which end at the calf, and are piped in gilt leather, with metal studs.

Accessories: A baldrick of red and gilt leather is slung from left shoulder to right hip and supports the scabbard which is ornamented in the same colours. The sword-hilt and shield are of bronze.

IV.7. Roman Legionary. Republic and Empire

Hair: This is unseen under the helmet.

Headdress: The plain helmet of iron or bronze with forehead piece and cheek-guards, has a small knob on the top.

Garments: The 'T'-shaped terracotta-coloured tunic is worn over thick brown leggings, worn by Roman soldiers in cold climates, though they were thought unnecessarily sybaritic in Rome. The cuirass is of metal strips, hinged on the right side and fastened on the left. It has brown leather strips pendant from it as an added protection, the large centre strip being fringed and ornamented. Similar strips are attached at the shoulders.

Footwear: The natural-coloured leather sandals have two thongs over the insteps, two rising from a fastening in the sole between the two first toes and three round the ankles.

Accessories: The soldier carries a spear and a metal shield bearing the conventionalized device of a thunderbolt. His short sword is slung on a baldrick from left shoulder to right hip.

IV.8. Lictor with Fasces.
Republic and Empire

Hair: The hair is combed forward over the brow and downward all round the head. It is cut short and the beard and moustache are trimmed.

Garments: The loose, 'T'-shaped tunic of natural wool is girdled at the waist and ends above the knees. The leggings are worn as a protection against cold, a fashion borrowed from the Gauls and other more northern nations. The lictor wears a rectangular brown cloak fastened on the right shoulder.

Footwear: The shoes cover the toes and the backs of the heels and are bound on with wide leather thongs attached to the sole over the front of the foot and wound round the legs to the level of the lower calf.

Accessories: The lictor carries on his shoulder the axe with rods bound round it, a symbol of his office.

IV.9. Roman Patrician.
200 B.C.–A.D. 200 approximately

Hair: The hair is cut short and brought forward over the forehead.

Headdress: A fold of the toga could be draped over the head if a head-covering were needed.

Garments: The tunic of cream-coloured linen, on the lines of the Greek kolobos, or chiton, with the arm-opening below the shoulder-line, is girdled at the waist, but at home the Roman often took off the girdle so that the tunic hung to the calves or ankles according to its length. The cream-coloured woollen toga has a border of 'purple' along its straight edge, as worn by magistrates and senators. The method of draping is described in 'Garments—Men', Chapter IV.

Footwear: The white calcei, or bootees, have an opening at either side and thongs of leather coming from the top of the heel-piece, a little above the ankle, and from the arch of the foot on both sides. These meet and are tied in the front, above the ankle.

Accessories: A scroll of parchment is carried in the left hand.

IV.10. Roman Lady with Leaf Fan.
1st Century A.D.

Hair: There is a thick fringe of short, slightly curled hair over the forehead. The shape of the chignon at the back of the head can be seen under the head-covering.

Headdress: A fold of the palla is drawn over the head.

Garments: The stola of cream-coloured linen has sleeves formed out of the fullness of the upper part and brooched or seamed on the outside of the upper arms. Its skirt is sewn or pressed in fine pleats. The palla, of soft pale blue wool, is hung forward over the left shoulder, the remainder of the material being brought round the back, across the body and over the left shoulder to hang down the back. The part that crosses the chest diagonally is turned over at the edge. Part of this portion of the drapery is used to cover the head.

Footwear: The sandals are of a simple type, showing the toes, and are made of white leather.

Jewellery and Accessories: Long drop earrings of gold are worn. A fan, probably made of parchment with a stem of painted wood, is shaped like a leaf and is carried in the right hand.

IV.11. Roman Standard Bearer.
2nd Century A.D.

Headdress: A round leather cap, with a stiffened crown and a neck-piece of leather hides the hair. Over it is the head (without the mask), the front paws and part of the back of a wolf-skin.

Garments: The brick-coloured woollen kilt is draped up at the sides. Over it is worn a corselet of brown leather with borders of leather in narrow vertical pleats at the ends of the short sleeves and at the hem. The belt is of leather with gilt metal studs and fastening. Four strips of leather, with metal ornaments at the bottom, intended to give some protection to the abdomen, hang down from the centre of the belt.

Footwear: Crepidae of natural-coloured leather, with thongs across the open fronts, cover his feet, exposing the toes.

Accessories: The soldier carries a metal standard bearing, with other ornamentation in bronze, a laurel wreath and a Roman eagle. A sheathed sword is attached to the left side of the belt and a sheathed dagger to the right.

IV:12. Emperor. 2nd Century A.D.

Hair: The hair is moderately long and is fringed over the forehead with a lock in front of each ear.

Headdress: A wreath of gilt laurel leaves, tied at the back with gold ribbon, encircles the head.

Garments: The tunic of gold cloth, with long tight sleeves, ends below the ankles. The clavi and wrist-bands are crimson. The toga umbo of white wool is put on like the toga praetexta, with some differences, and has the crimson border on the straight edge. The drapery hanging forward from the left shoulder is arranged in folds. The length that is brought round the back to be thrown over the left shoulder is turned over to show the border, which also shows on a fold brought forward to cover the right shoulder.

Footwear: The bootees, covering the ankle, are of white leather tied over the instep.

IV.13. Roman Empress. 2nd Century A.D.

Hair: The hair is parted in the centre and rolled back at the sides over a band that passes round the head under the headdress. The hair at the back is drawn up into a chignon projecting at a fairly high level at the back of the head.

Headdress: A long veil of blue gauze is worn over the head, one side of it being held in the right hand. A gold stephane, edged with pearl ornaments and decorated in front with green enamel, is put on over it.

Garments: The stola of violet silk, ornamented round the hem with gold thread, is worn beneath a palla of gold tissue, which is tucked into a waist cord on the right side, brought round the back to be tucked in on the left and round again to be thrown over the left shoulder and arm.

Footwear: The slippers, fitting the natural shape of the foot, are of gilded leather.

Jewellery: Drop earrings of gold, a bracelet of chased gold and another representing a snake are worn.

IV.14. Roman Emperor in Armour.
2nd Century A.D.

Hair: The hair is grown longer than during the Republic and brought forward on the forehead.

Garments: The emperor wears a 'T'-shaped tunic of brilliant red woollen stuff. Over it is a cuirass of gilded metal or leather, moulded to the body and ornamented with a gorgon's head and other decoration. Strips of white leather, ornamented in gold, hang from the shoulders. At the base of the cuirass is a circular basque of white, gold-ornamented leather, with strips of the same stuff depending from it, ornamented like those at the shoulders. A narrow rectangular wrap of purple silk is fastened at the left shoulder, with some folds coming forward. The rest normally hangs down the back, or might be draped over the right arm, but in this case is brought under the left arm and then thrown across it.

Footwear: Calcei of white and gold leather, laced in front, are worn on his feet.

Accessories: The emperor holds a sheathed sword in his left hand.

IV.15. Youth in Tunica Talaris.
3rd Century A.D.

Hair: The hair is brought forward in a fringe over the forehead and left fairly long, covering the ears, at sides and back.

Garments: The youth wears the tunica talaris, unbelted and with long, close-fitting sleeves. It is of orange woollen stuff. The clavi or vertical stripes are represented by bands of embroidery in brown and red, repeated at the wrists. Circular ornaments are embroidered on the right and left fronts of the tunic and on each shoulder.

Footwear: The brown leather open-fronted bootees, covering the legs at the back to mid-calf, have bands of leather across the front and are worn over white hose.

Accessories: The youth carries a scroll on an ivory rod.

IV.16. Man in Dalmatic. 3rd Century A.D.

Hair: The hair is brought forward in a short fringe over the brow and is longer at the back than at the sides, leaving the ears exposed.

Garments: The young man wears the dalmatic in green woollen stuff, with the purple clavi (vertical stripes) repeated near the edge of the sleeves. The garment hangs loosely and the three-quarter-length sleeves, made in one with it, are loose. It ends just below the calves. Beneath it is an under-tunic of white linen, with long, close sleeves.

Footwear: The sandals are of white kid, with thongs over the front of the foot horizontally and vertically, over the instep and round the ankle, where they are tied in front.

Accessories: A lighted oil-lamp of bronze is carried in the right hand.

IV.17. Man in Chasuble. 3rd Century A.D.

Hair: The hair is cut in a circular shape turned inward at the ends and covering the ears.

Garments: A white tunica talaris, ornamented with red embroidered clavi and wrist-bands, can be seen at the neckline, wrists and hem. Over it is worn a vermilion chasuble or circular cloak with a head opening in the centre. It is decorated by plain clavi of dark crimson.

Footwear: Bands of natural-coloured linen, wound round the legs, form a kind of hose. The shoes of red leather have high fronts and are tied at the top of the instep by thongs of the same colour.

IV.18. Roman Woman. 4th Century A.D.

Hair: The hair is parted in the centre, brought down in a wave on either side and then turned back, loosely enough to leave the ears covered, and formed into a roll across the top of the head.

Headdress: A veil of thin yellow silk is fixed to the roll of hair on the top of the head with pins, one of which shows as an ornament.

Garments: The dalmatic of pale green silk has clavi and sleeve-ornament embroidered in black and yellow. The hem is formed of a gored flounce edged in black and yellow. It is worn over a tunica talaris of cream-coloured linen with black wrist-bands. A palla of deeper green silk is hung forward over the left shoulder, brought round the back and thrown over the left shoulder to hang down the back. The front length is folded and held in place by a narrow green belt, fastened by an emerald and gold ornament. The belt also encircles the waist of the dress.

Footwear: The shoes, flat-soled and slightly pointed, are of green leather.

Jewellery: A necklace of green stones with an emerald pendant is worn.

IV.19. Man in Consular and Ceremonial Toga. 5th Century A.D.

Hair: This is short at the back and brought forward from the crown to the forehead. It is longer than in Republican times.

Garments: The toga is longer and narrower than the Republican version, with the 'purple' band on the straight edge. It is draped as follows: Arrange the toga in folds about eight inches in width and wind one end round the left arm to be held out of the way while the garment is being draped. Throw the drapery held in the right hand over the left shoulder and draw it diagonally across the back to the right side of the waist. Loosen the hold of the right hand on the folds so that some drapery falls to the ankles, then throw the remainder over the left shoulder. Draw it across the back to the right side of the waist again. Loosen the drapery from the left arm and let it hang forward from the left shoulder to the ankle. Take the rest of the drapery across the body and over the bent left arm. The toga could be of natural-coloured woollen stuff or made as a decorated 'toga picta'.

Footwear: The man wears calcei in red leather.

Accessories: A scroll is carried in the right hand.

V BYZANTINE DRESS

The dress of the Byzantine Empire, rich in colour, gold embroidery and jewels, developed from that worn in the last phases of Imperial Rome. The city of Byzantium, or Constantinople, founded upon an ancient Greek colony, later re-colonized by the Romans, was made the capital of the eastern part of the Roman Empire in A.D. 394. The city itself, built in a magnificent position on the shores of the Bosphorus, commanded the commerce as well as the culture of both East and West. The power of the Eastern Empire increased as

---

V.1. 5th–11th Centuries A.D. Byzantine Women

Hair: (b) The hair is parted in the centre and put up in a chignon on the top of the head. (c) The hair is parted in the centre and pinned in a chignon at the back, fairly low. (e) The hair is coiled round the head and has a short fringe in front. (f) The hair is parted in the centre and only the waves on the forehead and temples are seen.

Headdress: (a) (5th century A.D.) A double roll of white silk, patterned in lines of vermilion embroidery, hides the hair. The top of it is filled in by a cap, as in (f). (b) (7th century A.D.) A wide circlet of gold, edged with pearls, with a jewelled ornament in front, holds the chignon in place on the top of the head. A long veil of cream-coloured silk, fringed with gold, hangs from the circlet. (c) (10th century A.D.) The foliated coronet is of gold, set with a pearl in the centre. (d) (5th century A.D.) The voluminous semicircular wrap has a fold drawn over the head. The edge that comes over the forehead is taken round the head and fastened at the back. (e) (6th–7th century A.D.) A broad gold circlet set with green and unfaceted stones supports the coil of hair pinned round the head behind it. (f) (11th century A.D.) A single roll of yellow silk, banded with gold lines, has a cap of dark green felt or thick silk attached to it. Large ornaments of gold and strings of pearls hang from it at the sides.

Garments: (a) The stola and small palla are of ivory silk, with a tunica talaris of which only the close-fitting sleeves of vermilion wool are seen. (b) The tunica talaris of sea-blue silk has clavi in gold and green. The oblong panel embroidered in gold, green and blue hanging in front of it is attached to the palla. The top of the panel is fastened at the waist line and the drapery of the palla thrown backwards over the right shoulder. A portion of its edge is secured at the back of the waist. The rest of the drapery is brought round under the right arm and thrown diagonally across the body and over the left shoulder to hang down the back. The front drapery is held in place by a jewelled belt, with a

large ornament in front. A fold across the front is turned over to show the pale green lining. One of the jewelled wrist-bands of the tunica talaris is seen at the right, also the draped sleeve of an azure blue chiton shorter than the under-stola. The wide collar of blue-green jewelled silk is partly covered by the drapery of the palla. (c) The dalmatic of deep red-purple silk is ornamented round the neck, down the front and round the arms and hem with a wide band of gold tissue edged with pearls and set with large ruby and amethyst-coloured stones. The belt is narrower but of the same design. There is a narrow band of gold and amethyst at the edges of the wide sleeves. The semicircular cloak, held with one arm, covered, across the body, is of gold brocade lined with scarlet and has a border sewn with pearls and amethysts. The close sleeves of the tunica talaris are of gold tissue. (d) The tunica talaris reaching the ground, of cream-coloured wool with clavi in dark red, is covered by a large rectangular wrap of blue-grey wool. (e) The tunica is of saffron silk with clavi embroidered in brown and green: the silk semi-circular cloak is patterned in brown and green with the addition of gold thread. The collar and wrist-bands are of beads, silk and enamel in the same colours, but the collar is set with red stones. (f) The tunica talaris is of dark green silk bordered at wrists and hem with lighter green, sewn with pearls and emeralds. The dalmatic is of gold tissue shot with flame-colour and edged at sleeves and hem with orange silk bordered with amber and red stones, repeated in the broad collar. The pale yellow silk chiton has draped sleeves and is shorter than the two gowns.

Footwear: (a) The red leather shoes are soft and flat-soled. (b) The shoes are of green silk. (c) The shoes are of purple silk. (d) The shoes are of white leather. (e) The shoes are of dark green silk. (f) The shoes are of gilded kid.

Jewellery: (a) The drop earrings are of gold and the necklace a double row of clear red amber beads. (e) The earrings are large pearls.

V.1. 5th–11th Centuries A.D. Byzantine Women

that of Rome dwindled and finally came to an end. The result was an imperial system of great splendour, attracting the highest exponents of science, scholarship and the arts of many nations and at the same time the most glittering traffic of Eastern and Western trade. After the fall of Rome in A.D. 476 Byzantium became the centre of the civilized world. In ensuing centuries, however, it was assailed and finally overthrown by repeated Islamic incursions, but by this time the ornate Byzantine styles had laid the foundations of Western European dress for some centuries to come.

The tunic and dalmatic retained their late Roman form, to begin with, and the folded rectangular wrap continued for a time. Long hose, originally a Persian fashion ending at the ankle but now made in one with the covering for the foot, were an important feature. The paludamentum continued almost unaltered, except for increased ornamentation, throughout the centuries of Byzantine power.

Hair—Men: The short hair, brushed forward without parting, of Republican and Imperial Rome, formed the basis of men's hairdressing in Byzantium, but was usually rather longer and curled inward round the head. By the 10th and 11th centuries hair often hung down from a centre parting, again curling inwards at the ends.

Beards and moustaches could be worn from the 9th century onwards.

Hair—Women: In the 5th and 6th centuries A.D. Byzantine women often wore their hair concealed by a turban-like headdress (see 'Headdress—Women'). When visible, it was parted in the centre and combed into a roll on either side away from the face, with a veil hiding it at the back, or it might be piled in a knot on the top of the head or coiled round the head in a plait or twist. Another method was to roll the hair into a twist on each side of the head, bring them together at the brow and fasten them there. These ways of arranging

---

V.2. 6th–12th Centuries A.D. Byzantine. Six Figures

Hair: (a) (6th century A.D.) The hair is cut in a circular shape round the head and turned in at the ends. (b), (c) and (d) (7th–10th centuries A.D.) These three men have short hair, brought forward, unparted, in front in the case of (b) and (c). (e) (10th century A.D.) The hair has a fringe in front and is longer at sides and back than formerly, covering the ears and the back of the neck and turned in at the ends. (f) (12th century A.D.) The Byzantine girl has a short fringe over the forehead and loose hair worn at shoulder length.

Headdress: (b) A white fillet, with ties at the back is set high on the head. (c) The soldier wears the wide-brimmed helmet with metal crest worn in many countries at this time. (d) The Emperor, in military dress, wears a hinged crown of gold set with pearls and decorated in bars of red enamel. (f) The girl wears a fillet of silver ribbon set high on the head.

Garments: (a) (6th century A.D.) A consul. The tunica talaris is of pale yellow silk, with clavi and wrist-bands of gold and orange. Over it is a shorter dalmatic of gold brocade bordered in gold and red. Over this is worn the vestigial toga picta of scarlet silk embroidered in gold and bordered in gold and orange. Its lining is of pale yellow silk. (b) (8th century A.D.) The man, a citizen, wears a green woollen tunic with breast-band and borders of grey and violet embroidery. His plain cloak is of black cloth. He wears grey woollen braccae gartered with bands of green and violet embroidery. (c) (9th century A.D.) The soldier's tunic is of brownish-pink wool. He wears a leather corselet, moulded to the shape of the body, with leather strips hanging from it at shoulder and hips. The corselet and strips could be gilded or of plain leather. (d) (10th century A.D.) The Emperor's long-sleeved tunic is of crimson wool, bordered at hem and wrists with gold embroidery. He wears a

corselet of links of mail with guards of the same on his upper arms and linked plaques of silver forming a border at the hips. His cloak is of purple wool. (e) (11th century A.D.) The Byzantine man wears a tunica talaris of dark red-brown wool with wrist-bands of green and dull gold embroidery. Over it is a dalmatic of green silk, with the sides slit and ornament at all the borders including the shorter type of clavi, ending at the hips in this case, in flame-colour and gold. (f) (12th century A.D.) The girl wears an under-gown of crimson silk, draped up a little in front and ornamented in silver and blue. The over-gown of blue silk dips at the sides. It is sewn with pearls and motifs of silver braid. The belt, borders and collar are of crimson silk, ornamented with pearls.

Footwear: (a) The Consul wears bootees of red leather, with ties crossing the insteps and tying round the ankles. (b) The citizen wears boots of yellow leather, with ornamental ties on the outside of the calf. (c) The soldier wears bootees of brown yarn, which stretch and need no fastening, with leather soles. (d) The Emperor wears boots of crimson leather sewn with pearls. They are higher over the knee than at the front. (e) The 10th-century man wears shoes of soft brown leather, with openwork strapping and a jewelled ornament in the centre of the instep.

Jewellery and Accessories: (b) The Byzantine citizen carries a scroll. (b) The soldier has a circular metal shield embossed with petal-shaped ornament and wears a sword attached to his leather belt. (d) The Emperor carries a lance and supports a bronze shield with his left arm. He wears a sword attached to his red leather belt, a gold brooch, fastening his cloak, and large pearl earrings.

V.2. 6th–12th Centuries A.D. Byzantine. Six Figures

the hair seem to have lasted until the 11th century when hair was again concealed by a veil or other headdress.

Headdress—Men: Byzantine men went bare-headed, apart from the hood that could be attached to the semicircular cloak when needed, or a fold of the rectangular wrap, when it was worn, pulled over the head, until hats and caps came into fashion about the 10th century A.D. Before this date a conical cap with a round, upturned brim had been known, but its use was infrequent.

Headdress—Women: The 'turban' headdress consisted of a cap fitting the crown of the head, surrounded by a thick roll of material. A moderate stephane could be worn with the rolled-back type of hairdressing, also a veil.

Hair piled on top of the head had an ornamented band fastened round it with a veil depending from it.

Royal Crowns: The jewelled coronet of the 5th century was soon replaced by a deeper crown a little wider at the top than at the brow, sometimes in hinged segments and ornamented with jewels. This became higher and more elaborate in the following centuries with one or more 'bridges' over the top and puffed material making it into a complete head covering.

Garments—Men: In the 5th century the paludamentum, worn over the tunica talaris and fastened on the right shoulder, finally superseded the toga picta as an outer garment of royalty, courtiers or officials of note and military leaders, but only the Emperor might wear it in purple. An oblong ornamentation of gold, enamel and jewels, called the tablion, decorated this mantle about half-way down the straight edge which hung in front and also that at the back. Men of lesser rank wore a rectangular or semicircular cloak. The toga picta was still worn by consuls, in a longer, narrower and partially folded form, and was put on in the following way: it was folded along the straight edge (of which the decoration might now be wider and patterned) into a fairly thick strip about a foot wide and placed on the right shoulder with part of the fold hanging down the centre of the body to the ankle or just above it. The remainder of the fold was taken loosely across the back, hanging there in a curve, brought over the left shoulder, across the chest, under the right arm and round to the back again where it was looped over the loosely hanging curved fold, brought to the front again at hip level and held loosely draped over the left arm. After the looping, the drapery was allowed to unfold to some extent.

At the time when the consular office was abolished in the 6th century the toga picta had become narrower until it formed only a long, narrow stole which, richly ornamented and draped in the way described above, became a part of the Imperial dress.

The dalmatic still usually ended at the calf but might now end just below the knee. It nearly always had wide sleeves to the elbow or wrist, cut in a deep rectangular shape in one with the garment, or slanted so that they widened at the wrists.

In the 5th and 6th centuries the tunica talaris came to the knee or just below or ended at the calf. It was still variously ornamented, with square, circular or rectangular applications of embroidery, with or without jewels, borders at hem, sleeves and neck, and a new type of angustus clavus ending a little above the waist.

In this epoch the wearing of hose became usual.

For practical pursuits the tunic was plainer and might have a fringed scarf as a girdle and a leather pouch hanging at one side.

In the 7th, 8th and 9th centuries no major change is noted in men's garments; but from the 9th to the 12th the tunic was often of ankle- or instep-length.

In the 10th and 11th centuries the pallium, worn over the dalmatica or talaris with an under-tunic if needed, was once more in fashion. In this instance it was of moderate size and was draped rather intricately. One method was as follows: a corner of the long side was attached at the right side of the waist. The rest of the drapery was taken across the body in front, round the back at waist level to the right side, across the body diagonally in front, over the left shoulder and round the back of the neck to the right shoulder, where it is brought forward to hang down the front. By fastening the lower edge of the drapery to the original waist-level folds it was possible to create a 'pocket' to support and envelop the left arm.

In the 11th century the paludamentum gave place to the semicircular cloak, equally ornate and fastened at the front of the neck. The sleeves of the dalmatica were less wide than formerly and it was a little narrower and shorter.

Garments—Women: In the 5th and 6th centuries A.D. the stola, or Greek chiton, was worn again after being eclipsed by the dalmatic since the 4th century. It was girdled so that the drapery over the upper arms formed loose sleeves held in at the waist. The long talaris was worn under it, with the palla as an outer wrap, sometimes drawn up over the head when out of doors, with the fold over the brow fastened at the back of the head to keep it in place. The Empress was the only woman allowed to wear the paludamentum, but a similar cloak, semicircular, was worn by Court ladies.

For more practical occasions a plain dalmatic was worn over a long-sleeved talaris and might be ungirdled.

In the 7th, 8th and 9th centuries the talaris and palla were the mainstay of Byzantine feminine costume. A royal method of draping the paludamentum was to hang it straight down over the left shoulder, bring the rest round the back, fastening a part of the top edge to the dalmatic at the back of the right shoulder, under a decorative collar, and allowing the rest of the cloak to trail in the form of a train. The semicircular cloak was now frequently worn fastened in the centre rather than on the right shoulder and the drapings of the palla were as before (see pallium, 'Garments—Men').

In the 10th, 11th and 12th centuries the paludamentum was still worn and kept its place in royal dress, though Empresses are seen in this period wearing the locam, or narrow stole evolved from the original toga picta, wound round the body over the dalmatica (see toga picta as worn by consuls).

A gown of the 10th century had a close, round neck and long, wide over-sleeves, showing the close sleeves underneath and a belt at waist level. A dalmatic drawn up under the waist-belt to form a front drapery was a feature of 11th-century dress. It was longer than the second dalmatic worn beneath it, and had short, fairly wide sleeves, with a talaris providing the usual close-fitting long sleeves.

Shortened over-gowns with long, tight sleeves and undergowns that flowed to the ground were worn in the 12th century.

Footwear—Men: The elaborate sandals and open-work bootees of Imperial Rome were worn in Byzantium in the 5th century. Shoes of soft leather or material, with leather soles and a strap across the instep, with fastening on the outside, and soft bootees, were also worn, The same footwear continued in the 6th, 7th, 8th and 9th centuries, the shoes varying in design and often sewn with jewels. The fastening was sometimes a jewelled clasp at the front of the ankle. A revival of the toeless Greek bootees was a feature of the 6th century. In the 10th the Frankish boots called pedules, of soft leather or cloth, turned over at the top below the knee, and boots reaching the knee on the outside and the calf on the inside, with leather soles and the uppers sewn with pearls, exemplify new types of footwear. At this time shoes developed definite long points.

Footwear—Women: Women wore soft shoes of the same designs as those of men.

Materials, Colours and Ornament: Silk was a main item in the clothes of the upper classes, with linen in all the different weights known to the Ancient World, wool and a certain amount of cotton. Silk was produced in Byzantium after its weavers were established there in the 6th century, but long before this time the Eastern Empire was rich in silken stuffs brought from the Orient. Brocade was produced in the city from the 6th century onwards, mainly in conventionalized Persian designs. Silks patterned with woven representations of flowers, leaves, trees, birds and animals, which were also of Persian inspiration, as well as simpler motifs, and other silks with embroidered as opposed to woven patterns, were produced in a quantity of beautiful colours, with constant use of gold tissue, cloth of gold, sometimes woven with flattened strips of pure gold, and gold brocade.

As is often found in early centuries, contrasting colours were freely put together, but it was also usual to find a dalmatic and paludamentum or other type of cloak matching in material and colour, or the main colour in a pattern repeated in plain silk in the same ensemble.

Predominating colours were many shades of red and purple, violet, blue, green, orange, amber, maroon, white and brown. Black was used chiefly for patterning.

All outer garments of royalty and the nobility were richly ornamented with jewels and goldsmith's work, which indicates the use of heavy, durable silks which would hang well and support the weight of jewelled ornament.

Jewellery and Accessories: Earrings, brooches, bracelets, mantle-fastenings, jewelled ends for belts, reliquaries, pectoral crosses and large jewelled collars like those of the Egyptians were the chief items of Byzantine jewellery. Rings were often set with the wearer's seal or with cameos or intaglios.

Military Dress: Byzantine soldiers wore a replica of Roman military dress (q.v.), continuing to do so until the 9th century. Their helmets, however, resembled those of early Western European warriors (q.v., Chapter VI). Chain mail and conical or pan-shaped helmets were in use after the 9th century.

Ecclesiatical Dress: The talaris, dalmatic and paenula became in the early Christian Church the foundation of ecclesiastical vestments of today (see 'Imperial Rome,' Chapter IV).

V.3. Byzantine Emperor. 6th Century A.D.

Hair: The hair is thick and of moderate length, with a short lock in front of each ear and a fringe on the forehead.

Headdress: The emperor wears a gold crown, set with pearls and rubies. Two strings of pearls hang on each side.

Garments: The tunic of ivory silk has ornaments of violet and gold at the hem and edging the slit at each side. Similar decoration can be seen on the right shoulder and on the wrists. The paludamentum is of purple silk lined with crimson. A large ornament of gold, pearls and rubies fastens the cloak on the right shoulder. A tablion in red and gold ornaments the cloak.

Footwear: The hose are red and the shoes purple, sewn with pearls and rubies with fastenings of the same jewels on the insteps.

Accessories: The emperor carries an open book.

V.4. Byzantine Empress. 6th Century A.D.

Headdress: A padded circlet of brilliant red silk hides the hair. It is ornamented with pearls and strips of gold. The crown that surmounts it is of gold, edged with pearls, and set with emeralds and amethysts. It has three gold ornaments on the top, at the centre front. Two of these have a pearl at the apex. Two long strings of pearls at each side of the circlet hang down in front.

Garments: The gown, a tunica talaris, of ivory satin is ornamented with gold and red on the skirt. The paludamentum is of purple silk, embroidered at the hem with figures of men and elaborate gold ornament. The wide, jewelled collar is of gold, emeralds and amethyst.

Footwear: The shoes are flat-soled, of red leather sewn with pearls.

Accessories: The empress carries an open book, its leather cover tied with ribands.

V.5. Byzantine Emperor. 9th Century A.D.

Hair: The hair is of moderate length, and is parted in the centre. A short beard and moustache are worn.

Headdress: A crown of hinged plates of gold, set with unfaceted gems and decorated with figures of saints, has a 'bridge' over the top to which a gold cross is fastened.

Garments: The under-tunic or talaris is of scarlet silk, bordered at the wrists with gold embroidery and pearls. Over it is a dalmatic, with three-quarter sleeves, in gold brocade, with a deep border at the hem of bands of gold braid and jewels and a pattern of squares set with green and red enamel. The vestigial toga draped over the dalmatic, is of scarlet silk embroidered in gold, sewn with pearls and rubies and lined in dark green. The paludamentum is of gold brocade and is lined in purple silk. The hose are scarlet.

Footwear: The shoes are of red silk ornamented with gold and jewels.

Jewellery and Accessories: A large brooch of gold and jewels fastens the cloak on the right side of the chest. The emperor wears a ring on the third finger of his left hand.

V.6. Byzantine Empress. 9th Century A.D.

Hair: The hair is parted in the centre and puffed out on either side. The rest is coiled on the top of the head.

Headdress: Bands of crimson silk, edged with pearls, are attached vertically to the crown and to the hair. The crown is a circlet of gold set with rubies and has a gold ornament in the centre front. The top is filled in with red silk and edged with pearls. Three strings of pearls on each side hang down over the collar.

Garments: The long-sleeved tunica talaris is of purple silk. The stola of crimson silk has sleeves on the lines of the Ionic chiton. It is ornamented on the shoulder and sides with pearls and rubies attached to squares and circles of bright red silk, and is edged with pearls. The paludamentum is of violet silk, bordered with two rows of pearls and lined in crimson with a large tablion of crimson silk set with pearls and rubies on the front. The jewelled collar is of gold, green enamel, pearls, amethysts and rubies and has a high neckline.

Footwear: The shoes are of dark red silk, sewn with three rows of pearls.

Jewellery and Accessories: The jewellery has already been described as an integral part of the costume. The empress carries a gold sceptre and a golden orb surmounted by a gold cross bordered with pearls.

V.7. Allegorical Figure, Byzantine. 10th Century

Hair: The hair hangs loose, and has a fringe on the forehead. This method of doing the hair is seen in later Byzantine or other early Christian art, in figures of angels, saints or abstract qualities and is not defined as masculine or feminine.

Headdress: A fillet of deep blue ribbon is set high on the head.

Garments: A long stola of white linen flows on to the ground. Over it is a wide rectangular wrap of soft mid-blue, draped as follows: one corner is fastened at the back of the right shoulder and the remainder of the drapery brought forward to fall diagonally across the body, a corner appearing at its lowest point on the right side. It is then lifted to waist-level, folded and wound round the waist and fastened at the back. The rest is brought over the left shoulder, unfolded, to hang forward over the left arm. The deeper blue appears again in the long, close sleeves, banded with gold embroidery, of the tunica talaris.

V.8. Byzantine Emperor. 10th–11th Century A.D.

Hair: The hair is combed downward at the sides and turned in at the ends.

Headdress: The gold crown has pendant strings of large pearls, and is studded with green and red jewels. The flat top is of red silk.

Garments: The dalmatic of purple silk is sewn with jewels on the loose sleeves and lower part of the skirt. Over it is worn the tabard-shaped vestige of the toga, which has ceased to resemble the original garment. Its back length is brought round to the front of the body and laid over the left forearm. It is of cloth of gold, with large square-cut ornaments of jewels, enamel and glass. The under-tunic of white silk has close-fitting sleeves edged with pearls and gold embroidery. The hose are red.

Footwear: The shoes are of purple silk, decorated with jewels.

**V.9. Byzantine Empress.
10th–11th Centuries**

Hair: The empress's hair is divided from a centre parting and turned back in a roll on either side of the face.

Headdress: The crown is a replica of the emperor's, but jewelled in blue and green, with double strings of pendant pearls and jewelled decoration.

Garments: The empress wears a tunica talaris like the emperor's and a dalmatic resembling his, but in the blue variant of 'purple', with decorations identically placed. Over it she has a scarlet paludamentum heavily sewn with jewels and fastening on the right shoulder. Its jewelled tablion in blue, green and gold is placed a little way down the long front edge of the cloak. The hose are scarlet.

Footwear: The scarlet shoes have pearl-sewn edges meeting over the instep.

VI EARLY WESTERN EUROPEAN DRESS (600 B.C.–A.D. 1100)

The costume of prehistoric times in Western Europe, where civilization lagged a long distance behind that of Mediterranean and near-Eastern lands, is too well-known and too simple to need much description. The wearers of rough garments of fur, with bone ornaments, clay cooking pots and implements of stone or flint, were still in a state of savagery at the beginning of the Bronze Age. About 2,500 years later, however, approximately in 600 B.C., they had emerged to the point of having garments of coarse cloth as well as of fur, with primitive looms for weaving them and bone needles for sewing two oblongs of stuff or skin together to make the first tunics. Celtic tribes had long before entered Western Europe from Asia, where they originated, had later conquered the Iberian settlers they found in Gaul and moved on to Britain. They had elementary dwelling houses, two-wheeled chariots, a coinage copied from those of more mature civilizations and iron vessels and implements. A mingling of tribes produced by the 4th century B.C. a Celtic–Gallic–British race in the south more advanced than the still savage Picts and Caledonians of the north.

CELTIC DRESS

The southern community established the Celtic or Iron Age, though bronze remained in use. The people themselves had advanced from a state of nakedness covered only by a blue stain known as woad, which may have been tattooed into their skins, with fur coverings when needed, to the wearing of tunics and leg-coverings of coarse wool or flaxen stuff, with fur or woollen mantles added.

Hair—Men: Celtic men wore their hair long, plaited or loose. Moustaches were also long and drooping. Beards are unusual in the representations that have come down to us.

Hair—Women: Women wore their hair long, and either braided or loose.

Headdress—Men: Men went bare-headed or in a pointed cap resembling the Phrygian. Helmets worn with fighting dress were round and made of bronze, with a comb of bronze in the centre, or a down-turned brim and horns on either side.

Headdress—Women: Women went bare-headed, but the rectangular shawl known to all ancient civilizations was in use in early Celtic centuries and must sometimes have been drawn over the head.

Garments—Men: The tunic or 'crys' ended just above the knees and was worn with a stout belt to which was attached a sword or dagger. It could have short sleeves, ending just below the shoulders, or long ones to the wrists. Leg-coverings resembling trousers ('braccae'), sometimes bound with criss-cross strips, could be worn with the tunic or alone. They were held up by a draw-string at the waist or began only at the knees or just below them. A sleeveless garment of fur, an animal's skin worn as a cape, or a large rectangular cloak fastened on the right shoulder might cover the tunic. The warrior's breastplate and shield were of bronze and his spear of iron. Shields were oval, circular or oblong with rounded ends.

Garments—Women: Women wore the 'gwn' or gown, which could end above the ankles, touch the ground, or flow on to it. It was belted and often made with the top separate from the skirt, leaving the mid-riff bare. The skirt was held up by a draw-string and could have broad 'braces' and be worn without an upper part, leaving the breasts bare. The gown could be sleeveless or have fairly wide sleeves ending above the elbow or long close sleeves. A gown that had long sleeves might be worn with an over-tunic with short sleeves. A sleeveless bodice of fur was also worn in place of the over-tunic.

Footwear—Men: Celtic shoes were of untanned leather with the fur left on the inside. They were made with the upper and sole in one and were fastened with leather thongs put through holes made near the edge of the upper and wound together over the instep and round the ankle.

Footwear—Women: Women wore shoes resembling those of men.

Materials, Colours and Ornament: Tunics and gowns were made of wool of varying weights or of coarse linen, which was the material most used for the braccae, or trousers. Cloaks were made of wool, sometimes of felt.

The Celts understood the art of dyeing in a number of colours, including scarlet, orange, green, blue, black and purple. Garments were ornamented in checks or stripes of bright colours, sometimes spotted or trimmed with bands of coloured patchwork. The Celts of Ireland wore wrap-round kilts, forerunners of the actual kilt of later days, as an alternative to braccae.

Bronze and gilt bosses adorned shields and belts and the coils of large gilt bracelets that were twined round the arms. Burnished bronze ornament decorated the hilts and scabbard-ends of swords and daggers and heavy necklaces of twisted gold wire were worn. Pins and brooches used as cloak-fastenings were large and decorative, as were the ornate earrings.

DRESS OF BRITONS UNDER THE ROMANS

Under Roman rule Britons continued to wear Celtic dress with Roman adaptations. The Roman fashion of bare legs and sandals was adopted in warm weather, superior and better-woven woollen cloth and linen were imported from Rome by the wealthier classes and were later produced in Britain as methods and facilities improved. British men wore their hair longer than that of the Romans, but not so long as before the conquest. British women of rank copied the dress of Roman women, while those of the poorer classes continued for the most part to wear Celtic dress.

The Roman laena, a large rectangular cloak of thick, soft wool, was worn by travellers, shepherds, peasants and workers who needed protection from cold. Women wore it belted, with the top part drawn over the head.

Jewellery was again a mixture of Celtic and Roman, though gold was scarce among the Britons, who used bronze, jet and enamel, in which their work was highly skilled.

The military dress of the Britons was like that of the Romans, with the lorica or cuirass made of mail or of metal or leather strips. Their helmets were probably of the same type as those worn by the Celts. By the 7th century this helmet had been adopted by Frankish and Byzantine warriors, or was contemporaneously invented.

BRITISH DRESS IN POST-ROMAN BRITAIN

In the continued warfare of the 5th and 6th centuries A.D., after the Romans had left Britain, it is probable that little change took place in British costume. The helmet of this period still resembled that of the Celts, but in the 6th century the brim took on an upward curve at the front and back and a point at either side, or was made in a square shape.

It is at this time that King Arthur is said to have lived, though the Arthurian legends are generally costumed in the dress of the 13th century.

By the end of the 7th century, when the invading Jutes, Angles and Saxons had founded their various kingdoms and were engaged in a never-ceasing struggle to maintain their territories, and when the British Celts had been suppressed if not entirely exterminated, the dress worn by them persisted in that worn by their Teutonic invaders, mingled with the dress of the Franks across the Channel.

It was the gradual incursion of Byzantine influence into this barbaric mixture that later produced the Western European costume of the 11th, 12th and 13th centuries.

By going back a little in time in considering these two cultures it is not difficult to trace the development of Teutonic and Frankish dress to the point where it became that of Britain.

TEUTONIC DRESS, 5TH TO 8TH CENTURIES A.D.

The early phases of Teutonic costume were not very different from the Celtic. Their first woven rectangular tunic was open-sided, being joined only at the shoulders and belt. Their warriors put the heads of animals on their own heads, as well as using the hides to cover their bodies when they went to fight; and their clothes were heavily ornamented (see 'Materials, Colours and Ornament').

Footwear: Teutonic shoes were the same, for men and women, as those worn by Celts.

Materials, Colours, Ornament and Jewellery: Linen and wool in varying weights were the materials used. Brilliant colours lined weighty fur cloaks and decorated women's gowns with appliqué work in conventional designs, stripes, dots and representations of birds and animals. Women of position wore an extra belt, ornamented with metal bosses or other decoration, over the belt at waist-level or girdling the hips below the waist-belt. Colours generally were the same as those known to the Celts. There was an abundance of heavy, barbaric ornament on helmets, shields, scabbards, the surface of pedules (see 'Frankish Dress'), the straps of cross-gartering, belts and baldricks, as well as necklaces, arm-bands, mantle-fastenings and earrings.

FRANKISH DRESS

The dress of the Franks from the 5th to the 8th century was like Teutonic dress in many ways, though it had far less cumbrous ornament. The following points, however, may be noted:

The men of some Frankish tribes in the early part of the period had the custom of shaving the back of the head and twisting the long hair on the top into a knot from which sprang either one or two 'tails' of hair.

At this time, too, a short-sleeved, one-piece garment combining braccae and a tight-fitting 'vest' was known.

In the latter part of the period 'pedules', soft bootees of leather or cloth, ending below the knee and sometimes bound on with strips of woven stuff, became part of the national Frankish dress. The classical fashion of the toeless bootee was also adopted by the Franks.

From the 8th century onwards, Byzantine influence impinged on Frankish costume, owing to the rise in importance of the Franks under their Merovingian kings, which had brought them greater wealth and power. The nobles and their dependents were able to wear the richest of Byzantine stuffs and to command the finest workmanship. By the 9th century Frankish clothes had taken on the improved cut, the finer hose, the shapelier shoes and more exotic ornament of Byzantium. Men wore their hair in the shorter Byzantine style and the coiffure and dress of women of the richer classes were indistinguishable from those of the Eastern Empire. It is largely to the Franks that we owe the spread across Western Europe of these more civilized and sophisticated fashions, though drawbacks of climate and harder living conditions limited the whole-hearted adoption of a Byzantine way of dressing.

ANGLO-SAXON AND NORMAN DRESS

In the 9th, 10th and part of the 11th centuries the Western version of Byzantine styles evolved by the Teutons and Franks continued to be worn in the costume of Britain. Before

VI.1. Early Western European. Six Figures

Hair: (a) and (b), a Celt and a Gaul of very early times, have long, thick hair touching the shoulders. (b) shows unparted locks on the forehead and both have long moustaches. (c) is Frankish, also of primitive times. He has the back of his head shaved, with a tress knotted at the top hanging down over the left ear and a fringe in front. (d) (a Saxon of the 8th century A.D.) has straggling hair, covering the nape of the neck. He has a short beard and a moustache. (e) (a Norman of the 11th century A.D.) The hair is covered by the helmet. The moustache droops downward. (f) (Frankish, of the 9th century A.D.) The hair is short and shows only in front beneath the helmet.

the end of the 11th century, however, Anglo-Saxon and Norman dress began to take on a new assurance, as though now established in a life of its own. Individual characteristics, such as the draping of skirts, began to make their appearance.

In England and France changes ran more or less parallel to one another. The Danish incursions had little influence on English dress, the Danes being more prone to follow the fashions of the country they had invaded than to impose their own.

Hair—Men: In the 9th and 10th centuries men's hair was worn in a 'bob' with a centre parting or with the front hair brushed forward in a fringe; occasionally it was left to grow to shoulder length. At the time of the Conquest the more moderately cut or even cropped hair of the Conqueror's nobles was copied for a time, but the English seem never to have taken to the strange Norman custom of shaving the back of the head and brushing all the remaining hair forward. Very soon, however, long hair was again the fashion among Normans and English alike, and lasted into the next century.

Hair—Women: Except for young girls, who wore their hair loose and flowing, women covered their hair almost entirely during this period. It may have been plaited or coiled and allowed to hang down the back under the veil.

Headdress—Royal Crowns: The foliated crown was rivalling the Byzantine type by the 10th century.

Headdress—Men: The Phrygian cap was reintroduced in this epoch and was in wide use. A conical cap was another fashion.

Headdress—Women: The veils worn by women might be square, oblong or circular. To form the Anglo-Saxon 'head-rail' a square or oblong veil was put on over the head with one end hanging over the left shoulder in front. The other end was taken from the right side under the chin and round the neck. This was repeated, if the veil were large, and the right-hand end left to hang over the right shoulder in front or taken loosely over the chest and over the left shoulder once more. For the ordinary veiled headdress held in

---

Headdress: (a) The Celt wears a rough version of the Phrygian cap in dun-coloured felt or coarse woollen stuff. (d) The Saxon has an iron helmet with a metal coxcomb or crest. (e) The Norman's helmet rises to a point and is decorated with metal studs round the rim. (f) The Frankish soldier wears a development of the Byzantine helmet, with a metal coxcomb. This type of helmet was worn in several countries in the centuries following the fall of Rome and may have been of Celtic or Scandinavian origin.

Garments: (a) The Celt wears a plain, rough tunic, with long sleeves, of sage green woollen stuff. His cloak, fastened on the right shoulder, is of bright red and white stripes in heavy wool. He wears rough braccae from below the knees, which are bare, to the ankles. (b) The Gaul's only garment is a pair of braccae of coarse brown woollen stuff tied at the ankles and folded over a belt (unseen) at the waist. (c) The Frank wears braccae or loose hose of natural-coloured wool, bound on with strips of webbing. Over this is a one-piece garment of brown woollen stuff, possibly knitted, with a yellow border, drawn on over the braccae. (d) The Saxon soldier wears a blue woollen tunic with long sleeves and a corselet of chain mail with points at the hips and the ends of the sleeves. His coarse hose are of brown yarn, bound over with webbing strips in a way that resembles puttees. (e) The Norman soldier has a suit of mail that includes a hood with face-opening and breeches, made as one garment. The sleeves end in metal or leather wrist-guards. His hose are grey,

bound with webbing strips. (f) The Frankish soldier has a long-sleeved tunic of red-brown wool and over it a hip-length corselet of mail, with a broad collar. Brown leather strips hang from the shoulders and hips. Beneath the tunic are thick braccae of brown woollen stuff, ending below the knees and tied there.

Footwear: (a), (b) and (c) all have clumsy shoes of reversed leather, the fur still left inside. Those of (a) are laced with thongs and those of (b) are pulled up with leather draw-strings. Those of (c) are tied over the insteps. (d) The Saxon soldier has well-shaped leather shoes coming over the instep to the base of the ankle. (e) The Norman has shoes of the same type and wears spurs. (f) The Frankish soldier has leather sandals bound over the feet and up the legs to the calves, but exposing the toes.

Accessories: (a) The Celt carries a spear. (b) The Gaul has a short sword and a circular shield with a leather strap to put his arm through. As the inside of the shield is shown, the reverse of large metal bosses can be seen. (c) The Frank has a long shield of leather stretched on wood, with bronze ornament, and carries a double-headed axe. (d) The Saxon has a spear and a circular shield with a large boss and spike in the centre. (e) The Norman has a bow and arrow and wears a quiver containing arrows attached to his leather belt. (f) The Frank carries a lance.

place by a fillet or circlet, the square or oblong veils were put on the head with one edge slightly overhanging the brow. The two sides hanging on each side of the face might be joined at the throat by a brooch. The circular veils had a hole cut in them, roughly a foot from the edge, so that the veil was thrown over the head with the face showing through the hole and the longer part of the material hanging down the back. This type of veil was super-seded altogether by the rectangular type in the 11th century.

Garments—Men: Men wore the rectangular cloak fastened in the centre or on the right shoulder. occasionally on the left. The semicircular cloak, now often closed down the front,

a   b   c

VI.2. Anglo-Saxon. Three Figures

Hair: (a) (9th–10th century.) The hornblower's hair is arranged to come forward in a fringe on his fore-head and to cover his ears. It is cut in a short 'bob'. (b) (9th–11th century.) The king's hair is parted in the centre and long enough to touch his shoulders. He wears a long, drooping moustache and a bifid beard. (c) The hair is hidden by the headdress.

Headdress: (b) The king wears a square gold crown, ornamented at the four corners and set with uncut jewels. (c) (10th–11th century.) The queen's crown is of gold, set with uncut jewels and her head-rail of gold tissue. This is fastened on the right side of her head beneath the crown. It is brought down over the right side of the face, under the chin and over the top of the head, arranged in folds there and brought down on the right over the back of the head to cover the shoulders, the end being thrown over the left shoulder.

Garments: (a) The hornblower wears a tunic of red-brown woollen stuff with a round, close neckline, slightly draped, and long, plain sleeves. The skirt is draped up on the hips. The hose or leggings are of black wool. (b) The king's tunic is of green wool, ornamented in gold. His cloak is of purple cloth,

lined in scarlet, and is fastened on the left side of the chest. The leggings, from below the knees, are of scarlet wool, with tops ornamented in gold thread. (c) The queen wears an under-tunic of deep blue cloth and a circular cloak of scarlet wool embroidered in black and gold and bordered in black. A black sash, contrived from a narrow rect-angular veil or wrap, is fastened round the waist, leaving a large part of the circumference of the circle to form wide, draped sleeves. The drapery on the left side covers the left hand and arm.

Footwear: (a) The hornblower wears boots of buff leather, higher at the back than in front. (b) The king's shoes are of black fabric, bordered in gold. They cover the insteps and end just below the ankle-bones. (c) The queen's shoes are hardly seen, but would be of soft fabric, in this case gold, scarlet or blue.

Accessories: (a) The youth is playing a horn with several holes in it to produce different notes. It is supported on a forked stand held up by his left hand. (b) The king is playing a harp of gold. (c) The queen carries a book in her right hand, supported also by her covered left hand.

had a hole for the head made nearer the edge than formerly, so that a graceful but not too big fold was laid across the chest on to both shoulders, and the remainder of the garment covered the back. Capes for all ceremonial occasions were very large and were lifted from the floor on their wearer's arms when he needed to move freely.

The short tunic remained in fashion throughout the 9th, 10th and 11th centuries and could be draped upward at the hips. Elder statesmen and scholars, with members of the King's council, wore a longish gown with narrow, long sleeves, reminiscent of the tunica talaris of the late Roman epoch. The tunic still had long narrow sleeves.

The gown or tunic might have several under-tunics worn with it, the one next to the skin being called the 'sherte'. Sleeves were more often set in than in earlier times, instead of being cut in one with the garment (a fashion which still continued) and the seams just below the shoulders were often hidden by a strip of embroidery. Hose or braies were worn beneath the tunic or gown with or without cross-binding.

Garments—Women: Women's mantles at this time could be semicircular, fastened on the right shoulder or at the front with a brooch or, in the 11th century, across the chest with cords, or they could be circular, with a hole for the head (see 'Garments—Men').

In the 9th, 10th and 11th centuries the over-gown for women of the nobility was long, in some cases trailing on the ground, and the skirt was very voluminous, but it could be drawn up by fastenings at the waist on either side or by an unseen girdle to form a drapery and to show the skirt of the under-gown, which could be equally long.

The neckline of the outer gown was at the base of the throat, and was ornamented with embroidery, which also outlined the vertical opening in front. This was opened for the head to go through but was worn closed. It was often hidden by the veil or cape. Sleeves could be moderately wide or narrow, but if wide the long close sleeves of the under-gown were visible at the wrists. Close-fitting sleeves were made long enough to be rucked on the forearm. The beginning of the fashion for very deep borders to the over-sleeves was seen in women's dress, as in that of men, in the last part of the 11th century.

Footwear—Men: Pedules (see 'Byzantine Dress', Chapter V) over hose or, in the 10th century, sometimes leaving the knees exposed, were in general use, as were soft shoes which often came up round the ankle. Either might be worn with the short tunic, but shoes were more usual with the long gown. Short hose resembling stockings, ending below the knees, were also worn.

Footwear—Women: Women's soft shoes and bootees were like those of men.

Materials, Colours and Ornament: Wool, linen and silk (the last at a great price), also some cotton, were available. Garments were decorated at the neck and at the borders of skirts and sleeves by means of appliqué or embroidery, and gauze and silk were used by the wealthy for veils, otherwise fine linen was used. Damask was already known. Fustian and home-spun made ordinary garments. Colours were much as in the late Byzantine era.

Jewellery: Necklaces, earrings and bracelets were not worn. Brooches, rings, girdles and mantle-fastenings made up the chief jewellery worn in the Norman period and for a time afterwards.

VI.3. Teutonic Warrior

Hair: The hair is long and straggling in uneven lengths, some of it lying on the shoulders.

Headdress: The warrior wears a helmet of bronze or other metal with horns attached at the sides.

Garments: The tunic is of rough, dun-coloured woollen stuff, with borders of narrow appliqué in blue and white at the sleeves and hem. Over it is worn a brown leather corselet, with shoulder straps, fastened at the chest with buckles. The borders at the top and bottom are of black leather, with brass ornament. The stout belt is of natural leather, also ornamented in brass. The skin of a large animal is worn as a cloak, covering the back and with the paws joined at the front of the neck. Leggings of coarse wool or hempen stuff in its natural colour have crossed bindings of red webbing.

Footwear: The shoes are of reversed leather, with the fur still left inside.

Accessories: The bronze shield is oval, with ornament of the same metal. The sword-hilt and scabbard are covered in leather with brass ornament and slung on a strap from the left shoulder to the right side of the waist, by a metal chain.

VI.4. Woman of Teutonic Tribe.
A.D. 400–800

Hair: The hair is roughly cut in a fringe in front and falls loose on the shoulders.

Garments: The skirt of dun-coloured hempen or woollen stuff has a separate bodice worn separately above it, with an ornamented belt and with gold ornament at the neck and on the lower part of the bodice. The child wears one garment of animal's skin.

Footwear: The shoes are of natural-coloured soft leather, fastened on by ties over the insteps and at the base of the toes.

VI.5. Anglo-Saxon Warrior. 9th–11th Centuries

Hair: The hair is rather shorter at the sides than at the back, and turned in a little towards the face.

Headdress: The red Phrygian cap has a decorative border in black and yellow, set with unfaceted jewels.

Garments: The yellow tunic is pouched over a girdle at the waist and has close-fitting sleeves cut in one with the garment, with borders of black and green at the wrists partly repeating that round the hem. The red rectangular cloak is fastened on the right shoulder. The legs are encased in green braccae with cross-binding.

Footwear: The shoes of thick, soft, natural-coloured leather have no separate soles. They are fastened at the top of the instep by narrow straps encircling the back of the ankle above the heel.

Jewellery and Accessories: The warrior carries a broad-sword in his right hand and rests his left hand on a circular shield with a central boss.

VI.6. Anglo-Saxon Woman. 9th–11th Centuries

Hair: The head-rail conceals the hair entirely.

Headdress: A short, oblong blue veil has been put over the head and crossed over on the left shoulder. For methods of draping this and larger veils see Chapter VI, 'Headdress, Women'. The edge of the veil hanging over the forehead forms small folds above the brow.

Garments: The green under-tunic touches the ground and has long, close sleeves and a round, close fastening at the neck which is hidden by the mantle. The blue over-gown has a full, gored skirt, shorter than that of the under-gown and pulled up on one side under the belt to form a drapery. Its sleeves are loose, three-quarter length and widening at the ends, with a decorative border in blue and yellow repeated at the hem. The green cloak is circular, with an opening cut some distance from the edge, but not in the centre, to admit the head.

Footwear: The shoes, with flat soles, are made of soft green leather.

VI.7. Anglo-Saxon Labourer or Artisan. 9th–11th Centuries

Hair: The hair is cut fairly short, brought forward on to the forehead without parting and gives the impression of rough-and-ready cutting. A moustache and moderate beard are worn.

Garments: The brown or grey woollen tunic is belted and slightly pouched at waist-level. Its sleeves are cut in one piece with it and are rolled up to the elbow. The neckline is rounded and close-fitting, with a short vertical opening in front.

Footwear: The thick, coarse dun-coloured hose, rolled down to the lower calves, are supported by cross-binding. The brown leather felt or cloth shoes are fastened by front lacing.

Accessories: An axe is carried in the right hand.

VI.8. Anglo-Saxon Queen

Hair: The hair is parted in the centre and wound into plaits on either side. These are tucked inside the headdress and their ends hidden by the cloak.

Headdress: The circular veil of pale yellow linen has an opening for the face and covers the back of the head and the neck. The gold crown is set with unfaceted green stones and has moderate foliation in gold.

Garments: The under-gown is of yellow wool with borders at the hem and wrists of flame colour and gold. The over-gown is of green silk, with wide sleeves, ending below the elbows. Its hem and borders are yellow and set with green stones in gold settings. Both gowns are long and full, the over-gown being pulled up into the belt at the waist in front. The long circular cloak is of black wool, lined with pale yellow silk. It has an opening for the head near the upper edge.

VI.9. Norman Soldier. 11th Century

Hair: The helmet covers the hair.

Headdress: The metal helmet, put on over the head-cover-ing of mail, is ornamented by strips of studded metal meeting at the top, which is pointed. A band of metal at the base encircles the head and a nose-guard depends from this.

Garments: A tunic with long close sleeves and long cross-bound hose are worn beneath the three-quarter-length coat of mail. The hauberk or coat of mail is of leather or other stout material, with small metal plates or rings sewn on to it.

Footwear: The leather shoes have metal spurs attached.

Accessories: The soldier carries a broad-sword, with its scabbard slung on a baldrick at his left hip. The tall, narrow shield, with pointed base, is of metal, probably lined with leather. Leather bands are attached on the inner side at three points. A strap fastened to the scabbard is joined to one of these bands.

VII   12TH-CENTURY DRESS

Although it is clear that rather bulky voluminous garments were still worn at the opening of the 12th century, there was a certain dignity in the length and the simple folds of the gowns worn by both sexes. Before long better cut in gowns and tunics, finer hose and more shapely shoes showed the elegant Byzantine influence more clearly. It gave a look of opulence and some Oriental influence to the clothes of the more advanced countries of Western Europe. The deep jewel colours of Byzantine fashions illuminated the cruder vermilion, bright blue, green and yellow of Anglo-Norman dress with richer and more lustrous values, and the two cultures mingled in an adaptation that was more practical, less ornate and gem-encrusted than the original, but handsome and effective in its own way.

Hair—Men: At the opening of the 12th century the fashion for long hair followed by the English had become a French style as well. It flowed on to the shoulders and in front was parted in the centre or brushed forward from the crown in short locks. In some cases a plait was made at each side of the head, taken round to the back and joined there, sometimes being attached to the back of the circlet if this were worn. The beard was often forked or in three parts.

The hair was worn much shorter in the second half of the century, and unparted, with the front hair tumbled on the brow, in a 'bob' or with a fringe which sometimes took the form of a downward peak on the forehead. Beards and moustaches were less in evidence and when worn were usually neatly trimmed. A Norman fashion was to comb forward the hair in the front of the head, and shave the back of it.

Hair—Women: At the beginning of the century women's hair was almost entirely hidden by veil or wimple, or both. It may have been braided to hang down the back beneath the veil without being seen, or coiled at the back of the neck.

About 1130 women began to wear their hair parted in the centre and braided into two plaits, which were fastened and weighted with ornaments at the end. By 1135 the hair was divided into two tresses which were held together by a ribbon wound in and out and round them. This necessitated the addition of false hair for many women, and eventually silk cases, stuffed, took the place of the visible false hair.

Headdress—Men: The Phrygian cap and the hood with a peak, usually made in one with a neck piece and small shoulder cape, were the chief forms of men's headdress. During the times when hair was worn long, at the beginning and again at the end of the century, the fillet or circlet was popular. Round caps, with a small peak or point on top and only the suggestion of a brim, characterized the latter half of the century.

Headdress—Women: The circular or rectangular veil worn by all women varied in size and was sometimes very long, at others hanging only a short distance down the back. It was put on with an edge coming forward towards the brow and hanging on each side of the face, held in place by a circlet or fillet, or, in the case of royalty or the nobility, by a coronet or crown. With the body-fitting gowns promoted by Norman fashions, a high dome-shaped cap was worn, with a wimple and also a short veil.

About the middle of the century the barbette—a strip of linen, narrow at the centre and wider at the two ends, put under the chin with the ends fastened on the top of the head—became popular and was worn under the veil. This became a prominent fashion of the succeeding century.

In the last years of the century, the wimple came into very frequent use. This was made, like the hood, in one with a small shoulder cape and neck piece, and had an opening for the face. The veil or other headdress could be put on over it. It was not worn by young unmarried girls, but by married women, spinsters and nuns.

Garments—Men: The mantle of Byzantine, Norman and Saxon fashion continued in use, fastened in the centre of the front or to one side with a brooch or special mantle-fastening. At the opening of the century the long mantles of royalty and the nobility had to be held up so that the wearer could walk. These were of more manageable length again by the 1130s, and reached to the calf or the heels, only being worn very long on ceremonial occasions. After the middle of the century many short mantles, falling only to the upper part of the thigh, were seen.

The men's gowns and tunics of this century followed the current Byzantine pattern. After the opening years of the century they tended to fit the body closely, or the over-gowns were draped in such a way as to produce the effect of doing so, though looser, belted gowns could still be worn. The skirt of the under-tunic was often shown to some extent and the gown ended above the ankles or at the instep. The neckline was round, sometimes with a closed 'V' in front, and was ornamented by a broad, round collar. The sleeves of the under-tunic were still long and close-fitting and those of the over-gown could be the same or could widen at the wrist, as formerly. Some over-sleeves had a deep bell-shaped cuff that fell over the hand, covering it. Others widened suddenly into a very deep hanging cuff. A 'dolman' type sleeve, wide at the top and tapering to the wrist below the elbow, was added to the fashion late in the 12th century and persisted into the 13th.

The masculine form of the bliaut was in fashion from about 1130 to 1150. It had a figure-fitting 'bodice' which had a slight downward curve across the abdomen and the same at the back and which ended at the hips, where it was joined to a 'skirt' cut in two overlapping triangles, with curved sides, apex downwards, one used for the front and the other for the back. This was draped from the down-hanging central point upwards to each side where it joined the 'bodice'. The skirt was usually shorter than the under-gown, which might match it or be entirely different. Sometimes the central point was omitted and the skirt of the bliaut was circular, only slightly draped upward at the hips. It had the same round, embroidered neckline, with closed 'V' in front, as other men's garments of the time, and full-length sleeves moderately wide at the wrists to show the under-sleeves. In the middle of this century the first examples of parti-coloured dress and dagged edges are seen, though these fashions were not yet to become general. Long hose, tied on at the waist, followed the Byzantine trend. Knee-length breeches and leggings could also be worn and hose were fastened to under-drawers by strings.

Garments—Women: Women's gowns followed a late Byzantine influence and derived indirectly from Saxon dress as well. The long gown or under-gown with close-fitting sleeves to the wrist, the modest neckline and veiled head were all Teutonic and also Byzantine. Mantles were very long, like those of men. Early in the century gowns could be fitted to the body or loose and girdled at the hips, but the skirts in either case were very full and lay upon the ground. The skirt of the body-fitting gown was usually lifted a little at the sides, over the hips. Wide sleeves, resembling those of the dalmatic, were more prevalent among women than among men.

After the First Crusade, when many fine Oriental silks were obtainable owing to the consolidation of European conquests abroad, the feminine version of the bliaut became fashionable and reached England and France about 1130. It was made of fine silken material, crimped and goffered all over, and was of a length to trail on the floor, though it was not of the immense length hitherto worn in this century. The neckline was ornamented by a narrow round collar with vertical opening in front (worn closed) to leave room for the passage of the head. Over it was a close-fitting bodice, ending at the hips, of some stretching material,

VII.1. 12th Century. Six Figures

Hair: (a) The king's hair hangs down on to his shoulders from a centre parting. He wears a long drooping moustache and a bifid beard. (b) The hair covers the ears and is fringed in front. (c) The hair is brought forward over the forehead and is shoulder-length at sides and back. (d) The traveller shows a few locks of hair on the forehead and has a moustache and short beard. (e) The queen's hair is hidden by her crown and veil, but is probably plaited or left to hang down her back. (f) The German emperor has comparatively short hair, covering the ears and turned in at the ends. He has a moustache and a short beard.

Headdress: (a) The king wears a gold foliated crown in six points, set round the rim with rubies. (d) The

often worked in a honeycomb design of gold or coloured thread. It could cover the shoulders or start over the bosom, and was usually belted by a girdle that was wound from the front of the waist, crossed over at the back, brought round again and knotted in front. The over-sleeves were very wide from the upper arm downwards. The top of the sleeve was often caught in the upper part of the arm into one or more puffs. Contemporaneously with the bliaut a closely fitted gown, with long, gored skirts draped up over the hips, was in fashion. It had the deep, hanging cuffs mentioned in 'Garments—Men'.

Plainer versions of the gowns described, constructed to clear the ground or turned up, were worn for workaday pursuits.

Footwear—Men: The pointed shoes in soft leather or cloth, in some cases coming over the ankle to form bootees which could reach half-way up the calf of the leg, were the usual wear. Shoes were sometimes made with a high back and low front, or with a tall pointed piece back and front but low over the ankle bone. Some were made with a strap to fasten over the ankle or instep and were cut rather high on the inner side and low on the outside. Towards the end of the century there was a brief vogue for shoes with exaggeratedly long toes, twisted up into strange shapes. At this time soft boots reaching to just below the knee, laced on the inner side, were also worn.

Footwear—Women: Women wore soft shoes or bootees like those of men, but not those with the very exaggerated toes.

Materials, Colours and Ornament: Many kinds of woollen cloth, linen, cambric, silk and cloth of gold or silver were used at this time. After the first quarter of the century, when the effects of the First Crusade improved the supply of silks and gauzes from the East, these became less expensive and were more widely used.

---

traveller has a hood with a face-opening and moderate peak at the back and a neck-piece coming well down on to the shoulders. (e) The queen wears a hinged gold Byzantine crown set with sapphires and pearls over an oblong veil. (f) The emperor wears a hinged Byzantine crown of gold, set with rubies and yellow topaz, and with a 'bridge' and cross on the top.

Garments: (a) (Early 12th century.) The king's gown is of saffron yellow wool with wide borders of green and gold at the hem and sleeve-ends. The sleeves are very long and cover his hands when his arms are lowered. The gown flows on to the ground and is belted at the hips. Beneath it is an under-gown of dark red woollen stuff. The cloak, fastened on the right shoulder by a gold ring, is of brilliant green wool, edged with dark red. (b) (Mid-century onwards.) This is an early example of parti-coloured dress and dagged edging. The plain side of it is of black cloth, with dagged edges bordered in yellow, repeated at the neck, cuff and arm-band, which match the patterned side of the gown. The patterned side also has dagged edges and is of yellow woollen material embroidered and bordered in red. The cuff and arm-band of black wool are bordered in yellow. The narrow sash-belt and the hose are yellow. (c) (Early 12th century.) This man wears an under-tunic of dark purple and an over-gown of blue, with a crimson sash knotted in front. The skirt of the over-gown is pulled up into the sash to form a drapery. The broad collar, cuffs and hem are of crimson, blue and purple embroidery and the sleeves of 'dolman' shape. The hose are blue. (d) (Throughout century.) The traveller wears a long-sleeved tunic of grey wool and over it a kilt of fur. Over these he has a large circular cloak of dun-coloured wool or felt. He wears cross-bound hose of coarse

natural-coloured fabric. (e) (First half of century.) The queen wears a bliaut in coral-red silk. The overskirt is cut in a point at back and front. The swathed, close-fitting bodice is made of the same stuff as the rest of the dress. The close undersleeves are of cloth of silver. The over-sleeves are wide and loose, and the whole dress is crimped into an appearance of small pleats. The wide, round collar and the band encircling the under-skirt at calf-level are of cloth of silver, sewn with red enamel and rubies and edged with pearls. The semicircular cloak is of heavy dark green silk, lined with cloth of silver. (f) The German emperor wears a direct copy of Byzantine royal dress. The dalmatic, worn over a dark indigo-blue under-tunic, is of parchment-coloured silk, with a round collar, arm-bands and sleeve-borders of scarlet silk embroidered in gold and silver thread and sewn with pearls. A deep border edges the skirt, embroidered in a design of circles in scarlet, green and indigo blue on a gold ground, with blue and green jewels.

Footwear: (a) The king's shoes are unseen. (b) This man wears bootees to the calf of yellow and red fabric, matching the patterned side of the gown. (c) This man wears ornate shoes of gilt leather, turned up in front to resemble fish-tails. (d) The traveller wears stout leather shoes. (e) The queen's shoes are almost hidden, but would be of coral-red fabric. (f) The emperor wears shoes of gold fabric sewn with pearls.

Accessories: (a) The king carries a sceptre. (b) This man holds a cross-hilted sword. (c) This man has a wine-cup in his left hand. (d) The traveller has a crook-handled traveller's staff. (f) The emperor carries a sceptre.

All the main colours known to the dyer's art, including many shades of red—rose-colour, terra-cotta, purple and wine-colour—orange, saffron-yellow, blue, green, brown, grey, russet and black were known. In the 12th century much of the material worn in England was dyed abroad.

Embroidery in colours and gold thread, also appliqués, adorned edges of garments, belts and necklines, and were also used as all-over decoration.

Jewellery and Accessories: Belts, girdles, coronets, circlets, gloves and dagger-sheaths could be ornamented with gold, enamel and unfaceted jewels. Chief items of jewellery were brooches, rings and mantle-fastenings. In this century the first gloves with separate fingers were worn. They were in a gauntlet shape, often embroidered and jewelled.

VII.2. 12th-Century Man in Pointed Cap

Hair: The hair is long and hangs down over the shoulders at the back.

Headdress: The red felt cap, reminiscent of the Phrygian, has a heraldic animal on the front in gold appliqué and a gold embroidered border.

Garments: The man wears a scarlet silk bliaut to the knees and an under-dress to the instep, with borders and belt of gold, red and green. The skirt of the over-dress is flared and the sleeves are long and close fitting. Over it is a long cloak of black wool, bordered all round in gold and green and lined with scarlet, fastened on the right shoulder.

Footwear: The hose are green and the shoes of red leather ornamented in front with gold and green.

Accessories: A drawn sword is held upright in the right hand and the left arm supports a metal shield emblazoned with heraldic animals. A baldrick of buff leather, decorated in red, is worn from right shoulder to left hip.

VII.3. Norman Man. 12th Century

Hair: The hair is long enough to cover the ears. It is un-parted and three locks appear on the forehead.

Garments: The bliaut of dark red silk is shaped loosely to the body and draped slightly at the hips. Its skirt falls in formal folds forming a point at the centre of the front and back, and is lifted at the sides. It has a matching under-skirt of fine pleats. The broad circular collar is of yellow silk, and is decorated in red embroidery and red stones. The sleeves are loose but of moderate width, banded with red and yellow embroidery at the wrists, where the close sleeves of a yellow under-tunic are seen.

Footwear: The hose are yellow and the shoes of dark red leather banded in yellow.

VII.4. Norman Woman. 12th Century

Hair: This is parted in the centre with the rest probably coiled on the head inside the headdress.

Headdress: The wimple of cream-coloured linen is covered by a domed cap of the same colour on a stiffened founda-tion. Folds are laid close together on the head and the cap devolves into a short veil reaching the shoulders. A gold coronet set with unfaceted rubies and green enamel is worn over the wimple and veil.

Garments: The under-gown is black and shows the sleeves at the wrists. The gown is of scarlet woollen stuff, shaped to the body and unbelted. It is long enough to trail on the ground. The long, close-fitting sleeves are made in one with it and have deep, narrow cuffs, longer than the arms. The right cuff has been knotted to keep it out of the way. Another form of these sleeves was closed all the way down except for a hole to admit the hand.

Footwear: The toe of one shoe, of soft black leather, is seen.

Accessories: The woman holds a spindle and thread.

VII.5. 12th-Century Princess or Noble Lady

Hair: The hair is brought down over the ears from a centre parting and plaited on each side.

Headdress: The plaits of hair are put into long cases of twisted silver ribbon, which end in small fringes. The long veil is of fine silver gauze and is surmounted by a foliated gold coronet set with unfaceted sapphires.

Garments: The bliaut is of pale azure silk, finely pleated and long enough to trail on the ground. The long wide sleeves are puffed twice in the upper arm with ties of silver ribbon. The close, round neckline and sleeves of a white silk under-gown are seen at the neck and wrists. Over the bliaut is worn a close-fitting corselet in a honeycomb pattern of silver thread. It has a 'V'-shaped opening to admit the head, with ornamentation in silver and deep blue in the centre of the bodice. The belt, wound twice round the body, is of blue and silver embroidery with silver cords and tassels.

Footwear: The flat soft shoes are of blue silk.

VII.6. Norman with Head Shaved at the Back

Hair: The hair is cut short and combed forward, without parting, into a fringe. The back of the head is shaved to a point on a level with the eyebrows.

Garments: The under-tunic is of black wool. The over-tunic of dark red woollen stuff is unbelted and lifted up in folds at the hips. It is bordered at the 'V'-shaped neckline, the upper arms, wrists and hem with ornament in purple and white. Loosely cut breeches of fawn-coloured leather end below the knees.

Footwear: The short grey woollen hose are banded in red and the shoes are of red leather.

Accessories: A spear is carried in the right hand.

VII.7. Crusader. Late 12th Century

Hair: The hair is hidden by the metal casque. The slightly drooping moustache is of moderate size.

Headdress: The suit of mail has a hood, lined and bordered with leather. Over this is put the round helmet or casque of metal, with metal studs and border.

Garments: The suit of chain mail covers the body, legs and feet. It is in two parts, the lower consisting of leggings and the upper of a tunic. Over it is worn the cyclas, usually of white linen or woollen stuff, with the red Crusader's cross appliqué and a belt at waist-level.

Accessories: The Crusader carries a spear and a shield with his insignia on it. His broad-sword hangs in its scabbard from a baldrick slung from right shoulder to left hip.

VII.8. Labourer. 12th Century

Hair: The hair is combed downward all round from the crown of the head.

Headdress: The Phrygian cap is of red woollen stuff.

Garments: The dun-coloured tunic has sleeves cut in one with the garment, very full at the top, where they form part of the body of the tunic, and narrowing towards the wrist. It is bloused over a belt at waist-level and ends half-way down the thighs. The neck is cut down into a point at front and back.

Footwear: The thick hose of coarse grey yarn are rolled at the calf and have leather soles.

Accessories: The labourer is wielding a scythe.

VII.9. 12th-Century Woman

Hair: The hair is worn in a short fringe over the forehead. It is plaited on each side and the plaits covered in ornamental cases of green and gold silk, much longer, probably, than the plaits themselves.

Headdress: A long oblong veil of white semi-transparent linen is held on by a gold circlet set with green stones.

Garments: The under-gown of dark red wool ends at the insteps and has long, close-fitting sleeves. The orange woollen over-gown trails on the ground, but has some of its folds hung over the belt at the hips. The upstanding collar has a 'V' opening which continues into a vertical opening to admit the head. It is ornamented in green, blue and black. The over-sleeves end at the elbow and hang down from a moderately wide opening. The hem is bordered with large appliqué motifs in green, blue and black on a white ground.

Footwear: The soft, flat shoes are of green woven stuff.

Jewellery: A gold necklace is worn.

VII.10. 12th-Century Archer

Headdress: The archer wears a hood, with neck-piece, of chain mail and over it a round cap-shaped metal or leather helmet with metal studs as ornament.

Garments: A shirt of chain mail, with wide sleeves ending above the elbows, is worn over a close-sleeved scarlet tunic of wool. The lower part of the suit of mail is a kilt ending above the knees. Under this is a short cyclas of scarlet, with a leather belt. On the left wrist and forearm is a long cuff of leather to act as a guard when shooting arrows. The round collar is of brown leather.

Footwear: The hose are scarlet. The shoes are of brown leather tied on the outside of the instep.

Accessories: A light, sheathed sword is attached by a leather sword-carriage to one side of the belt, with the quiver, containing arrows, on the other side. An arrow is fitted to the drawn bow.

VIII   13TH-CENTURY DRESS

The dress of the 13th century was characterized by a certain conservatism in line and cut, while richness of colour, sometimes in startling contrasts, lightened the sober effect. Long, flowing lines distinguished the costume of both men and women. Gowns, not clinging to the figure, could be belted or left to hang loosely. Modest necklines still showed a Byzantine influence and the long close-fitting sleeve that was to last for another four hundred years showed little alteration. An innovation was the cyclas or gardcorps, an over-gown of varying length that was usually sleeveless. The alterations in fashions from those of the preceding century were more evident in the better quality of some of the materials used and the improvement in dressmaking and ornamentation than in any drastic changes of style.

Considerable wealth in Church and State, increased prosperity in commerce, particularly in the wool industry, and more varied importations of stuffs from abroad with the opening up of further trade routes must have contributed to this advance.

Hair—Men: The hair was cut in a convenient 'bob' with centre parting or unparted with a short fringe over the forehead. A fashion arose in the second quarter of the century for parting the hair across the top of the head and rolling the front lock into a curl turned under across the forehead, or combed into a fringe. Men could be clean-shaven or bearded and beards were often forked.

Hair—Women: Women wore their hair braided round the head or over the ears. It could be parted in the centre or across the top of the head, the front portion being brought forward and curled. Queens and unmarried girls might wear their hair loose.

Headdress—Men: The Phrygian cap gave way by degrees to the coif, a plain hood without a peak, like a baby's bonnet, tied under the chin. This headdress was worn by all classes and is frequently seen in representations of huntsmen and field-workers. It was to continue in use for several centuries, often worn with a hat or cap over it. Another form of headgear was a round, soft cap with a small tag on the crown. It was sometimes sewn into a narrow band. The hood, which could be attached to the cloak, formed one piece with a large round collar, and had a peak at the back or the long liripipe or tail, which could be wound round the head and later formed the chaperon of the 14th and 15th centuries. A round, stiff-collared cap with an upturned brim slightly wider at the top than at the head opening was also worn.

Headdress—Women: The barbette was worn widely by women throughout the century. This was a band of linen, put on under the chin and brought up over the head, the two ends being fastened a little to one side of the top of the head. There were some variations in width, but as a rule the part under the chin was narrow, growing wider over the jaws, and covered the ears. It could be worn with a fillet round the head or covered with a cap shaped like a wide pill-box. The rim of this might be jewelled or have a circlet or coronet worn over it. Towards the end of the century this cap became wider at the top and could be worn with a short veil (couvrechef) thrown over it, with or without the barbette. It might also be shaped like a shallow hat, with brim turned down. Two other methods of covering

VIII.1. 13th Century. Six Figures

Hair: (a) This is parted in the centre and hangs down in a moderate 'bob', turned in a little at the ends. (c) The ends are seen, with ears exposed, below the bishop's mitre. (d) The hair is covered by the nun's wimple and veil. (e) The monk's head is tonsured, the hair remaining below the bald crown being left fairly thick. (f) The hair hangs down to a 'bobbed' length, turned outward at the ends.

Headdress: (a) The round black cap has a pointed crown and a border of red braid ornamented with gilt circlets. (b) The 'saucepan' helmet has a neck-piece covering the collar-bones. There is a slit for the eyes, also small holes and slits for breathing and speaking, in the visor. (c) The bishop's mitre, covered in cloth of gold and studded with red and blue jewels, is shorter, and wider at the sides, than

the hair when it was worn over the ears were the 'ramshorn' headdress and the gorget. To make the 'ramshorn' effect a long band, of silk or linen, was placed across the top of the head and the hair rolled in its ends on each side, the resulting coils of material, fastened over the ears, resembling a ram's horns and the width of the stuff forming a cap covering the back of the head.

The gorget was a form of wimple, possibly made as a hood with an opening for the face in the first instance, but used a little differently. The hood was drawn down at the back and sides, not covering the head; the material was then pulled up on each side and fastened to the hair above the ears, covering the braids and the base of the back of the head only and drawing the stuff tight at the back of the neck and under the chin. Or it could be boned or wired at the top. It is illustrated in Chapter IX, No. 5.

The crespinette or caul was a jewelled net which could cover the hair entirely, either when it was worn coiled over the ears or braided round the head. It might be covered by the 'pill-box' type of cap or worn with a fillet, with or without a barbette beneath. This jewelled net was the forerunner of the reticulated headdress of the next century.

Unmarried girls would often crown their unbound hair with flowers or a jewelled circlet.

Garments—Men: The large semicircular cloak with centre opening for the head which dated from the ancient world, was a favourite covering for riding and for protection from the weather.

The mantle or cloak made in the shape of an ellipse, with a wedge-shaped piece cut out to shape the garment in front, could be fastened by a brooch in the centre front or on one shoulder.

From the beginning of the century an under-tunic with long, close sleeves was still worn with a belted robe whose wide sleeves displayed those beneath. This over-gown called the surcote, might end at the calf or be long enough to sweep the ground and was full-skirted. A sleeveless version of this was the cyclas, now developed in civilian styles. Sleeves were frequently very full at the top, in a dolman shape, and tightened from elbow to wrist.

Short braccae (breeches) and the long hose described in previous chapters were worn

---

those of succeeding centuries. (d) The nun wears a white linen wimple and headband, covered by a black woollen veil. (f) The soft-crowned cap is of red woollen material.

Garments: (Applicable to the greater part of the century.) (a) The full breeches, gathered and tied below the knee, are of buff-yellow woollen stuff. The 'cote', of red cloth 'rayed' horizontally with black, has a close, round neckline without a collar. It is fastened from neck to waist and left open from there, ending below the calves. The narrow black belt is hidden by the blousing of the upper part. The sleeves are of the 'dolman' type, tapering towards the wrists. (b) A suit of chain mail, with gloves of mail, is covered by a sleeveless white linen cyclas, ending at the calves and with a slit in the centre front. It is pouched over an unseen belt. (c) The bishop wears an 'alb', or white tunic to the instep, with close-fitting sleeves; it is ornamented with gold and blue thread on an oblong panel in the front of the hem. An open-sided garment of red silk embroidered in gold forming a panel back and front but with loose short sleeves (unseen), is worn over it, ending below the knees and seen at the neck, where the head opening is surrounded by a turn-over collar with matching ornament, the loose neck-line of the alb showing in the centre; an embroidered stole worn round the neck hangs down to the calves so that the ends show in front. The chasuble, a version of the circular cloak, with an opening for the head, is of gold-coloured satin, embroidered in gold, red and blue. (d) The nun wears a loose white robe of woollen stuff which flows on to the ground;

it has long, loose sleeves, showing at the wrists the close-fitting sleeves of a white under-gown. (e) The monk wears a habit of coarse brown wool, with a cowl thrown back at the neck and a hempen girdle; it has loose sleeves, with the fitted sleeves of an under-garment showing at the wrists. (f) The musician wears a loose surcote of dark green woollen stuff, ending above the ankles; it has a loose, upstanding collar fastened in front with buttons on a narrow panel of red material.

Footwear: (a) The hose are red and the bootees of soft black leather. (b) The leggings and shoes are of chain mail. (c) The flat-soled shoes are of golden silk embroidered in red and blue. (d) The nun's black shoes are flat-soled and of black material or leather. (e) The monk's feet are bare. (f) The musician's hose are of red yarn.

Accessories: (a) The youth is playing an eleven-stringed harp with a gilded wooden frame. (b) The knight holds his unsheathed sword in his right hand and supports a small shield, bearing heraldic insignia, on his left arm. A sword belt and carriage of red leather, ornamented with gilt, hold his sword-scabbard. He wears spurs. (c) The bishop holds his pastoral crook in his left hand while the right is raised in blessing. (d) The nun is playing a psaltery with a plectrum. (e) The monk plays a form of guitar. (f) The musician has a portable organ, which is slung from a leather strap across his left shoulder and supported by his right arm, his right hand working the bellows (unseen).

beneath the under-tunic. Some of these may by now have been knitted and they could be worn with cross-binding.

Garments—Women: Women's gowns in this period were not very different from those of men. The under-tunic and over-robe, or alternatively the cyclas, were worn, and their mantles were the same as those of men. Their dresses were voluminous and might be belted at the waist or hips or left unbelted. When the dalmatic or cyclas was very long, the skirt might be gathered up in the arms for freedom of movement.

Footwear—Men: The shoes of the period, made of leather or cloth, occasionally of silk, followed the shape of the foot and had a moderate point. They could be jewelled or embroidered and might be edged at the back with fur in the case of well-to-do people. The fastening was by a buckle over the instep or a button at the outer side of it, in which case the shoe was cut away a little on that side for greater elegance. Usually they reached to the ankle-bone, sometimes covering it. Soft boots to the calf or below the knee were turned over at the top to form a boot-top, underneath which a strap was fastened round the leg to prevent the boot from slipping down. Stout shoes or short boots were worn for heavy work.

Footwear—Women: Women wore soft shoes comparable to those of men. Countrywomen and those engaged in active pursuits wore stout boots ending above the ankle.

Materials, Colours and Ornament: Linen and wool of all weights and qualities were the materials most used. A durable cotton, grown in Italy, was imported for making into padded jackets to be worn under chain mail. Silk and possibly satin were worn by the well-to-do, though wool and linen were recognized everyday wear. Velvet came into being during the second half of the 13th century and was welcomed for royal robes.

Differing shades of most colours were now worn and might be put together in considerable contrast. Scarlet, crimson, purple, violet, blue, yellow, green, brown, russet and dun-colour, relieved by white or black and with lavish use of gold and silver cloth by royalty and the wealthy, were among those most in demand.

Embroidery and appliqué, in gold or silver or in colours, enriched gowns, mantles, shoes and headdresses. All were sewn with jewels for those who were sufficiently wealthy and important and the resultant work was often of great beauty.

Purses and gloves could also be embroidered.

Jewellery and Accessories: Circlets, brooches, bracelets, necklaces and rings were of the most delicate workmanship. Precious and semi-precious stones were still unfaceted. Purses, gloves and dagger-sheaths were often jewelled as well as embroidered.

Crowns were foliated and set with jewels, as they had been from the 10th century.

VIII.2. Man with Sword and Gloves. Early Years of 13th Century

Hair: The hair is cut in a long 'bob', turned in at the ends.

Headdress: The soft, full-crowned cap of saffron-yellow cloth has a close-fitting rim and a small tab in the centre of the crown.

Garments: The saffron-yellow over-tunic, ending just below the calves, is full-skirted and open in front, showing the hem of a woollen under-tunic, ending above the knees and ornamented in blue and green. The neckline of the over-tunic is slightly folded round the base of the neck. The sleeves are of the 'Magyar' or 'dolman' type, wide at the top and tapering towards the wrists. The cloak is of dark green cloth, with a lighter green lining.

Footwear: The hose of dark green yarn are bound with saffron yellow and natural leather soles are visible.

Jewellery and Accessories: The over-tunic is belted at the waist, in green and gold leather, with a matching sword-carriage. The scabbard and sword-hilt are of gold and are ornamented in gold, green and blue. The gloves are of yellow-buff leather, ornamented with green jewels and gold braid. The cloak is fastened by a gold brooch, with green and blue jewels.

VIII.3. Man with Sword and Shield. Early 13th Century

Hair: The hair curls a little at the ends and is worn long, touching the shoulders, with a short fringe in front.

Headdress: The circular cap is of red felt ornamented in gold thread, and has a stiffened brim and crown.

Garments: The long gown is of purple woollen stuff, with ornamentation of gold and green on the belt and hem. The neckline is round, edged with gold braid and has a 'bar' fastening of gold, with jewelled ends, over the vertical opening in front. The three-quarter-length oversleeves are hidden. The cloak is of red woollen stuff, edged with gold braid.

Footwear: The bootees of red leather have flat, stout soles.

Accessories: The shield, sword-hilt and scabbard are of silvered metal, ornamented in gold.

VIII.4. Woman in Head-rail. 13th Century

Hair: This is hardly seen, but is probably wound over the ears in small coils.

Headdress: The rectangular head-rail of deep blue soft woollen stuff is hung over the left shoulder to hang down the back; the remainder is brought over the head, with some folds left loosely arranged to frame the face, brought round the back of the neck and thrown over the right shoulder to the back.

Garments: The gown of blue woven stuff is similar in every way to that of 'Woman in Fluted Headdress', except that the blousing at the waist hides the narrow waist-cord and the waist-line is a little higher. The folds of the circular cloak, of green woollen stuff are supported in front by the arms.

Footwear: The pointed, flat-soled shoes are of green leather.

VIII.5. King. Early 13th Century

Hair: The hair is curled a little, hangs to a long 'bobbed' length and is brought forward in curled locks on the forehead from a parting across the head.

Headdress: The foliated crown is set with green and red jewels.

Garments: The under-tunic is of black cloth, with long, close-fitting sleeves, and ends just above the ankles. The gown of vermilion cloth is longer, touching the ground when not caught up, but has some of its material pulled up on the right side and held by the belt. It is bordered in red, gold and green. The round neckline, bound in gilt braid and set with red jewels, has a short vertical opening to admit the head. The sleeve-border is placed above the elbow, possibly hiding a seam. The cloak is of dark red silk, lined with gold tissue and bordered in gold, green and yellow.

Footwear: The hose are scarlet and the bootees of red leather are bordered and ornamented in black.

Jewellery and Accessories: The belt is of red leather, bordered in black and set with green jewels. The king wears a gold ring set with a red jewel.

VIII.6. Woman in Cloak Covering Hands.
1230–50

Hair: The hair is unseen beneath the headdress.

Headdress: A wimple frames the face and covers the neck. A round 'pie-shaped' cap of stiffened, bright blue linen is ornamented in appliqué of deep red.

Garments: The long, unbelted gown, flowing on to the ground, is of red cloth. It has a round neckline, with a border of gold and blue. The sleeves are not visible, but would be long and close-fitting. The blue cloth cloak has an edge turned back at the neck to form a collar and cords hanging down at the front of the neck. The hands are completely enveloped in it.

Footwear: The red leather flat-soled shoes have rounded toes.

Accessories: The woman carries a leather-bound book in her left hand.

VIII.7. Woman in Fluted Headdress.
1st Quarter of 13th Century

Hair: This is rolled up in large loose plaits and is supported by the barbette.

Headdress: A barbette increasing in width at the sides is placed under the chin and fastened on the top of the head. A stiffened, fluted off-white linen cap, wider at the crown than at the head opening, is worn over it. The side-plaits are covered with a jewelled net or caul.

Garments: The gown of yellow wool flows on to the ground and is bloused and belted at a low waist-level. The rounded neckline shows the top of the folds of the bodice. The long, close-fitting sleeves are made in one with the gown. The semicircular cloak is of dark red woollen stuff, lined with flame-colour. It is held by its fastening and by the right-hand front corner in the left hand, a frequent method of holding a cloak in place at this time.

Footwear: The soft, flat shoes are of dark red fabric.

Jewellery and Accessories: The belt is of dark red leather, set with gold ornaments. The cloak has a band of dark red material crossing the chest and fastened by jewelled gold brooches on the shoulders.

VIII.8. Woman in Barbette.
2nd Half of 13th Century

Hair: This is parted in the middle and wound in coils or plaits over the ears.

Headdress: A round white cap of stiffened linen in a 'saucepan' shape is put on over a barbette, in this instance widening towards the ends.

Garments: The gown is of pale blue wool, closely belted at the hips. It is thought that an early form of corset was worn under a dress of this type. The neckline is rounded, drawn close by a draw-string. The long, close-fitting sleeves are made in one with the dress. The semicircular cloak is of dull grape-purple, lined with scarlet. It is held to the body with the left hand and draped over the right arm.

Footwear: The soft, flat-soled shoes are of scarlet fabric.

Jewellery and Accessories: A circular gold brooch is worn at the neckline. A long, narrow belt of gilded leather, set with red and blue jewels, is worn at the hips. A purse of purple velvet with a gold frame and gilt tassels, is slung from the belt on gold cord.

VIII.9. Shepherd Boy with Lamb.
13th Century

Hair: The straight hair hangs in a medium length 'bob' and has a centre parting (unseen).

Headdress: The pointed hood of brown woollen stuff covers the neck and shoulders.

Garments: The loose tunic is of dun-grey woollen stuff. The sleeves are cut in one with the tunic and are turned back at the wrists, showing the reverse of the material. The belt is of brown leather. The boy wears loosely fitting leggings of brown wool.

Footwear: The short bootees of brown leather have loose tops wrinkling over the ankles.

Accessories: He carries a young lamb in his hands. A wallet of brown leather hangs from his belt.

VIII.10. Boy in Cyclas. Late 13th Century

Hair: The hair is cut in a loose 'bob', with the ends turned in and a lock coming forward on either cheek. A short fringe shows on the forehead.

Headdress: The pointed cap of dark blue cloth has the part intended to cover the neck and shoulders hanging down at the back, though the face appears through the correct opening.

Garments: An under-tunic of dark blue cloth with long, close sleeves is worn under the open-sided, sleeveless surcote of scarlet wool. It is piped in white, with white buttons.

Footwear: The hose are of dark slate blue yarn and the shoes of scarlet leather.

VIII.11. Girl with Basket of Eggs. Late 13th Century

Hair: The hair is wound (unseen) in a twist on either side of the head. A short fringe shows over the forehead.

Headdress: A white linen cap covers the head and has long ends on either side, which are wound over the ears and contain the twists of hair, forming the 'ram's-horn' headdress.

Garments: The under-gown is of dark red woollen stuff. Its oval neckline is covered by the over-gown. The sleeves are full to the elbow and close-fitting from elbow to wrist. The hem is turned up all round for freedom of movement, showing the buff-yellow lining. The over-gown, of a lighter red, has an oval neckline and no sleeves. Its full gored skirt is draped up over the hips showing the lining of pale pinkish red.

Footwear: The flat, pointed shoes are of black fabric.

Accessories: The girl carries a basket of eggs.

VIII.12. Man in Ganache. Late 13th Century

Hair: The hair is fairly long and turned in at the ends. The front hair shows in a curled fringe over the forehead. A moustache and beard are worn.

Headdress: A white linen coif is tied under the chin.

Garments: The long-sleeved under-tunic is of brown woollen stuff and ends just above the ankles. The over-garment, called a ganache, is of buff-coloured wool. It hangs loosely to calf-length and has a hood collar. Wide cape sleeves are formed out of the width of the material which is joined to make side-seams from the hips.

Footwear: The hose are of dun-coloured yarn and the shoes of black leather.

Accessories: The man carries a traveller's staff and has a black leather purse slung from his right shoulder and held in his left hand.

VIII.13. Man with Cup. Late 13th Century

Hair: The centre parting is unseen under the cap. The hair hangs over the neck at the back, and is turned inward a little at the ends.

Headdress: The round cap of dark green felt has a narrow upturned rim in white.

Garments: The calf-length under-tunic of dark green cloth has close-fitting sleeves to the wrists. The loose surcote of pewter-grey silken-faced stuff, ending below the knees, has a hood-collar and wide hanging sleeves lined in pale green with their seams joined at the hem.

Footwear: The hose are of grey worsted and the shoes of black leather or fabric, piped in white over the instep.

Accessories: The man carries a covered cup, containing wine or medicinal cordial.

IX 14TH-CENTURY DRESS

The 14th century followed the conservatism of the 13th with a gradual swing towards elaboration in dress, combined, as the years passed, with great beauty of line and distinction of cut.

Some important changes took place in dress during this century. The close-fitting cote-hardie, and later the robe called the houppeland, were worn in their different forms by men and women. Women's gowns in the height of fashion were very long for the greater part of the epoch. Parti-coloured and heraldic dress came into fashion, also the open-sided dress for women. 'Dagged' edges to sleeves and garments and long pointed shoes characterized the last part of the century.

The picturesque quality of its dress is recorded in the increased output of European sculpture, painting, brass memorials and tapestries.

Hair—Men: Men's hair was cut in a 'bob', with the ends rolled evenly inwards or outwards and a centre parting or fringe. Alternatively, it might be brushed back without a parting and arranged loosely to frame the face. It was of moderate length, varying only a little, throughout the century.

Men could be clean-shaven or wear beards and moustaches, or occasionally moustaches alone. Beards were frequently forked, sometimes divided into three.

Hair—Women: Women's hair could be braided round the head or over the ears, as in the preceding century, a centre parting predominating. The hair was arranged in various ways when worn at the sides of the head. One was to wind it into sausage-like shapes on each side of the head, pinned horizontally, presumably on cylindrical foundations; another to cover it in cylindrical jewelled nets worn vertically over each ear and held in place by the headdress; and yet another to place the braids vertically at each side of the head and turn up the ends under a headdress. Queens and unmarried girls might still wear the hair loose.

Headdress—Men: The hood, often made in one with a short shoulder-cape, and with a long liripipe or tail, continued in use, as did the coif. Towards the end of the century, men began to wind the liripipe round the head to form a kind of hat known as a chaperon. A hood with peak and shoulder-cape, but no liripipe, was also worn. The round hat or cap with a tag on the top and upturned brim, sometimes segmented so that one or another portion could be turned down, could be worn alone or over the hood or coif. Soft-brimmed hats capable of many changes, and usually made of beaver or felt, were useful workaday appurtenances. A tall hat widening a little at the top, with a band of contrasting colour forming the brim and with a feather or ornament in front, was another fashion. It appeared towards the end of the century and is illustrated in Chapter X, No. 12.

Headdress—Women: The reticulated headdress of jewelled net in its different forms was developed in this period. The 'nebulae' headdress that framed the face could be made of net or of gathered material. The remainder of this headdress was a veil, which could hang down the back or be gathered into a bag. The hair could be enclosed in the bag, or if the

IX.1. 14th Century. Six Men

Hair: (a), (d) and (f) The hair is hidden by the headdress. (b) A short fringe of hair is seen over the forehead. (c) The hair is parted in the centre and cut to a moderate length, turned in at the ends. (e) The hair ends just below the ears, which are exposed. It is unparted and taken back loosely from the forehead.

Headdress: (a) (First quarter of century.) A hood of yellow wool is worn over the head and neck. Over it is set a felt hat with a flexible brim. The crown is a dark slate blue and the brim of buff-yellow. (b) (First half of century.) The hood of vermilion wool covers the head and neck. Over it is worn a cap with a dagged brim in vermilion felt and a soft, draped crown, making a form of chaperon, of dark purple velvet. (c) (latter part of century.) The round cap with a stiffened brim wider at the top than at the head-opening and with a flat crown showing above it, is made of dark green velvet. (d) (Latter part of century.) The hood and shoulder cape made in one, with a dagged edge to the face opening, is made of

veil hung down loosely could be left loose or braided under it. The barbette and gorget are less often seen than in the preceding period after mid-century, except on elderly women. Circlet and coronet continued to be worn, as did wreaths of real or enamelled flowers. The wimple, made on the same plan as the hood, in one piece with a small cape fitting the neck and covering the collar-bones, and with an opening for the face, was worn for utilitarian purposes, also by the elderly and by nuns. A square or oblong veil might be thrown over it or wound round the head and neck.

Garments—Men: The large circular cloak, with an opening for the head, was in use from the beginning of the 14th century. During its early years men's tunics and gowns did not change much from those of the 13th. By 1325, however, the cote-hardie, a tunic made in varying lengths and fitting the body was in vogue. It had a belt at the hips and was fastened down the front and from elbow to wrist of the tight-fitting sleeves with small buttons. 'Tippets' or white bands with a single fall or streamer were worn just above the elbows in many instances. A hood-collar was usually worn.

Over the shirt and under the cote-hardie was worn a waist-length garment, called the pourpoint, with long, tight sleeves. The hose, made as two separate legs, were attached at the waist to this garment by laces, or points, as they were called. Short under-drawers were also worn and garters, which had to some extent gone out of fashion during the era of long robes, now reappeared, more as ornaments to men's dress than for use, and put on below the knee.

A version of the surcote, now often fitted closely to the body, with full skirt and a hip-belt or none, was also worn at this time. The skirt was normally slit at sides, back or front to give room for riding, and could have vertical slits looking like pockets through which the hands could reach the purse, which was worn on a belt beneath. It has a shoulder cape and sleeves ending at the elbow with a 'tippet' effect and the close sleeves of the pourpoint visible below.

In the last quarter of the century the cote-hardie became very short, sometimes ending only a short distance below the hips. Hose were made all in one to the waist for wearing with it, and for a time it had a very low belt. The shoulder-cape disappeared in favour of a

---

yellow wool and has small circular ornaments and dagges at the edge. (e) (Latter part of century.) The chaperon of crimson velvet is sewn permanently into the form of a hat. (f) (Latter part of century.) The hood of amber-coloured velvet has the liripipe twisted round the head.

Garments: (a) The under-tunic is of cinnamon-coloured cloth and has long, close sleeves. The surcote is slate-blue and brick-red on the right side and buff-yellow on the left. Both garments are pulled upwards on the left side and held by the belt, the buff-yellow lining of the surcote showing where it is turned over at the hem. The neckline has a wide upstanding collar of slate-blue. The cape sleeves are made in one with the garment. (b) The short cote-hardie of vermilion wool is stitched in horizontal lines in its upper part. The skirt is of strips of the same stuff sewn together at the sides. It has a close, round neckline and long, tight-fitting sleeves. It fastens down the front with purple buttons and the outer seams of the sleeves have buttons of the same colour. The belt of purple velvet forms part of the garment. The cloak is of dark purple velvet, with a round upstanding collar of vermilion cloth. (c) The pourpoint of dark green wool is seen at the ends of the long, tight sleeves. The courtepy is of black velvet with a high collar, 'V'-shaped in front, and wide sleeves lined with lime-yellow satin pinned back on to the shoulders. It is belted in its own material at waist-level. (d) The cote-hardie is parti-coloured in black and vivid yellow. It has long, tight sleeves and a dagged hem.

(e) The under-tunic of crimson silk shows at the ends of the long, close sleeves. The surcote is of sapphire blue velvet. It hangs unbelted and has a slit at either side of the skirt. Its sleeves are of moderate width and three-quarter length. They are edged with grey fur. A high-collared tabard of grey fur, open at the sides, with dagged edges, is worn over it. (f) The tunic is of dull orange-coloured woollen stuff, fastened down the front with tucks ornamenting the skirt and with a close, round neckline unseen under the hood. The sleeves are of 'dolman' shape and taper towards the wrists. The belt is of dark amber velvet.

Footwear: (a) The hose are parti-coloured in slate-blue and yellow and have long pointed toes. (b) The hose are vermilion, with moderately pointed toes. (c) The hose are lime-yellow and have moderate points at the toes. (d) The hose are parti-coloured in black and yellow and shaped to the natural contour of the feet. (e) The crimson hose, have slightly pointed toes. (f) The light amber hose have comparatively long points to the toes. The six figures could all be wearing leather soles, unseen.

Accessories: (a) The man carries a hunting horn, on a leather cord and round his neck. His belt and gloves are of buff leather. (c) The youth carries a leather-bound book. (d) An arbalest, or cross-bow, is carried. The belt and pouch are of purple leather. (e) A small sack containing money is held in the hands. (f) The man carries a bow.

high collar and tippets were no longer seen, but long, full over-sleeves covered those of the pourpoint, which at this time had some padding to throw out the line of the chest. Very full bag-like sleeves tapering to a close-fitting shape half-way down the forearm or near the wrist, and known as 'bag-pipe' sleeves, were a feature of the period. At the end of the century the waist-line was at a normal level, or just below it. Sometimes it was merely indicated by a join and a low-set belt was also worn. The purse and dagger were worn attached to the belt, sometimes at the back or in front rather than to one side.

The most important innovation contemporary with the courtepy, as the very short cote-hardie was called, was the houppeland, a gown with long full sleeves and voluminous skirt, a well-tailored 'bodice' with a high collar, a pourpoint with padded chest worn beneath it, and, in the first instance, a belt at normal waist-level. It sometimes had a shoulder-cape, or the cape belonging to the hood was worn pulled down over the collar of the houppeland. It varied in length from the calf (often with slits in the skirt for riding) to a length that trailed on the ground, had a buttoned front fastening, or was without fastenings, an opening being left for the head. In the shorter houppeland the belt might be low-set.

A loose gown hanging unbelted from shoulder to hem, which touched the ground or was a little shorter, was a suitable dress for the elderly and those of conservative tastes, though its colours might be brilliant. Any of these masculine garments except the houppeland could be parti-coloured, have heraldic designs on them, or be embroidered in rich patterns. Parti-colouring was also used in utilitarian dress.

Dagged edges to capes, over-sleeves and the edges of garments were in general wear in the last quarter of the century.

Garments—Women: At the opening of the 14th century women, like men, still wore the loose, full gowns. An innovation in the 1330s was the loose sideless gown, and over-dress with the side seams open to the hip, sometimes laced together and showing a closely-fitting

---

IX.2. 14th Century. Six Figures

Hair: (a) The bishop's hair just covers the ears and is turned in at the ends. (c) The priest has a tonsured head with hair left thick at sides and back, covering the ears. (d) The labourer has hair of moderate length, with a beard and moustache. (f) The youth has hair brushed straight back, raised a little from the forehead and turned outward at the ends.

Headdress: (a) The bishop's mitre is of ivory satin bordered in gold braid and set with amber, pearls and unfaceted sapphires. It is narrower and taller than in the 13th century. (b) (Latter part of century) The knight has a hood of mail covered by a helmet with long back and side pieces and a pointed crown. (d) The labourer wears a tall pointed hat of black felt, with an adjustable brim, turned up in front and down at the back. (e) About 1350–80. The woman playing the rebeck wears a 'nebulae' headdress of white gauze, gathered on a wire foundation, with a short, wide streamer edged with gathers falling on to either shoulder.

Garments: (a) The bishop wears an alb of linen finely criss-crossed with silver thread and ornamented above the front of the hem in blue and silver. The dalmatic with narrow front panel is of blue silk, ornamented in amber-coloured silk and pearls. Its sleeves are unseen. The ornament on its turnover collar is in dark blue and gold. The ends of the gold-embroidered, fringed stole are just visible in front. The chasuble is of ivory satin ornamented with pearls and with blue, green and amber-coloured stones. He wears a maniple, a strip of ornamented silk, over his left wrist. (b) The knight wears complete armour of hinged metal, with a heraldic beast in red decorating the front of the body and a narrow, scalloped fringe of blue leather at the hips. (c) The priest wears an alb of white linen, surmounted by a

form of dalmatic with a rounded, turned-over collar and long, loose sleeves. A stole of plain white silk can be seen in front. The cloak is of gold brocade with the pattern repeated on the border in red and gold. (d) The labourer wears drawers of natural unbleached linen and a white linen shirt with a rounded neckline and sleeves rolled up. (e) The girl wears an open-sided gown of brown woollen stuff with gilt buttons and light brown fur edging over a green under-gown with long, close-fitting sleeves. Her cloak, attached just under the edge of the fur trimming, is of black wool, lined with yellow. (f) The youth wears a surcote of scarlet wool ending below the knees, 'rayed' with a horizontal pattern of black and green and bloused over a belt. The turned-over hood-collar and the lining of the elbow-length sleeves are black. The under-tunic is green with black edging at the wrists.

Footwear: (a) The bishop's shoes are of gold satin, embroidered in pearls and blue stones. (b) The knight has shoes of hinged strips of armour, and wears spurs. (c) The priest's shoes are of white kid. (d) The labourer wears bootees of coarse brown yarn. (e) The girl has flat-soled, pointed shoes of black cloth. (f) The youth has red hose and black leather shoes.

Accessories: (a) The bishop carries a gilded pastoral crook. (b) The knight has a jewelled gold belt with green stones, set low on the hips. His sword scabbard, covered in blue velvet and ornamented with silver, is attached to it on the left and a dagger with a silver hilt and green leather scabbard on the right. He carries his unsheathed sword in his right hand. (d) The labourer is wielding a spade with a pointed blade. (e) The girl is playing a rebeck, an early type of fiddle. (f) The youth is playing a double pipe, with several notes for each hand.

IX.2. 14th Century. Six Figures
(The masculine costume is applicable to the greater part of the century.)

IX.3. 14th Century. Six Women

Hair: (a) The hair is parted in the centre and formed into a roll at the back of the neck. (b), (c), (e) and (f) The hair is hidden by the headdress. (d) The headdress covers all but a short fringe in the front. It is apparent from the shape of the headdress that the hair is formed into coils or plaits over the ears.

Headdress: (a) (about 1340.) The rondel of rose-coloured velvet is slightly higher in the centre-front than at sides or back. (b) (1350–80.) The 'nebulae'

headdress of cream-coloured wired net, with ends lying on the shoulders, has a baglike cap (unseen) fitting over the head at the back. (c) (Last quarter of century.) The turbanlike headdress is of coral-red velvet chequered in gold thread. There is an oval motif of gold embroidery in the centre of the upper rim, and three gold, jewelled ornaments below it. Strands of gilt beads hang from it on either temple and pass under the ears to be fastened to the turban again behind them. (d) (First quarter of century.) A

gown beneath. The sideless gown was sleeveless but covered the gown completely except for the sides and sleeves. Its neckline was boat-shaped and decolleté.

A gown of the early part of the century which made a useful style for the elderly hung loosely to the ground and was unbelted. It had a wide, boat-shaped neckline, which could be covered or filled in by a wimple. The sleeves were three-quarter length, only moderately wide, and as usual showed the tight sleeves of the under-gown.

Women wore their own version of the cote-hardie, with wide decolleté necklines, often dropping below the shoulders, and, in many instances, tippets just above the elbow of their long, tight sleeves. Sometimes the sleeves of this feminine cote-hardie ended at the elbow, showing the long, close sleeve beneath. It fitted the shape of the figure, flowing into long, flared skirts from the hips, and frequently had vertical slits resembling pockets which, in the case of women, who did not necessarily carry a belt and purse under the cote-hardie, could be used for lifting the skirts when walking. For more practical wear the feminine cote-hardie had a 'round' skirt clearing the ground.

The sideless gown, after being rivalled by the cote-hardie for some years, was developed in the middle and latter part of the century into many elaborate and beautiful forms, worn over a close-fitting cote-hardie and shaped now in itself to follow the lines of the figure. Like the cote-hardie, it could have a shorter, 'round' skirt.

The houppeland worn by women differed hardly at all from that of men, apart from being more tightly fitted at a high waist-level, and invariably having skirts that trailed on the ground. It was occasionally worn unbelted.

Women's gowns for utilitarian pursuits were made with 'round' skirts and otherwise followed the same lines as those of more elaborate gowns, excluding the houppeland. A method of shortening a dress for practical work was to turn the hem up facing outwards and pin or stitch it at regular intervals. Hose gartered at the knee were worn.

Footwear—Men: The moderately long pointed toes of the 13th century gave place early in the 14th to longer and more pointed shoes made of soft leather, velvet or cloth and much ornamented. The toes were stuffed to keep their shape and in the last quarter of the

---

wimple of white linen surrounds the face, partly covering the cheeks, and is tucked into the oval neckline of the dress. Over it is laid a rectangular white veil of linen or lawn, which reaches the shoulders at sides and back and covers the coils of hair over the ears. (e) The wimple of natural-coloured linen covering the neckline of the dress has a rectangular piece of the same stuff tied round the head above the brow and knotted on the left side of the head. (f) The wimple of natural-coloured linen is surmounted by a hood of blue woollen stuff with a short liripipe or tail. The dresses of (e) and (f) were worn by workers and country people for the greater part of the century.

Garments: (a) A cote-hardie of azure-blue woollen stuff fits the figure to the hips and flows out into a full gored skirt touching the ground. The neckline is rounded and the long, close sleeves made in one with the dress. (b) The gown of dark olive-green silk has long, tight sleeves with 'goblet' cuffs. The loose coat of salmon-pink silk has olive-green buttons and is lined in olive green. The left sleeve is fastened from elbow to wrist with the cuff of the gown turned back over it, but left open on the upper arm. The right sleeve is left open from the shoulder to form a 'hanging' sleeve. (c) The long-sleeved under-gown is of gold tissue and the high-waisted houppeland of coral-red velvet, with a full skirt flowing on to the ground. The high collar has a turn-back of dark green velvet. The sleeves, made in one with the gown, fit closely to the elbows, where they are turned back with green velvet. (d) This costume is

intended for an older woman. The long-sleeved under-gown is of silver-grey silk, and the over-gown of pale violet wool with small heraldic emblems in crimson, silver and blue. Its neckline is a wide oval. The sleeves end well above the wrists. (e) The calf-length woollen dress of scarlet wool has a round neckline, hidden by the wimple and plain rolled-up sleeves, inset. Over it is worn a pinafore of coarse brown stuff tied in at the waist by an apron of natural-coloured linen. (f) The under-dress of dark red wool ends at the ankles. The over-dress is of rust-coloured woollen stuff fitted to the figure and turned up over the hips showing the light blue lining. Its round neckline is hidden by the wimple. The sleeves are inset and close fitting. The left sleeve is buttoned to the wrist, the right rolled up for work. The costume of (e) and (f) is applicable to the greater part of the century.

Footwear: (a), (b), (c) and (d) The shoes, unseen, would be soft and flat-soled, toning with the dress and made of leather or fabric. (e) The black leather boots are laced in front and above the ankles. (f) The hose of red yarn are slightly elongated and pointed and have leather soles.

Accessories: (a) The belt of twisted rose-coloured velvet has a purse of the same stuff suspended from it by a gilt cord. (c) A citole (a form of guitar) is held in the hands. (e) The woman rests her elbow and one hand on a butter-churn made of wood. (f) A wooden wash-tub is carried.

century became exaggeratedly long. They might be separate from the hose or made in one with them.

Long boots do not seem to have been a feature of this period, though the bootees of workers could extend well above the ankle. Hose of mail or of armour went with the complete armour worn for tilting or in battle.

Footwear—Women: Women wore soft shoes on the same lines as those of men, but not so extreme in the points.

Material, Colours and Ornament: All weights and textures of woollen stuff were now in use, from the finest cloth to the coarsest homespun. Silk of many kinds, velvet, taffetas and cloth of gold and silver made up the dress of the well-to-do. Linen and cotton of various qualities were obtainable. Fur was lavishly used for trimmings and linings. 'Scarlet' was the name given to a brilliant red cloth, also to a fine silk in the same colour. Most colours and shades of colour could now be found and the Oriental silks introduced after the Crusades were in particular demand by the wealthy. Large heraldic blazonry, regular diapered patterns and all-over designs of flowers, leaves, birds and animals, either repeated in reverse or all facing the same way, adorned both masculine and feminine dress.

Jewellery and Accessories: Gloves, purses, dagger sheaths, belts, women's headdresses, men's hats and caps, royal or noble crowns and coronets were set with jewels. Neck-chains of heavy gold links set with jewels were worn by men over the cote-hardie or houppeland. Neck jewellery was less worn by women. Rings with unfaceted jewels were worn by both sexes. Bracelets were not usual, since arms were entirely covered.

IX.4. Man with Torch.
1st Quarter of 14th Century

Hair: The hair is parted in the centre and covers the ears, with ends slightly turned in.

Headdress: The round cap of crimson silk has ermine trimming the stiffened rim. Over it is worn a rectangle of purple velvet, lined with crimson, the folds hanging on each side of the face and fastened down in the front of the cap.

Garments: The gown of purple velvet has a close, round neckline and long, close sleeves edged with silver braid. The large circular cloak of crimson silk is edged with ornamented braid in silver, red and purple. It is put on with the head emerging through what should be the left sleeve-opening, the front opening with aperture for the head (closed by a long silver brooch set with amethysts and rubies) hanging from shoulder to hem down the right front of the body. The right arm is put through the opening intended for it. The wide circular hem of the cloak trails on the floor on the right side, but is supported on the left arm, lifting that side of the hem from the ground.

Footwear: The flat shoes, with long, pointed toes, are of red leather.

Accessories: The man carries a lighted torch.

IX.5. Woman with Gorget Covering Ears.
Opening Years of 14th Century

Hair: This is parted across the top of the head and the front portion brought forward to form a lightly curled fringe. The hair is again parted, down the centre of the back from the crown of the head and coiled over each ear.

Headdress: A gorget of white linen is wired and shaped so that it forms a covering for the coils of hair and is fastened to the hair above them. It covers the neck and is itself covered at the lower edge by the oval neckline of the over-gown.

Garments: A long, dark plum-coloured cloth under-gown, with close-fitting sleeves to the wrists, is covered by a loosely fitting, unbelted over-gown in silver-grey silk flowing on to the ground. It is bordered at hem, sleeves and oval neckline in dark rose-colour. Its sleeves end at the elbow and are cut to form a pointed effect on the outside.

Footwear: The flat-soled shoes are of grey woven stuff.

IX.6. Queen with Fur-lined Sleeves.
Opening Years of 14th Century

Hair: This is parted in the centre and fastened in plaits over the ears.

Headdress: The broad-brimmed, shallow-crowned hat of stiffened linen or canvas, covered in cloth of gold, has a gold foliated coronet added.

Garments: An under-gown of bronze velvet, with long, close sleeves to the wrists and a full skirt flowing to the ground, is worn beneath a long, full-skirted cote-hardie of cloth of gold. The sleeves are semi-fitting to the elbows and have long 'tippets' lined with fur. A gorget formed of two rectangles of ivory silk crosses from side to side at front and back to the brim of the hat.

Footwear: The flat-soled shoes are of gold fabric.

Jewellery and Accessories: The queen carries a gold sceptre in her left hand and wears a ring on her right hand. With this hand she holds up her gown.

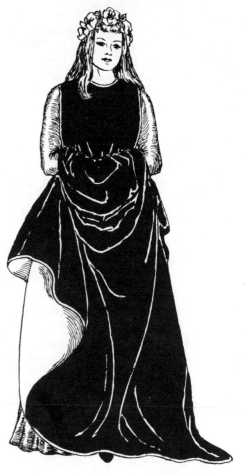

IX.7. Girl in Wreath of Flowers.
1st Quarter of 14th Century

Hair: This is cut in a thick fringe to come forward onto the forehead, the rest of the hair being allowed to hang loose.

Headdress: A wreath of pink flowers is worn, real or in enamelled metal with silver leaves.

Garments: The under-gown of cloth of silver touches the ground and has long close-fitting sleeves. The sleeveless cyclas, very long and hanging loosely from the shoulders, is held up over the crossed arms. It is made of dark green velvet, the rounded neckline and the arm-holes piped in silver. Its lining is of dark rose-colour.

Footwear: The soft, flat shoes are of cloth of silver.

IX.8. King. About 1330

Hair: Slightly waved and turned in at the ends, the hair hangs from a centre parting to a moderate 'bobbed' length.

Headdress: The foliated gold crown is delicately wrought and set with sapphires, pearls and rubies.

Garments: A cote-hardie of cloth of silver embroidered in gold, ending just above the knees, fits closely to the body, is belted at the hips and has little width in the skirt. The neckline is loosely folded and oval. The sleeves are long and close-fitting. The mantle is of purple velvet, lined with ermine, and is fastened on the right shoulder. A deep shoulder-cape of ermine hides the shoulder fastening and has a border at the top of gilt leather, with silver ornaments and red and blue jewels.

Footwear: The hose are scarlet and the shoes of purple velvet, embroidered in gold and silver.

Jewellery and Accessories: The belt is of gold plaques linked closely together and ornamented. The king wears a ring on each hand and carries a gold sceptre.

IX.9. Woman in High, Boned Gorget. 1330

Hair: The hair is parted in the centre with plaits on either side loosely brought together and fastened at the top of the head.

Headdress: The gorget of white silk is boned at the top to cover part of the chin, the neck and the back of the head.

Garments: The gown of ivory white silk, bordered in red and silver, has long, close-fitting sleeves. The circular cloak of black velvet has a collar of ermine coming down below the waist in two long points. It has a border of red jewels. The crimson silk hood depends from it unseen at the back, while a small part of its lining is visible on the shoulders. The hem and the vertical sleeve-openings are also bordered in red jewels. The left arm appears through one of these, while the right supports part of the circular breadth of the cloak, with the hem over the wrist.

Footwear: The flat-soled shoes are of red leather.

Accessories: The woman holds her purse in her left hand and is distributing a largesse of coins from her right.

IX.10. Man. Mid-14th Century

Hair: The hair hangs from a centre parting to a moderate 'bobbed' length. The moustache meets the slightly pointed beard.

Headdress: The white felt hat is conical, with a rolled brim.

Garments: The low-waisted cloth cote-hardie slightly fitted to the body and ending just below the knees, is parti-coloured in mulberry and a lighter shade of wine-red. It has a white hood-collar with a white streamer hanging from it, and white buttons. One leg of the hose is dark mulberry and the other wine-red.

Footwear: The shoes are of white leather with a criss-cross pattern of dark red.

Accessories: The twisted mulberry-coloured belt placed at hip level has piping of white. The mulberry-coloured pouch attached to it has white piping and a white conventionalized flower ornament with a red centre.

IX.11. 14th-Century Woman with Basket of Vegetables

Hair: This is not seen under the headdress.

Headdress: A small rectangular head-covering is dropped forward over the right shoulder, taken over the head and beneath the chin and the end thrown over the right shoulder to the back.

Garments: The plain dress of russet wool has an un-decorated rounded neckline (unseen) and long, close sleeves. An apron of coarse cotton cloth is worn at hip-level. It has a border of criss-cross patterning across the top.

Footwear: Hose of coarse brown yarn with leather soles are worn.

Accessories: A boat-shaped basket of vegetables is carried on the head.

IX.12. Man with Sword on Shoulder. Mid-14th Century

Hair: This is parted across the top of the head and brought forward in a fringe. The sides and back are of moderate length, turned in at the ends.

Garments: The under-tunic of copper-coloured satin has long, close-fitting sleeves bordered in red and gold and sewn with pearls. The surcote of black velvet fits the body and has moderate width in the skirt. It has a deep shoulder-cape, bordered with pearls and gold braid, and a small hood-collar. A narrower border of pearls and gold braid edges the sleeves, which end just below the elbows and is repeated on the hem and the front slit on the skirt.

Footwear: The hose are copper-coloured and the shoes of black velvet have red leather fronts with black lacings.

Accessories: A baldrick of stiffened copper-coloured material is decorated with diamond-shaped plaques of gold set with pearls and bars of gold. It supports a long dagger sheathed in gold and red leather. The man carries a sword with a scabbard of gilt metal, banded with red leather, resting against his left shoulder.

IX.13. Queen or Princess. Mid-14th Century

Hair: This is brought downward in two loose swathes from a centre parting, then taken towards the back and fastened in a roll together with the back hair.

Headdress: The foliated gold crown is set with green and blue unfaceted jewels.

Garments: The cote-hardie is of green and silver brocade with a décolleté oval neckline, unseen under the ermine top of the surcote. It fits closely to the body, has long, close-fitting sleeves with cuffs coming well over the hands, and is seen touching the ground below the lifted skirt of the surcote. The latter has a loose, sleeveless upper part of tailless ermine with a plastron of silver button-shaped ornaments. The long full skirt is of black velvet lined with silver tissue.

IX.14. Royal Lady in Parti-coloured Dress. Mid-14th Century

Hair: The hair is not seen, but is contained in the cylinders on either side of the head.

Headdress: A foliated gold crown set with green and blue unfaceted jewels is broadly shaped to accommodate the attached cylinders of gold and gilt lattice-work, lined with ivory silk.

Garments: The parti-coloured cote-hardie of black velvet and silver tissue fits closely to the body and has a full, gored skirt which flows into a train at the back. The neckline exposes the shoulders and is bordered with a band of silver stuff set with green and blue jewels. The close-fitting sleeves, with 'goblet' cuffs are also parti-coloured. The mantle is attached to the dress at the back of the shoulders and is of silver tissue shot with blue and green.

Footwear: The feet are not seen, but one soft, flat shoe could be of black velvet and the other of cloth of silver.

Jewellery: The belt set at hip-level is of linked silver plaques set with green and blue jewels.

IX.15. Young Prince or Nobleman. Mid-14th Century

Hair: Parted in the centre, the hair hangs in a thick, waved 'bob'.

Headdress: A circlet of gold, showing noble birth, is worn on the head.

Garments: A close-fitting cote-hardie of sherry-coloured velvet ends at the top of the thighs and is fastened down the front with large gold buttons. It has long, close sleeves, decorated on the seams with gold buttons from wrists to elbows. The belt of gold links set with red jewels and pearls is set at a low level. The cloak is of cloth of gold lined with ermine, fastens on the right shoulder with gold buttons and has 'dagged' edges.

Footwear: The hose are of dull orange colour and the shoes of gold and silver brocade.

Accessories: The youth holds a goblet of gold in his left hand.

IX.16. Girl with Lily. Late 14th Century

Hair: This is parted in the centre, with plaits fastened up in a vertical line on either side of the face.

Headdress: A band of silver material, studded with blue jewels and gold ornaments, encircles the head at forehead level.

Garments: A cote-hardie of dark purple satin, powdered with silver stars, shows at the sides, fitting closely to the body. It has long, tight sleeves, the lower part of the sleeves being joined just above the elbows to the upper part by seams in a 'dog's tooth' pattern. The sideless gown is of purple velvet with a white fur upper part which has a plastron of purple stuff with silver edging and ornaments.

Footwear: The flat-soled shoes are of purple fabric.

Accessories: A tall stem bearing lilies with leaves and buds is carried in the right hand.

IX.17. Girl with Spindle and Thread. About 1370

Hair: The hair hangs loose from a centre parting.

Headdress: A circlet of twisted dark green woollen stuff is worn.

Garments: The cote-hardie of light green cloth ends below the ankles. It is fitted closely to the body and has a wide oval neckline, exposing the shoulders, piped with darker green. The hem is bordered in gold and green and the buttons are gold. The long, close sleeves have white 'tippets' attached to the upper arms. There are vertical slits for reaching a knife or purse attached to the under-gown, on either side of the front of the skirt. The belt, set at hip-level, is of rectangular gold plaques, set with green jewels, with a circular ornament to form a fastening in front.

Footwear: The hose are of dark green cloth, with leather soles.

Jewellery and Accessories: A spindle and thread are carried.

IX.18. 14th-Century Woman with Candlestick. 1375

Hair: This is hidden entirely by the headdress.

Headdress: The round cap of stiffened linen and covered with red velvet ornamented in gold, has bands and a net, also in red and gold with red jewels, to confine the plaits or coils of hair over each ear.

Garments: The gown is fitted to the body and falls in a short train at the back, just touching the ground in front. The oval neckline exposes the points of the shoulders and has a slight declivity in the centre front. It is of ivory satin, the neckline bound with gold. The heraldic emblems on the left side of the figure are in deep blue and on the right are in scarlet. The heraldic beast on the right side of the skirt is in gold, on a black ground. The long sleeves are close-fitting and made in one with the dress. The white 'tippets' with long ends put on at the upper arms possibly conceal a seam attaching the lower part of the sleeves.

Footwear: The flat slippers are of cloth of gold.

Accessories: A silver candlestick, with candle lit, is carried.

IX.19. Man in Long Houppeland. Last Quarter of 14th Century

Hair: The hair is turned in at the ends, hanging from a centre parting.

Headdress: The hat is of green fabric, a development of the chaperon, made on a stiffened foundation.

Garments: The under-gown is of green silk; it has scalloped edges to the high, buttoned collar, the hem and the long, loose sleeves. The outer garment is a houppeland in brilliant red woollen stuff. Its rounded neck-opening is edged with gold cord. The chest is slightly padded and the sleeves are dagged and lined with matching red silk. The close sleeves of a black under-tunic show at the wrists.

Footwear: The long, pointed shoes are of black leather.

Accessories: A baldrick of green silk, embroidered in gold and edged with red stones, has golden bells along its lower edge. A purse of green silk, ornamented in red and gold, is slung from a narrow black belt. The waist is belted in green leather ornamented in black.

X 15TH-CENTURY DRESS

The first quarter of the 15th century saw few changes in costume. The flowing lines, huge sleeves, dagged edges, exotic headdress, high collars and long pointed shoes of the late 14th century trailed their extravagance into a new epoch. As time went on, however, the cult of elegant eccentricity took on fresh trends in the search for something new.

The sideless gown disappeared in the first half of the 15th century, though it was worn until the 1480s as a state dress by royalty and the nobility. The houppeland persisted, becoming a favourite dress for women as well as for men, and superseded the cote-hardie, the women's gown fitted to the figure, after the first quarter of the century.

Headdress grew even more varied, extravagant and fantastic, with an undeniable romantic beauty. Both men and women wore the large bag-sleeves already seen in the 14th century, or wide, curved sleeves with the long, close sleeves beneath showing at the wrists.

In the second half of the epoch, when the houppeland was out of fashion for men, they wore long gowns over their short tunics, or without tunics as complete outer garments. Between the 1450s and '80s, women wore the houppeland with long, tight sleeves, while puff-shouldered sleeves were in vogue for men. The '80s and '90s brought them open gowns and skirtless doublets while for women there were the innovations of the boned and fitted bodice and the first forms of the French hood.

Hair—Men: Men's hair remained at first as it had been in the 14th century: cut to a 'bobbed' length and parted in the centre or brought forward in a fringe in front. By about 1413, however, the custom of shaving the back of the head, now to the level of the ears, had returned. With this hair-cut the hair was brushed downward from the crown all round the head, turning inward at the ends. The fashion lasted until the middle of the century and was also worn without the shaving of the head.

In the latter part of the century, from about 1460 onwards, the hair of the nobility and upper classes was in many instances much longer, falling on to the shoulders.

The more conventional short 'bob', however, persisted to the end of the epoch.

Hair—Women: Women's hair was partly visible through the strands of the side-nets when these were not lined with silk, as long as the reticulated headdress was still worn.

With the various types of headdress worn in the remainder of the century, hair was either not seen at all or only to a very small extent in front of the ears or on the forehead. It was usual among elegant women to shave the hair above the forehead and to pluck the eyebrows to a thin line. Young girls and some royal ladies still wore their hair flowing.

It is easy to judge whether hair was dressed in coils or plaits over the ears, piled on top of the head, wound round the head or even in some instances cut short, to accommodate the headdress.

In the fashions of the Italian Renaissance the circlets, head-bands, veils and hats of the women showed the hair neatly bound and smooth. This fashion extended in a few instances to France. Under the bag or veil at the back of the French hood it may well have hung down the back but was not visible.

X.1. 15th Century. Six Figures

Hair: (a) A serving-man. His hair is in a fringe in front and is turned outward at the ends.

Headdress: (a) (About 1470.) The serving-man wears a conical cap of black felt, with a round up-turned brim of scarlet. (b) (1460–70.) A fisherman. He wears a large hood with a shoulder-piece, of black leather or coarse cloth. (c) (1460–70.) A traveller or peasant. He wears a large hood, with a deep shoulder-cape made in one with it, of coarse rust-coloured woollen stuff. It is pulled up over his mouth and chin. Over it is a black 'byecocket' felt with a brim turned up at the back and projecting, turned down, in front. (d) (First quarter of century.) A female farm-worker. She wears a round white linen cap with lappets on either side wound round the head with ends tucked in. (e) (Mid-century.) A serving-woman. Her red woollen hood comes down to her shoulders and is turned back in front with a 'liripipe' or tail hanging down at the back.

Headdress—Men: The chaperon, contrived from the hood with liripipe, or tail, gave rise to a great variety of 'made' hats whose designs were innumerable and showed much originality and grace. A form of turban was one of the developments of this style. Soft caps with or without upturned brims or bands of their own material could be folded into many shapes or were made with high tapering crowns, stiffened or soft. The byecocket, a hat with a round or tapering crown, the latter upright or backward-leaning, and brim turned up at the back with a long peak in front, was worn by all classes after 1460–70. A version of this, with shortened, often segmented brim, made useful and practical headgear. Hats of beaver, felt or straw shapes with brims partially turned up, were worn by countrymen, peasants and artisans.

The jewelled circlet, worn as a head ornament by the nobility, was out of fashion by mid-century except for ceremonial.

The very high-crowned, brimless cap was seen more frequently in the second half of the century and the chaperon went out of fashion.

In the final years the round flat-crowned cap with upturned brim was an important feature, varied by large round hats, also with upturned brims and huge feather trimmings. A close skull cap or scarf tied over the head was worn underneath these and might be worn without the hat, which is illustrated in Chapter XI, No. 12.

Headdress—Women: Women's headdress showed as much variety as that of men. At the beginning of the century, flat-topped, padded, or at times reticulated headdresses were worn, usually with nets for the hair at either side and a short veil at the back which might also cover the top. Early in the century a tendency for the headdress to widen and rise at the sides and to dip in the centre brought a change in the fashion. This dip grew deeper and by 1420, with the sides brought upwards, became the 'heart-shaped' headdress.

By 1440 a liripipe often depended from one side and a piece of folded stuff overhung the top, showing the relationship of this headdress with the chaperon. By this date, also, the two sides were brought even more closely together, forming the 'forked' headdress.

At about the same time the butterfly headdress, an arrangement of translucent lawn, gauze or silver or gilded tissue on a light frame, joined the current fashion and continued in varied designs until the 1480s. Between 1460 and 1480 a cylindrical cap, worn on the back of the head, often accompanied this headdress.

A rectangle of linen or lawn was sometimes put on the head with a length hanging down at the back, for practical purposes. It could also be folded in all round to cover the hair entirely.

The hood, or capuchon, was worn by women servants, country women and others. Its lappets often came down on to the shoulders and it sometimes had a stuffed 'tail' hanging

---

(f) A serving-woman, 1470. Her hood of black woollen stuff can be arranged in many ways. In this case she wears it in a peak in front.

Garments: (a) The tunic is slit for a short distance at the sides. It is of scarlet woollen stuff, with an up-standing collar of black velvet and black buttons. The sleeves are inset and are turned back at the wrists to show a yellow lining. The loose white cotton shirt-sleeves also show at the wrists. The white apron is fastened at the back of the waist. The hose are parti-coloured, the left red and white, the right yellow. (b) The fisherman has on a loose belted tunic of rough grey material, with long sleeves. His hose are of dark greenish-grey yarn. (c) The traveller or peasant wears a belted tunic in fawn-coloured wool, with a belt of black leather. His stout hose are of rust-coloured yarn with brown leather gaiters over them. (d) The dress of blue wool is turned up all round and tucked in. It has a round, wide neck-line, low at the back. The sleeves end a little way below the shoulders. The lower part of the white linen shift is seen, also its sleeves. (e) The serving-woman wears an under-gown of red woollen stuff,

and an over-gown of dark blue wool. It ends at calf-level and is slit at the sides from hip to hem, laces holding the two sides together. The neckline is plain and rounded and the sleeves long and close-fitting. A white apron is tied on at hip-level. (f) The serving-woman wears an under-gown of black woollen stuff and an over-gown of dark green wool, with turned-back cuffs of white. Her white cotton apron is tied on at the waist.

Footwear: (a) The serving-man wears black leather bootees, open in front but ending above the ankles at the back. (b) The fisherman has heavy thigh boots of black leather. (e) The serving-woman's shoes are of black fabric, pointed and flat-soled. (f) The shoes of black leather have fairly thick soles.

Accessories: (a) The serving-man is in charge of a dog, with collar and lead. (b) The fisherman holds his net in his hands. (c) A dagger in a plain leather sheath is attached to the belt. (d) The farm-worker holds a hay fork. (e) The serving-woman holds a three-footed cooking-pot. (f) The second serving-woman holds a metal tray.

forward or backward from the top. A round cap, gathered by a draw-string at the nape of the neck and turned back to frame the face, was another form of workaday headdress.

A 'turban' headdress, often sewn with jewels, characterized the middle of the century. It could be sewn or draped on the head, the two ends finishing the drapery hanging down on to the shoulders. A version of the turban, the roundel, a band of padded stuff, could be worn by young girls with their hair loose at the back.

X.2. 15th Century. Men's Headdress

Hair: (b) The hair covers the ears and curls inward at the ends. (c) The hair is parted in the centre under the hat and formed into two horizontal curled rolls, one above the other, round the back and sides of the head.

Headdress: (a) A 'made' chaperon of the opening years of the century, in cream-coloured woollen stuff, has its end draperies, dagged at the edges, coming forward from the back over the front and right side of the brow. (b) (Mid-century.) The hard-crowned hat of grey felt is wider at the flat top of the crown than at its base. The brim turns up at the back and down in front. It is decorated with a band of its own material and a small silver ornament in front. (c) (About 1406.) The byecocket, with an upright crown of black felt has a long, pointed white brim, turned up at the back.

Garments: (a) The neck and shoulders of a houppeland in black cloth, with a cream-coloured turnover to the high collar and raised shoulders, are in view. (b) The gown is of blue cloth, with a rolled collar of its own stuff meeting at a front opening and raised shoulders. (c) The dark red woollen tunic has an upstanding collar open in front.

The hennin, or steeple headdress, was in fashion from about 1430 to 1485. It was shaped like a pointed cone and was made of stiffened material covered in silk, brocade or tissue of silver or gold. It was tilted backwards on the head or sometimes put on upright when the 'round' dress (q.v., 'Garments—Women') was worn. A circular veil was attached to the hennin at its point or at the edge over the forehead and draped in various ways. At its greatest height the hennin could measure nearly four feet. In mid-century the rectangular veil was often used, two veils being employed to achieved intricate drapings. A frontlet of velvet could accompany the hennin. In the latter part of the period truncated forms were introduced.

The 'horned' headdress, a cap with projecting gauze brim, was adorned with forward-pointing horns and was in use from the middle of the century until the change that took place towards the end.

In the years between 1480 and the close of the century, a form of reticulated headdress was worn for state occasions, usually with the sideless gown. It was of a backward-sloping, oval shape, with a caul closely fitted to the head, which concealed the hair, and was worn with an elongated coronet on the top.

With the final years the headdress of young girls, with the hair flowing down the back, included a soft, full-crowned cap of jewelled silk set on the back of the head, with an ornamental loop or tag on the crown. No hair was shown in front. The first versions of the gabled or pyramidal headdress, varied by a bell-shaped cap on the back of the head with a deep frontlet, hooded most of the hair on the forehead, and all at the back.

Garments—Men: The houppeland, developing in several different styles, continued in fashion during the first half of the 15th century. Dagged edges were still seen and the long, very wide sleeves, disclosing the under-sleeves, and bag-pipe sleeves, often edged with fur, were still in favour. The houppeland might have slits in the centre of the front, at sides or

X.3. 15th Century. Men's Headdress

Headdress: (a) (1450.) The close-fitting hood of tomato-red cloth has an edging of brown fur, and continues downward as a neck and shoulder covering. Over it is worn a cap of dark brown velvet with a large puffed crown tipped forward over the left side of the forehead. (b) (First quarter of century.) A cap of white, green and black artificial leaves is worn, with a circular jewelled ornament, over the centre of the brow. (c) (Mid-century.) The hat has a large crown with a point surmounting its dented top. It is of grey felt, with a turned-up brim of purple.

Garments: (b) The high collar of the black velvet houppeland is edged with a white silk frill and the tops of white silk sleeves are visible. (c) The tunic of light green cloth has a loosely-folded collar of purple meeting in front.

Jewellery: (b) wears a necklace of silver links set with emeralds.

back. The length of the garment varied, some houppelands sweeping the ground, others ending at the ankles or calves, and some above or below the knee. The shorter forms of it could be belted at the waist or low on the hips.

After the first quarter of the century the neckline of men's garments became more open in a 'V' shape with a border of fur or small upstanding collar. The pourpoint or under-tunic sometimes showed its high collar. Wide sleeves were now often open down the back, forming a sort of cape over the arms. Bag-pipe sleeves had an extra opening at elbow level so that the arms could be put through at this point and the rest of the sleeves allowed to hang free. The low-set belt on the knee-length or calf-length gown was often put on well below the hips.

A much shorter tunic was in vogue by mid-century, ending at the hips with a basque in pleats or folds. At this time short, puffed over-sleeves or high-shouldered gigot sleeves tapering towards the wrists had come into fashion for men's gowns and tunics.

A new form of the long gown ended at the instep, and could be worn without a belt. Pleats from either shoulder, meeting at the waist, or starting at the waist itself, fell to the hem of the gown.

In the 1460s a straight, loose, unbelted gown of a similar length gave an unfamiliar line to the prevailing fashion for well-tailored bodies and and flaired skirts. It fastened down the centre front. A tabard-shaped gown of similar length, with hanging sleeves, came into fashion about 1470.

The journade, a very short, full, unbelted tunic, added to the vogue for some loose-fitting garments. It had moderately full wrinkled sleeves, loose at the wrists, with the close-fitting sleeves visible at the ends. The neckline, round or slightly square, showed the collar of the under-tunic. The neck, hem and sleeves were usually bordered with fur.

X.4. 1410–20–50. Women's Headdress

Headdress: (a) (1410.) Gold nets, sewn with gold beads, hide the plaits of hair and are joined by a close-fitting cap of blue silk (unseen). It is surmounted by a padded roll of brocade in blue and gold dipping towards the centre and rising a little at that point. A coronet of gold, shaped to fit the undulation of the roll, is worn over it. (b) (1420.) Large horizontally placed barrel-shaped cauls, bound at the ends with bands of silver, with a crisscross pattern of silver ribbon sewn with pearls over the ears, are joined by a silk cap which is not seen. They are lined in purple silk and hide the hair completely. A veil of cream-coloured silk supported on a light framework, with scalloped edges, hangs below the shoulders. It follows the same undulations as the roll worn by (a). A coronet of silver, shaped to fit the front curve of the headdress, surmounts the veil. It is set with amethysts, rubies and pearls. (c) (1450.) A cap of yellow silk joins cauls of gold net lined with yellow and sewn with pearls, with borders of gold and pearls. The shaped gold coronet, set with pearls, crystal and rubies, covers the cauls above the temples. They rise above it, forming a top to the headdress resembling rabbits'

ears. The yellow lining is turned outwards on the inner sides.

Garments: (a) The under-gown is of scarlet woollen fabric. The houppeland is of azure-blue wool, with a collar of its own stuff. This stands up at the back of the neck but may be worn lying flat. It is open in a 'V' in the front, with a small 'V'-shaped piece to fill it in. (b) The open-sided off-shoulder gown is of green and silver tissue, with a surcote of ermine, edged on the inner side of the front with purple satin. The cloak is of purple satin, also below the shoulders. (c) The sideless gown is of dark red velvet, with a surcote of ermine, and the cloak of gold tissue with a gold border sewn with crystal.

Jewellery: (b) The chain joining the sides of the cloak is of silver links, with jewelled silver fastenings, of different designs, set with pearls, rubies and amethysts. The necklace is of silver plaques, edged with pearls and set with rubies and amethysts. (c) The necklace is of gold, pearls, rubies and crystal. The ermine surcote is sewn with rubies, pearls and crystal.

Large, puffed shoulders and wrinkled sleeves appeared in other fashions, notably in a gown with round neckline and high collar, the fullness of the upper part gathered into the waist at the side-fronts and opening from the waist or thigh, with the 'skirt' trailing on the ground.

Tucks or folds were now used to bring the fullness in to the waist from the side-fronts of short belted tunics.

Padding was used at this time not only on the shoulders but to increase the size of the chest, thus emphasizing the slim waist-line.

The costume of the burgher and artisan classes followed in general the more picturesque trend of the clothes worn by the well-to-do, while keeping to more utilitarian line and stuff. 14th-century features such as dagged edges, hoods with larger shoulder capes and plain tunics ending well below the knee persisted rather longer than in the more fashionable world, but the ordinary citizen had his share in the brilliance and gaiety of the epoch, despite the sumptuary laws revived in 1403.

Hose for all classes of men could be parti-coloured or contrasting in the first quarter of

a   b   c

X.5. Mid-15th Century. Turban Headdress. Women

Headdress: (Mid-century). In all three instances the hair is entirely hidden by the headdress. (a) The turban is of parchment-coloured silk, draped so that both ends hang down on the left side. It is made as a hat and is bound in strips of two different kinds of ribbon—the plain in scarlet shot with gold and the patterned in scarlet and gold on a cream-coloured ground, with borders of darker red. (b) The hat is of blue-grey felt with a wide up-turned brim and a large crown level with it, giving the general effect of a turban. It has an ornament of silver set with red stones in the centre front. The scarves draped over it are of dark red silk patterned in white. Beneath it is a caul made of silver net and ribbon, covering the ears. (c) The made and draped turban is of saffron yellow linen, with draperies of the same stuff passing under the chin from the right side, crossing the crown, with part of an end

hanging backwards on the left side, and tied on the right side with ends hanging on that side.

Garments: (a) The high-waisted houppeland is of parchment-coloured silk with a neck edging of gold and scarlet ribbon. The sleeves are set in and if entirely visible would be of the wrinkled, evenly wide type worn at mid-century. (b) The under-gown, seen at the top of the sleeves, is of blue-grey silk, and the houppeland of deeper blue cloth, with an upstanding collar of dark red velvet opening in front. It has a yoke, below which the bodice is laid in pleats and is high-waisted, with a wide dark red belt. The sleeves end a little below the shoulder, showing undersleeves, and are edged with grey fur. (c) The houppeland, again high-waisted, is of brown velvet, with a front opening to the bodice crossing from left to right. The collar is of brown fur.

the century and again at the end. Fine wool was used for the best quality, while cotton, yarn and coarse wool were used for the poorer classes and soft leather for those engaged in active work.

They were now made as complete 'tights', ending at the waist. The skirtless doublet was introduced in the 1490s. It could be open to the waist showing the front of the shirt or a decorative stomacher. Its sleeves were of different types: narrow from wrist to elbow, the upper part being full and gathered on; close inner sleeves, with long dagged over-sleeves, open from the upper arms and put on with fullness at the shoulders; plain sleeves, opened at intervals along the seam to show the white sleeves of the shirt puffed out; and wide long over-sleeves turned over at the wrists to show the differently coloured lining. A plainly cut tunic, ending at the knees or a little above or below, was worn with the open gown. Its square or boat-shaped neckline sometimes showed the top of the shirt. It usually had plain, long sleeves and the skirt was rather narrowly cut. It was first seen in the 1480s and continued into the next century for ten years or so.

The loose gown worn as an outer garment from the 1480s had a collar broad at the shoulders and tapering in long revers, continuing to the hem. The gown could be long, sweeping the ground, or it could end above, below or at the knees. It has long, hanging sleeves with openings in the upper arms as well as at the wrists. It was usually open and unbelted, but could be wrapped over and belted.

X.6. 1460–80. Women's Headdress

Hair: (a) The hair is drawn back from the forehead and wound into a chignon covered by the headdress. One curled, flat lock appears above the brow. (b) The hair is dressed as in (a); but in this case only the crown of the head is covered by the headdress.

Headdress: (a) The small hennin is of blue and gold shot tissue, decorated with bands of gold. A gold coronet encircles its base. The frontlet is of blue silk to match the hennin, edged with a deeper blue and a pattern of gold. (b) The cap is of stiffened silver fabric which spreads outward in segments towards the top where it is edged in small points. A stiffened veil of rose-coloured gauze shades the face, comes to a point in the centre and ends in a point on each shoulder. (c) The cap, set on the back of the head, is of black velvet, with a flame-coloured star on the crown. The veil is of oyster-grey stiffened gauze, curving over the forehead and ending in two points at the back of the neck. Over this is a roll of flame-coloured velvet banded in silver and sewn with pearls. Its ends are shaped into horns on each side of the head.

Garments: (a) Part of the white fur collar of the houppeland is visible. (b) The rose-coloured collar of the houppeland, stitched with ornamental lines, is partly seen. (c) The black velvet houppeland has an unusual neckline, coming straight across the base of the throat from shoulder to shoulder, but cut low at the back.

Jewellery: (a) wears a necklace of gold, turquoise and pearls. (b) has a necklace closely fitting the throat, of silver ornaments with pearl drops.

Garments—Women: The sideless gown was not generally worn in the 15th century, except by royal or noble ladies on state occasions. The cote-hardie was much in favour for the first twenty years and fairly voluminous, falling in soft folds to the floor, the upper part fitted to the body and often with tippets attached at the upper arms. It was superseded by the houppeland in the 1420s.

The houppeland was now widely adopted in a feminized version by women. The very high collar was at first retained, but was also worn opened and turned down. The girdle was put on at a high-waisted level, with the fullness above drawn into it and allowed to flow into sweeping folds below it. The sleeves were immensely long and wide, trailing on the ground in many instances, and could be lined with fur or, in the first quarter of the century, have dagged edges. 'Bag' sleeves were worn with the houppeland in mid-century and remained in fashion until the 1480s, though they were rivalled by wrinkled sleeves, the same width throughout, with fur at the wrists, and by long close-fitting sleeves.

By about 1445 the collar of the women's houppeland had become much larger and wider and was frequently faced with fur. It turned back on to the shoulders, its points meeting only at the wide high-waisted girdle back and front. The decolleté space in front was filled in if necessary by the top of the under-dress.

In the 1460s the waist was at a more normal level, the belt broad and stiffened, and the skirt, though it still flowed all round on to the floor, formed a long train. Close-fitting sleeves, often bordered like the hem with fur that matched that of the collar, were worn with this development of the houppeland, until it went out of fashion altogether in the 1480s. From the 1450s onwards cuffs of some kind were worn with the long close sleeves,

a   b

X.7. 1460. Two Women in Hennins

Hair: (a) A curled strand on the forehead and part of the hair at the sides are all that can be seen. (b) A curl on the forehead is the only hair visible.

Headdress: (a) The short hennin, covered in gold tissue, has a border of gold braid, sewn with red and pink stones. Two veils are mounted on gilt wire above the hennin. The lower is of gold gauze, bordered in gold and silver edging and powdered with crystal dots. The upper is of silver gauze, bordered in gold edging and decorated with parallel lines of minute silver beads. (b) The very tall hennin is covered in red silk, criss-crossed in black and gold braid, and has a frontlet of black tinsel cloth, shot with gold, and an under-cap of white lawn, descending in two short streamers on to the shoulders at the back. A long veil of red gauze depends from the point of the hennin.

Garments: (a) The dress, visible to the hips, is of deep peach-pink silk, embroidered in motifs of gold and silver. It has a collar of pale-coloured fur below the shoulders, filled in across the bosom with dark rose-coloured velvet. The belt, at a high waist-line, is of this material, with a gold buckle. The sleeves are long and close-fitting, with goblet cuffs (not seen) of the same velvet. (b) The dress of black velvet, seen to the hips, has a wide collar, close at the neck, of stiffened red silk, ornamented in gold and black. The belt, at a slightly lower level than that of (a), is covered in gold tissue. The sleeves are long and tight-fitting, with turned-back cuffs (not seen) of gold tissue.

X.8. 15th Century. Six Figures

Hair: (a) The sower wears his hair covering the ears, ending at the back of the neck. (d) The man in the long gown has shoulder-long hair, brought down from a centre parting.

Headdress: (a) (Mid-century.) The sower wears a hat of brown felt, with a soft crown and a pliable circular brim turned up all round. (b) (About 1470.) The man in armour has the visor of his helmet closed. (c) (Latter half of century.) The man-at-arms wears a metal casque which protects the forehead and the back of the neck and has a knob at the top. Under it is a hood of chain mail covering the chin and the shoulders. (d) (About 1485.) The man in the long gown has a square, stiffened cap of ivory white velvet, with vertical pleats or lines of stitching. (e) (Latter part of century.) The jester wears a three-pointed cap, with shoulder-cape, parti-coloured in red and green. There is a gilt bell at the end of each point and bells on the points that edge the cape. (f) (About 1485.) The girl with the fiddle has on a soft cap of yellow silk with a close-fitting

sometimes circular and turned back, in other instances coming forward over part of the hand.

In the 1460s the 'round' dress provided a gown that was easier to manage than the immensely long skirts of the houppeland. Its skirt cleared the ground and was put on with even, moderate fullness all round, generally with a deep border of fur or of contrasting colour. It had a broad belt and long, close-fitting sleeves. The neckline varied, the line of wide décolletage, with the points meeting back and front, seen in the houppeland, being followed to some extent, but often filled in by folds of silk or lawn meeting down the front of the chest. The top of the under-gown was seen above the low fur collar. The dress was worn with the horned headdress, the truncated hennin with a stiffened veil shading the forehead, or the upright hennin with a veil and a frontlet or a small stiffened veil over the brow.

Another gown, dating from 1470 to 1480, was a precursor of transitional changes. It had a long skirt, fairly full over the hips, with slightly more fullness at the back than else-where, close-fitting sleeves with the cuffs that were now fashionable, and a tightly fitted bodice which provided an almost corset-like effect. Various fairly high necklines were worn with this dress, one being a small upstanding collar with 'V' opening filled in with folds of lawn on either side. A pointed neck-opening was usual, as the bodice was fastened down the front, and in some instances the points of a long turned-over collar met at the waist-line in front as in the round dress and the houppeland.

The four types of costume just described, the cote-hardie, houppeland, round dress and gown with fitted bodice, made up the prototypes of dress in this century. In their simpler forms, as worn by burghers' or farmers' wives and daughters, by peasants, servants and shopkeepers, they were made more practical by the bunching up of outer skirts and wearing of aprons.

Women's mantles in this period were still semicircular, fastened across the chest by cords and ornamental buttons or by jewelled brooches. The plainer surcote also acted as an out-door garment. There are examples of women wearing the short, loose, open gown worn by men in the latter part of the century, with furred sleeve openings near the shoulder.

In the 1480s a change of fashion brought in a transitory period. Skirts grew fuller at the back, but not yet at the sides. Bodices, which were now mostly fitted to the figure, had

---

rim that hides the hair. It is sewn with lines of pearls and a jewel is attached at the front. The small tag on the crown is also ornamented with pearls.

Garments: The sower wears a loose red woollen tunic, bloused over its belt. The sleeves taper moderately from shoulder to wrist. His hose are blue. (b) The man in armour is wearing a complete suit of plate armour, with pointed elbow and knee-pieces and narrow overlapping and pointed plates covering his hands and feet. A section of chain mail is in the centre front. The circular pieces on the shoulders are for resting his lance. (c) The man-at-arms wears a dark brown cloth tunic, and a tunic and leggings of chain mail. He wears a loosely fitting jerkin of padded brown leather as an outer garment, with loose sleeves shorter than those of the chain mail. (d) The man in the long gown wears a waist-length doublet of cloth of gold, with upstand-ing lapels showing the white shirt-frill. The close-fitting sleeves have puffs of the white shirt-sleeves showing at the elbows. The edges are ornamented with pink topazes and garnets. The hose are white, striped with dark rose-colour. The over-gown is of bronze, dark rose and white brocade with long revers of bronze velvet and a matching girdle. It has hanging sleeves, one of which encases the left arm, while the other hangs free. (e) The jester wears a tunic parti-coloured in red and green. It has a narrow green belt at the waist and its skirt is divided into six points, each with a gilt belt at its

end. Its sleeves taper to the wrists and have a bell on each elbow. The hose are parti-coloured in red and green. (f) The girl wears an under-gown of yellow silk, with full sleeves gathered into bands at the wrists. Over it is a sleeveless gown of black velvet, edged at neck, shoulders and hem with gold galon. Its open front is filled with a stomacher of gold tissue in horizontal pleats.

Footwear: (a) The sower has bootees of black buck-skin. (b) The shoes are separate from the suit of armour, made of flexible and overlapping plates. (c) The man-at-arms has thigh-boots of black leather. (d) The man in the long gown has soft bootees of rose-red fabric.

Accessories: (a) The sower has a bag of white cotton slung by shoulder-straps and a yoke from his shoulders, containing grain, which he scatters with his right hand. (b) The man in armour has a sword with a silver hilt and silver-ornamented scabbard attached by straps to a leather belt at his waist. (c) The man-at-arms has a sheathed dagger slung on a strap from right shoulder to left hip and is holding in front of him a tall shield of leather stretched on wood. (e) The jester holds a 'bauble' with a small jester's head on it. (f) The girl wears a necklace of yellow stones set in gold and a girdle of small gold links with a gold chain and large gold ornament hanging in front. She is playing a fiddle, holding it in the manner customary at the time.

square or rounded necklines, plain when there was no stomacher and often joined without ornament down the front. Some dresses were still made all in one, the waist-line only indicated by darts, and some skirts were slit or caught up at the back, side or front. One example has a buttoned fastening all down the front.

Sleeves could be of three main types: a version of the 'bag' sleeves of the earlier part of the century, now inserted below the shoulders; close sleeves, usually cuffed, of a length that made a slight wrinkling necessary throughout their length; and moderately wide over-sleeves, put on below the shoulder and showing the close sleeves beneath.

Footwear—Men: At the beginning of the 15th century the exaggeratedly long toes of the shoes worn at the end of the 14th were growing shorter, though still pointed. This more normal length did not last, and the very long toes returned in the first twenty years, gradually increasing in length until they reached their worst extreme about 1460–80.

Shoes were made of soft leather and of various pliable stuffs, including velvet, embroidered cloth and brocade, or they were made in one with the long hose. When separate from the hose, they were made in the first half of the century in the form of short bootees, reaching or covering the ankles and usually rolled at the top. These were laced at one side or fastened with a strap and buckle.

The second half of the century showed more variety in the styles of shoes. One covered part of the instep and fitted snugly over the heel without ornamentation or fastenings; another had points covering the back and front of the ankle, with the shoe itself cut down deeply between them. A third type of shoe cut down at the sides lacked the points back and front but covered the instep and heel.

A useful 'galoche' was a shoe mounted on a long, pointed wooden sole which was thickened under the ball of the foot and had a raised heel to keep the feet dry and out of the mud. The pouleyn was originally a long, pointed sole, slightly turned up at the end, with strips of leather attached at two points on either side, over the little toe and under the heel, joined by a tie over the instep. The name was also given to the very long pointed shoes.

After 1460, soft, wrinkled boots ending in a turn-over at the calf, just below the knee, or at mid-thigh, were another feature of the costume of this time. Some were attached to the hose at the front of the knee and allowed to droop towards the back.

After 1480 the toes of shoes and boots became shorter and broader until in the last years of the century the distortedly broad toes of the epoch which was to follow made their appearance.

Footwear—Women: Women's shoes and bootees followed the styles of those worn by men, but with their long skirts they did not wear the extremely long-toed shoes. Pattens and clogs were worn by those who had to be out in muddy weather.

Materials, Colours and Ornament: Wool of all grades, some cotton, linen of various qualities, satin, velvet, taffetas, rich silks in plain colours or embroidered, cloth of gold, silver and gold tissue, brocade and damask, with every type of fine lawn, gauze or thin silk for veils and headdress, were the materials used.

Many gradations of colour were used, soft shades as well as those of great brilliance being equally in favour. Saffron, rose, blue, green, pale yellow, flame and orange hues, scarlet, crimson and wine-colour, as well as greys, browns and blacks appear in the art of this epoch, with white used often in headdresses, veils and tippets, also in partlets which showed at the necks of dresses and to some extent in gowns and hose. In the more sombre women's clothes in the last years of the century darker colours such as deep red, purple, slate grey, brown and black were employed. Scarlet was in frequent use as relief and as trimming, facings and the turned-back lining of sleeves and skirts.

Ornament was lavish in this period, garments being sewn with jewels, embroidered in all-over patterns, trimmed with fur and, in the last ten years or so of the century, slashed and puffed. Gowns were 'powdered' with circles, stars, flowers, flying birds or other small motifs, and often with monograms or heraldic insignia, this way of using blazonry gradually taking the place of the large appliqués emblems. Patterns could also be diapered or in diagonals.

Material itself might also be used in decoration, for example a collar faced with satin on a velvet gown. A certain amount of parti-colouring was used during the century and came back in full force in the puffed-and-slashed period at the end. Large flower and foliage designs are found and the vine leaf, pomegranate and pineapple are favourite motifs.

Jewellery and Accessories: Royal crowns had grown higher, but kept their foliated shape or were filled in with velvet and 'bridged' with curved gold bands. Jewelled circlets and coronets were still worn by the nobility on state occasions.

Buttons, pins, belts, sword- and dagger-hilts, gloves, baldricks and purses could all be ornamented with jewels. Rings and necklaces were now set with faceted as well as with unfaceted jewels. Men wore jewelled necklets over the collars of their gowns or tunics. Outer garments were sometimes sewn with small gold or silver placques as an alternative to jewels.

Women in France and Italy in the latter half of the century wore a plain circlet or band with a pendant jewel in the centre of the forehead. Jewelled cauls and frontlets, drop-earrings where the headdress allowed them, necklets which lay fairly closely round the throat, and chains with pendants were also worn by women.

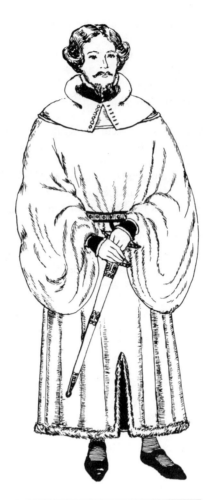

X.9. Man in Houppeland. About 1400

Hair: This is parted in the centre and turned outward at the ends, which cover the ears. A moustache, a fringe of hair along the jaws and a bifid beard are worn.

Garments: The under-gown is of dark green cloth. It has a high neck, with a collar fastening in front with gilt buttons and edged, like the goblet cuffs, with binding of dull orange. The skirt ends just above the ankles. The houppeland is of sand-coloured woollen stuff. It has a hood-collar, turned down over the yoke of the gown, with buttons and buttonholes in front to fasten it at the neck when it is turned up over the head. The brown leather belt worn at waist-level is ornamented in green. The gown ends at the ankles. The hem and the slit in the front are bordered with brown fur. The 'bag' sleeves are made in one with the gown and sewn into wrist-bands. The hose match the gown.

Footwear: The shoes of dark green leather are flat-soled, with a strap across the instep.

Accessories: A gold-hilted sword and a scabbard of green leather decorated with gold is attached to the belt by a strap of green leather.

X.10. Woman in Unbelted Houppeland. 1400

Hair: Only a little hair is seen on either side of the forehead; but it is reasonable to suppose that it is wound round the head under the headdress.

Headdress: The headdress is presumably a 'made' one, with the oval veil arranged so that short folds fall on each side of the forehead and longer folds frame the face. Ends of these folds disappear into the ends of folds coming from the sides. The back of the veil hangs down over the shoulders.

Garments: The under-gown is of scarlet silk, seen only in the goblet cuffs, which have cream-coloured edging. The long, unbelted houppeland is of cream-coloured wool. It has a high collar, fastened in front with scarlet buttons, and large 'bag' sleeves, made in one with the garment and sewn into bands at the wrists.

X.11. Man's Dress. 1400

Hair: The hair covers the ears and ends just below them. The ends are turned in a little and the front is cut in a short fringe.

Headdress: The cap, with a round upturned brim of brown felt, has a pointed crown of soft pinkish-tan woollen stuff.

Garments: The under-tunic of thin parchment-coloured silk shows its wrinkled sleeves from above the elbows to the wrists. The over-tunic is of pinkish-tan wool with a hem, hood-collar and turned-back cuffs of brown wool ending the sleeves above the elbows.

Footwear: The hose are light brown and the shoes, with long pointed toes and fronts coming up over the insteps, are of brown leather.

X.12. Youth in Feathered Hat. Opening of 15th Century

Hair: The hair is fringed in front and the ends are turned in a little.

Headdress: The tall cap with the crown wider at top and base than in the centre, is of dark red felt, with a round, turned-up brim covered in peach-coloured velvet. A jewelled brooch of gold, pearls and an emerald is fastened to the front of the cap and holds a green plume.

Garments: The short, high-necked tunic (courtepy) is of peach-coloured silk, decorated all over with motifs of green silk leaves sewn with gold thread. It has bag sleeves with wrist-bands of green silk, which also edges the neck, where it is scalloped. The hose are green. The belt is of twisted dark red velvet.

Footwear: The shoes are of dark red velvet, bound and laced in green silk.

Accessories: A purse of dark red velvet hangs from the belt. It has edgings and a criss-cross pattern of green, with gold ornament. The unsheathed stiletto held in the right hand has a hilt of gold and dark red enamel.

X.13. Young Man with Bow and Arrow. 1407

Hair: This is parted in the centre and hangs down to the jawline.

Headdress: A tall hat of black velvet has an indented crown and a narrow upturned brim.

Garments: The courtepy, of deep violet velvet, has a high collar and is joined at the waist to its short, close-fitting skirt, which is arranged in narrow, horizontal wrinkles, and belted at the hem. The sleeves are of the 'bag' variety, very large and deep, and joined half-way down the fore-arms to close-fitting, wrinkled lower sleeves. The ornament on the neck and shoulders is in silver, crystal and amethyst.

Footwear: The hose are parti-coloured; one violet, the other silver-grey, with long pointed toes and soles of leather.

Jewellery and Accessories: The linked belt is of silver, set with crystal and amethyst. The man carries a bow and arrow.

X.14. Woman. 1410

Hair: The hair is unseen beneath the headdress.

Headdress: A triangular framework of wire, slightly bowed in front, is covered by pale green silk, criss-crossed in silver thread, and edged with pink rosettes. The green silk cap attached to this framework, to cover the back of the head, has a rectangle of black velvet, ending just below the shoulder-blades, hung over it.

Garments: The cote-hardie of silver-grey silk is edged with green. It has close sleeves with 'goblet' cuffs in white lawn. The over-gown fits the body but has a long, full gored skirt made in one with the top part of the dress. The neckline is a moderate oval and the sleeves are made in one with the dress and widen out a great deal from the upper arm to hang down to calf-length. The over-gown is pale green and has an all-over decoration of blue, green, silver and pink flowers, with a deep border in the same colours to edge the neck, sleeves and hem. It is lined in black.

Footwear: The flat shoes are of green and silver brocade.

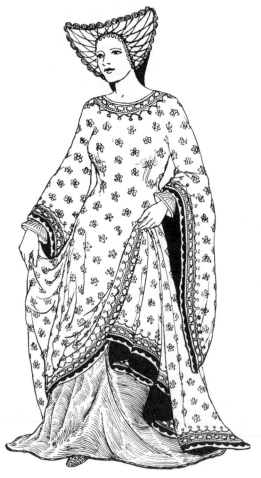

X.15. Woman in Butterfly Headdress. 1417

Headdress: A framework of wire or whalebone supports the light headdress of white lawn which is draped on it. A gorget, drawn closely round the neck, is worn beneath it.

Garments: The under-gown is of dark sapphire blue velvet, with long close sleeves which are the only part of it visible. The cote-hardie is of pale blue finely woven woollen stuff. It has a wide oval neckline, edged with dark blue velvet and filled in by the white lawn gorget. It fits the body to the hips and the skirt is long and full. The sleeves open at the elbow and hang down in 'tippet' form. The belt is of dark blue velvet.

Accessories: A purse of blue velvet with a silver frame is hung from the belt.

X.16. Man in Houppeland, with Sword
1st Quarter of 15th Century

Hair: The hair comes down to the collar, covering the ears. It has a fringe over the forehead, the front hair being combed forward from the crown.

Garments: The under-tunic is seen only in the high collar and goblet cuffs of scarlet and silver. The houppeland is of dark blue velvet, slit from the knee at both sides. The slits, hem and sleeve-ends are bordered with pale grey fur. The round neckline has a deeper border of silver-bordered fabric set with pearls and red stones. This is continued in a long strip from neck to hem. The belt is of scarlet leather, with a buckle and an ornament at the end of silver. The sleeves are of moderate width, lined in scarlet. The hose are scarlet.

Footwear: The shoes are of scarlet leather, ornamented in silver.

Accessories: The sword has a hilt of silver and a scabbard covered in red leather, decorated in silver.

X.17. Man in Low-belted Houppeland. 1st Half of 15th Century

Hair: The hair is cut to be combed down in circular fashion all round the head, showing the ears. The head is shaved at the base of the skull.

Garments: The houppeland, which ends above the ankles, is of dark brown woollen stuff, edged at neck, sleeves and hem, also lined, with lighter brown fur. It is open from mid-thigh to the hem. The up-standing collar is open in front to the base of the neck. The belt at the hips is of brown leather, with a long end hanging in front, set with yellow uncut stones and with a gold, weighted ornament to finish it. The hose (unseen) are light brown.

Footwear: The bootees are of brown velvet, laced on the inner side with gold cord.

X.18. Woman in Heart-shaped Headdress. 1420s

Headdress: The sides of the headdress, forming a close-fitting cap at the back, are of dark wine-coloured velvet. The padded roll of ivory silk that creates the 'heart shape' diminishes towards the back of the head. It is dotted with small gold roundels.

Garments: The high-waisted houppeland, belted in ribbed silk of the same colour, is of dark wine-coloured velvet, with a plain collar of ivory silk fastened at the throat. The wide, long sleeves are lined with pale rose colour, patterned in crimson. The close-fitting sleeves of the under-gown are of dull green silk and have ivory silk cuffs.

Footwear: The pointed, flat-soled shoes are of dark rose-coloured brocade.

Accessories: A leather-bound book is held in the hands.

X.19. Man with Scarf Draped over Hat. About 1440

Hair: The hair is of moderate length, turned inward and covering the ears.

Headdress: The black hat in turban style, but actually of felt with a wide upturned brim and a crown of equal height, has a long scarf of golden satin, with dagged edges, draped over it, and held up in the right hand.

Garments: The under-tunic is of black satin. The houppeland of dull orange cloth, belted very low, has three rows of overlapping dagges to form the skirt. In addition to the upstanding collar, a wide collar of overlapping dagges encircles the shoulders, and two long streamers of these pass under the belt and mingle with the dagges that make the skirt. The belt is of black, gold and orange. The large bag sleeves, of which one is hanging loose, have dagged cuffs. The hose are dull orange.

Footwear: The bootees have rolled tops and are of buff-coloured leather.

X.20. Woman in Large Bag-sleeves. 1440

Headdress: The side-nets or cauls are of gold net and bronze velvet, concealing the hair, and the veil of yellow silk.

Garments: The under-gown of bronze velvet is seen only in the full sleeves, gathered into bands at the wrists. The over-gown, a form of houppeland, is of heavy brownish-pink silk, belted in gold and bronze. The round, close-fitting neckline has a deep round collar of brown fur. The sleeves, hanging down in bag form almost to the hem of the dress, are bordered in the same fur from the shoulders to the bend of the elbows in front and more deeply at the back.

X.21. Man in Loose, Unbelted Gown. 1450

Hair: The hair is brought forward in a fringe in front, and is moderately long.

Headdress: A 'made' chaperon of dark brown velvet hangs behind the right shoulder. Loops of velvet, intended to lie across the crown, depend from it. The liripipe, unwound, is brought forward across the body and held in the left hand.

Garments: The tunic is of pale blue-green satin. The gown worn over it is loose, full and flared from neck to hem, and is made of flame-coloured velvet decorated all over with large appliqué motifs in gold. It ends at the top of the calves and is open down the front. Its neckline is low at the back and it is sleeveless, with large oval armholes. Light brown fur edges the garment all round and borders the armholes.

Footwear: The hose of stretching fabric are blue-green to match the tunic, and have leather soles.

Accessories: A gold ring is worn on the left hand.

X.22. Man in Black 'Chaperon' Hat. 1450

Hair: The hair is parted in the centre (unseen) and turned in at the ends.

Headdress: The round cap, made on a stiffened foundation, is of black velvet. Folds are draped over the left side, across the top and allowed to hang down in the form of a long scarf which is held in the right hand.

Garments: The under-tunic is of pewter-grey ribbed silk, with a close-fitting, rather high neck, open in front. The houppeland, ending at the top of the calves, is of deep crimson cloth, bordered at the 'V' neck, sleeve-ends and hem with grey fur. It is belted at the normal level with a narrow belt of crimson leather, ornamented in black and silver. The sleeves are long and very wide at the ends, though narrow at the top, and are lined with grey silk.

Footwear: The hose are grey, with leather soles.

Jewellery and Accessories: A sword with a decorative silver hilt depends from a sword-belt matching that at the waist. A ring is worn on the right hand.

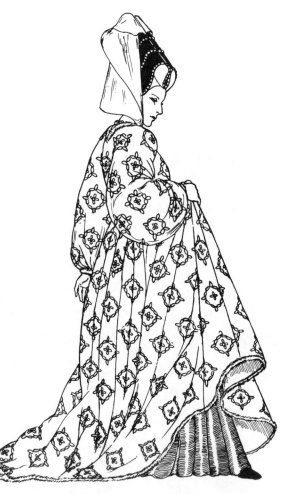

X.23. Woman in Double Hennin. About 1450

Headdress: The hennin in black velvet with pearls on a stiffened foundation is in two 'cornets', close together, with a short veil of pale blue-green silk thrown over it.

Garments: The skirt of the under-gown is of grey and green shot silk. The houppeland is of finely woven blue-green woollen stuff, embroidered in an all-over pattern of motifs in dull silver. The neckline, in a moderate 'V' at back and front and the sleeve-ends and hem are bordered in grey fur. The full bag-sleeves are gathered into bands at the wrists.

Footwear: Part of one shoe, in black velvet, is seen.

Jewellery: Part of a necklace of silver can be seen.

X.24. Man in Gown with Hanging Sleeves. About 1450

Hair: This touches the collar and is turned in at the ends.

Headdress: The hat of pinkish-fawn felt has a dented crown decorated with small gilt rings and a small brim turned up at the back and down in front. A black satin scarf is wound round the base of the crown and brought forward over the left shoulder, across the chest, to hang down behind the right shoulder.

Garments: The under-doublet of black cloth has tight-fitting sleeves, with fawn-coloured turned-back cuffs. The gown is of pinkish-fawn cloth, decorated with black piping and diamond-shaped motifs in black. The body and skirt are arranged in padded pleats converging at the waist and the high collar is turned down at the top. The hanging sleeves depend from raised shoulders and are edged, like the hem, with light brown fur. The right wrist is enclosed in the cuff of the hanging sleeve, while the left sleeve hangs loose. The narrow belt is black.

Footwear: The long, pointed shoes are of black velvet.

Jewellery and Accessories: A necklace of jet covers the join between the collar and the gown. A black velvet purse, with gilt metal bars and handle, hangs from the belt. A coin is held in the right hand.

X.25. Youth with Pennant. About 1450

Hair: The hair is long enough to touch the collar and is fringed on the forehead and turned in at the ends.

Headdress: The round stiff-crowned cap of rust-brown velvet has a flat top and a small upturned brim of mustard yellow.

Garments: The parchment-coloured silk yoke of the under-tunic is gathered into a close-fitting band of rust-coloured velvet. The tight sleeves are of rust-coloured velvet. The loosely-fitting, beltless tunic or 'journade', is of cloth in mustard yellow, edged at the square neck, the loose long sleeves and the hem, with light brown fur. The hose are of a brownish rust colour and have leather soles.

Accessories: The pennant is of scarlet silk, with the staff painted gold.

X.26. Man in Short Tunic. 1460s

Hair: The hair is parted in the centre, brought down to cover the ears and rolled up at the ends.

Headdress: The hat of mushroom-coloured velvet has a soft, indented crown and a pliable, upturned brim in a double roll.

Garments: The under-tunic is of dark brown velvet. The over-tunic is of velvet in coral red, ornamented with motifs in gold edged with black. It is bordered at the neck, hem and sleeve-edges with sable-coloured fur. The body of the tunic has flat tucks from shoulder to hem on both sides of the front, converging to some extent at the waist and parting again in the short, flared skirt. The narrow belt is dark brown. The sleeves are made in large puffs, ending at the elbow at the back and cut away in a point in front. The hose are mushroom colour.

Footwear: The pointed shoes are of coral-red velvet.

Jewellery and Accessories: A gold-hilted dagger in a brown leather sheath hangs from the belt. A short stick, often carried at this time, is held in the right hand.

X.27. Woman in Houppeland. 1460

Headdress: The hennin is covered in pale yellow velvet, with gold piping, a veil of ivory gauze and a frontlet of black velvet.

Garments: The under-gown is of black velvet and is seen at the décolletage and the hem. The gown is of deep parchment-coloured satin, 'powdered' with pale golden stars. Its collar and cuffs are of gold cloth and the belt of the same, edged with gold and decorated with motifs of black velvet and parchment-coloured silk set with small gold ornaments.

Footwear: The shoes are of gold fabric.

X.28. Man with Hooded Falcon. About 1460

Hair: The hair is long enough to lie on the shoulders and is parted in the centre (unseen).

Headdress: The tall conical cap is of stiffened fabric covered in cloth of silver.

Garments: The long gown of dull purple velvet, lined with green silk, is fastened at the back of the upper part, but open in front from mid-thigh. It has a small upstanding collar with a front opening. The narrow belt is of silvered leather. The sleeves are puffed at the shoulders and long enough to cover the hands if desired. The hose are of a purplish pink.

Footwear: The long-toed shoes are of green leather.

Jewellery and Accessories: A triple chain of silver, set with amethysts and uncut green stones, is worn round the neck over the gown. The gloves are of green leather with a silver motif embroidered on the back. The falcon perched on the left hand has a hood of green, with a silver ornament on the top of the head.

X.29. Woman in 'Round' Dress, with Children. 1460–80

Hair: A curl of hair is worn in the centre of the forehead. The rest is taken back tightly and presumably dressed on top of the head. Some hair in the front of the head is probably shaved.

Headdress: The truncated hennin covered in gold satin and bordered in gold, black and orange, has a veil of thin gold gauze.

Garments: The 'round' dress of bronze velvet has a deep hem of light-coloured fur and a collar with a chemisette of parchment-coloured silk. The skirt just touches the ground. The sleeves, long and close-fitting, are cut in one with the dress and have fur cuffs.

Footwear: The soft, flat slippers, with long, pointed toes, are of bronze velvet.

Accessories: The belt, worn at a high waist-line, is decorated in the same colour as the hennin.

Boy's Dress—*Hair:* The boy's hair is parted in the centre and covers his ears. *Garments:* The doublet of blue-grey silk ends at the waist. The scarlet 'points' that tie in the sleeves and join the hose to the doublet are visible. The white velvet tabard, with a scarlet neckband, has a jewelled belt clasped round the front of it, over the doublet, but the back hangs free. This could also be an adult dress. The hose are scarlet. *Footwear:* The shoes are of blue-grey velvet.

Girl's Dress—*Hair:* The hair is dressed in a fringe in front and curls outward over the neck. *Headdress:* The girl wears a white or natural linen coif, with a slight forward peak in front, embroidered in red and blue. *Garments:* The red silk dress ends below the knees; with the hem scalloped, and has bands of black velvet at the neck, shoulders, upper arms and wrists. The pinafore is of white linen, with a scalloped border of blue. *Footwear:* The stockings are pale grey and the shoes of red leather. *Accessories:* The belt worn over both dress and pinafore is of stiffened material. It has a red ground, a narrow black border and is patterned in blue beads. The child carries a ball.

X.30. Man in Tabard-style Gown. About 1470

Hair: The hair is turned in at the ends and touches the collar at the back.

Headdress: The round cap of dark brown felt has a turned-up rim in two bands, one amber-coloured and one pale yellow. A yellow plume stands up at the back.

Garments. The short tunic, ending at the top of the thighs, is of amber and yellow shot silk. It has a neck-band of yellow silk and the top of the tunic is slightly draped. The sleeves are long and close fitting with narrow wrist-bands of yellow silk. The narrow belt is of amber-coloured fabric. The gown is of heavy dark brown silk, made in tabard fashion, with a draped neckline and open sides. The hanging sleeves have puffed shoulders and are lined in pale yellow. The hose are yellow.

Footwear: The long, pointed shoes, with a point coming up at front and back of the ankle, are of brown leather.

Jewellery: Gold rings are worn on the thumb and forefinger of the left hand.

X.31. Youth in Top Boots. 1470

Hair: The hair is almost straight and hangs down on to the shoulders.

Headdress: The soft cylindrical black velvet crown of the tall cap is wrinkled. The upturned brim is of vermilion felt.

Garments: The tunic is very short ending at the hips. It is of vermilion cloth, with a small, open, upstanding collar of black velvet, and a border of green velvet outside it. The belt is of green leather, edged in black and set with green and red stones. The sleeves are raised at the shoulders and full at that point, diminishing to the wrists, where they have cuffs of green. The hose are green.

Footwear: The top boots are of wrinkled black reversed calf, giving the effect of suède. The heels are low and the toes long and pointed. The turn-over at the tops is of green leather.

Accessories: A dagger with a gold hilt is held in the left hand. Its sheath, attached to the belt on the right side, is covered in green leather and ornamented in gold and red.

X.32. King's Robes. Late 15th Century

Hair: The king's hair is parted in the middle and curls outward at the ends. He has a moustache and a small trimmed beard.

Headdress: The gold crown resembles that of English sovereigns towards the end of the century. It has a 'bridge' surmounted by a cross and is set with precious stones.

Garments: The gown is of gold brocade, ending at the instep and edged at the hem and cuffs with ermine. The sleeves are plain and of moderate width. The belt is of gold fabric. The cloak is of crimson velvet, with a collar and border of ermine and a lining of the same fur. The collar crosses the chest and fastens on the left shoulder.

Footwear: The shoes are of gold brocade.

Jewellery and Accessories: The king wears gloves of ivory velvet, decorated on the backs with gold thread and red and blue stones. He wears rings over his gloves, and carries a gold sceptre.

X.33. Woman in Cloth of Silver Houppeland. 1470–80

Hair: The hair is drawn back from the forehead and above the ears and is dressed in a chignon inside the cap.

Headdress: The cylindrical cap of silver fabric is bound in dark rose-coloured velvet and set with blue stones. Over it is a double-winged headdress of the 'butterfly' type, in rose-coloured gauze.

Garments: The under-gown is of rose-coloured velvet. The houppeland is of cloth of silver bordered round the collar and hem with sable-coloured fur. The deep, stiffened belt is of dark rose-coloured velvet, edged with deep blue and sewn with pearls. These are also sewn to the panel of rose-coloured velvet in the centre of the bodice above the belt and to the rose-coloured velvet cuffs, piped in blue, of the long tight sleeves.

Footwear: The shoes are of silver cloth, with flat soles.

Accessories: A sapphire ring is worn on the third finger of the left hand. The silver necklace is set with large blue stones bordered with pearls.

X.34. Woman in Fitted Bodice. 1470–80

Headdress: The white linen cap, with a frontlet forming two streamers at the back, has a shaped and stiffened crown with a flat top.

Garments: The gown of dove-grey wool has a wide oval neckline edged with black and a bodice closely fitted to the figure by means of seams and darts. This style is a precursor of the gowns with fitted bodices that were to oust the houppeland in the 1480s. The skirt is long, with a good deal of the fullness at the back. The sleeves are close-fitting, made in one with the bodice and with black turned-back cuffs.

X.35. Man in Short Gown. About 1483

Hair: The moderately long hair hangs from a centre parting (unseen under the cap).

Headdress: The round segmented cap is wider at the crown than at its base. The brim is black velvet and the crown scarlet cloth.

Garments: The tunic is of red, green and gold brocade, with a boat-shaped neckline. Its border of gold cloth, set with green and red jewels, matches the belt. The sleeves are plain and close-fitting. The gown is of black velvet, lined with scarlet and bordered with ermine. It has hanging sleeves open from the upper arms. The hose are green.

Footwear: The long, pointed shoes are of red velvet.

Jewellery and Accessories: A gold ornament set with pearls and rubies is fastened to the front of the cap. A dagger with a gold hilt is in the right hand. Its sheath, of gilded leather, with a scarlet tassel, is attached to the belt. A gold and ruby ring is worn on the forefinger.

X.36. Woman in Sideless Gown. 1485

Hair: A flat, curled lock is seen on the forehead. The rest of the hair is dressed high inside the cap.

Headdress: The oval-shaped, backward-leaning cap of gold net covers the ears and the back of the head. It is bound with gold braid and decorated with pearls and gold thread. A shaped coronet of gold, set with pearls and emeralds, is worn on the top.

Garments: The cote-hardie is of gold brocade. Its square neckline is edged with ermine. The long, close-fitting sleeves have goblet cuffs. The sideless gown is of black velvet, its long skirt edged with ermine and lined with brilliant green. The cloak of black velvet, also edged with ermine and lined in green, is cut from three-quarters of a circle and fastened with a gold brooch on each shoulder.

Footwear: The shoes are of gold brocade.

Jewellery: A necklace of gold and emeralds is worn. The belt of gold links at hip-level is set with large green uncut stones.

X.37. Youth with Lute. 1485

Hair: The hair descends to the shoulder-blades and has a fringe in front.

Headdress: The soft-crowned cap of black velvet has a folded turned-up rim of cardinal red silk. A matching feather is fastened on the right side.

Garments: The square-necked shirt is of white lawn, frilled at the top. Its sleeves are seen in puffs at openings in the doublet sleeves and at the waist below the hem of the collarless black velvet doublet, of an Italian fashion, which is open to the waist. The sleeves are edged and tied at three points with cardinal red silk. Bands of the same silk join the sides of the doublet in front. The cloak is of silver grey silk, with a lining of white silk turned over at the collar. The hose are cardinal red, laced in front and with a codpiece.

Footwear: The broad-toed, flat shoes are of grey leather.

Accessories: The youth is playing a lute, slung by a white leather strap from his right shoulder. His red leather belt is ornamented with silver. The black velvet purse has a dagger attached to it. An ornamental silver garter, set with red stones, is worn below his left knee.

X.38. Youth with Harp. About 1495

Hair: The hair is long and thick, curving inwards and touching the shoulders. It is parted in the centre, under the cap.

Headdress: A black silk scarf is tied over the head and knotted at the back. Over it is worn a round cap of grey fur.

Garments: The under-tunic of black silk has tight-fitting sleeves, with narrow white cuffs. The over-tunic of deep blue ribbed silk has a boat-shaped neckline with an edging of white. The large over-sleeves are sewn with pearls along the dagged edges and lined in black. Pearls also edge the hem of the short, pleated and flared skirt. The belt is black, with a silver buckle. The hose are parti-coloured, white on the left leg and white with cerise stripes on the right.

Footwear: The broad-toed mules are of black leather.

Accessories: The harp is gilded and is slung from the neck by a cherry-coloured scarf.

X.39. Woman in French Hood. 1495

Hair: The hair is smoothed down from a centre parting and shows only at the forehead. It may hang loose under the veil at the back of the hood, but is more probably wound round the head.

Headdress: The French hood, an early example, has a double border of pleated gold tissue to frame the face and behind this a band of red silk edged with gold and set with garnets and amethysts to form a border for the hood, which is of black velvet. Its sides are slit, with an embroidered ornament of gold thread at the top of the slit.

Garments: The under-gown is of gold brocade. The overgown is of deep violet silk, with a fitted bodice and flowing skirt. Much of the fullness is at the back of the waist and the front is held up in the hands. The neckline is square, edged in black velvet, with an ivory muslin partlet gathered up to the base of the neck into a band. The loose sleeves are edged with grey fur.

Footwear: The blunt-toed shoes, with flat soles, are of black velvet.

XI   16TH-CENTURY DRESS

The trends of fashion in France, England, Italy and Germany combined at the opening of the 16th century to produce the slashed, puffed and parti-coloured costume of the first quarter. By this time Spanish influence had established itself, particularly in the introduction of the bell-shaped farthingale. It continued in the second half of the century, creating with English, French and Italian modes the exotic panache of the later fashions. A mixture of formality and bravura was achieved by the stiffened dresses and doublets, the jewelled scintillating stuffs, the widened shoulders and tapering waists. This effect was heightened in the last twenty years of the century by the tall-crowned hats and short flared cloaks of the men and the wide French farthingales and great standing ruffs of the women.

Hair—Men: Men's hair was worn long at the beginning of the century, with a fringe or centre parting. It was allowed to grow thick and was generally turned in a little at the ends, left almost straight apart from this or arranged in loose waves.

By 1515 hair was shorter, ending at the nape of the neck, with the fringe more usual than the centre parting. Some men already had their hair cut short, and by 1530 short hair was in vogue and continued until the end of the century, with other styles accompanying it. In 1570 a fashion arose for wearing the hair brushed upward and back, and in 1580 for having it closely curled all over the head, brushed to one side with a lock falling over the temples, or brushed back in a wide arc. It was often allowed to grow longer at the back with this style, and was curled and frizzed if necessary. Men at the French court at the same time had their hair arranged in a central downward peak on the forehead, and do not seem to have favoured the widened shape and wore it short at the back for some time longer than in England.

Men were usually clean-shaven at the opening of the century. By 1530 a short, fringed beard and narrow, untrimmed moustache meeting it were sometimes worn, and trimmed short beards and moustaches had come in by 1540, though many men were clean-shaven and the moustache might be worn alone. A long pointed beard was in vogue from 1560 onwards, and from 1570 a full or small pointed beard went with an upward-brushed moustache. Forked or large, spade-shaped beards were characteristic also from the 1570s, though they did not gain much currency with young men. The short, fringed beard was revived at this time and the equivalent of the 'Imperial' was known, also a wisp-like goatee beard worn by elderly men.

Hair—Women: Hair showed very little with the headdress of the early part of the century. Smoothed back from a centre parting, it was shown in the front by the original hoods and pyramidal headdress.

After 1525 the long hair at the back, which had often hung down at the back under the 'veil' of the headdress, might be turned up in two swathes inside the 'gable' of the English hood and pinned across the top of the head, confined in silk bags attached to the 'gable' or bound in place by ribbons twined round it.

With the development of the French hood the hair was coiled or plaited closely at the back of the head and usually covered by the headdress.

Hair was waved and curled more often after 1540 and showed at the temples. It was parted in the centre and from about 1540 pads or frames at the sides were used by many women to widen the appearance of the hair in front. After 1570 the parting was less usual, the hair being taken back in a wide, padded arc, often with the effect of a dip in the centre. Sometimes in the latter part of the century the front of the head was shaved to enhance the effect of an uncovered forehead which was characteristic of the whole epoch, but this was never a common custom.

In the last few years of the century an effect of height added to width, especially with formal dress, was achieved with the aid of frames and pads. This fashion was to continue at the opening of the 17th century.

XI.1. 1520s–30s. Women's Headdress

Hair: The hair of (a), (b) and (c) is parted in the centre and smoothed down. It is hardly visible.

Headdress: (a) (1520.) Wears a hood made of two rectangles of white linen seamed together. One of the short edges is laid over the forehead a little above the hair-line. It is then taken round to the back of the neck and fastened there. The remainder of the material hangs down at the back. (b) (1530.) This is a similar hood to that of (a), but is fastened to the hair and hangs down to the shoulder-blades. A corner on each side of the face is pressed or stitched back. (c) (1534.) The hat worn by (c) is of white felt made in a beret shape with a head-band. It has a lappets of its own material curving inward over the cheeks.

Garments: (a) The gown is of tomato-red cloth, with inset sleeves. It has a square décolletage, edged with black velvet. Within it is a partlet of white lawn, gathered into a band at the base of the neck and finished by a frill and a black velvet neck-band. (b) The gown is of dark green cloth with a plain turned-down collar of white linen. (c) The black wool gown has a square décolletage filled in with a white lawn partlet which is in fact a part of the dress. The border of crimson satin that edges the top of the décolletage goes down the middle of the bodice and up the centre of the partlet to the base of the neck, where it continues as a neckband. Small crimson buttons decorate the bodice. The cape-scarf is of crimson taffeta.

Headdress—Men: The late 15th century cap, with a soft round or rigid crown, was among the important forms of headdress at this time. It could have a brim turned up at the front, with another segment at the back turned down, or segments turned up at sides and back, with no brim in front. As the brim segments could be fastened back, it was known as the 'buttoned' cap.

After 1520 this cap was less fashionable and was worn chiefly by countrymen and by elderly men of the learned professions. The crown was now sometimes square and segments of the brim could be fastened over it. These could be joined by lacing or by a brooch in the front or to one side.

A hat popular from 1505 to the 1540s had a full, soft crown gathered into a band and a fairly deep brim unsegmented or in two segments only, overlapping slightly at the sides.

A cap, or bonnet, as caps were now called, which was in vogue from 1520 to mid-century was of a shallow pill-box shape, wider at the outer edge than at the inner and trimmed with a feather edging or with plumes. It was worn tilted, with a band round the back of the head

XI.2. 16th Century. Three Figures

Hair: (a) (About 1525.) Man-at-arms. The hair is of moderate length, showing the ears and meeting the collar at the back. Some locks come forward over the forehead and in front of the ears. (c) (1533.) Statesman. The hair is cut fairly short, with short locks covering the ears. A moustache and short beard are worn.

Headdress: (a) The soft-crowned hat of the man-at-arms is of black velvet with a moderately wide, flat brim and a scarlet plume attached on the right side. (b) (First half of century.) A labourer. The hat of brown felt with brim turned down is worn over a coif of unbleached linen. (c) The statesman has a four-cornered hat of black velvet, worn with one corner over the centre of the forehead.

Garments: (a) The sleeves of the doublet of buff-coloured cloth slashed with green are full in the upper part, with close-fitting lower parts of dark green wool. The high-collared jerkin is of scarlet cloth, slashed in the body and skirt and edged with yellow at the shoulders, hem and front skirt-opening. The sleeves end below the shoulders. From the shoulder-opening the short sleeves of a shirt of mail worn under the jerkin can be seen on the upper arms. The breeches of scarlet cloth slashed with yellow are close-fitting, with three puffed rings of material encircling the legs. The hose are scarlet. (b) The farm labourer wears a tunic of russet wool, buttoned down the front from the close uncollared neckline to the low waist and ending at mid-thigh. The long sleeves are rolled back, showing the loose sleeve-ends of the white shirt. The cloak is fastened at the neck in front and is of dark green wool. Loose, long breeches of light brown canvas or coarse hempen stuff end at the ankles and are bound with straps at that point and below the knees. (c) The doublet is of black cloth, with a high collar of white linen. The loose outer gown is of black and brown damasked velvet lined with brown fur which is turned outward to form a roll collar. The garment is drawn across the body in front and ends at the instep. The sleeves widen towards the elbows, then taper towards the wrists.

Footwear: (a) The man-at-arms has shoes of black buckskin with the vamps cut into three points at the top. Slashes over the insteps and toes show the scarlet lining or the hose. (b) The farm labourer wears stout shoes of brown leather. (c) The statesman has round-toed shoes of black velvet.

Accessories: (a) A sword is slung from a black and scarlet sword-belt attached on the right side of the waist. An arquebus is held in the right hand. (b) A sling-shaped pouch of unbleached linen is worn fastened to the waist of the tunic. A hoe is held in the left hand.

or over an embroidered skull-cap or caul. The coif, in black or white, was worn, indoors and out, by elderly men.

The 'flat cap', a head-covering in use by all classes from the 1530s onward, had a shallow, soft crown and a small unsegmented brim lying flat. It could be put on straight or tilted. It was worn by apprentices and artisans in utilitarian materials, but by the well-to-do in velvet, often with a jewelled band or a brooch and plume. The flat cap remained in use throughout the century.

XI.3. 1528–40. Women's Headdress

Hair: The hair of (a), (b) and (c) is parted in the centre and worn smoothly pressed down on either side.

Headdress: (a) (1540.) The cap is of white lawn and is made in three overlapping layers: a plain band to frame the face, a close-fitting cap fitting the back of the head, and covering the ears, and a raised additional cap giving the headdress both width and front-to-back depth. (b) (1540.) The cap is similar to the two first layers of that worn by (a), but is parchment-tinted and is surmounted by a flat, circular, plate-like hat of natural straw, attached in the centre to the crown of the cap. (c) (1528.) This is known as a 'lettice' cap and is of white fur. It comes to a peak at the crown of the head and fits the back of it closely. The sides protrude at the level of the temples and curve inward over the cheeks.

Garments: (a) The gown is of black cloth with a fitted bodice. The 'V'-shaped standing collar of white lawn is tied in front by short scarlet cords.

The high-necked white lawn partlet has a small turn-over in front and scarlet embroidery. The cape-like scarf of scarlet silk is put round the shoulders and attached to the gown under the arms. (b) The gown is of brown velvet. The fitted bodice has an arched décolletage with a border of parchment-coloured silk sewn with yellow stones. An oval shoulder-yoke covers the centre front of this. The upper sleeves are close fitting with full lower sleeves joined on. The 'V'-shaped standing collar is of parchment coloured velvet and the plain partlet of off-white lawn fastens at the throat and is surmounted by a high collar of narrow frills. (c) The gown is of indigo blue cloth with a 'V'-shaped standing collar of white fur and a folded white lawn partlet. The cape-scarf of white silk is held together in front by one hand (unseen).

Jewellery: (a) A small gold ornament covers the collar fastening. (c) A silver ornament is worn at the base of the collar.

A raised crown was characteristic of hats in fashion from about 1560 onwards. A version of the flat cap with its crown heightened was an early example of this mode. The 'copotain' had a tall cone-shaped crown with a small rolled, flat or turned-down brim. It was trimmed with a band round the base of the crown. A later version of this, near the end of the century, had a lower, flat-topped crown and wider brim and was worn towards the back of the head.

In the 1570s a 'bowler' type of hat, with a stiff crown, a rolled brim and a narrow jewelled or decorated band round the base of the crown, was added to the wide variety of hats that were now developed from the basic fashions of the latter part of the century. Narrow but flexible brims and differences in the height of the crown, as well as in feathered or jewelled ornament accounted for a good deal of this variety. At the French court small-brimmed hats or berets, perched well back on the hair, carried a feathered and jewelled ornament at the front.

Headdress—Women: The hood became the main feature of women's headdress at the beginning of the 16th century. It was semicircular, draped over the head, and in one of its early forms turned back to show a long band of embroidery and in some cases the front of an under-cap and a little hair. The back of the hood hung down to the shoulder-blades and had lappets hanging forward at the sides of the face, divided from the back length by slits in the shape of an inverted 'V', but after 1515 the back and the lappets were shorter. In the first years of the century in England the turned-back front was stiffened into the 'gabled' form that became the pyramidal or gabled headdress. A band of embroidery, laid across the top of the gable, hung down on each side and took the place of the side-lappets. These two types of hood were in fashion at the same time.

A plain hood of lawn or linen, undecorated, was also worn. This had the suggestion of a forward peak on the forehead and was shaped to come forward towards the cheeks in front of the ears. It later became the 'Marie Stuart' cap, but at first had a length hanging at the back like the hoods already described.

After 1525 a custom arose of pinning the side-lappets or back-length, or all three, of the gabled headdress over the top of the head. The back-length by this time was divided into two pendants from the box-shaped back of the headdress, covered with the same stuff. This facilitated the pinning up. In the 1530s the two streamers at the back became sheaths sewn up at the ends, which could be draped more easily.

About 1500 the French hood, seen in its first forms in the 1480s, became popular. It had a stiffened, horseshoe-shaped front, worn well back on the head and towards the crown, with the two points of the horseshoe curved forward on to the cheeks. Its back-length, hanging down to the shoulders, was straight, not semicircular, and could be pleated or plain. It could also be stiffened and turned up over the head from the back, its ends forming a shady brim over the forehead.

A separate headdress known as the 'bongrâce' was evolved from this development and was worn tied on over a coif, cap or plain hood, or by itself, for the greater part of the century. Hats of various shapes were worn over caps or alone in the '20s and '30s.

The back-length as worn with the French hood was very often dispensed with by mid-century, but was worn again more frequently in the final quarter. In the 1540s the hood was given a square outline over the forehead.

The caul in its 16th century form was an ornamental cap with jewels sewn on to net or real hair, worn towards the back of the head and sometimes lined with silk. In this form it came into fashion early in the century and persisted until the 1590s.

The escoffion, a cylindrical cap of silk and jewels, set back on the head, was worn between the late '50s and early '70s.

The 'Marie Stuart' hood or cap was shaped so that its edge dipped over the centre of the forehead and extended its curves outward on either side to show some hair. The curves then came forward towards the cheeks. The hood curved over the back of the head and ended at the nape of the neck. It came into fashion in 1550 and was worn, with modifications, until about 1630.

A large hood, covering the cap or other close-fitting headdress and the ruff as well, was in fashion late in the century, from 1580.

Hats and 'bonnets' in imitation of those worn by the men, but smaller, were put on over coifs, under caps and cauls in the 1570s and for a longer period with utilitarian dress.

In the final twenty years the Marie Stuart cap was widened and had more pronounced curves, or was made smaller and raised on the head to accommodate the higher and wider arc of the hair which became fashionable.

Single ornaments affixed to the hair, or to a hairnet of real hair, were in vogue by the end of the century when no cap was worn.

Wigs and false hair were freely used to attain the rigid effect of the hairdressing at this time.

Garments—Men: At the opening of the century until about 1520, the garment known as 'bases', a sleeveless bodice put on over a sleeved under-doublet, with a flared skirt composed of lined and padded corrugated folds of even size, was worn by soldiers, noblemen and various functionaries. The bodice was sometimes separate from the skirt, which tied at the waist and was open at back or front. It was made in brilliant, contrasting colours and was copied in metal in suits of armour.

The neckline fashionable for men early in the 16th century showed the top of the shirt, which was usually gathered into a band. This was often decorated with black or coloured embroidery.

A small goffered frill or a collar could be added. In French and Italian styles the décolletage of shirt and doublet was both wide and deep during the first years in the extreme of fashion for young men, and sometimes had a wide curved neckline at the back as well. While the neckline of the doublet had risen above the base of the throat in more northern countries by the 1530s, the low-necked style in France and Italy continued until about 1540. Shirts were usually white but were also made in coloured silks. The sleeves of the shirt were long and full, gathered into a band at the wrist. By 1530 a narrow frill could be added which was visible below the edge of the outer sleeve.

The doublet could be skirtless in the opening years, or made with the short basque that became a lasting fashion. The sleeves could be plain, though not close-fitting, full throughout and banded at the wrists, or puffed in various ways.

The jerkin, worn over the doublet, was usually open to the waist, and could be skirtless at the beginning of the century or have a skirt open from waist to hem, showing the codpiece and ending just above or below the knee. It could be sleeveless or have puffed sleeves ending at the elbow.

Both garments could be collarless until about 1540, when a low standing collar, not always fastened, was usual.

Among servitors and some citizens in the first years of the epoch a tunic covering the knees was worn instead of the doublet. It was less fitting to the figure than the closely fitted doublet, had a fairly full skirt put on at the waist, sleeves full over the elbow but fitted from elbow to wrist, and a neckline opened in a square or a moderate 'V' with the neck of the shirt or under-doublet reaching the base of the throat.

German influences, which had introduced puffing and slashing, also brought into fashion breeches separate from the hose. These were puffed and slashed, though close-fitting, and ended just above or below the knee. Frequently the breeches were sewn to the hose, but the two garments became known as upper and nether stocks and could be made of differing colours and materials. It seems obvious that the breeches could be a separate garment, put on if desired over full-length hose.

Nether stocks, or stockings, were made of silk or wool, cut on the cross and seamed. Knitted stockings, often without toes and with open heels, were known by mid-century and were made of yarn or wool, more rarely of silk. They were not in general use until the following century.

The main outer garment in the first forty-five years of the period was the open gown, ending at the ankles, knees or calf. It was sometimes girdled and could have long wide sleeves in the opening years. Hanging sleeves depended from the shoulders and were often supplemented by the 1530s by large puffed sleeves ending above the elbow, so that the hanging sleeve became chiefly a decoration. As an alternative, the hanging sleeve from the shoulder could be the only sleeve to the gown, with large puffed sleeves belonging to the jerkin protruding from the arm-holes.

Cloaks were unusual at this time, the gown taking their place, but in the latter part of the century the situation was reversed.

In the second half of the century the doublet had a standing collar, edged with scallops or tabs which were ornamentations or supported a small ruff. The narrow turn-over collar, fastened in front, which was worn as a collar to the shirt and to the plain doublet or jerkin throughout the century, appeared sometimes on the high-standing doublet collar in the years following 1540 usually in utilitarian dress. The ruff became the almost universal finish to the high collar. It was higher at the back than in front, but was made a little lower in

XI.4. 16th Century. Six Figures

Hair: (a), (b) and (c). These three figures have short hair coming forward on to the forehead in the case of (a) and (c). (a) has a moustache and a short fringe of beard. (d), (e) and (f) have hair covering the ears and in the case of (d) and (f) coming forward on to the forehead.

Headdress: (a) (1560.) A carpenter. The cap of red felt is shaped like a truncated cone and has a close-fitting, flexible brim turned up all round. (b) (1560–70.) A city youth. The hat of brown felt has a cone-shaped crown. The flexible brim is turned up on the right side and down on the left. A yellow feather is attached on the left side. (c) (1570–80.) A wharf-man or sailor. The round cap is covered in strands of wool in grey, blue and white. (d) (1570.) A farm lad. The dun-coloured, round-brimmed hat is of felt. (e) (1570–80.) A shepherd. The wide-brimmed hat of grey felt has the brim turned up in front, at the right side and at the back, while the left side is turned down. (f) (1560–70.) An apprentice. The cap is of black felt. It has a flat, soft crown and a narrow brim.

the 1570s, when the ruff grew larger and was supported at the back by an 'under-propper' of wire or wood.

The falling-band (a turned-down ruff or collar), moderate in size, was worn with the lower standing collar of the 1580s and '90s.

Doublets and jerkins were generally fastened in front, with concealed lacing or hooks and eyes or with loops and buttons which were usually visible.

The body of the doublet was now padded with 'bombast' (a term given to various kinds of padding such as cotton, flock, horsehair or even bran) and further stiffened with canvas or buckram. The garment was narrow at the waist with a deep point in front. Rounded waists were also worn but were not generally in fashion until 1590, when they became more usual. An effect of breadth on the shoulders was achieved by cut and padding, in contrast to the pinched-in waist. From 1575 the 'peascod belly' was in vogue. The doublet had extra padding in a ridge over the abdomen which ended in a downward bulge sometimes overhanging the belt. This fashion was not always in evidence. In more practical dress it hardly existed, since the amount of stiff padding necessary in front would have impeded movement. By the 1590s the doublet had reverted to a more normal shape, though some trace of the peascod belly continued into the 17th century.

From 1540 onwards the doublet-skirt was as a rule attenuated to a short basque; it was cut on the cross and stood out a little, but was often almost concealed by the narrow girdle or leather belt and the lower part of the heavily padded body. It could be made with a gap between the front edges or with the edges meeting or overlapping. Alternatively it could be slit into plain, looped or scalloped tabs. It was also sometimes made in two layers, the upper a little narrower than the lower. One or more sleeveless and padded under-doublets might be worn for warmth or as a defence against sword and dagger thrusts.

The doublet nearly always carried 'wings', that is miniature capes or rolls of material at the shoulders, covering the tying-in of sleeves by 'points', during the second part of the century. Sleeves were generally padded and in some cases stiffened as well. They could be wide at the top, narrowing towards the wrist, or of even width, frequently close-fitting, with a wrist-frill. Fuller sleeves from 1575 onwards could be of the 'trunk' type, heavily padded, with considerable width in the upper part, tapering towards turned-back cuffs at the wrists. The last type of sleeve did not have shoulder 'wings' or rolls. Hanging sleeves, sometimes for decoration only, were fashionable in the second half of the century.

The jerkin, lined but not as a rule padded, and with a high, standing collar, was frequently worn over the doublet, following its shape and just covering it, though in the

---

Garments: (a) The workaday doublet of russet-coloured woollen stuff ends at the waist and has a wide, uncollared neckline. It fastens down the front and the sleeves are rolled up, showing the rolled sleeves of the white shirt. The short, full breeches of brown wool are gathered into bands well above the knees. An apron is tied on at the waist. The hose are light brown. (b) The white shirt-collar shows at the neck. The jerkin is of buff-yellow cloth, fastening down the front, with a basque made up of joined segments, and has short, puffed sleeves. The brown sleeves of the doublet beneath are visible. The round-hose are brown, paned in yellow, and the hose buff-yellow. (c) The sea-going youth wears a white shirt with full sleeves gathered into wrist-bands, a red sleeveless jerkin of woollen stuff, ending at the waist, and loose, long breeches of stout blue-grey cotton material. He wears a red leather belt with a sheath-knife attached to it. (d) The white shirt-collar of this farm lad shows over the top of his short, full 'cassock', which is sleeveless except for shoulder-rolls and shows the full shirt-sleeves. It is of fawn-coloured woollen stuff with black edging at the hem and neck fastening, which has black buttons. He wears brown 'Venetian' breeches fastened below the knees. His hose or stockings are of coarse brown yarn. (e) The young shepherd has a short, loose, grey woollen tunic, belted at the waist and showing the white shirt-collar. His legs are bare to the calf, where his grey woollen stockings are turned down over the tops of his boots. (f) The apprentice wears a deep-skirted jerkin of blue woollen stuff buttoned down the front. The high collar, finished with a small ruff, and the close-fitting sleeves of his scarlet doublet are visible. His hose are of blue wool. The large cloak, held together by a band or cord crossing the chest, is of dark blue cloth. A red leather belt is worn at waist-level.

Footwear: (a) The flat shoes are of brown leather. (b) The shoes, with fairly high vamps, are of brown buckskin. (d) The boots are of brown buckskin. (e) The boots are of brown leather or yarn. (f) The shoes are of red leather, with high vamps.

Accessories: (a) The carpenter carries a hammer. (b) The city youth carries brown gloves. (c) The sailor has a coil of rope in his hands. (d) The farm lad carries a crooked staff. A horn is slung from his left shoulder to his right hip. (e) The shepherd has a pouch on a strap from right shoulder to left hip and carries a combined crook and hoe. (f) The apprentice has a purse of red leather attached to his belt.

XI.5. 1570s and '80s. Women's Headdress

Hair: (a) (1575–85.) The hair is parted in the centre and brought upward into a caul which covers the back of the head. (b) (1575.) and (c) (1575.) The hair is arranged as in (a).

Headdress: (a) The hat is of blue satin made on a stiffened foundation. It has a small, rigid brim and a crown wider at the top than at the base, with pleats arranged in the Italian fashion and a band of pearls. Three short grey plumes are set on the right side. The caul is of blue net ornamented in red silk. (b) The hat has a tall, shaped crown and a brim curving down at the front and back and up at the sides. It is worn tipped forward and is of black plush-like material, with a band of red stones and a tall scarlet plume set in the front. A caul of black velvet covers the back of the head. (c) The hat is of black satin on a stiffened foundation, with pleats as in (a), and a tall crown with its brim turned up at the back and down in front. Five amber-tinted plumes ornament the top and sides. The band is of amber beads and the caul of amber-coloured silk.

Garments: (a) The open standing collar is of ivory-tinted pleated lawn, with a close-fitting, high, frilled collar worn inside it. The grey cloth gown fastens in front with silver buttons set with small blue stones. (b) The partlet of white lawn has a high, full neck-piece gathered on at the base of the neck. It is surmounted by a close-fitting white ruff. The gown is of dull greyish-green cloth, with revers in matching silk meeting a front fastening. (c) The partlet of (c) resembles that of (b) but has a narrow neck-frill in place of a ruff. The gown is of tan-coloured wool decorated with matching silk braid. The standing collar is backed with the same stuff but faced in pale biscuit-colour edged with black.

Jewellery: (a) Pearl drop earrings are worn and a triple necklace of blue stones put on over the shoulders. (b) The earrings are large black pearls. A necklace of red stones made in two strands looping over each other is worn round the base of the high collar. (c) The earrings are of gold and amber and the necklace a double row of amber beads, worn round the high collar of the partlet.

late '50s and the '60s, it might end at mid-thigh. It was often sleeveless, or with a short, puffed sleeve that left a large part of the doublet sleeve visible. It sometimes had long, plain sleeves or sleeves that were wide in the upper part and narrowed towards the wrist. Hanging sleeves only could also be a feature of the jerkins, sometimes of the imitation variety, having no wrist-opening, but only being meant to hang loosely from the shoulders.

Upper and nether stocks could still be worn as separate garments or sewn together. The upper-stocks or close-fitting breeches could differ entirely in material and decoration from the nether-stocks or stockings, which were often drawn over the breeches at the knees. In the second half of the century trunk or round hose were evolved. These were full, short breeches, again not necessarily of the same material or patterning as the upper and nether stocks, and were padded, stiffened with coarse linings and almost invariably slashed, with a differently coloured lining showing through. From about 1550 to 1570 these breeches ended a little way down the thighs or at mid-thigh. In their later form they sloped outward from the waist, the fullest part coming near the finishing point. In the last twenty-five years of the century they were sometimes very short indeed, a mere puffed and slashed adornment round the hips, with the upper-stocks, now reappearing, forming the actual breeches. Conversely, if the round hose were in fact breeches, the upper-stocks might be separate part-hose, reaching from the upper thigh to the knee, and drawn up under the round hose. In this form they were known as 'canions'.

The codpiece, now diminished in size from its conspicuous proportions in the early part of the century, was still made to go with round hose, but was not visible in the final quarter of the century.

'Venetians', worn from 1570 onwards, were pear-shaped breeches swelling out over the hips and decreasing to the point just below the knees where they ended. They were generally of plain silk, satin or velvet, without slashing, though stiff linings must have padded them over the hips.

Hose ending above the knees were often of silk, with embroidered clocks, after mid-century and could be tailored or knitted. Garters were usually narrow sashes with fringed ends or bands of material decorated with embroidery and sometimes jewels. In 'cross-gartering' the garter was put on below the knee, as was usual, but instead of being tied on the outside the ends were crossed at the back, brought round and tied on the front of the leg just above the knee.

By 1530 the short gown was occasionally worn covering the left arm as though it were a cloak, the garment being kept in place by a jewelled chain across the chest. By mid-century the gown in its loosely hanging form was largely superseded by the cloak, except for wear by scholars, lawyers, elder statesmen and other men of learning and importance, also by merchants and well-to-do tradesmen. As worn by them it ended at the calf or ankle, could be fur-lined or have long lapels faced with fur, had arm openings with imitation hanging sleeves and was worn open down the front. It was still worn *en négligé* or as a dressing-gown. The short, full version of the gown, previously worn by men of rank of all ages, did not go entirely out of fashion and was apparent as the 'sleeved cloak', with the sleeves worn hanging, until about 1575.

The cloak, ending usually at the top of the thigh, was widely flared, being cut from three quarters of a circle. It could end at the waist and was a favourite fashion in this form from 1580 onwards. After 1570 a longer cloak, reaching to the ankle, foreshadowed the long cloaks of the ensuing century. Short shoulder-capes, called tippets, or ornamental folded hoods could be added to cloaks. Standing or turned-down collars could be worn or the cloak could be collarless. When worn over both shoulders cords on either side were passed under the arms from the front and tied at the back. When the cloak was worn over one shoulder only the cords were taken under the opposite arm and tied at the armpit.

The mandillion, or short, open-sided coat with sleeves, popular after 1570, was often worn with the body of the garment across the shoulders and a sleeve hanging at back and front or straightforwardly with the sleeves left hanging.

The gaberdine, a long, loose coat which could be worn girdled, with wide sleeves, was at first made as a fashionable garment, of velvet, cloth or silk, though used mainly as a casual extra wrap. After 1560 it was no longer an item of modish wear, but was entirely a useful garment, a sound protection against bad weather and widely adopted by people doing practical work.

Versions of the jerkin, made loose instead of close-fitting, or the thigh-length open gown, plainly made, with moderately wide sleeves, and other variants and combinations of the garments described must be considered as part of the male costume of this time.

Garments—Women: The transitional fashions of the final years of the 15th century, continuing into the 16th, existed for a time side by side with the development of the new fashion. This was the gown with closely fitting bodice, low, square décolletage with a slightly arched shape across the bosom, wide over-sleeves turned back above the elbow to show bishop-style sleeves beneath and long full skirts gathered into a miniature 'bustle' at the back of the waist and forming a train. Combinations and variations of these contrasting fashions were known, but by 1525 the new outline had crystallized and the transitional costume was found mainly in country places and among the elderly.

The newer fashion consisted of a kirtle—at first a complete under-dress with sleeves, but later made with the bodice and skirt separate—and an over-gown whose rigid bodice might be worn over the shift or chemise without the bodice of the kirtle or a separate corset. The under-sleeves could then be detachable, fastened by points to the shoulders of the over-gown beneath the wide over-sleeves, which, when fastened back above the elbow, showed a lining of fur or rich material. The decorative edge of the chemise-top could show at the square décolletage. The neckline of the bodice at the back of the neck was usually a 'V'. Until 1530 the skirts of the gown might be caught up over the arm or in front or on either side by fastenings at the waist-line, or it might be turned up at the back and fastened to the top of the 'bustle'. After 1530 trains were shorter, only being worn very long for state occasions. By 1540 many skirts were circular, without a train, just touching the floor. The Spanish farthingale, nearly always worn beneath these gowns, was a wired or whaleboned funnel-shaped petticoat which caused the gown to hang without folds, or, in a bell-shaped form, to let the folds hang over it. It created, with the heavy, much ornamented stuff of the dress hung over it, an effect of stiffness and weight.

About this time a partlet with a small standing collar, turned back and left open to the top of the bodice, where a brooch or other ornament was worn, brought a variation to the décolletage. The partlet in this case was usually dark, and the turn-back of the collar white or of a light colour. Full 'bishop' sleeves were generally worn with this type of dress, fastened at intervals along the outer seam, with aiguillettes (small cylindrical ornaments sewn on in pairs) to mark the fastenings, and with puffs of the chemise sleeves or of rich material showing between the fastenings. The decorative cuffs of the chemise were visible as usual at the wrists. Wide, turned-back over-sleeves matching the over-gown were still worn.

Bodices ended in a rounded waist-line, and were worn with a narrow jewelled or ornamental girdle.

Most gowns were open from the waist down to show an ornamental kirtle.

Long mantles joined across the chest by cords or jewelled chains, and worn mainly for ceremonial occasions but sometimes for travelling, tippets (small shoulder-capes), and square or oblong wraps folded double or cornerwise and put round the shoulders were the outer garments worn until mid-century.

By 1545 it was more usual to wear the half-kirtle than the type that formed a complete dress, and the bodice and skirt of the over-gown were separate. The bodice by this time had a moderate point at the waist. The partlet was often very ornate, matching the sleeves and kirtle.

Narrow ruffs had appeared by 1560 and the partlet could be finished by an upstanding band round the neck and a small ruff. The ruff might be worn alone, without a partlet, in which case an ornate necklace was sometimes seen below it. The partlet with the open upstanding collar could have this closed and the frill or lining that showed at the top of it could be replaced by a ruff, or it could still be worn open.

A typical sleeve of the second half of the century was fairly close-fitting, but raised in puffs, rolls and wings at the shoulders and sometimes, to begin with, puffs at the elbows as well. Once the ruff had become popular, 'hand-ruffs' finished the sleeves at the wrists. Later, from the 1570s onward, hanging sleeves appeared on many dresses and were still in fashion at the opening of the 17th century.

A padded bodice differing in material from the skirt and generally embroidered in an all-over pattern was in fashion from the mid-1560s onwards and was known as the doublet. Towards 1600 its pointed base changed to a rounded one with a short basque.

In the 1580s the 'trunk' sleeve, heavily padded throughout, raised high at the shoulder and tapering from a full top to the wrist, was added to the mode. Soft, full sleeves, ending in hand-ruffs and with 'wings' at the shoulders, also became a part of the fashion during this decade.

From about 1580 the 'cart-wheel' ruff, often raised at the back and supported by an 'under-propper' of wire or wood covered in stuff toning with that of the dress, was worn with high or low décolletage. The 'rebato', a large standing ruff of lace, wired to frame the head from the back, and the pear-shaped ruff were worn with low décolletage from the 1580s onwards.

This decade saw changes in the shapes of women's gowns. The stomacher, a stiffened, inverted triangle of material attached to the front of the dress so that its upper edge formed the low décolletage, greatly lengthened the bodice in front, its apex forming the lowest point. Its place was sometimes taken by the front of a chemise, laid in pleats, with a high neck and small ruff.

The French farthingale, coming into fashion about the same time, altered the styles of skirts. It was of two types: the 'roll', a sort of bolster tied on at the waist to pad out the skirt at sides and back, or, in a shorter form, the back and part of the sides only; and the 'wheel', a wheel-shaped contrivance of covered wire, also put on at the waist, which created a kind of shelf all round under the skirt. A circular frill was added on the outside of the skirt to cover the outline of this farthingale.

With a large 'roll' farthingale the skirt usually touched the ground, sometimes with the suggestion of a train, but with a smaller roll, or with petticoats instead, it might be well clear of the ground, especially if worn for practical work. With the 'wheel' farthingale the skirt was shorter, just showing the shoes.

The gown, a feminine version of the man's outer robe, came into fashion about 1550. It was long and usually loose-fitting, worn open over a dress. In some instances it had a closed, front-fastening fitted bodice, with the front half of the skirt joined on at the waist.

XI.6. 16th Century. Three Figures

Hair: (a) and (b) The hair is hidden by the headdress. (c) (1590s.) The hair is taken back from the forehead, above the ears. It is thick, wavy and fairly long at the back of the neck.

Headdress: (a) (About 1570.) A kerchief of dull orange silk is worn over the head and knotted at the back of the neck. Over it is a 'bowler' type of hat in beaver-coloured felt. (b) (1560.) The closed metal helmet has a crest from front to back. (c) The hat of grey felt, carried in the right hand, has a tall, flat-topped crown and is decorated with five red plumes. The wide, flexible brim is turned up at one side.

Garments: (a) (1570s.) A townswoman. The dress is of dull orange cloth with a laced corset of black velvet worn over it. The bodice is low cut, with part of the white chemise top showing. The white lawn collar, turned down and meeting at the throat, is surmounted by a small ruff. A larger collar meets over the top of the dress and covers the shoulders. The skirt is moderately full, worn over a kirtle or petticoat. The sleeves are close-fitting and have hand ruffs. A white apron is tied on at the waist. (b) (1560.) The complete suit of armour has wide

shoulder-plates, elbow-pieces and knee-pieces. The metal gauntlets protect the forearms as well as the hands. The metal 'skirt' is wide enough to allow for the round-hose, which are of black satin, paned in amber with gold piping. (c) (1590.) The matching doublet and breeches ('Venetians') are of black velvet. The collar of white embroidery is a 'falling band', tied in front, and the cuffs are turned back. The outer garment is a mandillion, a tabard-shaped garment with open side-seams. The sleeves are worn hanging loose. It is of pewter-grey satin, bordered in black velvet at the sides, hem, sleeve-ends and along the shoulder wings and shoulder-seams. The tailored hose are of pewter-grey silk.

Footwear: (a) The shoes are of light brown buck-skin. (b) The armoured shoes have high-vamped uppers. The leg-armour comes down to cover the heels. (c) The shoes are of pewter-grey satin with red ties.

Accessories: (a) A small covered basket is held in the right hand. (b) A sword hangs from a strap attached at the waist. (c) A sword hangs from a strap attached to a belt beneath the doublet.

A standing collar with a small ruff and a 'Medici' collar (high at the back and opened in front) could be worn, and long revers of fur from shoulder to hem were often added.

The sleeves were generally round and puffed at the top and might end there, those showing from the upper arms to the wrists being those of the dress. Alternatively the gown could have wings or rolls at the shoulders and have real or imitation hanging sleeves.

XI.7. 1570s. Men's Headdress

Hair: (1570s) (a) A lock of hair shows on the forehead. The waved hair is cut short and combed back. A trimmed moustache and a fringe of beard, slightly pointed in front, are worn. (b) The hair is short and combed back above the ears. (c) The hair is cut short and combed back as in (a) and (b).

Headdress: (a) The hat of sapphire blue velvet with a narrow, flexible brim and a tall, soft crown is worn at an angle. A short, bright green plume is attached to the right side and the band is of blue and green jewels. (b) The 'bowler' hat of black felt has bands of scarlet giving the crown a segmented effect, and a band of scarlet. (c) This example of a 'copotain' is

of purple velvet, with a turquoise blue plume and a jewelled band of amethysts set in silver.

Garments: (a) The doublet is of dull blue cloth banded in green, with a high collar edged with pointed cream-coloured embroidery. (b) The doublet is of mustard yellow cloth stitched in scarlet with a small standing collar, open in front. Within this is a larger one of saffron-tinted linen standing up to frame the neck and face. (c) The doublet of violet cloth has a high collar edged with ivory-coloured goffered linen and fastened with silver buttons set with turquoise.

Occasionally, after their inception in the 1580s, 'trunk' sleeves might be worn with the gown.

Slits at the side-fronts of the bodice from breast to waist or at hip-level in the skirt were features of the gown, so that the wearer could reach objects suspended from the waist of the dress. In its loose-bodied form the gown was worn as a dressing-gown or 'bed-gown'. Elderly ladies also found it both comfortable and becoming.

In the 1570s the large diaphanous veil, covering the back and sides like a cloak, became a fashion for formal occasions. It was square in shape, made of metallic tissue or gauze, with ornamentation of lace or needlework and was put on at the shoulders or draped over a fan-shaped, semicircular or 'rebato' ruff. As a rule a large standing ruff, circular or open, was worn within it.

In the 1580s the first examples of the turned-back lace cuff were seen. They were generally worn with the ruffs enumerated in the foregoing paragraph.

Aprons, worn throughout the century for domestic or other manual work, were without bibs and were attached at the waist.

An extra skirt of plain, hard-wearing stuff was put on over the kirtle and dress for protection against cold or bad weather. Apart from this a long semicircular cape and feminine adaptations of the casual outer wraps described at the end of 'Garments—Men' were occasional outdoor wear. Gartered stockings ended above the knee.

Footwear—Men: The splay-footed shoes which came into fashion about 1494 were worn until about 1540. Some shoes had thick soles and in the early days of the fashion often a strap and buckle over the instep. Those worn for the popular game of tennis were soled with felt. Another type of shoe was very low-cut round the heel, and many were made like 'mules', with no back.

XI.8. 1590s. Headdress

Hair: (a) The hair is covered by the coif. A drooping moustache and long bifid beard are worn. (b) The hair (possibly a wig) is drawn up to the top of the head in the shape of a cone, exposing the ears. Small curls are arranged over the forehead. (c) The hair is taken back from the forehead, loosely arranged so that it forms an arc. A moustache and square-cut beard are worn.

Headdress: (a) The black coif is tied under the chin. A black velvet hat with a soft crown and brim curving down a little in front is worn over it. (b) A jewelled ornament, curved to fit from side to side over the top of the head, is worn over the coiffure. (c) The black felt 'copotain' has a tall diminishing crown and a flexible brim turned up in front. Scarlet plumes curve over the brim on the right side of the front.

Garments: (a) An oval ruff of white lawn, tilted up at the back, is fastened in front. The front of the black velvet doublet, with silver buttons, is seen at the chest. A black silk gown with a deep collar of brown fur is worn over it. (b) A large 'rebato' frames the head, with another circular ruff worn inside it. Both are of white gauze ornamented with silver lace, and are set upright at the back of the head. The dress, of gold satin has a low décolletage and is embroidered all over with pearls and yellow topaz. (c) A small circular ruff fits closely round the neck. A steel gorget is worn over the black cloth doublet.

Jewellery: (a) A jewelled chain is worn over the fur collar of the gown. (b) The elaborate necklace of pearls has pendants of pearls and rubies. (c) A single pearl earring is worn.

Boots to the ankle, calf or ending in turn-over tops above the knee, were of soft leather and much wrinkled, forming clumsy leg-coverings. They were used mainly for travelling, riding and hunting.

Early in the century decoration in the form of pinking, slashing, or scalloped edging to the vamp, was applied to shoes. From 1530 shoes of an elegant and normal shape, following the line of the foot and with a high vamp, were already being worn by men in the fore-front of fashion. These shoes, decorated with discreet pinking or slashing, or ornamented with diagonal strips in a contrasting shade, often with small scallops at the top of the high vamp, were to be the masculine style for the remainder of the century. They were some-times tied over the instep late in the century, but for the most part were without fastening. They might be of pliable leather or of silk, cloth, damask, brocade or velvet in colours to tone with the dress in the second half of the century. Slightly raised heels were known in the final years, with the higher heels of the 17th century just coming into fashion. Cork was beginning to be used for these heels and for the soles of 'mules'.

Boots in the second half of the century were more commonly worn than in the years before 1540. They were much better fitted to the leg, made of soft, well-dressed leather, ending at the calf or above the knee, and either of such pliability that they needed no fastenings or fastened on the outside by buckles, lacing or buttons. After 1585 boots were a part of fashionable dress, instead of being worn only for riding or outdoor pursuits.

Over-shoes of leather, with thick 'wedge' soles, deepening at the heel, were worn as a protection in bad weather.

Footwear—Women: Women's shoes followed men's fashions almost identically and they wore boots of fine leather for riding.

Materials, Colours and Ornament: Velvet, brocade, damask (often in two colours), taffetas, satin and plain or watered silk were among the most popular stuffs for making the clothes of the well-to-do. Cloth of gold, coloured silk or gauze woven with gold or silver thread, and gold or silver tissue shot with such colours as violet, green or crimson were among the stuffs worn by people of rank.

All colours were available and yellow was especially in favour, as were its variants of parchment colour, orange, amber and saffron. Taffetas was woven with a raised, velvety surface cut into patterns in a different colour from the ground and this treatment was copied in less expensive materials. Crinkled crêpe was known, also watered silk and a parti-coloured weave, made to look like marble and known as 'marbled' silk.

In more sober dress the fashion was for cloths with a thick pile, plush, mohair and tufted or knotted surfaces. Browns, greys, russets, dull blue and dun colour contrasted in them with brighter shades.

In addition, all the ordinary kinds of wool, linen and some cotton were in use. Lace, introduced into England about 1545, was in great demand for the delicate edgings of caps, collars, cuffs and standing ruffs.

Hats and 'bonnets' were made of beaver, felt, smooth fur, velvet, damask and any durable woollen or silken stuff, and stiffened with buckram or canvas, or sometimes starched or stuffed with paper.

Slashing, the most characteristic ornament of the period, was at its height in the second quarter of the century, but was used throughout.

Pinking was the piercing and edging of small holes, arranged in a pattern. Conversely, small circular ornaments such as metal rings, buttons or beads could be applied in patterns.

Tabbed or scalloped edges and borders of fur were very usual trimmings. Bands of embroidered or plain stuff (guards) might be sewn on in parallel lines, or parallel slashings (panes) used to give the opposite effect.

Embroidery and fine needlework were widely practised arts in this century and were often done in colours, in black on a coloured surface, or in metal thread. Jewels, particularly pearls, were lavishly used as trimming but were not necessarily real. Motifs included conventionalized as well as naturalistic presentations of flowers, fruit, birds and animals. Cut-work (the edges of material joined by strips in a cut-out geometrical design) was used as a method of seaming as well as for decoration, and seams were frequently covered by ornament of one kind or another.

Jewellery and Accessories—Men: Large jewelled neck-chains, made to fit across the collar-bones or shoulders rather than round the neck, and sometimes to hold the two sides of a cloak in place; pendants, lockets and miniatures hung over the doublet on similar chains; finer chains, holding less conspicuous jewels; rings for fingers and thumbs; and, late in the century, the insignia of Orders, worn on the breast from a wide, scarf-like ribbon round the neck, and a single earring, usually a pearl drop, made up the sum of the jewellery worn by men. In addition, belts, sword and dagger hilts and their scabbards and sheaths, hat-bands and gloves could be jewelled; and jewels were sewn into the decorative patterns of garments.

Gloves, of gauntlet shape, were made of leather or of silk, wool or velvet and were often perfumed. They could be carried in the belt, which could also hold the purse and the large lawn handkerchief, edged with lace or fringe, often with a tassel at each corner.

Very elegant young men occasionally wore patches on the face from 1595.

Jewellery and Accessories—Women: In the early part of the century, with the 'gabled' headdress or the French hood, women wore necklaces of large jewels set in goldsmith's work, whose second row disappeared into the bodice; large jewelled ornaments affixed to the top of the bodice in the centre; jewelled girdles, ornamented across the front or all round, with a long jewelled chain hanging in front from waist to hem and a spherical or circular pomander or a pendant at the end; rosaries, also hung from the girdle, and embroidered or beaded purses, with gold tassels to pull their draw-strings. This fashion of hanging jewelled objects from the waist was revived in the 1570s and '80s, though the girdle was not always worn in the second half of the period. Throughout the century jewelled bands or bands of embroidery in colours and metal thread decorated the hood, cap, caul or coiffure, with the exception of white caps made of lawn, gauze or lace; and throughout the century also women wore rings on their fingers, stud or short drop earrings when the headdress allowed it and magnificent necklaces, while jewelled chains or ropes of pearls were festooned on the bodice or hung down over the dress. Jewels were also sewn on to their dresses and the rigid handles of their feathered fans, or the sticks of the folding fans that were in use from 1580.

Women's handkerchiefs were large, like those of men, and carried in the sleeve or the girdle when this was worn.

Patches for the face were known from 1595 onwards. They were cut from pieces of silk or velvet.

Small muffs of silk or velvet were carried after 1580.

Masks, covering the face, with a button attachment at the back for holding them in place with the teeth, were worn from mid-century onwards to conceal identity or protect the complexion from sun or wind.

Mufflers, tied over the mouth, were worn in country places in bad weather.

XI.9. 16th Century. Man Wearing 'Bases'. 1500

Hair: The hair is of shoulder length and parted in the centre.

Headdress: The soft-crowned black velvet cap has a flexible segmented brim with segments left unfastened.

Garments: The top of the white shirt is gathered into a neck-band. The under-doublet of bronze velvet has long, close-fitting sleeves. The over-garment may be in three separate parts, sleeveless 'bodice', full sleeves, and skirt which can be tied in at the waist, or it may be one garment. It is of heavy peacock blue silk, with a square-cut neck-line, and is ornamented with strips of embroidery in bronze, pale blue-green and dull gold. The band that ends the full three-quarter-length sleeves has the same decoration. The 'skirt' is made up of corrugated, padded, even-sized pleats, forming what were known as 'bases'. It is bordered with a deep strip of embroidery in the same colours as the other borders, with blue and green uncut jewels and pearls added. The hose are pale blue-green.

Footwear: The shoes are of green leather and have broad toes and thick soles.

Accessories: The man is playing a wide-mouthed flute.

XI.10. Man in Furred Gown. 1500

Hair: The hair is long enough to touch the shoulders, turned in at the ends, with a fringe over the forehead.

Garments. The man wears a waist-length doublet of black cloth, with a small collar-band of scarlet, open in front to show the top of a scarlet silk shirt. The hose are striped in black and scarlet. The gown is of dull greyish-green tapestry, patterned in black, with a collar and border down the front of brown fur. The ends of the long, loose sleeves are bordered in the same way and the gown is lined in red.

Footwear: The broad-toed shoes are of black buckskin, with thick soles and seams up the fronts.

XI.11. Woman in Bongrâce Headdress. 1500

Hair: This is taken back from the temples, above the ears and swathed or plaited across the head or allowed to hang down under the veil at the back.

Headdress: The cap is an early style of French hood, with a border over the front of the head of silver tissue, another behind it of red silk, and behind that a thick segmented roll of azure blue satin, with a looped length hanging down to the shoulder-blades. On the top is a bongrâce headdress of black silk over a stiffened oblong framework, with a short veil of its own material depending at the back. This addition to the headdress was to shade the face.

Garments: The under-dress is of black velvet and the over-gown of azure blue cloth. It is fitted to the body but the skirt is full and flowing from the hips down. The décolletage is square-cut, with a double border of silver tissue and black velvet. The sleeves are long and full, turned back with silver tissue.

Footwear: The broad-toed, thick-soled shoes are of red leather.

Accessories: The heavy necklace of silver cord has a silver pendant set with a red jewel. The girdle is of silver cord with a rosary attached.

XI.12. Youth with Plumed Hat. 1510

Hair: This is parted on the left side and descends to the shoulders, with ends turned in.

Headdress: The large white felt hat is turned up on one side and decorated by three purple plumes, with pearls fixed to their spines.

Garments: The white lawn shirt has narrow pleats sewn to a plain, oval neckband. The black satin doublet ends at the waist and has a cross-over in front piped in white silk. Three diagonal frills of this are attached on the right side of the chest. The moderately full sleeves are sewn into wrist-bands of white silk. The seams are open and piped with white silk, showing the sleeves of the shirt through the openings. The close-fitting breeches, with triangular codpiece, are striped in black, purple and white, ending at mid-thigh with black and white fringes. The hose are purple and the open outer gown of red, purple and silver brocade. Its white satin collar forms revers from shoulder to hem. The artificial hanging sleeves of brocade hang down to the calves.

Footwear: Loosely fitting boots of white leather are worn under broad, clumsy shoes of black buckskin with a strap over the instep.

Accessories: A purse of white leather is fastened over a belt of the same material.

XI.13. Girl in a German Type of Gown. 1514

Hair: The hair is parted in the centre and hangs loosely down the back.

Garments: The gown is of crimson velvet, ornamented in gold. The low décolletage is off the shoulders, with strips of gold tissue appliqués on either side to outline the shoulders and bosom. The close-fitting bodice has a border of gold tissue at the top and a central design in the same material. The waist is laced with gold cord. The full, round skirt, touching the ground, is gathered on at the waist, the folds flowing out from the gathers. The sleeves give the effect of short over-sleeves, with puffs sewn into a band and close-fitting lower sleeves, with three puffs at the elbows and goblet cuffs, but are probably made with joins in the upper arms and at the elbows. The puffs on the sleeves are outlined in gold tissue and the bands are of the same stuff.

Footwear: The round-toed shoes are of crimson velvet.

XI.14. Woman in Gabled Headdress. 1516

Hair: The hair is taken back from a centre parting. It may hang loose or in a plait at the back, or be bound in swathes or plaits across the head.

Headdress: The gabled headdress has a hood of black velvet which hangs at the back below the shoulder-blades. The 'gable' in front is in two parts, one descending to the collar-bones, in cream-coloured taffeta sewn with gilt beads and embroidered in orange silk, and another outside it, of black velvet, appliquéd with diamond-shaped motifs in amber and gold, with green and red jewels. It is edged with gold braid and fringe and is longer than the inner 'gable'.

Garments: The dress is of orange-tan wool, fitted to the body and flowing into a full skirt reaching the ground. It is bordered at wrists and hem with brown fur. The cream-coloured lawn partlet has a narrow border of black velvet. The gold belt has a long end hanging down from its buckle, with a criss-cross pattern of orange and black.

Footwear: The flat shoes are of black velvet, broad-toed and with thick soles.

Jewellery and Accessories: Attached to the belt are a rosary of gold and pearl beads and a purse of amber velvet ornamented in gold and black.

XI.15. Huntsman with Spear. 1520

Hair: The hair is thick and long enough to cover the ears and touch the jaw-line. It is brought forward in locks over the forehead.

Headdress: The shallow cap of brown felt has a close-fitting upturned brim fastened back in two segments, and three red-brown feathers fastened between the crown and the brim.

Garments: The doublet of terracotta-coloured wool is close-fitting, made all in one with its skirt which is cut in scallops at the hem. The high collar has a turned-down frill of white lawn. There are slashes, following a German fashion, showing a brown lining round the base of the neck. The belt is of natural leather, ornamented with oblongs of the same material and descending, with a buckled opening, to the codpiece. The sleeves are full, made in one with the doublet and sewn into bands at the wrists. The breeches or upper stocks are close-fitting and match the doublet. The hose are brown and the overlap between them and the upper stocks is covered by an early example of cross-gartering in terracotta-coloured woollen stuff.

Footwear: The blunt-toed shoes are of brown leather, tied over the insteps.

Accessories: A hunting knife is attached to the belt by natural leather buckled straps. A short spear is held in the hands.

XI.16. Man in Turned-back Sleeves. 1525

Hair: The hair is bobbed, with ends turned in.

Headdress: A white felt caul is worn beneath the soft-crowned black velvet hat with upturned brim in two segments and narrow white plume.

Garments: The top of the white taffetas shirt shows at the neck. The doublet, of blue taffetas appliqué with broad strips of black velvet and ending at the waist, fastens down the front with silver aiguillettes at intervals. Puffs of the shirt-sleeves show through the openings and through those in the full sleeves. The sleeveless jerkin of white silk is fastened at the waist, and has a belt and borders sewn with silver thread, pearls and crystals. The breeches of white silk end above the knees in bands tied on the outside. The codpiece is decorated in the same way as the jerkin. The outer gown is of black velvet bordered with white fur. Its wide sleeves are turned back and fastened at the shoulders, showing the blue satin lining. The hose are parti-coloured, the right tailored in white silk and the left in blue, with black stripes.

Footwear: The broad-toed shoes are of black velvet, with a band across the instep.

Jewellery and Accessories: The necklace is of silver, turquoise and crystal. A dagger of silver and turquoise is attached to the belt.

XI.17. Woman with Dress Pinned up at the Back. 1527

Headdress: The gable headdress has a double front of pale brick-red taffetas and ivory-coloured lawn, of which only the former can be seen. Two bands of taffetas, patterned in black thread with gilt ornaments, cover the top of the head. The back of the black satin cap is diamond-shaped, placed flat to the head, with two broad streamers.

Garments: The gown is of dark green silk, its fitted bodice slightly high waisted. A border of ivory lawn forms a 'V' at the back and would have a square-cut shape in front. The skirt is full, with a long train pinned up inside out to the back of the belt, showing the lining of sable-coloured fur and the train of a black satin under-kirtle. The inner sleeves are of brick-red taffeta appliqués with strips of black satin. They have wrist-frills of ivory lawn and puffs of it show at intervals through openings in the outer seams. The outer sleeves are made in one with the dress and fit closely over the upper arms. The wide, fur-lined lower sleeves are attached above the elbows and pinned up, inside out, to the outer sleeves.

Accessories: A rosary of large crystal, pearl and silver beads is fastened to the belt in front.

XI.18. Man in Slashed and Puffed Clothes. 1st Quarter of Century

Hair: The hair forms a fringe in front, covers the ears and is turned in at the ends.

Headdress: The shallow segmented cap of black velvet is adorned with three tall scarlet plumes.

Garments: The shirt of parchment tinted lawn has a turned-down collar and wrist-bands. Diamond-shaped panes in the body-fitting, skirtless black velvet doublet show a gold tissue lining. Bands of it decorate the full sleeves and the breeches, whose waist-band covers the base of the doublet. This is open in front as far as the top of the codpiece. The puffed gold-trimmed leg-coverings of black velvet, added to the breeches above the knees, may be attached to the scarlet hose and joined by 'points' to the waistband.

Footwear: The broad-toed shoes are of black velvet, slashed and ornamented with gold.

Accessories: The sword-scabbard and belt are of scarlet and gilded leather.

XI.19. Woman in Gabled Headdress. 1536

Headdress: The 'gabled' front of the headdress is of white velvet embroidered in red and gold and set with red stones. Behind it is a soft-crowned cap of gold material embroidered in scarlet thread. The black velvet 'veil' of the headdress has been pinned up across the crown of the head.

Garments: The under-kirtle is of ivory satin, with an appliqué criss-cross pattern of scarlet silk and small gold ornaments. The over-gown of black velvet has a close-fitting bodice, and arched décolletage edged with gold embroidery and a gold gauze frill. The same embroidery edges the open skirt. The ensemble is worn over a Spanish farthingale. The full under-sleeves, with puffs at intervals along the outer seams and frills at the wrists, match the under-kirtle. The black velvet outer sleeves fit the upper arm closely and have a wide lower part joined on above the elbow, which is fastened back to the upper part of the sleeve, showing a red and gold lining. A girdle of gold cord is worn round the waist.

Jewellery and Accessories: The necklace of gold and rubies is in two strands, one fitting the base of the neck and the other disappearing into the top of the bodice. A large ornament of gold and rubies is attached below the edge of the bodice. A pomander of red enamel and gold hangs from a gold cord attached at the waist.

XI.20. Man in Plumed Cap with Caul. 1534

Hair: The hair is short and unparted, brought forward from the crown of the head.

Headdress: The round, shallow cap of black velvet is worn at an angle, with a curled crimson plume on the lower side, over a close-fitting matching cap set on the back of the head.

Garments: The shirt of crimson silk is patterned with gilt dots. The doublet sleeves are made in small puffs, with wrist-frills. They are of crimson satin paned with gold braid. The black velvet jerkin, fitted to the body and partly open in front, is bordered with crimson and gold. The outer gown is of black and gold brocade, bordered with sable-coloured fur, which also forms the wide collar. It is lined with cloth of gold. The garment is worn as though it were a cloak, with the fur-bordered sleeves hanging loose and a jewelled chain from shoulder to shoulder. The close-fitting breeches, turned up at the hem with crimson silk, match the doublet-sleeves. The hose are crimson.

Footwear: The shoes of crimson leather with ties over the instep, have a seam down the centre and are sewn with small gilt beads.

Accessories: A dagger with a gold hilt and a sheath of crimson leather with gilt ornament, is slung from a narrow crimson belt.

XI.21. Man in Short, Open Gown. About 1539

Hair: The hair is cut short and brought forward over the forehead.

Headdress: The flat cap is of brown velvet, with a parchment-coloured plume.

Garments: The shirt is of ivory silk, and the under-doublet of parchment-coloured velvet, patterned in gold. The over-doublet is of biscuit-coloured satin banded vertically with orange silk braid and horizontally with gilt ribbon and red jewels. The belt is of gold fabric. The brown velvet outer gown is full and short with a wide collar and revers of parchment-coloured velvet. The large puff sleeves have broad slashes criss-crossed in gilt ribbon and red jewels, over ivory satin. The wrist-bands are of gilt ribbon and red jewels. The breeches, close-fitting and ending at mid-thigh, are of brown velvet. The hose are ivory white.

Footwear: The shoes follow the natural shape of the foot and are of brown velvet ornamented with cuts.

Accessories: Gloves of biscuit-coloured silk, ornamented in gold, are carried in the right hand and a gold pomander in the left.

XI.22. Woman in Sleeves with Aiguillettes. 1542

Hair: The hair is parted in the centre with a looped puff over each ear.

Headdress: The black velvet French hood has a border of silver tissue edged with pearls and two rows of pearls across the top. The back is made of two triangles of velvet forming a pointed bag. The under-kirtle is of black velvet and the over-gown of blue-green tapestry with motifs of blue, green and silver. Its black velvet yoke is arched over the bosom and the open standing collar of white lawn. The sleeves are padded, with the seams open, showing an insertion of black velvet, fastened to the sleeve at intervals by silver aiguillettes. The skirt is open and is edged with green and silver braid, which is repeated at the top of the bodice.

Footwear: The shoes are of blue-green stuff to match the gown.

Jewellery and Accessories: The girdle, the necklace and the chain looped to a silver ornament on the bosom are of silver set with green stones. A silver and pearl chain with a pendant ornament hangs from the waist. A ring is worn on the first finger of the right hand and a leather-bound book held in the left.

XI.23. Youth in Open Gown. 1547

Hair: The hair is short, brushed back from the forehead.

Headdress: The black velvet hat, worn at an angle, has a flat, soft crown and narrow, flexible brim. It is encircled by a chain of pearls and brilliants and has a curled white plume on its upper side.

Garments: The doublet of black satin has a standing collar of white lawn, and plainly cut sleeves with wrist-frills. The jerkin is of black satin, long in the body, with a fairly deep basque. The short, close-fitting breeches are of black satin. The outer gown of black velvet has curiously shaped arm-openings. Hanging sleeves come from behind these. The collar and revers are of white fur, which also edges the hem and the ends of the hanging sleeves. The ornamentation on the doublet, jerkin and outer gown is of pale grey satin, embroidered in silver. The hose are pale grey.

Footwear: The shoes are of black velvet, with cuts.

Accessories: A silver-hilted dagger is attached to a belt of silvered leather, with a large silver tassel fastened to the sheath. The gloves are of pale grey leather, embroidered in silver.

XI.24. Woman in Development of French Hood. 1547

Hair: The hair is parted in the centre and puffed out on either side.

Headdress: The front of the black velvet French hood is flattened and widened. Pearl drops and green jewels edge the top. The back of the hood comes forward in two points on to the cheeks.

Garments: The under-kirtle of black satin has wide sleeves edged with silver lace and aiguillettes devolving into close-fitting cuffs trimmed with silver embroidery and green stones. The over-gown is of green and silver brocade, with a full skirt, open down the front. Its fitted, arched bodice is surmounted by a shoulder-yoke of black satin. A ruff of pearl-coloured gauze encircles the neck, with a matching partlet and standing collar. The sleeves are close-fitting to the elbow and have wide bases, turned back to show a lining of cloth of silver. A belt of silver links and green stones is worn.

Footwear: The shoes are of black satin.

Jewellery and Accessories: A collar of silver, pearls and emeralds with a pendant encircles the neck. Rings are worn on the first and third fingers of the left hand. A silver ornament, set with green stones, hangs from a silver chain suspended at the waist.

XI.25. Man in Ankle-length Gown. Mid-century

Hair: The hair, that of an elderly man, has been left fairly long and covers the ears.

Headdress: The soft-crowned cap of black velvet has a round, close-fitting, upturned brim.

Garments: The round neck of the shirt is finished by a small, close-fitting ruff. The gown is long and plain, fastening down the front. It is of wine-coloured ribbed silk, the sides of the neckline meeting in a 'V'. The sleeves are full, sewn into bands at the wrists, which are covered by hand-ruffs. A narrow belt of wine-coloured fabric is worn. The outer gown is of black cloth, with the collar and revers of brown fur reaching to the hem. The shoulders are raised and the hanging sleeves end at the hem of the gown. The hose are grey.

Footwear: The black leather shoes are fastened on the outside of the insteps and come up almost to the ankle-bone.

Accessories: A quill pen is held in the right hand and an open book in the left. A black velvet purse is hung from the belt.

XI.26. Woman in Closed Gown. 1550s

Hair: The hair is parted in the centre and rolled back over a pad.

Headdress: The French hood is of gold tissue with the front in the form of a coronet of gold, pearls and diamonds.

Garments: The gown of gold and pink shot silk has an open, square-cut décolletage, wider over the bust than at the shoulders. The bodice is open a little at the bust and ornamented in coral-red, gold-embroidered silk. The sleeves of coral-red silk have epaulettes of puffs and petal-shapes and puffed hand-ruffs. Pearls are sewn down the length of the close-fitting sleeves and edge the épaulettes and hand-ruffs. The skirt touches the ground all round and is worn over a Spanish farthingale, with the hip-line raised. The skirt is closed and ornamented like the bodice.

Accessories: Pearl drop earrings are worn and a necklace of gold and coral is fastened to the shoulders of the gown. A string of pearls is looped at either side of the bust and hangs down in the centre. Rings are worn on the first and third fingers of the left hand. The fan has a frame and handle of gold and red enamel and a border of curled shell-pink feathers.

XI.27. Man's Dress. 1554

Hair: The hair is cut short and combed back.

Headdress: The round, shallow cap of plum-coloured felt, ornamented with scarlet and with a scarlet plume, is wider at the top than at the head-opening.

Garments: The doublet is decorated in the same pattern as the jerkin, but in scarlet on parchment yellow, with saffron-tinted wrist-frills. The jerkin is of plum-coloured velvet, ornamented in scarlet. It is long in the body, with short sleeves, a scarlet leather belt and a fairly deep basque. It has a high collar and fastens down the front, with small buttons placed on alternate sides at a distance from one another. The codpiece matches the doublet. The round-hose are of plum-coloured velvet strips, edged with scarlet, with panes of parchment-yellow silk. The hose are scarlet.

Footwear: The shoes are of plum-coloured velvet, with cuts.

Jewellery and Accessories: The necklace of gold links is set with rubies. The fringed gloves are of parchment-yellow leather. A sword with a red leather sheath and gold hilt is attached to the belt.

XI.28. Man in Utilitarian Dress. About 1560

Hair: The hair is cut short and brought forward from the crown of the head to hang in short locks over the forehead.

Headdress: The round, full-crowned cap of olive-green velvet has a narrow, flexible brim.

Garments: The doublet is of olive-green cloth, with plainly cut sleeves, edged with white wrist-frills. The sleeves are open down the seam to show a shirt-sleeve or lining of cream-coloured silk. The opening is edged with darker olive-green braid. The round-hose are of the same design. The sleeveless jerkin is of buff leather, with a standing collar, tied at the base of the throat, a narrow belt and a deep basque. The hose are olive green.

Footwear: The thigh-boots are of buff leather, fastened by straps to the waist of the round-hose or to an under-doublet.

Accessories: A sword is attached to the belt on the left side.

XI.29. Man's Dress. About 1570

Hair: The hair is cut short at the back but left longer in front, where it is brought forward in curls above the forehead.

Headdress: The black velvet hat has a soft crown, a rolled brim and an orange-coloured curled plume.

Garments: The doublet is ornamented in a pattern of squares in yellow, gold, cream-colour, black and orange, and fastens down the front under a strip of black velvet sewn with gilt buttons. The shoulder-wings and the short basque are of black velvet edged with gold. The white ruff is pleated and goffered. It is propped up at the back (unseen) by a 'pickadil' or under-propper. The turned-back cuffs are of white lawn, lace-trimmed or embroidered. One buff-coloured gauntlet glove, ornamented in gold, is worn. The round, padded 'trunk-hose' or breeches are of black velvet edged with gold and slashed with cream-coloured, yellow and orange silk. The hose are yellow and are fastened by 'points' (laces and eyelet holes) to the base of an under-doublet or are made as complete tights.

Footwear: The shoes of black velvet have oval slashings.

Jewellery: A single earring is worn in the left ear.

XI.30. Man in Short Gown. 1569

Hair: The hair is cut short, brought forward above the ears and in a short lock on the forehead.

Headdress: The cap is of leaf-green velvet, with puffs of velvet edging the crown and a band to fit the head decorated with pearls and an emerald.

Garments: The doublet is of off-white velvet with panes of green silk and a cream-coloured ruff. The belted jerkin is of pearl-coloured satin, edged down the front and round the hem with silver fabric appliqués with puffs of green silk. The round-hose are of pearl-white satin and silver, with green panings. The ornamental codpiece is of the same design and the hose off-white. The outer gown is of silver tissue, with long revers of white fur. It has hanging sleeves and short puffed sleeves, ornamented with pearls and with the openings edged with fur. The hem is bordered with pearls in the same design.

Footwear: The shoes are of pearl-coloured satin ornamented with slashing and pearls.

Accessories: A silver-hilted sword is slung from the belt. The guard is of silver and green enamel and the scabbard of green leather ornamented with silver. The gloves are of pearl-coloured silk, fringed in silver.

XI.31. Man in Sleeved Cloak. 1560–70

Hair: The hair is cut short and combed back from the brow, exposing the ears. A small moustache and pointed beard are worn.

Headdress: The hat of bronze velvet has a full, soft crown and small brim. A curled terracotta-coloured plume is attached to the left side of the brim.

Garments: The doublet is unseen. The round-hose are very short, of bronze velvet banded in rosewood and terracotta satin. The sleeved cloak is of rosewood-coloured satin. It is edged with two rows of terracotta ribbed silk, bordered with bronze velvet. The base of the standing collar, the shoulder-rolls and hanging sleeves are ornamented in the same way. Narrow padded rolls of rosewood satin edge the top of the collar and the shoulder-rolls. The general effect is of rose-tinted browns and fawns. The hose are fawn-coloured.

Footwear: The shoes, tied over the instep, are of fawn-coloured buckskin.

Accessories: A light sword is worn at the left side. The gloves are of pale fawn-coloured leather, embroidered in terracotta and gold.

XI.32. Woman in 'Mahoytered' Sleeves. 1560–70

Hair: The hair is parted in the centre and turned back smoothly.

Headdress: The cap ('Escoffion') is flattened across the front and sewn with pearls and red jewels. Its crown and upper part are of rose-red velvet and the lower part of silk in the same colour.

Garments: The wrist-frills and upstanding, open collar are of cream-coloured gauze and the partlet and close-fitting sleeves of the same, criss-crossed with pearls. The over-gown is of rose-red brocade with the skirt open over an under-kirtle of pale pink silk bordered with pearls and gold embroidery. The arched décolletage passes under the arms but is attached to the puffed 'mahoytered' sleeves by a shoulder-border. The décolletage, sleeve-endings, the front bodice fastening, the skirt-opening and the hem of the outer gown are bordered with gold tissue edged in red and sewn with gilt ornaments and red jewels. The belt is of gold links, set with pearls and garnets.

Footwear: The shoes are of rose-red velvet.

Jewellery and Accessories: The close-fitting necklace is of gold and garnets. A gold pomander on a gold chain is attached to the belt. The handkerchief is of ivory-coloured silk, with gold embroidery and fringe.

XI.33. Woman in Open Gown. 1560–70

Hair: The hair is puffed out at the sides from a centre parting.

Headdress: A black velvet 'Marie Stuart' cap lined with white satin frames the face.

Garments: The dress is of silver-grey satin decorated with diagonal bands of embroidered silver fabric. It has a square-cut décolletage and a skirt of moderate fullness. The open, upstanding collar is of white lawn, with a close-fitting ruff worn within it. The sleeves are plain and close-fitting, with ruffs at the wrists. The outer gown, worn open, is of black velvet, with a collar and border all round of pale grey fur. It is slightly shaped to the body in the upper part, but flows out into a full skirt touching the ground. The short puffed sleeves are banded and edged with the same fur.

Footwear: The shoes are of silver brocade.

Jewellery and Accessories: The necklace is of emeralds, pearls and silver. Rings are worn on the third finger of the left hand and the first and third of the right. A fan of grey, curled feathers with a frame and handle of silver, pearls and emeralds is hung from the waist on a chain of green stones.

XI.34. Man in Hooded Cloak. 1575–80

Hair: The hair is short, taken straight back from the brow behind the ears.

Headdress: The man wears a hat in contemporary Italian style, with a high, stiffened crown and small curved brim. It is of dark red-purple satin.

Garments: The high-necked doublet has a narrow frill at the top of the collar and is of pale grey cloth, trimmed with bands of silver braid and ornamented with pearls. The round-hose are of grey satin, with a design of silver braid, paned in dark red-purple velvet. The Spanish cloak is of silver-grey satin, with a deep hood. This has amethyst buttons with button-holes of silver braid, and the cloak has a double border of red-purple velvet embroidered in silver. The canions are red-purple and the stockings, rolled above the knee, are pale grey, with cross-gartering of silver ribbon, fringed at the ends.

Footwear: The shoes are of pale grey leather.

Accessories: The gloves are of pale grey leather, ornamented and fringed with silver.

XI.35. Man in Short Cloak. 1577

Hair: The hair is short but fairly thick, and wavy. It is taken back from the forehead, showing the ears.

Headdress: The hat is of grey felt, with a band of sapphire-blue velvet.

Garments: The doublet is of light blue-green cloth, ornamented in silver braid. The sleeveless jerkin is of pale grey cloth with slashings and vertical bands of light blue and sapphire-blue jewelled buttons. The chest is padded and the waist well-defined, as though corseted. The garment has a short basque and a grey leather belt. The breeches of sapphire-blue velvet are full 'Venetians', ending in a band below the knee. The cloak is of light blue-green satin with a border of silver braid, sapphire-blue appliqué ribbon and pearls. It is lined in sapphire blue. The hose are pale grey.

Footwear: The shoes are of sapphire-blue velvet, tied with silver ribbon.

Accessories: A light sword with a silver and sapphire hilt and a scabbard covered in sapphire velvet is slung from the belt.

XI.36. Woman in Trained Gown. 1570

Hair: The hair is taken back over a roll, unparted.

Headdress: The French hood is of black velvet, the edges sewn with small jewels, and has a black velvet 'veil' hanging to the shoulder-blades.

Garments: The gown is of pearl-coloured satin, worn over petticoats without a farthingale. It has rows of pearls sewn to strips of silver tissue on either side of the front bodice-opening, on the front of the skirt to the hem, on the sleeves and edging the square décolletage. The partlet of cream-coloured gauze has an upstanding open collar. Within it is a high, close-fitting collar made up of rows of cream-coloured gauze frilling. Roundels of frilled gauze form the cuffs. The over-gown is of black velvet, fitted to the waist but open down the front. It touches the ground in front and forms a short train at the back. It has a collar and edging all round of white fur and the short, puffed sleeves are edged and banded with the same fur.

XI.37. Woman in Spanish Dress. About 1570

Hair: The hair is drawn back from the forehead, and dressed in a coil inside the cap.

Headdress: The close-fitting cap or caul of green velvet sewn with pearls is set on the back of the head. Over it, at an angle, is a matching pill-box cap sewn with pearl drops and trimmed near the edge with silver galon. Two curled plumes of coral red are fastened by a brooch on the left side.

Garments: The gown, in the Spanish style, is of green velvet, fastening in front and worn over a Spanish farthingale. The bodice is trimmed with three rows of silver galon and a design in pearls, edged with silver galon, decorates the hem, the front seam of the skirt and the hanging sleeves, which are lined with coral-red silk. The collar is high and close-fitting, edged with ivory gauze cut in scallops. The inner close-fitting sleeves are of black. green and silver brocade woven in horizontal lines.

Footwear: The shoes are of black fabric.

Jewellery and Accessories: Black jet drop earrings and a necklace of silver links set with green and red stones are worn. The gloves are of pale grey leather, embroidered with green and coral silk.

XI.38. Man in Peascod-belly Doublet. 1583

Hair: The hair is brushed back over the ears and shaped in a 'widow's peak' over the forehead.

Headdress: The 'copotain' hat is of dark red felt, edged with gold braid. It has a band of gold medallions set with garnets and a brooch of gold and garnets pinned to the crown.

Garments: The matching doublet and breeches are of parchment-coloured satin decorated with bands of gold and red shot taffeta, bordered in dark red. The doublet has the padded overhang known as a 'peascod belly'. Its front fastening is defined by gold buttons set with garnets. The collar is a 'falling band' of ivory-tinted lawn and lace. The large 'trunk' sleeves are padded and end in turned back cuffs matching the collar. The breeches are padded 'Venetians' and the stockings, of ivory silk, with gilt clocks, are rolled over them and secured by dark red silk garters fringed with gold.

Footwear: The shoes are of dark red leather, tied over the insteps with ivory ribbon.

Jewellery and Accessories: A single pearl drop is worn as an earring. A gold-hilted sword, with a scabbard of ivory leather and gilt metal is slung by an ivory leather sword-belt from beneath the doublet.

XI.39. Woman's Dress. 1580s

Hair: The hair is parted in the centre and puffed out at the sides.

Headdress: The 'Marie Stuart' cap of ruby velvet has points coming down in the centre of the forehead and on both cheeks. It curves widely at the sides. The lining is of ivory satin and the edging of ivory lace.

Garments: The gown is of ruby velvet, worn over a 'bolster' farthingale. The standing collar of ivory lawn bordered with lace, edges the deep front opening of the bodice. The skirt forms a short train at the back. The 'bollonais' sleeves are made in four large puffs, banded in gilt ribbon, with small gold ornaments, and paned in ivory satin. The turned-back cuffs match the collar.

Footwear: The shoes are of black velvet.

Accessories: The fan is of ivory-tinted feathers, with a handle of gold set with rubies. The necklace is of gold, pearls and rubies, and pearl drop earrings are worn.

XI.40. Woman in French Farthingale. About 1580

Hair: The hair is taken upward at the back of the head and folded in swathes.

Headdress: The back of a black velvet Marie Stuart cap comes down to a point at the back of the neck. It is edged with pearls, inside another edging of white lawn.

Garments: The ruff is rounded and up-standing at the back with an under-propper. The bodice of the black satin gown is fastened down the front. The skirt, which forms a short train at the back and touches the ground in front, is closed and worn over a French 'bolster' farthingale. The 'trunk' sleeves are full, with raised shoulders, and have turned-back, embroidered cuffs, decorated with diagonal bands of silver galon studded with pearls.

Jewellery: A gold chain hangs at the back in two loops, the lower of which has a gold, jewelled pendant attached to it. There are probably two rows of the chain worn at the base of the throat and on the bosom in front.

XI.41. Man's Dress. 1580s

Hair: The hair is thick and wavy, and is brushed back diagonally from right to left.

Headdress: The 'copotain' hat of purple velvet has a tall oval crown and a circular brim rolled up at one side. The feather ornament is violet-coloured, held by a gold brooch set with garnets and amethysts. The band is of bronze and gold ribbon.

Garments: The doublet of purple velvet has a peascod belly and a short basque. The buttons and piping are of dull gold. The short round-hose, which could be merely a covering and not actual breeches, are of purple velvet paned in bronze satin, with decoration of purple velvet appliqué. The canions are purple, and the stockings of bronze silk criss-crossed in gold and purple. The unpleated standing collar and the hand-ruffs are of écru-tinted lawn. The stiffened cloak of purple velvet, with a double border of reddish-bronze tissue, is piped in dull gold and ornamented with gold thread, garnets and amethysts.

Footwear: The shoes of purple velvet have fastenings over the insteps covered by high vamps.

Accessories: The hilt and scabbard of the sword are of bronze and gilt.

XI.42. Woman with Broom. 1590

Hair: The hair is rolled back over a pad.

Headdress: The cap of unbleached linen has a stiffened, curved front, and a full gathered crown.

Garments: The shift of unbleached linen is gathered into a neck-band. A close-fitting saffron-tinted ruff is worn. The under-dress of brown woollen stuff has a fitted bodice, arched over the bust and a moderately full skirt worn over petticoats. It is edged at the top of the bodice and at the hem with green velvet. The open over-gown is of rust-coloured wool, with turned-back revers from shoulder to waist, and girdled with a strip of its own material. The full sleeves are sewn into a band at the wrists. The revers, open skirt, hem and sleeve-ends have a border of two strips of black velvet.

Footwear: The flat, wedge-soled shoes are of brown buckskin.

Accessories: A garden broom is held in the hands.

XI.43. Woman in Open-fronted Gown. 1580–90

Hair: The hair is rolled back over a pad and puffed out at the sides. The chignon meets the front roll at the top of the head.

Headdress: The French hood of black velvet has two borders of pale yellow silk and is decorated along the top with green and yellow jewels set in gold. It has a 'veil' of black velvet hanging to the shoulder-blades.

Garments: The pleated front, gathered at the neck, of a shift of pale yellow silk, shows from throat to waist in front. A saffron-tinted, close-fitting ruff encircles the neck. The bodice of the gown of black velvet is open from shoulders to waist, where it ends in a long point. Revers of black velvet are turned back. The skirt is moderate in width, full over the hips and clearing the ground. It is open from waist to hem, and bordered in gold and green. The under-kirtle is of yellow satin, bordered with a criss-cross pattern in green. The 'trunk' sleeves are also of yellow satin, decorated with appliqué flowers in green, with gold centres. Small double frills of saffron-tinted lawn form the wrist-frills.

Footwear: The flat, wedge-shaped shoes are of green leather, with cuts.

XI.44. Soldier. About 1590

Hair: The hair is short, curling forward over the forehead. A moustache and short pointed beard are worn.

Headdress: The morion-type helmet has a plain metal crest along the crown and a brim pointed upward at front and back with sides curving downward.

Garments: The dark green cloth doublet has a high collar with a white neck-frill and plain, close-fitting sleeves. The sleeveless jerkin, unseen except at the shoulder wings, is of buff and brown leather. The metal cuirass juts out a little down the front. Breeches are of dark green cloth, banded under the fullness above the knees. The hose are green.

Footwear: The thigh-boots are of buff leather.

Accessories: The gloves are of buff leather. An arquebus is held in the right hand. A sword is worn at the left side, slung from a strap attached at the waist under the breast-plate. A crimson sash is put on over the right shoulder and tied at the left hip.

XI.45. Man in Travelling Cloak. About 1590

Hair: The hair is long enough to touch the collar at the back and is brought forward above the ears and on to the forehead.

Headdress: The black felt copotain hat tapers towards the top and has a flat crown. The brim is wide and flexible and the band is of folded chestnut-brown woollen stuff.

Garments: The doublet is plain and buttoned down the front. It is of chestnut-brown cloth. The close-fitting, turned-down collar of white lawn is edged with a frill cut in points. The moderately full sleeves have turned-back cuffs to match the collar. The breeches match the doublet and are 'Venetians', fastened below the knee with two buttons. The hose are of chestnut-brown yarn. The black cloth cloak is put on sideways, the turned-back collar hanging down over the left side of the chest and crossing the back to the right shoulder. It is kept in place by a black cord, which passes under the right arm. The garment is lined in grey.

Footwear: The stout shoes are of black buckskin.

Accessories: A traveller's staff is carried in the left hand.

XI.46. Woman with Basket of Flowers. 1590s

Hair: The hair is rolled back over a frame or pad, to form a semicircular shape round the face. The hair at the back, not seen, is pinned up in a chignon at the top of the head.

Garments: A yoke of white, pleated lawn meets in a 'V' in front and is attached to a standing, open collar of the same stuff. The dress is of thin grey woollen material. The fitted bodice, starting just above the breasts, fastens down the front and the full skirt, just clearing the ground, is worn over a French farthingale. The moderate 'trunk' sleeves end in deep embroidered turned-back cuffs of white lawn. A narrow white apron is tied on under the bodice.

Footwear: The flat, wedge-shaped soles are of black fabric.

Accessories: A basket of flowers is held over the right arm and a posy in the left hand.

XI.47. Woman in Wheel Farthingale. 1590s

Hair: The hair is taken up over a pad and pinned at the top of the head, dipping in the centre. The hair at the back is pinned up in a flat chignon.

Headdress: The Marie Stuart cap is of bronze velvet edged with pearls. An ornament of pearl drops and gold hangs from the front of the cap to the forehead.

Garments: The dress is of bronze tissue, with 'trunk' sleeves and bodice-front of pinkish-fawn silk, decorated by puffed peach-coloured ribbon in vertical and horizontal bands, with ornaments of pearls and pink topaz at the intersections. Gold ornaments are sewn in the centres of the squares formed by the ribbon. The stomacher and centre front of the skirt are edged with pearls and gold braid. The skirt does not quite touch the ground and is worn over a 'wheel' farthingale. The fan-shaped ruff and turned-back cuffs are of cream-tinted gauze. The 'trunk' sleeves match the stomacher and have shoulder wings and hanging sleeves of bronze tissue, ornamented with bows, pearls and gold decorations.

Footwear: The flat shoes, with 'wedge' soles, are of gold and bronze brocade, with 'cuts'.

Jewellery and Accessories: Pearl drop earrings, a necklace of gold, pearls and pink topaz and rings on both hands are worn. The fan is of bronze feathers, with a gold handle.

XI.48. Man in Black Satin Suit, 1590s

Hair: The hair is taken back from the forehead in a wide arc.

Garments: The black satin doublet has a short basque, with a belt of black and gold leather following a downward-pointing line. Gold piping decorates the front fastening. The falling band or turned-down collar is of white lace matching the turned-back cuffs of the moderate 'trunk' sleeves. Artificial round-hose of black satin are put on at the base of the doublet and matching breeches fit the thighs closely. The short full cloak is of black velvet, with collar and revers of reddish brown fur. It is lined with gold coloured satin and ornamented on the outside with tapering lines of appliqué gold fabric and gold ornaments. The garment is put on sideways, over the left shoulder, with part of the fur collar hanging forward over the left side of the chest. The stockings are of black silk.

Footwear: The shoes are of black buckskin, with wedge-soles, uppers cut down at the sides, and black ribbon ties.

Accessories: A gold and black-hilted sword is slung from a gold and black strap attached to the belt. A gold and diamond medallion on a brilliant blue ribbon is worn on the chest.

XII   17TH-CENTURY DRESS

The rigid formality, combined with great splendour and dignity, of late 16th-century dress was followed automatically at the opening of the 17th. After the first quarter, however, despite the repressive influence of the Puritan sections of society, an era of careless freedom in dress, of swinging cloaks, full sleeves, curling plumes and gallantly tilted hats informed the masculine mode. Women followed suit with wide necklines, hidden at times by demure collars, ringlets and ribbons, gleaming satin gowns and softly wound scarves. The effects of the Civil War in England and of the Edict forbidding extravagant dress in France, introduced a more sober attitude to clothes. The Restoration of the Monarchy in England, however, and the reign of Louis XIV in France brought an intensification of many of the former fashions and even the formality of the coat and waistcoat could not dim the effect of romantic licence which late 17th-century costume always evokes. Only at the end of the century did some return to heavy stuffs, large, bold patterns and too much decoration again create an atmosphere of formal grandeur.

Hair—Men: The wearing of curls all over the head, as in the last twenty years of the 16th century, continued until about 1605. The style with hair brushed back in a wide arc, or to one side, and allowed to grow thick and a little longer than formerly, remained until 1630. The fashion for long hair just seen at the end of the 16th century, developed by 1628 into the flowing locks traditionally associated with the first sixty years of the 17th. One lock, drawn forward over the shoulder, was often tied at the end with ribbon. The hair over the forehead was usually cut in a straight or very lightly curled fringe, arranged with seeming negligence. Centre and side partings were also known and the forehead could be left bare.

The wearing of wigs did not become general until about 1660 (see 'Wigs—Men'). False additions to the hair, powder to alter its colour and scent to perfume it were commonplace aids to romantic attraction. The use of white or grey hair-powder in the 17th century was most unusual, but instances of it were known.

Cropped hair never quite died out in this century and was worn by many Puritans and adherents of Cromwell.

Elderly men did not as a rule appear with long natural locks and before wigs became the general rule were apt to have their hair of a 'bobbed' length or nearing the shoulders.

Countrymen, tradesmen and working-class townsmen usually had their hair 'bobbed' or of medium length.

Men with thick, well-grown hair could simulate a modified form of the fashionable coiffure without wearing a wig. Men wearing wigs had their heads closely cropped or shaved.

The 'Vandyke' or trimmed chin-beard and a moustache with the ends a little upturned were in fashion until mid-century. A 'lip-tuft' often accompanied or replaced the beard. A moustache alone might be worn from about 1635, but between 1650 and '85 was trimmed to a fine line drooping to the corners of the mouth. After 1685 the moustache was seldom seen. Beards were rare in the second part of the century, though some soldiers and ecclesiastics continued to wear the small chin-beard until the 1680s.

Hair—Women: The coiffure built high over a roll, which was at the height of fashion at the end of the 16th century, was in vogue at the opening of the 17th. A tall, narrow and tapering coiffure existed in England and France until about 1608 and a few years longer in Spain, but the fashion for hair brushed back in a wide arc, fairly high and spreading to cover the ears, remained until about 1635. The hair at the back of the head was put up at the back, on a level with the top of the head, in a flattened coil, sometimes plaited. A short, straight or curled fringe could be worn from about 1625, but was not a general fashion until the 1630s and was optional then. The hair curving over the ears was frequently shorter than that brushed back over the roll, and was curled or frizzed to complete the rounded frame for the face.

XII.1. Early 17th Century. Three Headdresses

Hair: (a) 1603, (b) 1600 and (c) 1613. The hair in each case is taken back from the forehead without parting and dressed in a high pompadour over a pad. In (a) there is a single pad, in (b) there are two, one behind and one above the other, with the front hair trained over both, and in (c) the coiffure is narrower with the front of a flat 'bun' visible on the top of the head. (a) and (b) would have similar chignons, but these are not seen.

Headdress: (a) A scarlet aigrette is worn over the left temple, fastened by a gold, jewelled ornament. (b) A halo-shaped headdress of gold and pearls is worn behind the front roll of hair. (c) A circular ornament, worn in the centre of the front roll of hair, is of black enamel and pearls, with an outer border of small curled grey feathers.

Garments: (a) wears a gown of pale fawn-coloured velvet, with two rows of scarlet panes and one of red buttons down the centre front. The standing ruff is made up of triangular frills of ivory gossamer lawn, in three tiers. (b) The gown is of rose-coloured satin, with a deep décolletage edged with gold galon and satin scallops, with a gold ornament in the centre. The inner ruff is made up of triangular segments of parchment-coloured silk gauze, in three tiers, with the edges scalloped. The outer ruff is in the same material, with its outer edges cut in large scallops. (c) The gown is of pale grey cloth, with two vertical bands of darker grey braid ornamenting the side-fronts of the bodice and three rows of pearls defining the front fastening. The standing collar is a 'golilla'.

Jewellery: (a) wears pearl earrings and a pearl necklace, put on over the gown and extending laterally towards the shoulders. (b) wears pearl earrings, (c) wears a close-fitting necklet of pearls.

In the early 1630s the lessening popularity of the roll resulted in the hair being drawn back from the forehead with side partings on both sides of the head and curls hanging from them, and sometimes at the back of the neck. Thin, small curls arranged separately, as though stuck down, across the forehead were a new form of the fringe. A small protuberant chignon was worn half-way up the back of the head.

In general shape the fashion continued the same after mid-century, but from 1660 until 1670 there was a custom of wiring out the curls dangling on either side of the head. These were often thicker and more numerous than formerly.

In the 1660s and '70s there was a fashion for wearing the hair short, in a mop of downward-pointing ringlets all over the head, arranged fairly thickly at the back.

A centre parting with bunched curls massed on either side and raised a little in feminine imitation of the dressing of men's wigs had a bun at the back and several thick ringlets depending from it. The curls at the sides did not come down much further than the lobes of the ears.

To accompany the 'fontange' headdress in the last ten years of the century the hair in front was built up on a wire frame in a tall arrangement of curls known as a 'tower'. In many instances this was a 'false front'. A flattened chignon could be worn low at the back or the hair could hang down in ringlets. Large ringlets from the back often lay over the shoulders in front. Wigs and artificial hair were worn in many cases.

Wigs—Men: Wigs were worn by men of the fashionable classes from 1660 onwards. The frizzed and crimped style, falling to the shoulders from a centre parting, had very little shape except that its ends were curled horizontally and that it was divided into three parts, one to hang down the back and the others to be brought forward over the shoulders. From 1660 to 1675 those hanging in front might be tied at the ends with bows. This arrangement also applied to another style, set in thick curls, which were clustered on the forehead and lay horizontally on both sides of the face. The two thick locks that descended to the shoulders in front were loosely ringleted.

The large, full-bottomed wig was made on the same plan, but was sometimes worn with a mass of its luxuriant curls drawn forward over one shoulder, while on the other only a few ringlets dangled, with the rest hanging down the back. To begin with the hair of this wig was dressed in a haphazard tumble of curls. After 1675 the curls were tighter and more evenly arranged. The front of the wig grew higher and the hair was usually raised in two points over the brow on either side of a centre parting after 1690. In some instances the wig was so large that the wearing of a hat became impracticable, and it was carried instead.

From 1675 onwards a shorter but equally full wig was worn for travelling, campaigning or other arduous outdoor life. From 1680 onwards it was occasionally tied back, especially by soldiers.

A plain bobbed wig was a feature of the end of the century, worn chiefly by men doing practical work.

Headdress—Men: The 'copotain' of the 16th century was still in fashion until about 1620. Its tall, conical crown and adjustable brim remained the same and it was trimmed as before with feathers and an ornamental hatband and with loops of ribbon in the 17th century.

The sugar-loaf hat much resembled it, the only real difference being that the brim was wider, less flexible and was worn flat, turned up in front or bent a little downward at back and front. Its vogue was finished by 1665 or 1670 at the latest.

The large hat of felt, beaver or velvet, with a moderate, dented crown and wide flexible brim (extended in width after 1620) was the most favoured wear from about 1620 to the 1640s. Its brim could be cocked in many ways and it was worn with plumes or unornamented.

A hat with a round, low but stiffened crown and a more or less hard brim was in wear from 1665 to 1675, but the round, soft-brimmed hat with a low crown rounded to the shape of the head was more popular and remained in fashion well into the 18th century. In the 17th it could be worn plain or trimmed with ribbons or with a band and plumes of moderate size.

The tricorne or cocked hat, which was to be in its varied forms the main headgear of the following century, was seen about 1690. In this phase it was turned up all round, its rim usually trimmed with a narrow feather edging and bound with braid.

Caps were for utilitarian or négligé wear in this century. The 'buttoned' cap of the 16th century was worn until 1610 and the 'flat cap' by apprentices and some citizens until 1640, after which it was used only as livery (see Chapter XI).

The so-called 'night-cap' was worn in the daytime, indoors or out, as a protection for the head more convenient than a hat. It could be made of plain, stout material or of silk, brocade, cloth, velvet or linen. It was sometimes quilted and could be embroidered in all-over patterns. It was made with a dome-shaped crown and its close brim was turned up all round.

Another cap, worn from 1645 onwards, also had a close-fitting brim of its own material, but this was divided at the sides and could be worn turned up or down.

Headdress—Women: The 16th-century 'bongrâce' headdress, worn over the high, rolled coiffure of the first quarter of the 17th, persisted until about 1630. It was usually worn alone, seldom with the French hood, which was seen only on the elderly and unfashionable after the opening years.

The Marie Stuart hood, widened and enlarged, with a 'U'-shaped dip in front rather than a 'V', continued until about 1620.

The wide, arched hood, of a size to cover the headdress and the ruff, which was fashionable in the latter part of the 16th century, continued to be so until about 1625. It might extend over the shoulders to the waist, or, for ceremonial wear, as a hooded cloak to the ground. Elderly women still wore it as mourning until 1640.

Rounded hoods, sometimes wired in front to produce a squared or bow-shaped line over the forehead, were worn tied under the chin or attached to cloaks out of doors from the 1630s onwards. From this time also a small, square veil was often thrown over the head and face. Another and larger type of square veil had one corner cut off and the edge turned back. This was put over the head and could be fastened under the chin.

Many varieties of caps and coifs in lawn, linen, lace and embroidery, set on the back of the head, were worn in the first half of the century, including, in Holland, the winged and halo caps which persisted into the 1630s. Dutch women of rank wore caps to a much greater extent than in England or France. A miniature ornamented caul or cap was frequently worn over the 'bun' of hair at the back. A lace-trimmed kerchief, folded cornerwise, might be pinned over the hair, not tied under the chin.

The copotain and the sugar-loaf hat, trimmed as for men, were worn by married women in the first twenty years of the century and the latter survived until 1665. They might be worn with the linen coif or other caps and were a feature of the dress of country-dwellers and Puritans, tipped down at front and back. The wider-brimmed Cavalier hat was a fashionable adjunct until mid-century or thereabouts, for riding or whenever a hat was necessary.

The cornet or shadow, fashionable in one form or another until the 1690s, was worn at first as a cap of lace and lawn, shaped to cover the top of the head and hang down a little at front and back, with the sides slightly outstanding or considerably enlarged. It changed after 1640 to a coif fitting the back of the head, with a deep edging of lace which framed the face and descended in lappets to the shoulders at the sides and at the back sometimes as far as the waist. Raised over the 'top-knot' (a bunch of ribbons pinned to the hair just above the forehead from the 1680s onwards), it bore some relationship to the fontange.

The fontange or 'commode', in fashion from 1690, was a tall structure of lace and ribbon supported on a wire frame and attached to the front of a coif-like cap. It had long side-lappets which hung over the shoulders in front. The only covering possible over a fontange was a shawl, mantilla or large veil, which was put on over the headdress and allowed to drape the shoulders. (For hair ornaments see 'Jewellery and Accessories'.)

Hats were unusual after mid-century, but a version of the wide-brimmed hat, with a tall, slightly tapering crown, was still worn over a coif by country-dwellers and citizens' wives.

Garments—Men: At the opening of the century the doublet was still long-waisted, rounded or pointed in front and, with the latter shape, a slight protuberance over the abdomen, the last vestige of the peascod belly. Many doublets had a deep point in front, so that the join of skirt and body was higher at the back. The garment was often slashed on the breast and sleeves and was less stiffly padded than formerly, but was lined and sometimes quilted. An alternative to slashing was braid trimming or embroidery. The doublet was usually fastened by buttons and buttonholes, or by loops, from neck to waist, with the skirt or border of tabs not fastened. The skirt was made up of short, separate, overlapping tabs, generally eight at the beginning of the century. Between 1610 and 1630 the tabs grew longer and the waistline higher. After 1630 the doublet was tight-chested, with the high waistline scarcely indicated and no longer pointed. The tabs were now six in number as a rule and much longer. Some doublets had a deep, plain border instead of tabs, with a vent at the back. The narrow waist-belt of the 16th century was not often worn at the beginning of the 17th, and with the high-waisted doublet was frequently replaced by rosettes or ribbon bows with points, put on at intervals round the waist.

By 1640 the doublet was short, with a turned-down collar, and among the ultra-fashionable had an increasingly cramped look about the chest and shoulders. In many instances the shirt showed all round below the edge of the doublet, which was now cut into shallow tabs, or had a narrow tabbed border added. The body of the doublet was shaped a little to indicate the high waist, sometimes with a slight outward flare at the hem, and was usually buttoned only at the chest.

A broad silk sash, with fringed ends, tied at one side towards the back, was frequently worn over the high-waisted doublet from the 1650s onwards. It was also worn at times from right shoulder to left hip as a baldrick to carry the sword. Other baldricks, worn from 1625 onwards, were of ornamented leather or of thick material, faced with silk or velvet and embroidered.

Collars were gradually changing. The circular ruff was worn contemporaneously with the 'falling-band' or turned-down collar. Ruffs could still be raised at the back by an under-propper, could be level or turn right down in the manner of a falling-band. Very large ruffs were unusual after 1610 and after 1645 ruffs of any kind were rare. The pleats of the ruff were sometimes asymmetrical in this century. Falling-bands were of various shapes, including a wide collar spreading to the shoulders, a small, plain, rather high collar and larger collars of the same kind, all fitted closely to the neck at the turn-over and dividing in an inverted 'V' from the ties that fastened them in the centre. Many had lace insertions and deep edgings of lace. The tasselled ties could be left visible or tucked in at the throat. Other collars, particularly a Spanish one ('golilla') cut in a semicircle, the straight side forming the front and the arc of the circle standing up at the back, met edge to edge. Some, called 'standing falling-bands', could turn down at one side or at the back with the sides still raised. The under-propper used for collars and ruffs was usually of wire, covered in gold or silver thread. A tabbed or 'pickadil' edging to the doublet neck-band could also support the ruff or collar.

The sleeves of the doublet were mainly of two kinds in the early years of the century. They could be close-fitting, often with a slit at elbow level in the seam, which could be buttoned and was used as a pocket. Another type was full from shoulder to elbow, with the lower part, close-fitting, added on. This kind of sleeve was usually slashed in the upper part, with the shirt-sleeve or a lining showing through. Hand-ruffs were still worn, but with the falling ruff and the standing or falling bands turned-back lace cuffs, starched like the ruff or collar and matching them, were more usual. The seam had a row of buttons and loops, so that it could be opened and turned back a little, the lining forming a cuff. Shoulder-wings were smaller and were not worn after 1640.

The sleeves of the high-waisted doublet were plain in shape, ending in hand-ruffs or turned-back cuffs, and with the seam still partly slit if desired. A new fashion was to have sleeves ending half-way down the forearm and slit for a little distance to show the full shirt-sleeves and the ruffles that trimmed their wrists.

Under-doublets were worn as a means of keeping out the cold.

The jerkin continued to be worn until about 1620, following the shape of the doublet, with a longer skirt and with hanging sleeves or wings only. After this date it remained only as a military garment, made of dressed leather.

The long, furred gown of the 16th century was still worn by men of the learned professions, but after 1625 or thereabouts the short puffed sleeves and the hanging sleeves disappeared.

'Trunk hose', with canions (see Chapter XI), were worn until 1620.

Some trunk hose were like those of the 16th century, others were very full and much longer than formerly, ending just above the knee with the greatest fullness at this point. They often had short canions and were fastened at the waist and the front opening by points. A little later the front opening had buttons and buttonholes. Venetians worn until the late 1830s, could be exaggerated in shape and heavily bombasted over the hips.

'Dutch' breeches with wide tubular legs, ending just below the knee or at the calf, and not

XII.2. Three Three-quarter-length Figures. Women

Hair: (a) (1630–40.) The hair is arranged in a curled fringe in front and in ringlets round the back and sides. (b) (1617.) The hair is taken back unparted and kept smooth to the head. (c) (1620.) The hair is drawn down over the ears and slightly puffed out.

Headdress: (a) The black velvet hat has a wide brim, dipping at the front and back, with a moderately tall, diminishing, flat-topped crown. A jewelled chain forms a hat-band. (b) The wide-brimmed hat is turned up on the left side and fastened to the crown with a jewelled ornament. It has a tall, diminishing flat-topped crown and is worn at an angle. It is made of the same stuff as the gown, with a lining and band of pale green. Beneath it is a 'halo' cap in white lace and lawn. (c) The hat of black felt has a wide circular brim and a tall, diminishing crown with a flat top. The narrow band is of tawny satin. Beneath it the front of a 'shadow' cap can be seen.

Garments: (a) The gown is of black satin, with a high-waisted, boned bodice, open in front and laced across with carnation-red ribbon, showing the white lawn shift beneath. The narrow waist-band of carnation red ribbon is finished with four loops arranged in a flower-shape. The skirt is long and full. The flat, oval ruff of white lawn is worn over a broad white lawn collar, with lace edging, fastening at the throat in front but with an opening between this and a second fastening across the bosom, where it is decorated with a bow of carnation red ribbon. The sleeves are full and end in a band and white frill, below the elbow. (b) The stomacher and under kirtle are of pale green ribbed silk. The stomacher is fastened down the front and ends in a deep, protuberant oval, edged at the base with blue galon. The kirtle has four bands of slate-blue fabric, embroidered in darker blue, down the front. The bodice is made like a tight-fitting jacket ending in a small flare at the hips. It is open in front, with rolled-back revers, and is of pale green silk diagonally striped in slate-blue. The close-fitting sleeves, with shoulder-wings, have a band of slate-blue embroidered in darker blue along the outside. The turned-back cuffs are of white lawn and lace. An upstanding ruff of white lawn covers the close-fitting neckline of the stomacher. The skirt is bell-shaped, just clearing the ground at the hem. (c) The gown is of orange-tawny satin, with folds of parchment-coloured gauze arranged low on the bosom. A band of orange satin ribbon encircles the high waist. The flat, pleated shoulder-wings have narrow artificial hanging sleeves. The sleeves are close-fitting, with turned-back cuffs of parchment-tinted lawn and lace.

Jewellery: (b) Round pearl earrings are worn, and rings on both hands. (c) Round pearl earrings are worn.

caught in at the knees, became fashionable. A form of these, more narrowly fitting at the knee and ending just below it, was worn from 1600 to 1610 and returned to fashion in 1640. They could be slit at the outside of the knee to show the tie of the garters or the garter-ends could be allowed to show beneath them. 'Cloak-bag' breeches were worn from 1620 to 1630. They were of ordinary fullness, trimmed on the outside seams by wide bands of embroidery or braid and ending, caught into a band hidden by decorative points just above the knee. Another form of these, in vogue until 1635, ended below the knee and had button-and-buttonhole fastenings along the outside seam. The coloured lining showed when these were left unfastened.

'Spanish hose', in fashion from 1630 to 1645, had a high waist-line and ended below the knee. Worn with the short high-waisted doublet, they gave an impression of considerable length. They were of reasonable fullness over the hips and tapered to a close fastening below the knee, covered by rosettes of ribbon or garters like small sashes, tied in bows on the outside, or to open ends edged with rows of loops, points or bows. Braid down the outside seams was usual.

Breeches were attached to the inner edge of the doublet by hooks and metal rings after 1630. When the shirt was allowed to show at the waist, the breeches were unattached, but cut so that they dropped a little from the waist, but were tight enough to remain in position over the hips.

Vertical pockets in the sides were customary from early years onwards and were sometimes divided into two or three compartments, with an opening into the breeches as well. Very small pockets, often fastened with a button, were sometimes made at the left and right fronts of the waist.

Garters were very decorative and in many different colours, still in 'sash' form, often with fringe of gold or silver, and made in silk, taffetas, ribbon and net as well as worsted and crewel work.

Stockings were of silk, worsted and wool of various kinds. Many were now knitted, though tailored stockings were still made. Blue, white, black, silver, grey, scarlet, 'carnation', green, yellow and flesh-pink were among the colours used. They were often decorated with embroidery and had embroidered clocks. Socks or extra pairs of stockings were worn for protection against cold or bad weather.

Stirrup-hose were like gaiters, but knitted of thick wool. They were worn to protect the legs or boots when riding and were kept in place by a strap under the foot.

Boot-hose were over-stockings worn between the stocking and the boot, usually of stout linen but occasionally of silk. They had borders of white lawn or linen, edged with frills of lace or embroidery or of gaily coloured stuff, turned over to show at the top of the boot.

Leggings of leather or cloth, sometimes of silk, could be worn out of doors. Boots with a leg constructed like that of a legging were called 'cockers' by country people.

Several outer garments of the 16th century were worn in the 17th (see Chapter XI). The short, full cloak with a folded hood which was chiefly for ornament, was in fashion for the first twenty years, and the sleeved cloak until about 1640. Loose coats such as the gaberdine and mandillion, which became a livery coat after 1620, were in fashion at the beginning of the century and the latter was often worn over one shoulder with the sleeves hanging over the chest and back.

A jacket known as a cassock, looser in fit than the doublet, was a utilitarian garment widening at the hem and fastened down the front. After 1620 its length was extended from the hips to the thighs.

The longer cloak was the other main outer garment until the coat became general later in the century. It was cut out of a half or three-quarters of a circle and varied in length from the top of the thigh to a point just above the ankle. It could be collarless or have a turned-down collar, round or of a square 'sailor' shape. Before 1620 it sometimes had a shoulder cape added. The ruff or falling-band was worn outside the cloak. This form of long circular cloak was in fashion until the 1670s. It fastened at the neck; the rest of it was generally left open. It was frequently put on casually, not fastened at all but draped in various ways, one of the commonest being to lay the collar over the left shoulder and allow the sides of the cloak to hang down over the left arm back and front. Other methods were to suspend the left end of the straight edge from the left shoulder in front, carry the rest of the cloak round the back, under the right arm, across the front of the body and over the left shoulder and arm, from which position it could be raised to enclose the right arm and shield part of the face; to hang the right end over the right shoulder and arm in front, take the remainder round the back, under the left arm and then over it; to drape the garment across the back with the collar uppermost, laying the cloak over the left shoulder and under the right arm and fastening it by cords diagonally across the chest; and, with the cloak in the same position, let the folds hang over the left arm, then roll the end of the drapery in front and tuck it into the belt on the right side. Roll the ends of the drapery hanging on the right, and tuck it into the roll made from the left-hand drapery. The bent left arm could then be left wrapped in a fold of the cloak. The process might be reversed to enclose the right arm, or folds of the cloak might be wound round this arm to protect it when fighting with the sword.

Cloaks as well as doublets and breeches were often made to match or to tone attractively with each other from the 1630s until the fashion for both ended about 1670.

The fashion called 'petticoat breeches' came in during the 1660s and lasted into the 1670s. Originally intended as a riding dress it consisted of very wide-legged breeches in the form of a divided skirt, suspended by a band at hip-level and ending at the knee or just above or below it. They were worn with a short-sleeved bolero jacket or a sleeveless doublet. The full sleeves of the skirt had ribbon appliqué from shoulders to elbows and were puffed below the elbows by ribbon ties, with loops of ribbon hanging all round. Similar loops hung from the front and back of the waistband, the hems of the breeches and down their side-seams.

The coat which came into fashion about 1668 is held to have followed the ancient Persian fashion and to have been in its turn the ancestor of the coats worn today. It was collarless, cut loosely or to fit the figure and ended just below the knee. It had slits at sides and back to give width, since it was often worn fastened with buttons and buttonholes from neck to hem, though occasionally with only the middle buttons done up. It had pockets, without flaps, low down on the skirt. These were vertical to begin with, but horizontal openings, generally with sham fastenings of buttons and buttonholes, soon took their place.

Between 1680 and 1690 the coat fitted the body more closely and was more often left partly unfastened.

The shoulder-knot, a bunch of looped ribbon or cords worn on one shoulder, was very fashionable from 1660 to 1700.

After 1690 the coat began to assume the shape that was to be carried on into the 18th century. The fit was improved, the waist more snugly shaped and the skirt more flared, with pleats from the top of the vent on either side.

The waistcoat was at first almost as long as the coat and could be worn closed when the coat was left open. Sometimes one was worn without the other. The sleeves of the waistcoat were longer than those of the coat and might be turned up at the ends over the coat-cuffs. It had pockets much like those of the coat. After 1690 it ended above the knee.

The sash, in a slightly narrower form, could be worn at hip level and a small sash could also be worn over the waistcoat with the ends tied in front.

Baldricks were now very ornate, often embroidered with gold thread. They were both wide and long and were still worn with civilian dress to carry a light sword.

The falling-band became very deep between 1640 and 1670, depending from a high neckband. Until about 1660 it might still be laid in stiff pleats. It could be square when not pleated, or, after 1660, rounded. The two edges met in front and the ties, tucked in at the top, were long enough to show below them as a rule. Lace, embroidery or transparent muslin edging were used.

The cravat appeared first as a delicately embroidered and edged muslin scarf, simply tied in front in a bow or loosely knotted. From the 1660s to the 1680s narrow cravat strings (lengths of ribbon) were fastened in a bow to tie the cravat. From the 1690s onwards the cravat was folded over itself, with even ends left hanging, and the cravat strings became a made-up double or treble bow on a band, fastening at the back, put on under the cravat and showing on either side of it. The 'Steinkerk', said to have become a fashion after French officers tied their cravats hurriedly before the battle of that name, was a plain cravat put on round the neck from the front with its ends brought to the front on each side, folded over one another and twisted several times before being put through a buttonhole or attached to the edge of the coat. It was worn from the 1690s onwards and persisted into the 18th century.

The sleeves of the early coat could end at the elbow (or above it among the very fashionable) in large turned-back cuffs, showing part of the shirt sleeve and its wrist-ruffle. Alternatively, they could be close fitting, ending a little above the wrist, with the cuffs turned down and widening in a 'goblet' shape.

With the coat and waistcoat the breeches were at first full over the knees and gathered into a band invisible under the fullness. They were of dark material such as black velvet or matched the coat and waistcoat. They were attached to a band at waist or hip level.

From the 1680s onwards knee breeches were worn, fastened with a strap and buckle at the outside of the knee and similarly at the waist-band. They were hardly seen under the coat. From 1690 onwards the stockings could be drawn up over them and rolled at the top, with plain garters below the knees. The breeches had large pockets with openings through vertical slits and small fob pockets at the left and right fronts of the waist-band in which coins of value and other small objects might be kept.

Leggings, boot-hose and stirrup-hose were much as formerly, except that while petticoat breeches were in fashion stirrup-hose had very wide tops, with eyelet holes for fastening them to the breeches by means of 'pointed' ribbons attached to the hems.

Stockings in the second part of the century were decorated only with embroidered clocks as a rule. After 1680 narrow garters with buckles and straps were worn in place of the 'sash' type.

The frills attached below the knees with wide, open-legged breeches were in reality the loose, ornate tops of stockings turned over the garters. They were called 'canons' as distinct from the 'canions' worn earlier with trunk hose.

The long cloak was still worn for travelling and in bad weather. It was no longer draped, but worn as originally intended on the shoulders.

A loosely fitting and loose-sleeved coat ending at the calf, with wide turned-back cuffs of moderate size and a flat, turned-down collar, also side pockets and a vent at the back, largely took the place of the cloak from 1670. It was known as the 'Brandenburg'. It was often worn at home as a sort of dressing-gown.

A short, loose, thigh-length jacket, known as a 'jump', also with a vent at the back, was worn for riding or other practical wear, becoming a feature of Puritan dress in the 1640s.

Garments—Women: The styles in dresses of the late 16th century were worn until about 1625–30, when the French farthingale, reduced in size after 1615, finally went out of fashion. 'Trunk' sleeves lasted only a short time in the 17th century, being replaced by close-fitting sleeves, often with large imitation hanging sleeves. A new neckline was evolved, consisting of a deep, oval décolletage filled in by an ungathered partlet or tucker fastening down the front from the base of the neck or folds of soft material forming a 'V' shape curved at the sides. Unmarried women sometimes wore this décolletage with a circular ruff, without anything else to fill it in, exposing a good deal of the bosom. Sometimes the gathered top of the chemise formed the 'fill-in', with a standing collar attached.

The standing and falling ruffs and collars worn with the low décolletage continued until about 1630, as did the rebato, but the golilla and the fan-shaped ruff went out of fashion before 1620. A large elliptical ruff was worn by women from about 1625 to mid-century.

The open, loosely hanging gown of the 16th century became very popular as a négligée and in the late 1630s had loose sleeves like a 'cassock'.

From 1615 a type of dress with a rather high waist and 'round' skirt, worn with petticoats and without the farthingale, acted as a forerunner of the new style. It was worn with the circular ruff or the standing collar, closed at the neck as a rule, and was short enough to show the shoes. The sleeves, though close-fitting, with turned-back cuffs, ended well above the wrists.

A basqued jacket or doublet, was worn with a full round skirt, just clear of the ground, over petticoats.

The new fashion kept the broad general effect of former styles, but was high-waisted, with a close-fitting basqued bodice girdled with a narrow sash. The high waist was not universally worn, however, and it is only seen in this form for about ten or eleven years, between 1629 and 1640. While it was in vogue, often with a small, oval-ended stomacher under the girdle, many dresses were still made with the long, pointed or oval stomacher of earlier years or with a deep, downward-pointing basque attached to a high-waisted bodice instead of the moderately sized tabbed border which was a part of the new development. Compromises and combinations of old and new styles were numerous and it may be said that the long stomacher never really died out. When the French farthingale was no longer worn, the protuberance over the abdomen which it occasioned, particularly in Dutch costume, was continued in the curve of the long stomacher. Normal-waisted modes obtained in the '40s and '50s. By 1660 the long, deep-pointed line had come into its own again, to remain until the late 1670s. It did not necessarily include a stomacher, however, and the very long bodice was often edged all round with looped tabs or the skirt was gathered on to it without decoration to cover the join.

The skirt throughout the century was comparatively full and rather heavy. It usually touched the ground and the back often formed a small train. It could be closed or open showing the under-skirt. It was frequently bunched up in various ways, again showing the under-skirt, and beneath this when it was lifted the silken fabric of under-petticoats. In utilitarian dress, if the skirt was not pinned up it was short enough to clear the ground.

The collars worn with the new styles were wide and could be of various kinds. In many cases they covered a low décolletage. A wide standing or half-raised collar from shoulder to shoulder at the back, turning over in front to a 'falling' shape, was worn, often with another smaller collar at the same angle within it. Sometimes the collar ended at the points of the shoulders and the bodice had a turned-down lace edging in front. This neck-trimming was in favour until about 1640. The neckerchief, a plain or lace-trimmed square folded corner-wise, and in use throughout the period, was fastened at the base of the throat or on the chest by a brooch, or it could simply be worn loose as a wrap; a scarf might also be put round the shoulders in this way. A deep, shaped 'Bertha' collar, circling the widely cut-out shoulders of the gown, was in fashion from 1660 to 1680. The large, plain turned-down collar, as worn by men, tied beneath the chin and extending to the shoulders, was worn by women until the 1640s and the big square collar, also a masculine fashion and tied in the same way, until the 1670s.

By the 1640s the wide and deep neckline was sometimes square, still lace-edged or with the top of the chemise just showing and caught at intervals by ornamental buttons to keep it to the shape of the neckline. It could also be wide and rounded and was worn without a collar, a mode which continued into the 1680s. The décolletage grew wider and lower, in the 1660s, exposing the shoulders back and front. The soft folds of the chemise-top lay at indeterminate levels, showing much of the bosom.

Sleeves were of various types, the early ones often having a double puff formed by the opened over-sleeve tied above the elbow across the slashed, ballooning inner sleeve. The turned-back cuffs were close at their openings and widened towards their outer edges. These ballooned sleeves, sometimes ending a little way above the wrists, were worn from 1625 to 1640. Another type was full and of three-quarter length, and could have the chemise-sleeve showing its edge or frill at the end, or have a turned-back cuff. It was worn from the 1630s to 1650s. A similar sleeve ending above the elbow and showing the puffed and frilled chemise-sleeve to three-quarter length was worn from 1630 to 1670, but was much shorter after 1650. A plain three-quarter-length sleeve, fairly loose, had a turned-back cuff. It was worn from the 1630s to the '50s. A longer sleeve of the same kind, ending at the wrist, with an elbow-length over-sleeve, came into fashion a little later and went out about the same time. Plain, long sleeves could be worn with practical dress.

A long, wide sleeve, which was turned back at the elbow and fastened just below the shoulder, was fashionable by the 1640s. A longer sleeve of the same type was fastened back to the upper arm. They were worn with the deep décolletage and showed wide, chemise-sleeves, frequently of satin, or a lining giving the same effect. They were worn until the fashions changed in the 1680s.

The tippet, a waist-length cape, might be worn for warmth or as a négligée and was

XII.3. 1640s. Six Figures

made in a variety of materials, trimmed with lace if it was of silk or lawn and with fur if of heavier stuff. Wide scarves and lengths of rich material were draped from the shoulders with deep décolletage and pinned-back sleeves.

The loose 'cassock', of ankle or ground length and with wide sleeves, was worn as an outer garment. The 16th century 'safeguard', or thick over-skirt, was still worn for warmth or protection from weather.

The long cloak, put on in the normal way and not draped, was in use throughout the century, but was used chiefly for travelling (see 'Garments—Men').

A hip-length jacket, often of velvet edged with fur, which could be fitted or loose, was the favourite wear apart from scarves and tippets, when an outer garment was needed.

In the 1670s the skirt became narrower, with a longer train in some instances and with the outer dress often fastened or bunched up at the back. With less width over the hips and with the narrow shoulders and sleeves that were soon in fashion the modish silhouette became elongated rather than broad.

From 1680 onwards the bodice was open to the waist in front and filled in by a

---

XII.3. 1640s. Six Figures

Hair: (a) The hair is dressed in long ringlets. (b) The hair is 'bobbed', parted in the centre and turned in at the ends. (c) The hair is hidden by the helmet. A heavy moustache is worn with a small lip-tuft. (d) The woman's hair is drawn back into a chignon at the back of the head and parted on both sides with ringlets hanging down. The child's hair is in loose ringlets and a fringe over the forehead. (e) The archbishop's hair is hidden by his coif. (f) The cardinal's hair is parted in the centre and brought smoothly downward, turning in at the ends.

Headdress: (a) The helmet has fluted decoration round the crown and a circular brim. The short cheek-guards have a chin-strap attached. White plumes spring from a small knob on the top. (c) The 'lobster-tail' helmet has a rounded crown, a flat peak in front, two curved bars of metal to protect the face, long cheek-guards with a chin-strap and a shaped metal 'tail'. (d) The woman wears a black velvet band round the base of the chignon and another at right angles to it. The child has a close-fitting coif of apricot velvet, edged with gold galon, with a yellow plume at the right side. (e) The arch-bishop wears a black coif and flat black cap. (f) The cardinal wears a scarlet skull-cap and carries a scarlet biretta.

Garments: (a) The Cavalier's armour is restricted to the necessities of riding. The body is protected by a cuirass and arm-coverings of plate-armour. Cuisses or jointed plates protect the thighs and armoured plates cover the knees. Leather straps bind on the armour below the waist at three points. The breeches are of black velvet. A broad collar of white lawn and lace covers the steel gorget. (b) The basqued doublet of rust-coloured woollen stuff has shoulder-wings and a front fastening of gilt buttons, which also edge the open sleeves. The white lawn shirt-sleeves and wrist-ruffles are shown by the sleeve-openings. The round turned-down collar is tied in front. The matching breeches are tied on the outside of the knees with brown ribbons. The stockings are of light brown wool. (c) The doublet and breeches are of dark green woollen stuff, and the plain collar of white linen. The skirts and shoulder-wings of the sleeveless jerkin of buff leather can be seen. Body-armour is worn over it. The tops of grey woollen stockings can be seen. (d) The woman wears a gown of aqua-marine blue satin, with a hem of gold and green

embroidery and a fold of ivory-coloured gauze across the top of the bodice. Her loose hip-length jacket is of black velvet, edged with white fur. It has three-quarter-length, fur-bordered sleeves. The little girl wears a dress of soft wool in pinkish-yellow, embroidered all over in apricot silk. Her round turn-over collar and the turned-back cuffs of her three-quarter-length sleeves are of cream-coloured satin. Narrow sham hanging sleeves of brown velvet hang from the shoulders. Her white muslin pinafore is edged with embroidery. (e) The archbishop wears a black cassock, and a surplice of white lawn with a lace-trimmed hem, a ruff collar and full 'bishop' sleeves frilled at the wrists. A loose, open outer gown of black silk is worn. (f) The cardinal's scarlet cassock is worn under a surplice of white satin edged with lace. The plain white satin collar is tied in front. The scarlet satin circular cloak has a shoulder-cape, partly turned over to show the white satin lining. His right arm is put through an arm-opening in the cloak, while the left arm supports its full width.

Footwear: (a) The thigh-boots of pale buff leather have 'butterfly' spur-leathers with spurs attached. (b) The shoes are of light brown buckskin, tied with composite bows of brown ribbon. (c) The 'bucket-top' boots are of stout brown leather, with 'butter-fly' spur-leathers and spurs. (d) The woman's shoes are unseen. The child's slippers are of yellow kid. (e) The archbishop's shoes are of black fabric. (f) The cardinal's scarlet silk shoes are unseen.

Accessories: (a) The Cavalier's baldrick is of black velvet, with applicqués chevrons of white satin and silver embroidery. His gloves are of pale buff leather and his sword has a silver hilt and scabbard. (b) The seated man is playing a bass viol. (c) The Parliamentarian soldier wears a dark red sash from right shoulder to left hip, with a sheathed sword depending from it. He carries a pike. (d) The child carries a horn-book. This is an oblong of polished wood, with a short handle in which there should be a small hole to take a string for hanging the 'book' around the neck. Attached to the wooden oblong is a sheet of parchment bearing the letters of the alphabet, simple words and rhymes or texts, covered with a thin layer of horn. (e) The archbishop carries an open book. (f) The cardinal's pectoral cross is hung on a wide ribbon of brilliant blue.

stomacher, trimmed with embroidery or ribbon bows, or an ornamental laced 'corset'. The waist-line was at normal level or a little below it, slightly deepened in front. The neck of the dress reached the nape of the neck at the back. It was outlined by folds of lawn or muslin or by lace edging. The skirt was gathered on and usually open down the front over an elaborate under-skirt. Decorative aprons, sometimes very short, became a feature of the mode after 1690. The skirt was folded and pinned back in various ways so that a large part of the under-skirt was in view. A small bustle was worn under this from 1680.

The sleeves ended at the elbow and usually had turned-back cuffs. They were finished by deep ruffles or puffs edged with ruffles.

A loose gown with sleeves like those of the dress was worn as a négligée and became, like the sacque of the 18th century, a garment for daytime wear. It could be girdled by a sash or buckled belt.

The hip-length jacket of the earlier part of the century was now shaped to the waist and enlarged at the back to accommodate the 'bustle'.

The tippet was as it had been earlier, except that a small one of fur, shaped to the neck, was a new development.

Capes ending at the knees were worn for warmth. They were usually made of velvet, but sometimes of silk, warmly lined, and trimmed with fur, fringe or embroidery.

Long, loose coats, like those of men, were also worn as outer garments.

Footwear—Men: Naturally rounded toes to men's shoes in the first thirty-five years or so of the century were supplanted by squared-off toes which continued in fashion until the end of the epoch.

Slightly raised and shaped heels, of leather or cork, could be worn from the second decade onwards.

Until about 1615, shoes might have their uppers slashed to show the stockings or linings. After this date decoration was chiefly concentrated on ribbon ties and 'shoe roses'. The latter could be very large and elaborate, made of ribbon and trimmed with lace and spangles, concealing the tie across the instep. When ties alone were worn they were also ornate, made up of double, treble or multiple bows, sometimes spangled.

Shoes often had open sides below the instep tie in the first half of the century. By 1635 shoe roses were rare.

Short tongues could be worn from about 1617.

Vamps were long by the 1630s. From 1640 to 1680 the ribbon loops across the instep extended widely on either side and could be limp or stiffened.

After 1680 the instep fastening was usually a strap and buckle, with the buckle in the centre or to the outer side. The fronts of the shoes were lengthened, and had a long tongue covering the front of the ankle, with a turn-over of red leather cut in a 'Cupid's bow' shape. Heels were thick and high, coloured red for formal wear.

Pumps had thin soles, were made of soft leather and were often worn with the addition of 'pantofles' or mules. The uppers of these and of soft slippers generally could be made of brocade, taffetas, velvet and silver cloth, but all more practical shoes were made of leather. Some pantofles were made with thick soles, as well as high heels, of cork and were intended to raise the feet from the floor, but not for outdoor wear in bad weather. For this pattens (overshoes with wooden soles raised on iron frames) and clogs, similar to pantofles but with wooden soles, were worn. Heavy bootees called 'start-ups', with buckled fastenings on the outside, were worn by country people.

Boots in the first years of the century reached the thigh and were elegant and softly wrinkled, with well-fitting tops. By 1625 wider, cup-shaped tops, ending just below the knee, had superseded the first type. These could be turned over to show the tops of lace-edged or embroidered boot-hose also turned over; or pushed down so that the leg part of the boot still gripped the upper calf and many-frilled boot-hose tops could be seen within the 'cup'. Wider, bucket-top boots, in vogue by 1630, could be pushed down to a lower level, in this case the leg part of the boot, standing up above the 'bucket', providing the site for the turned-over boot-hose top.

The oblong of leather with a strap under the foot and another round the heel holding the spur, which was known as the stirrup or spur leather and worn across the instep of the boot early in the century, developed into a large butterfly-shaped piece which served the same purpose and covered most of the foot.

Boots had the same fronts as shoes, and followed their fashions in heels.

After 1660 they were worn mainly for riding and were not often seen with fashionable dress. They were of thigh-length, fitting the leg more closely than in earlier years. One type was laced down the calf on the outside and its wide tops were often turned down to a point below the knee. Boot-hose and stirrup-hose were still worn with these boots, which continued in use until the 1670s.

Jack-boots of fine leather and elegant shape, laced, buckled or buttoned on the outside or front of the calf and ornamented along the edge of the tall, wide tops and down the front, were in fashion from 1675.

Heavier versions of this boot, dating from 1665, were for purely practical use.

Footwear—Women: Women's shoes were covered to a great extent by their long skirts. They followed men's fashions in the first part of the century, but after 1660 had long pointed or slightly squared-off toes and high, shaped heels. Their shoes were fastened across the instep with buttons or ties, and although most of them had long vamps; mules, or pantofles sometimes had shorter vamps. The fronts of shoes were ornamented and some with high heels had an extra, flat sole attached for walking with more comfort.

Pattens and clogs were worn in bad weather and long boots, of leather or sometimes of satin, for riding.

Materials used for women's shoes apart from leather were silk of various kinds, brocade, satin and velvet.

Women's silk or woollen stockings and their garters were like those of men (see 'Garments—Men').

Materials, Colours and Ornament: The materials available in the 17th century were much the same as those of the 16th, except for the introduction, late in the period, of printed calico. The use made of them, however, when 16th-century fashions were outmoded about 1625, was a little different. Brocade still held its place to some extent, but satin, velvet, taffetas, various silks, muslin, linen, cotton and lawn, and all unpatterned surfaces of a single colour, were preferred to heavily figured, damasked and ornamented stuffs. In the period between 1625 and the Restoration velvet and cloth were made up in deep, soft shades such as sapphire blue, crimson, dark green, purple, wine colour, 'mulberry', brown and black, while pearly satins in white, cream, grey, biscuit colour and pale blue were favourites, with rose, leaf green, violet, yellow and amber among the lighter colours used.

All neutral tones of grey, slate-blue and dun-colour, with brown and black, buff, tan, maroon, dark green, rust-red and dark blue, were worn for more practical clothes. Puritans wore all these in addition to the brown, buff, grey or black in which they are usually dressed for stage or film presentation. The linings of their cloaks and hoods, like those of other people, could be scarlet, and their wide collars and cuffs, if less exquisitely ornamented than those of the more worldly, could have embroidery or lace to make an edging for linen or lawn.

The Restoration brought many brighter colours back into fashion, and in the last decade heavy materials and bold decoration were once more in favour. At this time also flowered and patterned prints were manufactured in England and were in favour with women of all classes.

The use of lace for collars, cuffs, head-veils, caps, chemise tops, boot-hose, canons, shoe-roses and garter-ends, and for edgings to under-petticoats and the necks of dresses, is one of the most important features of 17th-century dress. Later, cravats, sleeve-ruffles, fontange headdresses, mantillas, neck-trimmings, edgings of various kinds and the decorative aprons worn by women were trimmed in the same way.

Ribbon was the other characteristic ornament of the century. Hair, sleeves, collars and shoes were tied with it, hats trimmed with it and narrow sashes made of it. It was used to make shoe-roses and to ornament the fronts and waists of doublets and the bodices of dresses in made-up bows. Bunches of ribbon loops decorated the front and back of the waist and the outside of the knees of men's breeches from about 1645 to the 1660s.

Ribbons adorned walking sticks, fans and garter-ends; shoulder-knots and sword-knots persisted into the '90s, and ribbon was lavishly used in this decade in the top-knot and fontange.

Braid was fashionable in the last twenty years of the century, chiefly to ornament men's coats in horizontal strips. Tassels were attached to sword-hilts and walking sticks. Fringe was popular, also gold and silver galon, for trimmings and edgings for both sexes.

Embroidery was used to ornament the edges of doublets and stomachers and later the edges of coats, waistcoats and aprons. It was also used to decorate baldricks and the gauntlets of gloves.

Quilting, particularly for underskirts, was very much in favour.

Jewellery and Accessories: Men's jewellery followed late 16th-century fashion in the first quarter. Jewelled hat-bands and brooches to fasten the collar were still worn by men in the 'Cavalier' period and a single earring was an occasional masculine fashion until 1660. 'Ear-strings', put through the pierced lobe of the ear and tied on either side below it, were a form of ornament in the first decade of the century.

Women wore chains of gold and jewels or of pearls alone festooned on the bodice or, in the early years, worn under one arm, from shoulder to opposite side, then taken round the waist. Close-fitting necklaces of even-sized beads, pearls or semi-precious stones were worn throughout. Rings were sometimes fastened from the ring-finger to a cord round the wrist. Jewelled brooches fastened the collar, held the long necklaces in place, ornamented the bodice or fastened draperies or sleeves on the shoulders or upper arms. Bracelets were worn, or strings of pearls wound round the wrists. Drop earrings, usually of pearls, were fashionable throughout the period.

Jewelled buttons were used as sleeve closures and jewelled combs were worn in the hair. Other hair ornaments included jewelled pins, pendants and hair bands, feathers, small bunches of real or artificial flowers and loops or bands of ribbon.

From time to time during the century women carried pomanders, also mirrors, on a short chain or cord from the waist.

Watches were worn on chains, chiefly in the second part of the century.

Men wore the insignia of their Orders on broad ribbons hung across the chest, from left shoulder to right hip.

Fringe, ribbon, lace, fur and gold or silver thread were used to decorate the gloves of both sexes. Shorter sleeves for women brought about the introduction of long gloves, a fashion copied by ultra-fashionable men. Mittens were worn in delicate fabrics, or made of leather or wool for practical work.

Purses were decorated with beads or embroidery and often tasselled. They were made like small bags and fastened with drawstrings.

Muffs of various sizes, from the very large to the minute 'wrist-muffs' worn by women, were made of velvet, satin or fur. Women wore their large hand-muffs on a cord round the neck. Men did the same at first, but in the 1690s they were often attached to a broad sash or belt at hip-level.

Walking sticks, carried in the second part of the century, were of normal height with knobs of silver or ivory, but taller sticks, adorned with ribbon or tassels, were favoured by the exquisites and were also carried by women. Parasols, non-folding, were used by women.

Masks covering the half or nearly the whole of the face, were often worn by women to protect their complexions and by both sexes if they wished to conceal identity. They were made of satin, velvet, silk and sometimes of fur, and frequently edged with fur in any case. They were hung from the neck or waist by cords or carried in the hand when not in use.

Boas of fur were worn by men and women after the Restoration.

Fans were still both of the rigid and folding type. Some were painted, but this fashion came into fuller force in the 18th century.

Patches were worn both by men and women, sometimes in too great profusion.

Handkerchiefs were large and lace-edged. They sometimes had tassels or buttons at the corners.

Sword hilts could be of precious metals and ornamented with jewels and enamel.

XII.4. Man in Dutch Breeches. 1600

Hair: The hair touches the collar at the back and is turned in at the ends, with a short fringe in front.

Headdress: The mole-coloured velvet hat has a turned-down brim and tapering, flat-topped crown. A yellow-green plume is fastened in front.

Garments: The sleeveless jerkin is of mole-coloured velvet, decorated with strips of gold braid. The doublet sleeves, of yellow-green satin with gold thread embroidery in diagonal lines, have wrist-frills of parchment-tinted lawn. The wide, loose breeches match the doublet sleeves. The square collar of parchment-tinted lawn fastens at the throat. The cloak of mole-coloured cloth is worn with the collar, edged with sable-coloured fur, across the left shoulder. A scarf of green and gold silk gauze, with gold fringe, is worn from the right shoulder to the left hip and tied in a bow on the right shoulder. The stockings are of yellow silk and the garters of yellow green silk.

Footwear: The shoes of brown buckskin have squared-off toes, flat heels and small gold ornaments covering the fastenings.

Accessories: The gloves are of brown buckskin with a border of green embroidery and gold fringe. A sword hangs on a strap from a belt of gilt leather.

XII.5. Woman in French Farthingale. 1610

Hair: The hair is taken back without a parting over a pad. The flattened chignon is at the crown of the head.

Headdress: Three ornaments of gold ribbon, with red stones and two scarlet plumes are fastened to the hair.

Garments: The gown of amber satin has a protuberant oval stomacher ornamented in gold galon and red jewels, and bordered with pearls which also festoon the front. Folds of yellow silk gauze edge the décolletage, with three ornaments of scarlet ribbon. The basque of amber satin is goffered to stand out at the hips. The open, amber satin hanging sleeves and shoulder wings are decorated with gold galon. The seam along the upper arm has two rows of red jewels. The inner sleeves are of yellow silk with stripes of gold thread and the cuffs of yellow-tinted lawn and lace, matching the open, standing ruff. The skirt hangs stiffly over the farthingale, ends above the ground and is ornamented with gold galon and red jewels.

Footwear: The gold cloth shoes have small 'cuts' and wedge soles.

Jewellery and Accessories: A necklace of even-sized pearls, a ring and pearl drop earrings are worn and a scarlet and gold fan is carried.

XII.6. Man in Long Trunk-hose. 1614

Hair: The hair is cut short, and taken back from the forehead.

Headdress: The hat of silver-grey velvet has a moderate brim and a tall conical crown, with rosettes of blue taffeta ribbon.

Garments: The doublet of blue-grey silk is tight-fitting and short-waisted, the basque coming to a point in front and the front fastening, shoulder-wings and sleeves decorated by bands of blue and silver embroidery and silver buttons. The lace collar is a 'golilla'. The round hose of blue silk fit over the hips but increase in fullness, ending above the knees. The blue silk stockings have clocks of silver thread. The black velvet cloak with a collar and border of grey fur, is put on with the collar thrown across the left shoulder. Some of the drapery of the cloak is drawn diagonally across the back and fastened on the right, the remainder wound round the left arm.

Footwear: The shoes of grey buckskin have squared-off toes, low heels, and shoe roses of blue taffeta.

Jewellery and Accessories: A black satin ribbon with a jewelled medallion is worn round the neck. The jewelled, silver-hilted sword has a scabbard slung on a grey leather strap.

XII.7. Woman in Arched Hood. 1614

Hair: The hair is parted in the centre and puffed out in small curls at the sides. It is dressed at the back in a flat chignon near the crown of the head.

Headdress: The hood of black gauze is wired out in a curve at the sides, with a dip over the centre of the forehead and continues as a veil over the shoulders. A bunch of black satin ribbon is pinned in the centre front.

Garments: The long-waisted, basqued gown of black satin has a front fastening outlined in silver cord. This also edges the oval décolletage, the waist and the hanging sleeves. These have the seam open, from above the elbow to the wrist, where they are formed into long cuffs. The inner sleeves of ivory satin are close-fitting with deep turned-back cuffs of ivory lace. The ivory silk gauze partlet is gathered into a high collar. The skirt is worn over a moderately sized French farthingale, and decorated with silver cord.

Footwear: The shoes are of silver cloth.

Jewellery: Pearl drop earrings are worn and the matching bracelets on the wrists are of silver and onyx. A collar of four rows of pearls is worn at the top of the partlet.

XII.8. Man in 'Cloak-bag' Breeches. 1625

Hair: The hair is taken back without parting, and is long enough to touch the collar. A short lock curves forward on each side of the forehead.

Headdress: The hat of fawn-coloured felt has an indented crown and flexible brim turned up on the right side, with a terracotta-coloured plume curved round the crown and drooping over the brim.

Garments: The doublet of green cloth, paned in terracotta velvet, is high-waisted and has a basque in six segments, two of which form a point in front. The front fastening and shoulder-wings are ornamented with strips of velvet matching the paning. Rosettes of the same velvet, with green tags, define the waist-line. The sleeves are full to the elbows, where they have a narrower portion joined on and tapering to the wrists. The 'falling band' is of pleated ivory-white lawn. The 'cloak-bag' breeches match the doublet and have rosettes above the knees like those at the waist-line. The hose are green.

Footwear: The boots of natural dressed leather have wide tops forming a cup shape, rounded toes, slightly raised heels and 'butterfly' spur-leathers with spurs attached.

Accessories: The sword, worn at the left side, is fastened by a strap to a belt under the doublet. The gloves are of natural leather.

XII.9. Woman in Open Ruff. 1620–5

Hair: The hair is arranged over a pad in front and swept upward at the back into a small chignon at the top of the head.

Headdress: The halo-shaped headdress is of gold and pearl.

Garments: The gown is of coral-red satin, the fitted bodice decorated with dull gold galon round the décolletage, at the base and down the front. The side-fronts of the bodice, the inner sleeves of coral-pink silk and the front of the bell-shaped skirt have narrow swathes of gold gauze appliqués and are ornamented with garnet-coloured artificial jewels. The inner edges of the skirt-decoration represent a fastening and are bound with gold galon. The hanging sleeves are of the same stuff as the gown. The parchment-tinted turned-back cuffs are of lace and embroidery and the open, loosely goffered ruff of lawn in the same colour.

Footwear: The shoes are of gold brocade.

Jewellery and Accessories: The earrings are of gold and pearls. The necklace is of two rows of pearls with a gold and pearl pendant. A gilt-framed fan and a gold embroidered handkerchief of ivory silk are carried.

XII.10. Woman in Dutch-style Dress. 1624

Hair: The hair is drawn back unparted and worn close to the head.

Headdress: The 'halo' headdress of stiffened white lawn and lace curves round the face. The back, unseen, is a plain lawn cap.

Garments: The under-kirtle of peach pink satin has five bands of light olive green silk braid at the hem. The over-dress is of olive green and gold shot silk. Small tabs of this edge the base of the bodice. The front fastening of the long, protuberant stomacher is edged with gold galon and the side fronts of the bodice with three rows of dark olive green braid, which also borders the open front and hem of the skirt, and the ends of the hanging sleeves. The inner sleeves are of peach-pink silk paned with gold tissue. The turned-back cuffs and the oval standing ruff, with its edge crossing the top of the bodice, are of ivory embroidered lawn.

Footwear: The shoes, hidden by the dress, are of olive green velvet.

Jewellery and Accessories: The drop earrings are of dark green enamel. A double necklace of even-sized uncut crystals and a triple string of pearls are worn. A rose is held in the left hand.

XII.11. Woman in Velvet Over-gown. 1625

Hair: The hair is parted in the centre and puffed out a little at the sides.

Headdress: The 'shadow' headdress is made up of rows of oyster-grey lace.

Garments: The dress of oyster-grey satin is slightly high-waisted and fits comparatively loosely. The bodice is sewn with pearl beads and amethysts in a criss-cross design and piped with oyster-grey satin. The skirt ends above the shoes and has an over-skirt of silver lace. The close-fitting sleeves are three-quarter length, ornamented like the bodice and with turned-back cuffs of oyster-grey lace. A gauze ruff in the same colour is worn. The over-gown is of dull purple velvet, reaching the ground. Its broad turned-back collar forms revers and is edged with silver galon, which also ornaments the hanging sleeves. The grey silk lining shows in one slightly open hanging sleeve.

Footwear: The shoes of grey satin have small 'Louis' heels and 'shoe roses' of purple ribbon.

Jewellery and Accessories: Large drop earrings of black pearl and a ring on the third finger of the right hand are worn. A lace-edged handkerchief is carried.

XII.12. Woman in Short Head-veil. 1630

Hair: The hair is parted across the head and dressed with some of the back hair in a small chignon near the top of the head. The hair over the forehead is parted in the centre, and formed into ringlets. More ringlets hang at the back of the neck.

Headdress: A small cap of yellow satin and brown velvet is fitted over the chignon. A square veil of yellow gauze is worn over the head and face.

Garments: The under-petticoat is of yellow taffeta and the kirtle of ivory satin, embroidered with yellow flower-sprigs. The skirt of the brown velvet over-gown is open in front, and the bodice laced with gold ribbon. The saffron-tinted lawn chemise shows through this and above the low décolletage. The embroidered collar of saffron-tinted lawn covers the shoulders and part of the collar of the fur-edged parchment velvet shoulder-cape. The three-quarter-length brown velvet sleeves end in two rows of embroidery, showing the close-fitting lawn and lace cuffs of the chemise-sleeves.

Footwear: The shoes of yellow satin, with high heels and vamps, are tied over the insteps with brown ribbons. Wedge-soled pattens are strapped over the front of the foot.

Jewellery: A gold and amber brooch is worn on the bosom.

XII.13. Girl in High-waisted Gown. 1635

Hair: The front hair is taken back unparted and dressed in a chignon half-way up the back of the head. A fringe of short curls is arranged on the forehead and ringlets of varying length hang at the sides of the head.

Garments: The gown of azure-blue ribbed silk is slightly high-waisted and the bodice has a deep basque and pointed stomacher. It is open to the waist with bands of black velvet across it over the white lawn chemise, and a band edging it on each side, forming a square-cut décolletage. Two bands of black velvet make the waist-belt and loops of it are bunched at the sides of the open front. The bodice is sleeveless, with small shoulder-wings, showing the full white lawn sleeves of the chemise. They are of three-quarter length and have turned-back cuffs of white lawn and embroidery. The full skirt is long enough to trail a little on the ground.

Footwear: The shoes are of grey fabric.

Jewellery: The girl wears a necklace of turquoise and silver, with a matching pendant.

XII.14. Woman in 'Virago' Sleeves. 1635

Hair: The hair is taken back over a pad, with short curls on the forehead and ringlets over the ears.

Headdress: A short veil of green-blue gauze is turned back above the face and covers the head. It is weighted with small blue beads.

Garments: The under-dress, padded inner sleeves and stomacher are of blue-green shot taffeta, ornamented with turquoise and silver ribbon, edged with dark blue-green galon. The long, full open-skirt of the over-dress of dark blue-green velvet is trimmed in the same way. It has a slightly high-waisted bodice, with a waist-belt tied in a bow at the left front. The skirt is open and ornamented in the same way as the bodice. It is long and full, touching the ground at front and sides and with the suggestion of a train at the back. The outer sleeves are open and tied at the elbows with dark blue-green ribbon. The turned-back cuffs of gossamer lawn edged with lace take in the ends of both inner and outer sleeves and match the open, flattened collar.

Footwear: The shoes are of dark blue-green velvet, with squared-off toes, and shaped heels.

Jewellery and Accessories: The necklace is of even-sized pearls. A silver brooch set with jewels is worn at the bosom. A fan of dark green feathers, set in a silver and turquoise handle, and a black taffeta mask are carried.

XII.15. Youth in Paned Doublet. 1635

Hair: The hair is arranged in a fringe over the forehead and loose ringlets lie on the shoulders.

Headdress: The black velvet hat has a wide brim, turned up at the sides and front and is decorated with grey and white plumes. The crown is undented.

Garments: The doublet of pearl-grey grosgrain flares slightly at the hem, and fastens down the front. It is trimmed with silver galon and paned on the chest with black velvet, bows of which ornament the waist. The falling band, or collar, is of pearl-tinted lace, fastening at the throat and extending to the shoulders. The full sleeves are paned in black velvet and have turned-back cuffs of lace. The 'Venetian' breeches match the doublet and end below the knees with a border of grosgrain cut in points. Black velvet ribbons fasten them on the outside of the legs. The stockings are of pearl-grey silk.

Footwear: The shoes are of pearl-grey corded silk, with squared-off toes, red heels and shoe-roses of silver ribbon.

Accessories: A sword with a hilt of black enamel and silver hangs from a belt of thick silver braid slung from the right shoulder to the left hip.

XII.16. Cavalier in Plumed Hat

Hair: The hair is arranged in a fringe in front with ringlets at the sides and back and one 'love-lock' brought forward and tied with red ribbon. A narrow upturned moustache and small, pointed chin-beard are worn.

Headdress: The black velvet hat has an indented crown (not seen) and five white and grey plumes showing above the pliable, upturned brim.

Garments: The doublet and breeches ('Spanish hose') are of pewter-grey corded silk ornamented with motifs of dull silver galon on carnation red silk. The white lawn collar has a lace edging. The three-quarter-length sleeves have open seams tied at the ends and showing the white lawn shirt-sleeves. The sleeveless jerkin of grey dressed leather has shoulder-wings and a skirt made in four overlapping sections. The cloak is of black cloth, lined with carnation red, and has a turned-down collar bordered with grey fur.

Footwear: The boots of fawn-grey dressed leather have 'bucket' tops, slightly squared toes and 'butterfly' spur-leathers with spurs attached, high heels and extra, detachable soles of cork. White, lace-edged boot-hose are turned down over the boot-tops.

Accessories: A baldrick of carnation-red stiffened material, embroidered and piped in silver, is worn from the right shoulder to the left hip and supports the silver-hilted sword. The gloves are of pale grey leather.

XII.17. Woman in Tall-Crowned Hat. 1640s

Hair: A little hair can be seen coming forward on to the cheek.

Headdress: A white embroidered lawn cap is tied under the chin. Over it is worn a wide-brimmed, tall-crowned hat of black felt, with a grey ribbon band tied at the back.

Garments: The under-skirt is striped in white and grey with black edges to the stripes. The over-dress is of black woollen stuff, a cape collar of white embroidered lawn meeting at the base of the neck and down the front of the bodice. The sleeves are plain and moderately full, with turned-back cuffs matching the collar. The skirt is turned back and fastened in place near the back of the waist showing a scarlet lining. A white apron is worn.

Footwear: The shoes are of black buckskin with shaped heels of moderate height and grey ribbon ties.

Accessories: The woman carries a rush basket containing vegetables.

XII.18. Man in Plain Dress. 1640

Hair: The hair covers the ears and hangs in straight locks from a centre parting.

Headdress: The wide-brimmed hat of black felt has a tall diminishing crown with a flat top and a plain grey band.

Garments: The jacket of grey cloth is buttoned down the front and ends just below the hips. It has plain sleeves with white turned-back cuffs and a turned-down square-cut white linen collar worn over the cloak, which is a little longer than the jacket and is lined in blue. The grey breeches are of the loose 'Dutch' variety and end below the knees, with a narrow border of lighter grey. The hose are of grey yarn.

Footwear: The shoes of black leather have short, wide tongues and bows of grey ribbon to tie them across the insteps.

Accessories: A small leather-bound book is carried.

XII.19. Woman in 'Cassock'. About 1644

Hair: Only the curls arranged on the forehead and cheeks can be seen.

Headdress: The hood worn over the head and tied under the chin is of black velvet. It is wired to form a curved shape framing the face.

Garments: The 'cassock' or outer wrap is of soft grey-green cloth with a collar of sable-coloured fur. It has a deep shoulder-cape and the wide sleeves are of a curious shape, with elbows protruding. The garment is slightly high-waisted and its long, full skirt trails on the ground.

Accessories: The woman wears pale grey gloves and carries a muff of the same fur as her collar. A black velvet mask, with a white frilled edging, hangs from her wrist on a black cord.

XII.20. Girl in Grey Silk Gown. 1640s

Hair: Short ringlets over the forehead can be seen. The rest of the hair, under the cap, is taken back unparted and bound up in a chignon at the back of the head.

Headdress: A cap of white lawn fits over the back of the head, its crown diminishing towards its flattened end. The front has a wide turned-back band edged with white lace or embroidery cut in points. It is tied under the chin.

Garments: The dress is of heavy dove-grey silk with a high waist and long, full skirt. The puffed sleeves are three-quarter length and have turned-back cuffs of white lawn edged with lace. The wide cape collar, fastening at the throat and again over the bosom with a bow of narrow black ribbon, is of the same stuff as the cuffs.

Footwear: The shoes, hardly seen, are of woven stuff in dove grey.

Accessories: The girl wears long white gloves and carries a sable-coloured fur muff over her left arm. She holds a gold watch which is attached to the waist of her dress by a narrow black ribbon.

XII.21. Man in Short Jacket. 1650s

Hair: The hair is parted in the centre and arranged in shoulder-length ringlets.

Garments: The open front of the sapphire blue velvet bolero jacket shows part of the white satin shirt, which has full sleeves, oval cuffs and a square-cut collar tied at the throat with silver cord and tassels. The sleeves of the jacket are open from shoulder to wrist, ornamented along the edges by cherry-red silk edged with silver and ending in narrow, oval-shaped turned-back cuffs with the same ornament. It also edges the open front, hem and side-fronts of the jacket, passing over the shoulders to continue at the back. The 'Dutch' breeches match the doublet, with bands of cherry red and silver decorating the side-seams. Loops of cherry-red ribbon border the loose legs and are attached to the top of the breeches, which are worn at hip level, and show the shirt bloused over them. The stockings are of cherry-red silk.

Footwear: The shoes are of black Cordovan leather with shaped heels. They have short tongues and ties of cherry-red ribbon over the insteps.

Accessories: The man carries a light unsheathed sword with a silver hilt.

XII.22. Country Girl or Maidservant. Mid-Century

Hair: The hair is taken back without a parting, and put up in a flattened chignon at the back.

Headdress: The white linen or cotton cap fits the head and is turned back in front.

Garments: The white cotton shift is fastened at the bosom and the sleeves are rolled above the elbows. A boned bodice of glazed brown cotton stuff is worn over the shift and laced down the front. It has shoulder-straps of black velvet and the top of the garment is edged with it. The full skirt of russet wool ends above the shoes and has two bands of black braid to ornament the hem. The stockings are of brown-grey yarn.

Footwear: The plain shoes are of light brown buckskin and have high vamps and flat heels.

XII.23. Woman in Satin Gown. 1650

Hair: The hair is drawn back without a parting, and dressed in a chignon level with the top of the head. There are short curls over the forehead and long ringlets at the sides and back.

Headdress: A strip of dark green velvet sewn with pearls is fastened to the hair on the right side by a circular gold ornament set with green stones.

Garments: The gown is of pearl-coloured satin with a fitted front-fastening bodice and a long, full skirt touching the ground. The pearl satin stomacher is ornamented with stitching in gold thread. Four strips of the same decoration are appliquées down the front of the skirt, and two round the hem. A broad collar of lighter cream-coloured satin comes up to the throat and covers the shoulders, with a triple bow of green velvet in the centre front. The turned-back cuffs of the full three-quarter-length sleeves match the collar. The outer sides of the sleeves are decorated with four strips of gold-stitched pearl satin.

Jewellery and Accessories: A small gilt-framed mirror is fastened to the waist of the dress by a green velvet ribbon.

XII.24. Man in Petticoat Breeches. 1660

Hair: Loosely curled ringlets lie on the shoulders. A narrow moustache and small chin-beard are worn.

Headdress: The hat of black felt has a tall diminishing crown with a flat top and a wide brim dipping at front and back. It has a band of violet taffeta ribbon and a bunch of the same ribbon on the left side.

Garments: The white lawn shirt has full sleeves gathered into bands and oval cuffs. The body of the shirt is visible between the base of the jacket and top of the breeches. The bolero jacket is of black velvet. Its short sleeves have an opening at the lower end on the outside. The shoulder-knot and the ties below the elbows of the shirtsleeves are of violet ribbon. The square-cut lace collar fastens at the throat. The breeches of black velvet are full and loose so that the effect is of a kilt or petticoat. They are put on, unattached, at the hip-line. Loops of violet ribbon hang from the top of the breeches all round and in four tiers at the sides. Lace 'canons', of the same pattern as the collar, hang from below the knees. The stockings are of black silk.

Footwear: The shoes are of black leather, with upstanding tongues, squared toes and high heels.

Accessories: A silver-headed cane and gloves of pale grey leather, with black and silver embroidery and fringe, are carried.

XII.25. Girl in a Spanish Dress. 1655

Hair: The hair hangs loosely, pomaded to keep its shape. It is parted on the right side.

Headdress: Carnation-red plumes are attached to gold artificial roses on the left side of the head.

Garments: The dress is of gold and black shot tissue, worn over a Spanish farthingale. The boat-shaped neckline is edged with parchment-tinted gauze. The top of the pointed bodice is bordered with pearls, a strip of gold-embroidered parchment satin and a band of gold galon. The skirt is open in front, showing an under-skirt matching the dress. The sleeves are made up of three large puffs of black and gold tissue paned with carnation-red satin, edged with gold galon and banded horizontally with black velvet. They are set in below the shoulders, a triangular piece of carnation-red jewelled satin covering the insets. The turned-back cuffs are of pleated parchment-tinted gauze, edged in gold.

Footwear: The shoes are of the same stuff as the dress.

Jewellery and Accessories: Large drop earrings and a circular brooch of gold, pearls and rubies are worn, with rings on the first and third fingers of the left hand. The handkerchief is of parchment-coloured silk embroidered and fringed in gold. The fan is black and gold.

XII.26. Woman in Classical Over-drapery. 1660

Hair: The hair is taken back unparted and dressed in a chignon at the back of the head. Wired-out ringlets hang at the sides.

Garments: The gown of mulberry satin has a full skirt with a short train. The low décolletage is dropped from the right shoulder. The draped top of the white satin chemise shows above the fitted bodice. The short, draped sleeves are open, but caught together with crystal buttons which also fasten back the chemise sleeves. Two separate rectangular draperies are arranged over the dress. The first, of silver tissue shot with black, is fastened with a silver brooch on the right side of the bosom above the top of the bodice. Three of its corners are joined at this point, so that the drapery descends diagonally across the body to the left hip, with its length reaching the ground, and passes across the back with the fourth corner forming a point there and the width of material between the other two joined corners billowing out in a looped-up fold over the right side of the back. The second drapery, of rose-pink satin, is hung forward over the left shoulder, held together at the shoulder by a silver brooch and brought across the back to be held in place or lifted in the right hand.

XII.27. Woman in Watered Silk Gown. 1665

Hair: The hair is drawn back and dressed in a chignon at the back of the head. Ringlets hang at the sides.

Headdress: A dark green satin ribbon is tied round the chignon.

Garments: The under-skirt is of pearl-coloured satin, ornamented down the centre and round the hem with rosettes of coral-coloured taffetas. The bodice of the green watered silk over-gown is ornamented with gold galon and a narrow border of pearl satin embroidered in gold, green and coral red. The open front of the long-trained skirt is bordered in the same way. The off-shoulder décolletage is swathed in pearl satin with small bunches of green ribbon below each shoulder. The puffed sleeves end above the elbow and have lower puffed sleeves of pearl satin, ornamented with frills of matching gauze bound with green ribbon.

Footwear: The shoes are of gold brocade.

Jewellery and Accessories: Pearl drop earrings, a necklace of even-sized pearls and a brooch of gold and pearl are worn. Narrow green satin ribbon is tied round each wrist. A fan is carried in the right hand.

XII.28. Man in Coat and Breeches. 1670

Hair: The wig is dressed in horizontal curls and hangs down over the shoulders.

Headdress: The hat of brown-purple velvet has a hard, shallow crown, a narrow, stiffened brim and decoration of grey-green ribbon.

Garments: The loosely fitting coat is of brown-purple velvet, with facings and turned-back cuffs to the short sleeves of oyster-coloured satin, ornamented with small gold buttons. The waistcoat and breeches are of grey-green corded silk, the latter very full and gathered into bands (unseen) below the knees, where bunches of brown-purple velvet ribbon are attached. The cravat and full inner sleeves, frilled at the wrists, are of ivory-coloured lawn. The bunches of ribbons on the shoulders and the loops protruding from under the coat-sleeves are of grey-green taffeta. The stockings are of oyster-grey silk.

Footwear: The shoes of greyish fawn buckskin have high shaped heels, an upstanding tongue and ties of brown-purple ribbon.

Accessories: An ivory-headed white-enamelled cane is carried. A baldrick of grey-green and brown-purple embroidery with dull gold edging supports a light gold-hilted sword with a gilded scabbard.

XII.29. Countryman or Artisan. About 1670

Hair: The hair touches the shoulders and is turned in at the ends. It is parted high up on the right side, with a few short strands coming forward on to the forehead.

Headdress: The wide-brimmed brown felt hat, held in the hands, has a flat-topped, indented crown, narrower at the top than at the base.

Garments: The loosely fitting coat is of dull slate-blue cloth, with cuffs of grey cloth turned back to the middle of the forearm showing the ends of the white shirt-sleeves. There are three buttons on the cuffs and five on the horizontal jacket flaps. The plain white linen cravat is tied with narrow cravat-strings. The full breeches of brown woollen stuff are sewn into bands, unseen, below the knees. The stockings are of grey yarn.

Footwear: The shoes are of light brownish-grey buckskin and have long, broad tongues and a fastening across the instep.

XII.30. Man's Dress. 1674

Hair: The wig is loosely curled, in contrast to the more usual closely curled type.

Headdress: The low-crowned, wide-brimmed hat is of brown felt, trimmed with two orange-coloured plumes.

Garments: The collarless coat of heavy brick-coloured silk has a moderately full skirt and is slightly fitted at the waist. Gold cord decorates it down the front and at varying levels above the hem. The wide sleeves are turned back at the elbow with fastenings of gilt cord and gold buttons, showing the biscuit-coloured lining, and loops of dull gold ribbon hanging from them. Below these are the puffed, banded and frilled sleeves of the écru lawn shirt. The waistcoat is edged with gold fringe. The full breeches are of brown velvet with loops of gold ribbon at the knees. The stockings are of biscuit-coloured silk and have clocks of gold thread. The cravat, of écru lawn, has ties of brick-red ribbon at the front of the neck.

Footwear: The shoes of brown buckskin have ties of brick-red ribbon, squared toes and raised heels.

Accessories: A green silk baldrick embroidered in gold supports the sword. An ivory-headed cane is carried.

XII.31. Woman in Draped-back Gown. 1670s

Hair: The hair is parted in the centre with a short fringe on the forehead. It is arranged in three horizontal rolls from the temples round the back of the head, from which long ringlets descend at the back and sides.

Garments: The under-skirt is of cloth of silver, with two adjoining panels of silver tissue sewn with crystals down the centre front and a matching border round the hem. The over-gown is of black satin. The fitted bodice ends in a deep point in front. The décolletage is off the shoulders and has a wide 'bertha' collar of silver lace. The front of the long skirt is bunched up at the back of the waist and the front breadth is held up in the right hand. The sleeves end half-way down the upper arm and their seams are left open. The under-sleeves of silver gauze are formed into three puffs banded with narrow strips of black satin, ending above the elbows, and are finished with frills of silver lace.

XII.32. Man in Long-waisted Coat. 1680

Hair: The full-bottomed wig of large ringlets is long enough to lie on the shoulders.

Headdress: The wide brim of the black velvet hat turns up on the right side and rather less on the left. It is edged with silver galon and trimmed with white plumes and a bunch of crimson ribbon.

Garments: The body of the prune-coloured velvet coat is long and the sash of crimson silk set low and tied on the left side. The front opening of the coat is edged with silver galon and fastened with amethyst buttons. Ornamental panels edged with silver decorate the slightly flared skirt of the coat. The sleeves are close-fitting at the top and widen below the elbows, ending in turned-down cuffs and unstarched wrist-frills. Bunches of crimson taffeta ribbon are attached on the outside at the knees of the breeches (unseen). The white lawn cravat, edged with lace, is tied in a bow in front. The stockings are of black silk.

Footwear: The black leather shoes have wide tongues fastening over the insteps, with small buckles on the outside, and red heels of moderate height.

Accessories: The gloves are of pale grey buckskin and the cane of ebony, with a silver top.

XII.33. Woman in Draped-back Over-dress. 1684

Hair: The hair is parted in the centre and dressed in five puffed rolls on either side. Ringlets come down on to the shoulders.

Garments: The under-skirt, visible from waist to hem, is of fine biscuit-coloured net, in tiers, the edges of which are decorated with gold fringe. The over-dress is of pale amber satin. The bodice is fitted to the figure and has a wide, rounded décolletage edged by a narrow frill of net. The stomacher is of satin in the same colour as the under-skirt. It is bordered with gold galon and decorated with bows in diminishing sizes of brown velvet. Bows of the same stuff hold back the hip-panniers of the open skirt, which is formed into a short train at the back. The sleeves are made in one with the bodice and end just below the elbow in deep frills of net.

Footwear: The shoes are of biscuit-coloured satin.

Jewellery and Accessories: A close-fitting necklace of even-sized clouded amber beads is worn round the throat. A small open jewel-casket is held in the hands.

XII.34. Man in 'Brandenburg' Coat. 1689

Hair: The wig is arranged in small horizontal curls, some of which are loosened a little as they lie on the shoulders.

Hat: The hat of black velvet has an upturned brim that curves downward and up again on the right side. A long, narrow, white plume shows above the brim.

Garments: Part of the front of the long waistcoat of grey grosgrain is visible. It is bound with silver braid and has small mother-of-pearl buttons. The loose 'Brandenburg' overcoat is of lavender-blue cloth. It has fastenings of dull silver braid with silver buttons on the open front of the coat and on the turned-back cuffs. The sleeves are made in one with the rest of the garment. The stockings are of grey silk.

Footwear: The shoes are of black leather, with shaped red heels. There is a fastening over the instep, covered by the tongue, which is doubled over it.

Accessories: The gloves are of pale grey leather. A cane with a silver top is carried in the left hand.

XII.35. Woman in 'Cornet' Headdress. 1684

Hair: This is taken back over pads from a centre parting and dressed in a chignon near the top of the head (unseen).

Headdress: The 'cornet' headdress is a simplified fontange. The cap of ivory lawn has an upstanding frill in front and lappets at the back. The veil of ivory gauze is wired to stand up above the forehead. A 'topknot' of wired black satin ribbon is pinned at the front of the cap.

Garments: The dress is of pale pink silk, horizontally striped in deeper pink. The rigid bodice has a rounded waist-line and a black satin belt. The décolletage is outlined by frilled ivory gauze, with a black satin bow in the centre. The short sleeves have puffed inner sleeves of frilled ivory gauze, bound in the middle with pink ribbon. The skirt is narrow over the hips and flares slightly towards the hem, forming a short train. Small panniers are looped over the hips.

Footwear: The shoes are of black satin.

Jewellery and Accessories: A necklace of even-sized pearls is worn and a small white fur muff, trimmed with a double bow of black satin, put on over the right forearm. The gloves are of ivory silk and the tall cane has an ivory knob.

XII.36. Man in French Style of Wig. About 1690

Hair: The wig is of straight hair curled loosely at the ends with large curls.

Headdress: The hat is of black felt, with a wide up-turned brim trimmed by a narrow pearl-grey plume.

Garments: The waistcoat is of garnet red and silver brocade. The coat is of garnet red velvet, lined with pearl-grey satin, flaring from the hips and open down the front. The fastenings are of silver fabric with silver buttons. The sleeves are of three-quarter length, widening towards the turned-back cuffs, which are of pearl-grey satin decorated with strips of silver ribbon and silver buttons. The pocket flaps are ornamented in the same way. The full sleeves of the white lawn shirt are gathered into frills at the ends. The two-tiered cravat is tied with a double bow of black satin ribbon. The breeches and stockings are of pearl-grey silk.

Footwear: The shoes are of fawnish-grey leather and have up-standing tongues with a turnover of red leather, red buckles and high red heels.

Accessories: The sword depends from a strap coming from a belt beneath the waistcoat. It protrudes from a side-vent in the coat.

XII.37. Man with Muff. 1695

Wig: The curled brown wig is dressed in ringlets which lie on the shoulders.

Headdress: The shallow-crowned hat of black felt has a wide brim, turned up a little all round and further on the right side of the front. It is decorated with short grey plumes.

Garments: The sleeved waistcoat is of buff-yellow silk, with maroon stripes. Its lining of parchment-coloured quilted satin is turned back in revers on the chest and over the coat sleeves at the wrists. The coat, which flares from the hips, is of maroon cloth, faced with grey. The buttons are silver and the button-loops and pocket-tassels are of silver thread. The epaulettes are of grey satin, ornamented with silver motifs. The sleeves, of moderate width at the top, grow wider towards the turned-back cuffs. The neck-cloth and shirt, showing ruffles at the wrists, are of white lawn. The breeches of black velvet are scarcely seen. The stockings are of grey silk.

Footwear: The shoes are of fawnish grey buckskin with broad tongues, silver buckles and red heels.

Accessories: A muff of grey fur is slung from a black satin sash round the hips and ornamented by a double bow of fringed black satin. The man carries an ebony cane and wears a silver-hilted rapier.

XII.38. Woman in 'Fontange' Headdress. 1695

Hair: This is parted in the centre and puffed out over the temples. Two large ringlets frame the face on each side.

Headdress: The 'fontange' headdress of ivory gauze is formed of tall fluted rolls leaning forward over the forehead and tapering downwards at the sides to continue as lappets attached to the cap (unseen).

Garments: The under-skirt of pale blue satin is encircled by a frilled band of its own stuff, puffed out between bands of black satin. Round the hem is a ruched frill of pale pink silk gauze. The over-gown is in stripes of pink and blue satin, edged in black galon. The bodice is open in front, with revers of black satin. The décolletage is edged with fluted rolls of ivory gauze. The pink silk stomacher has elliptical motifs in blue embroidered in black set across it, diminishing towards the waist. The open skirt is draped back over a bustle to form a train and has paniers on the hips. The short sleeves are turned back with black satin and the inner sleeves of blue satin have frills of ivory gauze.

Jewellery and Accessories: The necklace is of black pearls and the muff of grey fur, with a bow of fur and black satin.

XIII   18TH-CENTURY DRESS

The pale colours and delicate materials of the early Rococo Period replaced the late 17th-century fashions after the first decade of the 18th. Women's caps grew smaller, their skirts wider, the use of powder for the hair came in and the tie wig began to appear. Men wore the tricorne for fifty years or so, and women the hooped skirt in its varied forms. Dress became more elaborate and lavishly ornamented after mid-century and women's coiffures were built up to an immense height. A narrower style of gown in the late 70s was accompanied by a narrower-skirted coat for men.

In the 1780s an elegant version of countrified dress became fashionable wear for men, with hair of bobbed length, often unpowdered. Women wore the 'bouffant' mode, with puffed-out fichus and bustled skirts. A further change, in the 1790s, brought in high-waisted, long-tailed coats for men, worn with pantaloons or close-fitting breeches. Women abandoned the corseted appearance and wore high-waisted dresses with long, full skirts by 1795.

Hair, Wigs and Hats—Men

Hair: Wigs were worn as a matter of course by the majority of men during the greater part of this epoch, but some grew their hair long, having it curled and tied back to be in the mode. With the arrival in fashion of the tie wig a false front might be added to give the required height, or the back piece might be false, with the real hair used in front, making it difficult to be sure how much of a man's coiffure was his own. Exceptions were those country-dwellers, labourers, artisans and serving-men who did not in any case wear wigs. The 'bobbed' haircut of these men, casually and often attractively framing the face, was copied in the '80s and '90s in more sophisticated versions. Short hair, brushed forward from the crown in curls or straight strands, was introduced in the closing years.

Vestiges of the queue remained until the end of the period and grey powder, especially popular in the 1780s and 90s, or a light powdering, also persisted until this time.

Wigs: The full-bottomed wig, still worn at the beginning of the 18th century, was usually parted in the middle, a ridge of thick, waved hair on either side of the parting giving an effect of height. The rest of the wig was divided in three, one mass of waves and curls at the back and the other two falling forward on either side of the face.

By 1710 the wig was longer, smoother and less thick with straight hair behind the frontal curls and down the back, curled again round the edges. This fashion was seen in France as early as the last decade of the 17th century. Between 1710 and 1720 the use of powder became general and the custom of tying the wig with a ribbon bow at the back of the neck gradually gained ground. The first move in this direction was to divide the back portion in two and to tie the ends with ribbon. By 1720 wigs were definitely smaller and less cumbrous.

In the tie wig the back piece became curled locks or a queue, and the hair in front was taken back without parting or was parted in the centre with two, or sometimes three rolled curls placed horizontally at the sides. This type of wig remained in fashion, with some variations of size and dressing, until the 1770s. The practice of putting the queue of the

XIII.1. 1700–20. Six Figures

Hair: (a) (1700–10.) The hair is arranged in a mass of curls over the forehead and in a chignon at the back, unseen beneath the headdress. (b) (1715.) The wig may be powdered or of a natural colour. It is parted in the centre, the hair on either side being raised and then allowed to fall in ringlets of varying lengths on to the shoulders. (c) (1717.) The hair is unpowdered and is taken back from the forehead without a parting and swept up at the back and above the ears into a small chignon on the top of the head. (d) (1720.) The youth's hair is cut to cover the ears, falling in thick waves at the sides. It is tied back (unseen), and hangs down to the shoulder-blades and is curled at the ends. (e) (1717.) The hair is parted in the centre and is arranged in waves on either side, partly covering the ears. The chignon is hidden by the hat. (f) (1707.) An English officer. The wig may be powdered or natural. It is arranged at the ends in separate curled strands to lie on the shoulders.

wig into a black bag was in favour between 1720 and 1770. The queue could be wound into a narrow twist fastened at the end, or into a pigtail or coiled twist turned up on itself and fastened. Between the '30s and '70s a black ribbon was sometimes attached to the shirt frill on the chest and to the black bow or wig bag at the back and was called a 'solitaire'.

The untied 'bob' wig of rounded and simple shape, either curled tightly or with curls falling to the neckline of the coat or to the shoulders, brushed back or from a centre parting, was worn at first by men of all ages, later mostly by professional and elderly men, also by some clerks, apprentices and tradesmen until the 1780s.

Wigs were made in black, brown, auburn, flaxen, grey or grizzled hair, some of which was dyed.

In the early '70s the front hair on men's wigs was taken back from the forehead towards the top of the head, where it rose in a slightly pointed shape. Rolled curls still lay horizontally on each side of the face, and were sometimes placed behind the ears rather than over them. A roll of hair was worn round the base of the skull. The black ribbon tying the hair at the back of the neck remained, but was tied lower down and the 'tails' at the back were once again sometimes divided into two. A variation in this type of hairdressing was to create a tall crest of hair in front with a smooth, untied, slightly waved mass of hair descending at the back.

In the 1780s the queue became shorter and was eventually discarded. More grey powder than white was worn, and a light sprinkling of powder on a naturally coloured wig was often seen. By the 1790s, with hair cut to end just above the collar-line the wig was unusual

Headdress: (a) The 'fontange' headdress has a tall, flat front of starched and pleated white lawn, ornamented with bows and loops of peony-red ribbon. The cap and shoulder-long lappets attached to it are of white lawn. (b) The black tricorne hat is carried in the left hand. (c) A 'pompon' of small flowers is set forward on the top of the head. (d) The youth wears a cocked hat of natural-coloured straw, with a yellow flower set in front of the crown. A black ribbon ties the hair at the back of the neck. (e) The hat is of 'burnt' straw and is worn at an angle, with the brim curved upward. It is decorated on the left side with flowers. (f) The cocked military hat is of black felt or fabric, with an edging of gold lace.

Garments: (a) The under-dress is of peony-red satin, ornamented with ruched gilt ribbon, edged with galon, and with motifs of gold tissue and fringes of gold thread. The over-gown, open from the waist, is of brocade in gold, red and orange. Its reverse side, shown where it is draped back over a bustle, is of orange satin. Satin of the same colour edges the décolletage, the gold tissue stomacher, and forms the turned-back cuffs of the elbow-length sleeves. Three-quarter-length sleeves of white lawn, banded and frilled, show below these. (b) The coat is of pinkish-buff cloth, worn open, ending above the knees and widely flared from the low waist-line. It has a low-cut neckline, above which the neckline of the brown-corded silk waistcoat can be seen. This is shorter than the coat and is fastened down the front with small buttons. The pockets and turned-back cuffs of the coat are ornamented with buttons and button-holes matching those on the coat. The neckcloth is of cream-coloured lawn, forming a jabot in front, and matches the frilled and banded sleeves of the shirt. The close-fitting breeches are of brown corded silk. The stockings of fawn-coloured silk are rolled over them. (c) The gown of rose-coloured and silver tissue has a fitted bodice with a stomacher filled in with rows of ruched ivory chiffon. Its wide circular skirt touches the ground and is worn over petticoats or a pyramidal hoop. The off-shoulder décolletage is low, and is edged

with chiffon frilling. The sleeves end in turned-back cuffs and frills of ivory chiffon. (d) The youth's suit is of copper-coloured satin, with a matching waistcoat. The coat is short, like the jackets worn by artisans and peasants, and has three-quarter-length sleeves ending in turned-back cuffs open at the seams. The cream-coloured lawn shirt has a flat, round collar and full sleeves banded and frilled at the ends. It is visible at the hips below the waistcoat. The knee-breeches end below the knees and are tied on the outside with ribbons matching the suit. Silk frills of the same colour are attached at the outer seams. The stockings are of fawn-coloured silk. (e) The dress follows a French fashion and has a close-fitting basqued jacket of green taffetas. The low décolletage shows the points of the shoulders and is edged with narrow frilling. A 'ruff' of starched and pleated white muslin stands up at the back from shoulder to shoulder. The sleeves are long and close-fitting, with chiffon frills at the wrists. The full, circular skirt is of yellow taffetas, worn over a pyramidal hoop, and shows the shoes. (f) The military coat is of scarlet cloth ornamented with gold braid. The front flaps are fastened back on each side, showing a biscuit-coloured lining. The back vent is decorated with gold braid.

Footwear: (b) The shoes of fawn-coloured reversed calf have high heels and long vamps, with 'heart-shaped' tongues and gilt buckles. (d) The buckled, low-heeled shoes are of light-brown leather. (e) The shoes are of green fabric, with 'heart-shaped' tongues, silver buckles and moderate 'Louis' heels. (f) The thigh-boots of black leather have large 'bucket' tops and flat heels. Spurs and spur-leathers are attached.

Accessories: (a) A folding fan is carried in the right hand. (b) The man carries a cane in his left hand. (c) A folding fan is held in the left hand. (d) The youth carries a battledore and shuttlecock. (e) The girl carries flowers in her white muslin apron. (f) The officer wears a baldrick with sheathed sword attached. His gauntlet gloves are of white buckskin.

XIII.2. 18th Century. Women. Two Figures

Hair: (a) (1750.) The small powdered wig, with two horizontal curls at each side above the ears, is tied back and has a small curled queue (unseen). (b) (1740s.) The hair is parted in the centre and drawn into a flat chignon (unseen) at the back of the head.

Headdress: (a) The queue is tied with a black ribbon and the black tricorne hat, for riding, is edged with gold braid and tipped forward over the brow. (b) A pinner of ivory or écru lace is worn on the top of the head.

Garments: (a) The riding-habit is of scarlet cloth, ornamented with gold braid. It is worn over an oval hoop. The body of the coat fits closely to the figure and is fastened in front by buttons and gilt cord. It has a deep basque covering the top of the skirt. The sleeves are like those of a man's coat, with shirt-ruffles showing. There is a small standing collar with narrow lapels. A black bow is worn in the front of the neck, and a little of the frilled shirt-front is visible. (b) The 'sack' dress is of pale orange watered silk, worn over a fan-shaped hoop. The petticoat is of pale yellow satin, trimmed with écru lace. The bodice of the gown is open to the waist, showing a stomacher with a bow of yellow satin at the top, and rows of écru lace below this. The sleeves are made in one with the dress and have frills of écru lace.

Footwear: (b) Yellow satin mules are worn.

Accessories: (a) A riding-crop is carried. (b) A fan is held in the left hand.

except among the elderly and for Court dress. By the end of the century it was out of fashion.

Hats: The tricorne, or three-cornered cocked hat, was worn by all townsmen and gentry for the greater part of the century, varying in shape and size from time to time. Countrymen, more conservative citizens and elderly men wore a round, pliable felt or beaver hat with flat or turned-up brim. It became fashionable wear in the 1780s and '90s. Apprentices still wore flat round caps, various woollen hats were worn by street-boys and traders, and scholars and learned men wore square or round black caps or mortar-boards. In 1745 the kevenhuller, a cocked hat with a wide turn-up back and front, with the front point marked only by an outward curve and a cockade at the left centre, became the mode for 'young bloods'.

Turbans or embroidered caps were worn by men *en négligé* without their wigs.

A hat with a tall, flat-topped, diminishing crown and a moderately wide, flexible brim was worn in the 1780s and '90s. Another version of this had a lower crown and a narrower brim turned up at the sides and down at the front and back, and a band with a buckle in front.

A development of the cocked hat which took the place of the tricorne in the final decade of the century was the bicorne or chapeau-bras, a flat, crescent-shaped hat easy to carry under the arm with its front and back pressed together. Fashionable in England, this hat was favoured by French Revolutionary leaders and partisans, who also wore the tall hat, and the round beaver or felt, usually with the brim turned up in front and bearing the tricolour cockade. The 'sans-culottes', or male members of the mob in the French Revolution, wore a scarlet Phrygian cap, adorned like the others with the tricolour.

Hair, Wigs, Caps and Ornaments for the Hair—Women: It is difficult to tell from portraits in this era of wigs and powder when a woman is wearing a complete wig and when her coiffure is of natural hair or has false hair and padding mingled with it. It seems best therefore in the case of women to consider hair and wigs together and to include caps and ornaments, since these were adjusted so often to fashions in hairdressing that it is not easy to describe them separately.

At the opening of the century the hairdressing of the end of the 17th century was still in vogue. By 1715 the front of the fontange had dwindled to a curved upstanding frill or, alternatively, an ornament of wired ribbon loops tipped forward over the forehead, with a small, perched cap and streamers.

By this time a smaller coiffure had been evolved, the hair being drawn back into it in front and swept up at the back to the top of the head, where the flat, round cap called a 'pinner' rested. Quite frequently the small headdress was no more than a knot of ribbon, flowers and lace, known as a 'pompon'. Streamers with both were optional. The pompon survived in various forms until the 1770s, the pinner into the '80s. Hair was normally brushed off the ears at this time, though occasionally two or three small horizontal rolled curls, at the back, or a short ringlet at either side of the face, provided a slightly different dressing. By 1720 the 'round-eared' cap was in evidence. It fitted the crown of the head, where it was tied back with a draw-string, and in its early form had side-lappets which could be fastened up on the top of the head. A bonnet-shaped cap, fitting over the back of the head, with side-lappets which could be tied under the chin, had been evolved by 1720 and lasted into the '50s with some modifications.

The first mob-cap, in the opening years of the century, was probably an informal version of the fontange, with a commodious back into which the undressed hair could be bundled. With the development of the small coiffure the mob-cap became a shallow, perched head-dress owing something to the pinner. In the '30s a larger and more widely-frilled version appeared: The '40s produced a shallower type again. In the '50s it was still perched, with a close relationship to the round-eared cap. In the '60s and '70s a fusion of the mob and the bonnet-shaped caps created the 'dormeuse' cap in its many variations, suited to the larger, more rounded coiffure of the early '60s and the taller, more elongated line of the late '60s and the '70s. The basic types of cap given here were subject to some divagations in the course of the period.

The use of powder and pomatum was at its peak and during the twenty years of very eccentric coiffure the hair, inextricably mixed with false hair and padding, of the 'Macaroni' ladies was often not undone to be washed and brushed for weeks at a time. In the early 1780s the line of the coiffure grew wider, though less high, and very large mob caps were worn.

The decade that included the French Revolution saw the end of thickly powdered hair, except to some extent in Court dress, and a fashion of dressing the natural hair in ringlets, bound with a snood of ribbon, or with caps and turbans that allowed curls to show round the face and on the shoulders, established itself in England and France. A certain amount of powder was used for a time, but this was discarded before the end of the century. For formal occasions tall ostrich feathers were worn and caps were ornate. Height was still important to the general effect and a large version of the mob-cap, sometimes with a very tall crown, became a feature of the mode. Hair was cut in 'hedgehog' or 'poodle' fashion or dressed in a mass of curls, often with one or more queues descending to the shoulder. Much shorter hair was fashionable in the closing years of the century, so that only a few curls showed beneath the turban or cap.

XIII.3. 18th Century. Six Figures

Hair: (a) (Coachman, 1760s.) The coachman has his natural hair brushed back from the forehead, with a small roll of hair pinned above each ear and with the queue tied at the back of the neck. (b) (Inn-servant or man-servant in working clothes, 1780s.) The hair of the inn-servant is dressed in the same way as that of (a). (c) (Farm labourer, mid-century.) The farm labourer's hair is of 'bobbed' length, un-curled. (d) (Fish-seller, 1711.) The fringe over the forehead is the only part of the hair to be seen. (e) (Maid-servant or working girl, 1738.) The hair is

parted in the centre and puffed out a little at the sides. The remainder of the hair is put up under the cap. (f) (Citizen's wife, 1735.) The hair is arranged in the same way as that of (e).

Headdress: (a) The tricorne of black felt is set towards the back of the head, with its blunt central peak pointing upwards. (c) The farm labourer wears a round hat of brown felt, with a flexible brim. (d) The fish-seller has a wide-brimmed, flat-crowned hat of black felt. (e) The cap of white muslin, a blend

Hats and Hoods—Women: Hats were not worn in the first years of the century as they could not be put on over the fontange, which served for headdress indoors and out. Hoods, tall enough to go over it, were worn attached to cloaks for travelling if necessary, but were not a usual form of headgear. Shoulder shawls, veils and lace mantillas might also be wrapped over the head when needed.

With the closer coiffure small, sideways tilted hats with upturned brims, often in the form of tricornes, were followed in the 30s by wide-brimmed hats, usually of straw simply trimmed with ribbon, tied on under the chin over a small under-cap. These remained in fashion, with some modifications, until the tall headdress of the 1770s altered their shape so that they were tipped forward on the head, turned up at the back and more lavishly trimmed. In the later '70s and greater part of the '80s hats were perched high on the already high coiffure and became very elaborate. They were of a toque or turban shape, or had curved brims, turned upward or tipped forward, and were made of all suitable materials, straw, felt, beaver, velvet, silk, satin, or stiffened muslin and lawn. Feathers, flowers, fruit, bunched ribbons, strings of beads, tassels and scarves were used as trimming. With the wider coiffure of the late '80s hats increased their width and although the turban or toque shape still appeared, more hats with large brims worn level on the head appeared. Picture hats adorned with plumes, tilted to one side and well raised on the coiffure, at the end of the '80s and the first half of the '90s, provided the most attractive headdress of the period. The simple, wide-brimmed straw hat now came into fashion again. Hats with tall, diminishing crowns and the brim dipping a little at the back and front, were often worn with the 'riding' dress which was adopted for ordinary wear. A lower-crowned, flat-topped version of this was also worn. Bonnets and turbans were the most usual wear with the high-waisted dresses from about 1794 to the end of the century.

Round, frilled hoods attached to cloaks of the 'Red Riding Hood' type were worn practically throughout the epoch when protection from the weather was needed. A detached hood with a small shoulder-piece not extending much beyond the collar-bones, could be worn as a casual head-covering until the 1760s or thereabouts. It had gathers meeting in the centre of the back of the head to provide a neat shape. When the coiffure grew too large for this in the 1770s it was replaced in fashionable circles by the calash, a hood with collapsible hinged segments like those of the hood of a carriage.

of 'mob' and 'round-eared' styles, is set high on the head and has a narrow black ribbon round it. (f) A 'round-eared' cap of white muslin that fits the back of the head and frames the face is worn under a black silk hood with a shoulder-cape, fastened under the chin.

Garments: (a) The coachman's coat of fawn-coloured cloth hangs open, showing the long waistcoat of claret-coloured cloth. The close-fitting breeches are of biscuit-coloured fabric. (b) The inn-servant wears a sleeveless waistcoat, striped in white and red, over a neck-cloth and shirt of white cotton. The knee-breeches are of brown cloth and the stockings of grey cotton. A white apron is worn. (c) The smock is of natural linen and covers the shirt, waistcoat and breeches. It has the stitching known as smocking in three rows on the back and sleeves, continued (unseen) in front. The stockings are of thick grey-brown yarn. (d) The fish-seller wears a laced corset bodice of black velvet over her white shift, which has the sleeves rolled up to the elbows. Shoulder knots of chestnut-brown ribbon are worn. Her skirt is striped in chestnut brown and yellow, with a white apron tied over it. Her stockings are of grey cotton. (e) The girl's corset-bodice is laced over the white cotton shift with rolled-up sleeves. A fichu of white muslin is tucked into the top of the brown fabric bodice in front. The skirt is of cotton print in green and white and the stockings of white cotton. A white apron is tied on at the waist. (f) The dress of the citizen's wife is of grey cotton patterned in bright blue. The narrow fichu of white lawn is attached down the sides of the bodice-opening and fastens with it. The sleeves are turned back at the elbows, showing the puffed and frilled three-quarter-length sleeves of the shift. A white apron is worn.

Footwear: (a) The boots of black leather have tan leather tops and webbing loops at the side for pulling them on. (b) The shoes of black leather have steel buckles and flat heels. (c) The shoes are of brown leather, with metal buckles. (d) The shoes are of light brown reversed calf, with shaped heels (unseen) and squared toes. They are tied across the insteps with brown ribbons. (e) The shoes of black leather have moderately high heels and steel buckles. (f) The shoes are of black leather.

Accessories: (a) The coachman carries a whip. (b) The inn-servant carries a small circular tray in his left hand and a cleaning cloth or napkin in his right. (c) The farm labourer carries a hay fork. (d) The fish-seller has a flat basket of fish balanced on the head and a pewter tankard for measuring out shrimps or mussels, in her hand. (e) The girl carries a wooden bucket, banded with metal. (f) The citizen's wife has a bunch of keys attached by a cord at her waist.

XIII.4. 18th Century. Men. Six Figures

Hair: (a) (Sedan-chair man, 1760.) The hair covers the ears, but is longer at the back, where it is tied back. (b) (Watchman, mid-century.) The 'bobbed', straight hair is left to hang down at the sides. (c) (1760.) The boy's hair ends just above the collar and is turned in a little at the ends. (d) (Hairdresser, 1760s–'70s.) The powdered wig, or blending of natural hair with false, is compact and neatly dressed with two small horizontal ringlets on each side, over the ears, and a queue at the back. (e) (1760s–'70s.) The hair is hidden under the night-

cap. (f) (Ballad-seller, 1770s–'80s.) The hair is long and lank and is left to straggle over the collar.

Headdress: (a) The tricorne hat of black felt comes to a point in front over the brow. (b) The watchman wears a wide-brimmed black felt hat with a shallow crown. (c) The black tricorne is of the 'Kevenhuller' type, with a fold in the upturned brim over the right temple. (d) A black silk bow ties the queue at the back of the neck. (e) The night-cap is of blue taffeta. Its soft crown and upturned, pliable brim can be

Garments—Men: At the opening of the century the coat with an almost equally long waist-coat was still worn with few modifications. A coat with a widely flared skirt appeared in the opening years of the 18th century. The slightly fitted waist was at normal level to begin with, but between 1710 and 1720 could be at hip level. The pockets were at first low at the sides with large flaps. There was no collar and no lapels but before 1720 the top edges of the coat could be turned back a little showing the lining. The neck-cloth, about a yard of linen or lawn, roughly twelve inches wide, sometimes with an edging of lace, took the place of the lace jabot early in the century. By 1715–20 the wide-skirted coat could be shorter and more closely fitted at the low or normal waist. Sleeves were long, with very large cuffs showing the wrist frill of the shirt. By 1715 the pockets were higher, about midway between the waist and the hem of the coat, and by 1730 were generally at about the level of the hips. The flaps were not so big, but the pockets themselves were large and deep. Early in the century also the slits in the sides of the coat were augmented by several pleats. Those on the left side admitted the sword. The flat pleats of the vent at the back remained as in the preceding century.

The waistcoat was slightly flared and varied in length with the caprices of fashion. In the early part of the century it had sleeves and could be worn indoors, and by servants, as an informal coat.

A plain, calf-length greatcoat, with a small upstanding neckband, and a cape extending to the points of the shoulder, or a round, flat collar was worn all through the century from these early years until the 1780s. It was slightly shaped to the figure and had flares in keeping with the width of the coat-skirts. It was usually unbelted, but a belt at hip-level is found in 1729. A semicircular riding cloak, with a collar fastened at the neck, was also in use for the greater part of the century.

An easily fitting coat, with a flat, round collar, known as the frock, was adapted from a working man's garment for general informal wear about 1730 and remained in use for the remainder of the century.

The close-fitting knee-breeches could be covered at the knees by the stockings, rolled and gartered. By 1725 the tendency was to fasten the breeches over the stockings, though the fashion for rolled stockings did not quite die out until the 1740s.

The Macaroni Club, whose members were exquisites devoted to the last word in fashion, was formed in 1730.

During the 1730s the fashion arose of leaving the waistcoat unbuttoned at the top to show the embroidered or lace-edged frill of the shirt, which the smaller cravat of the '40s also helped to display.

---

arranged in various ways. (f) The black tricorne hat of black felt has a well-defined point in front. The back is tilted up in a straight line across the back of the head.

Garments: (a) The open coat worn by the sedan-chair man is of brick-red cloth, with a buff-coloured waistcoat. The frilled shirt-sleeves and neck-cloth are white cotton. The stockings are of grey cotton. The breeches are unseen beneath the coat and long waistcoat. (b) The watchman wears a long belted coat of snuff-brown frieze or other woollen stuff. It has a deep shoulder-cape and ends above the ankles. (c) The boy wears the coat known as a 'frock', of maroon cloth. The round collar is turned down and the sleeves fit fairly closely and have no added cuffs. The waistcoat is of lavender-grey ribbed silk, and the knee-breeches of pale grey cloth. The silk stockings are pale grey. The white lawn shirt has a flat, turned-down collar of the type often worn by boys in this century. The shirt frill and wrist frills are visible. (d) The hairdresser wears a sleeved waist-coat of taffeta, striped in green and white. His shirt frill, neck-cloth and wrist frills are of white lawn. The knee-breeches are of black velvet and the stockings of grey silk. A white apron is tied on at the waist. (e) The man's dressing-gown is of royal blue satin, patterned in gold. It wraps across the body and has a collar and revers of black satin. (f) The ballad-seller wears a shabby coat of dark bottle-green cloth, with the turned-down collar in vogue in the 1770s. His fawn-coloured breeches are almost covered by his coat. The stockings are of brown cotton.

Footwear: (a) The shoes are of black leather with steel buckles. (b) The stout boots, wrinkled over the ankles, are of black leather. (c) The black leather shoes have silver buckles. (d) The black leather shoes have short tongues and silver buckles. (e) The slippers are of red leather. (f) The black leather shoes have small metal buckles.

Accessories: (a) The chair-man has the shafts of his sedan-chair hung from the back of his neck by a black leather strap and grasped in his hands. (b) The watchman carries a staff and lantern. (c) The boy is playing a recorder. (d) The hairdresser holds a hairbrush with a narrow curving ivory back and handle. (f) The ballad-seller has a sheaf of song-sheets under his left arm and one in his hand.

XIII.5. 18th Century. Six Figures

Hair: (About 1795.) The hair of the 'Incroyable' (a figure of the French Revolution) is long, straight and unkempt, straggling on to the shoulders. (b) (About 1795.) The hair of the 'Merveilleuse' (the feminine counterpart of (a)) is untidy and left to hang as it will, with a ragged fringe over the forehead. (c) (1785.) The man in the tricorne hat has his powdered wig arranged in a horizontal roll round the back of the head, with the queue tied at shoulder level by a black ribbon. (d) (1740.) The seaman's hair covers his ears and hangs loosely at the sides. (e) (Mid-century.) The infantryman's hair is powdered and is curled at the sides above his ears, partly covering them. (f) (1750s.) The naval officer's powdered hair or wig is taken back from the forehead in a roll, with a 'widow's peak' in the centre, and the queue tied back with a black ribbon.

There was little change in the cut of men's coats and breeches between 1725 and 1745, but by 1750 the waistcoat was shorter, displaying a good deal of the breeches. Cuffs were still large but less wide.

In the 1750s and 1760s the skirts of the coat were less widely flared and the back was narrower. Waistcoats ended in deep points in front and varied in length. Coats, breeches and waistcoats were now often made of the same embroidered or brocaded stuff. During this decade examples of the turned-over collar were seen. This collar was general by 1770. By this date the skirts of coats were much narrower, sloping away from a chest-fastening to narrow coat-tails. The waistcoat, ending at the hips, followed the line of the coat.

A sleeve without a cuff but ornamented with buttons and sometimes braid, or a small cuff, came into fashion. The frilled wrist of the shirt still showed. A stand-up, turned-over collar to the coat was a novelty foreshadowing change.

In the 1770s the dress of the extravagant 'Macaronis' reached its highest point of eccentricity. While men of conservative tastes wore coats of quieter colour and ever narrower fit, with tails approaching the cut-away shape, the Macaronis, following similar styles, made them startling with exaggeration of cut, with a wealth of embroidery on gaily coloured silk, and with buttons and shoe-buckles set with jewels or paste. A vogue for short, flared coats or for cut-away coat-tails suddenly abbreviated half-way down the back of the thighs had some popularity.

Headdress: (a) The man wears a chapeau-bras of black fabric with a red, white and blue cockade on the left side of the front. (b) The woman wears a black velvet bonnet with a rounded crown trimmed with a blue ribbon and a large protruding oval brim. (c) The tricorne has a wide brim turned up all round, with the front point sloping forward and the other two corners formed into a straight line across the back of the head. It is of black felt, edged with gold braid. (d) The seaman has a black tricorne hat with the brim turned up all round and edged with gold braid. (e) The infantryman's uniform hat has a tall front of blue fabric, with a white border at the sides and an ornament at the top. The arms of his regiment appear in red, gold and white on the blue ground. (f) The naval officer's black tricorne hat, held in the right hand, with a turned-up brim, is edged with gold braid and has a black silk cockade on the left side of the front.

Garments: (a) The redingote type of coat, with a flared skirt, is of blue cloth with collar and cuffs of black velvet. The broad lapels are faced with parchment-coloured satin patterned with small red flowers. The sleeves are close-fitting and show wrist-frills. The cross-over waistcoat is striped in two shades of maroon. The parchment-coloured breeches are close-fitting, ending below the knees and fastened by buttons and by ribbon ties on the outside of the legs. The shirt is of cream-coloured lawn, striped in red, matching the stockings. (b) The woman wears a high-waisted gown of pale blue muslin. The décolletage is low and edged with a narrow frill. A broader frill edges the skirt, which is held up in front over the arms. The sleeves are very short, with unfrilled edges. The stole is of wine-coloured net with a border of black stripes and black fringe. The stockings are white. (c) The coat is of lilac-grey cloth. It has a turned-over collar and narrowly cut skirts with a back seam flanked by two darts which end in pleats, with silver buttons at the top. The coat-tails are square-cut at the hem. The sleeves are close-fitting, with cuffs of their own material, showing wrist-frills. The knee-breeches match the coat and have three buttons on the outside of the knees. The stockings are of grey silk. (d) The seaman wears an open, collarless jacket of bottle-green cloth with fawn-coloured cuffs. His shirt and kilt are of discoloured white cotton stuff. He wears a red neck-cloth and a red leather belt. His stockings are of grey yarn. (e) The infantryman has a scarlet coat, the skirts turned back to show a light biscuit-coloured lining. The waistcoat and close-fitting breeches match the coat lining. The scarlet epaulettes are ornamented with strips of white braid. This is also used in vertical strips down the sides of the chest, with gilt buttons sewn on where horizontal strips of the braid cross the chest. The cuffs are of blue cloth, bordered with white round the edges and along the seam, which is ornamented with gilt buttons. A white pipe-clayed belt, with a stout metal buckle, is round the waist. Two similar belts are crossed over on the chest and back. The white cloth gaiters are fastened down the outside with gilt buttons. A brown leather strap is fastened round the leg below the knee. (f) The naval officer's coat is of dark blue cloth faced with cream-coloured satin and gold braid, with gold braid to define the collar. The sleeves widen a little towards the cuffs, where the frilled and banded sleeves of the white lawn shirt can be seen. The large turned-back cuffs match the coat facings and the flap pockets are edged with gold braid. The coat has a moderate flare and ends just below the knees. The waistcoat is of cream-coloured grosgrain edged down the front and on the pockets with gold galon. The breeches are of white satin and stockings of white silk.

Footwear: (a) The short boots of black leather have wide tops but fit more closely round the ankles. (b) The black fabric slippers have flat soles. (c) The shoes are of black leather, with flat heels and silver buckles. (d) The shoes are of black leather with large tongues and steel buckles. (e) The boots are of black leather. (f) The silver-buckled shoes have flat soles.

Accessories: (a) The man carries a short cane. (c) The man carries a silver-knobbed cane. (d) The seaman carries a cutlass. (e) The infantryman carries a rifle and has black leather ammunition pouches attached at both hips to the pipe-clayed belts that cross his chest. (f) The naval officer wears a cutlass in its scabbard attached to a sword-belt beneath the waistcoat.

By 1780 this ostentation in men's dress had had its day and a trend towards simpler and more sober male fashion was established. The dress of the English country gentleman, which had run concurrently with more elaborate styles, was adopted in London and Paris except where more formal dress was obligatory. Fine cloth was now just as important as satin, taffetas, brocade or velvet had been in the past, though velvet coats and breeches retained their hold on masculine fashion. Discreet embroidery decorated waistcoats only and a plain neck-cloth was the rule.

a   *b*   *c*

XIII.6. 1750–70. Women's Headdress

Hair: (a) (1760s.) The front hair is taken back from the forehead over a moderate sized semicircular roll that brings it forward a little at the sides. A ringlet hangs down from behind the left ear and another lies on the shoulder. (c) (1750s.) The hair is taken back from the brow and upwards, showing the ears, from the sides and back, to a small flat chignon (unseen) on the top of the head.

Headdress: (a) The hat of loosely-woven natural straw has a curving brim of moderate width turned back from the face. The crown is not large and has a curved depression at the top. Black satin ribbons from beneath the brim are loosely tied under the chin. (b) (1760s.) The back of a grey silk 'calash' is shown. It has a framework of cane in horse-shoe-shaped hoops, making it possible to fold the head-dress flat. The back is gathered in the centre into a

small black satin bow. There is a narrow frill round the base, fastened in front under the chin with black satin ribbons (unseen). The calash was made taller and wider when the coiffure was larger. (c) The small hat of 'burnt' straw has a flat crown and a narrow, rolled brim. It is perched high on the head and has a yellow carnation on the left side.

Garments: (a) The top of the bodice and sleeves of the satin gown in cerulaean blue is seen. A white muslin fichu is tucked into the top of the bodice. (b) The edge of a folded white fichu can be seen at the back of the neck. Over it is a frilled stole in black net. (c) The dress of apple-green taffeta has a square décolletage edged with ruching of its own material, with a green ribbon bow in the centre. A soft fold of écru chiffon is tucked into the top of the bodice on each side.

The stand-up collar without turn-over was an innovation of the late '80s, worn without revers, but the turn-over collar, now more upstanding at the back of the neck, had revers added to it. The skirts of coats were cut away from the waist in a style very like that of a morning coat today, except that some were double-breasted and rather negligently fastened by one or more buttons at or above the waist. Waistcoats ended at the waist or just below it, without points, and fobs depended from them. The plain cravat was varied by one tying in front in a knot or bow with the ends left loose, and was now often made of muslin. Sleeves were narrow and plain, or had moderate cuffs, showing only a little of the shirt-frill. By the '80s the greatcoat was shaped to the figure and often had a shoulder-cape in one to three layers. A development of this was very voluminous, fitted loosely and had straps and buckles inside to regulate its width. It was known as the 'Garrick' overcoat.

In the 1790s large revers came into fashion and lasted, with the high-turn-over collar, well into the following century. For a time the waistcoat also had revers, worn outside the

XIII.7. 1760–70. Three-quarter-length Figures

Hair: (a) The hair is closely drawn back into the cap. (b) The powdered wig is dressed in a pompadour with ringlets descending at the back and sides of the head and set vertically in front.

Headdress: (a) A close-fitting 'round-eared' cap of white muslin is worn under a 'bergère' hat of natural straw, with the brim tilted up at the back. A lavender blue ribbon arranged in small zig-zags encircles the shallow crown and is tied at the back in a bow. Strings of lavender blue ribbon from beneath the brim are tied at the back of the head. (b) A cap made up of loops of white silk organza falls in a festoon down the back of the head from two loops placed upright above the ringlets on the top. Short streamers of silver ribbon finish it at the back.

Garments: (a) The gown of greyish rose-pink, patterned with lavender-blue flowers with stems and leaves of grey-green, has a square décolletage with a wide collar of cream-coloured lace-edged chiffon, fastening in front and extending over the shoulders. The short sleeves, made in one with the bodice, end in a lace band above the elbow and have deep frills

of cream-coloured chiffon and lace. Bands of the lace are appliqués vertically on the front of the bodice. A train in the same stuff as the gown is attached at the back of the shoulders and forms part of the back breadth of the bodice and skirt. (b) The gown of black velvet has borders to the stomacher, the décolletage and the skirt-opening of dull silver ruched ribbon. The under-skirt is of white satin, which is also used to fill interstices in the bodice-trimming. A train of black velvet is attached at the back of the shoulders. The short sleeves are attached to lower sleeves of white silk organza which end at the elbows in wide oval cuffs. Two double sets of pleated and stiffened white satin are tied in the middle by silver ribbon on the upper arms. A black velvet ribbon round the neck forms the top of an inverted ruff of pleated white organza with two streamers in front.

Jewellery and Accessories: (a) The gloves are of white silk and fan of pink silk on ivory with a painted design in blue and gold. (b) Large silver drop earrings are worn. The gloves are of white kid or silk.

a   b

XIII.8. 1780s. Headdress

Hair: (a) The powdered wig has an exaggeratedly high pompadour. Large horizontal ringlets are set one below the other down the back of the head, with one descending on to the shoulder. (b) The powdered wig is dressed in much the same fashion as that of (a) but the pompadour is less high and a thick loop of hair hangs over the back of the neck.

Headdress: (a) A tricorne hat of 'burnt' straw, with a deep turn-up all round the brim, is perched above the pompadour. Loops and streamers of copper-coloured satin ribbon overhang the edge of the brim and some are formed into a bow on the right front. Six plumes of light brown, copper, yellow and cream-colour are set above the crown, also three posies of cream-coloured and orange flowers.

(b) The turban of gold tissue is set high on the wig. It has four plumes in blue, purple, pink and white attached at the top. Festoons of large pearl beads, with ornaments of mother-of-pearl and amethyst hang at the front and back. A string of gold beads is attached on the left side, ending in a bow of gold silk gauze, with a pink edging, and a mother-of-pearl and amethyst ornament in the centre.

Garments: (a) The top of the gown of pale orange satin has rows of frilled and ruched écru net across the bosom and on the small shoulder-cape. (b) The off-shoulder gown is of pale blue silk, the bosom edged with écru frilling which is repeated in the short sleeves starting at the upper arm. Small pink silk flowers form the shoulder-straps.

lapels of the coat. The front of the double-breasted coat was fastened with its three buttons and lost its former pulled-together look. Single-breasted coats with tails cut square at the bottom and ending just above or below the level of the knees, were also worn. Sleeves became tight-fitting, with small cuffs. A short-waisted, close-fitting jacket, called a spencer, was sometimes worn over the coat from about 1795.

The fashion for elegant though countrified dress persisted and grew more general. It was not affected in England by the eccentric dress of some extreme French Revolutionary partisans. These wore coat-tails that nearly touched the ground and the coat-collar and revers were enormous, with a wide cravat wound so high that it sometimes covered the chin. Their stockings or pantaloons were often garishly striped. Men of the French street mobs wore open shirts, loose 'slops' or trousers and sleeveless unfastened jackets.

XIII.9. 1780s. Women's Headdress

Hair: (a) The lightly powdered wig or real hair mingled with false, is dressed in a pompadour in front, with ringlets framing the face and festooned down the back and sides of the head and neck, the longest descending to the shoulder-blades. (b) The wig or mixture of real and false hair is puffed out and then rolled inward at the back of the head. Thick tresses, pomaded and slightly curled at the ends, hang down at the back to touch the shoulders.

Headdress: (a) The large black velvet hat is worn at an angle. The wide brim curves up on the right and down on the left. The crown is fairly tall, diminishing towards the flat top. Curled plumes of grey and white curve over the crown. (b) The hat of sherry-coloured velvet has a flat, circular brim and a large soft 'mushroom' crown, sewn into a band. A velvet bow is attached to the left side towards the back. Curling plumes in brownish pink are set in the centre of the crown.

Garments: (a) The 'riding' dress is of sapphire blue velvet. It has a long-waisted bodice with a rounded waist-line. The long, close-fitting sleeves are slightly raised at the shoulders. the standing collar is turned over and has wide lapels. Second lapels of grey satin striped in blue, as though belonging to a waistcoat, are turned back over them. The top of the skirt has fullness at the back. (b) The sherry-coloured velvet dress is hidden by the pelisse except for part of one sleeve and a fold of the skirt held up in the hands. The loose-fitting, three-quarter-length pelisse is of brownish-pink velvet, lined with gold satin. The hood collar and open front are edged with light-coloured fur. The short, wide sleeves are made in one with the garment and bordered with the same fur.

Pantaloons were generally in fashion by the mid-'90s, made in plain colours or stripes, and ended at calf or ankle. Stockings were often white or striped and always in pale colours.

Garments—Women: The costume of the late 17th century was superseded about 1710 by the prettier and more romantic dress of the early Rococo Period. In its first manifestations the hoop was pyramidal, widening very much towards the hem, but was soon rivalled by the bell-shaped hoop. Both touched the ground in most instances, but some skirts were made short enough to show the ankles or the shoes.

Bodices were closely fitted and rather long-waisted; their necklines were wide and décolleté, or had long revers and open fronts, filled in with the stomachers that had typified the preceding fashion. The oval neckline was left plain or was edged with ruching or frilling. The stomachers could be plain, laced, frilled, ruched or trimmed with diminishing ribbon bows.

Most sleeves ended at the elbows or just below them, in turned-back cuffs. Part of the banded and frilled chemise sleeve showed below them. Another fashion was for a short puffed sleeve ending above the elbow, with two or more puffs below it, the lowest being of white gauze or muslin, with a frilled edge. Some examples of the 18th-century plain sleeve ending at the elbow without a turn-back, but with a frill, were seen in the 1720s and were general from the '40s to the early '70s.

Many sleeves in the 1720s were long and close-fitting, particularly in France. This mode reappeared in French fashions in the '30s, '40s and '50s, and became general in the late '80s and '90s.

XIII.10. 1780s. Women's Headdress

Hair: (a) The unpowdered hair is cut short at the sides and frizzed out in a haphazard, partly curled mass which covers the head but is partly hidden by the hat. A lock knotted at the top hangs from behind the ear to the left shoulder and another, knotted at the bottom, on to the right. (b) The hair is seen only in a lock curled foward on the left cheek and the rolled ends of the hair hanging down at the back and lying on the shoulders.

Headdress: (a) The large, mushroom-crowned hat of white muslin has a 'lampshade' frill round the brim. Broad ribbon of silk gauze in turquoise blue with narrow stripes of scarlet and gold forms a band for the hat and is tied in a bow in front. (b) The hat of dark brown-purple velvet lined in yellow has a tall, flat-topped crown and a wide, drooping brim with the greater part of its width at the back. Yellow satin ribbon, with a bunch of loops in the front, is tied round the base of the crown. A length of it passes across and under the brim on either side, is fastened where it touches the inside of the crown and is left to hang in strings for tying under the chin.

Garments: (a) Part of the sleeves and bodice of the gown of turquoise-blue muslin, with narrow scarlet and gold stripes, can be seen. The white lawn fichu crosses over to tie at the back. Two smaller folds of white lawn are crossed to fill in the décolletage and an upright starched frill is worn inside them. (b) The gown is of velvet, matching the hat and has a narrow sash of yellow ribbon tied at the back of the waist. A fichu of yellow silk muslin is draped across the front of the bodice from one shoulder to the other with a similar fold lying more loosely across the back, giving the effect of a cape. The top of the long, close-fitting sleeves can be seen.

By about 1740 the oval hoop, wide at the sides and flattened at the back and front, had come into fashion and lasted through the '50s and '60s. An extremely wide-hipped version of this was worn in the '40s, '50s and early '60s.

In the '40s and '50s the fan-shaped hoop was popular. It was developed from the early pyramidal hoop and increased in width from the waist to a very wide hem. Because of its shape it was inclined to tilt as the wearer moved.

Hoops were made at first of cane or whalebone joined by ribbons, but by 1730 were covered in canvas, holland or other stout material, and occasionally by more expensive stuff such as silk damask. They were tied on round the waist by draw-strings. Oval hoops had hinges at the sides to facilitate the use of staircases and doorways.

Skirts in general touched the ground from 1720 to the 1760s, but in almost every phase of this epoch a dress was in vogue that cleared the ground, in some cases showing the ankles. 'Closed' dresses were frequently seen. With the 'open' dress the overskirt was divided down the centre to show the petticoat and was often looped up on panniers.

The sacque dress, in fashion soon after 1720, was worn originally as a négligée, but was soon adopted for general wear. It hung loosely in front at first and in loose flat pleats at the back, becoming part of the skirt of the over-dress. Part of a separate, hooped under-dress was revealed when the sacque was open from the breast down or from the top to a point below the waist. The bodice of the sacque could be made fitted to the figure by 1740, with the flat box pleats at the back attached to it from the shoulders. In the modifications of the hoop in the '60s and '70s the back of the sacque was often formed into a short train.

By 1730 the fichu was worn, tucked into the top of the bodice and sometimes folded over. In the '40s and '50s it could be fastened by a band or ties of ribbon attached to the front of the bodice over the bosom, the ends being allowed to hang down. The fashion for revers meeting at the waist lasted into the '50s. Bodices wrapping over in front were worn from the 1720s to the '50s. The square neckline was in fashion by the 1750s, worn with a closed or open bodice, the latter being filled in with lacing or a stomacher. In the '80s a 'pouter pigeon' effect was produced by a bouffant arrangement of the fichu. In this decade and in the '90s fichus were frequently crossed over on the bosom, and sometimes tied at the back of the waist.

In the late 1770s the hoop grew narrower and the whole line of the dress more elongated. The under-dress just cleared the ground, while the over-dress, with fullness chiefly at the back over a sort of bustle, formed a short train in many instances. In others an under-skirt with the hoop fairly full at the sides and protruding considerably at the back showed the tops of the shoes, and the open skirt of the over-dress was bunched up over it. This mode was also adopted with a more sloping and graceful hip-line to the hoop and a return to the sack-back fashion, with the skirt covering the tops of the shoes. In the 1780s the hoop was hardly worn except in Court dress, and thick, shaped pads, tied on at sides and back, distended the skirts in the required directions. At all times during the years in which hoops were worn many women dispensed with them and wore petticoats for practical purposes.

In the '80s a picturesque dress, with a puffed-out fichu surrounding the low décolletage, a long, tightly corseted waist, flowing, rounded skirts with fullness towards the back and long-close-fitting sleeves, was evolved. These dresses often opened at the waist to show the underskirt and many had a sash or belt. In some the opening began where the fichu met in the centre of the bosom and was stitched or fastened down to the waist in order not to spoil the closely fitting line of the bodice. Alternatively, the bodice of this dress was often a jacket with a basque which protruded over the back fullness of the skirt.

The attractive riding dress of the day, which had lapels and often caped shoulders, and fastened like a coat down the front, was adopted for ordinary wear, sometimes as a coat worn over a dress. This fashion was worn approximately from 1785 to 1795.

In the last five or six years of the epoch waists became very high and lost their corseted look. Skirts flowed to the ground and were still full, fichus still prevailed, but sleeves, though still long and close-fitting in some dresses, could also be slightly rucked and ending at the elbow or of three-quarter length. At the end of the century they could be formed of a small caped shape covering the edge of the shoulder, or be apparently sleeveless but with the shoulder just covered by the fichu or 'cape' collar. Long, elbow-length or three-quarter sleeves could have a moderate puff below the shoulder.

XIII.11. 1780s. Women's Headdress

Hair: (a) (1788.) The lightly powdered wig of thick curls stands out all round the head and has a curled roll at the base continuing from the sides round the back of the head. (b) The natural hair is arranged in short curled locks over the forehead, with loose ringlets lying on the shoulders.

Headdress: (a) The large-brimmed hat of black velvet is set on the back of the head. Four curled white plumes appear over the front of the brim and pale green satin ribbons droop over it and beneath it towards the back. (b) (1788.) The mob-cap of white muslin with a narrow edge of embroidery has a tall crown (unseen), and its unstarched frills hang over the forehead and at the sides and back in several tiers. The hat of natural straw has a tall diminishing crown with a flat top and a deep circular brim bound at the edge with coral satin. Large loops of coral-red silk gauze, with ends lying on the sides of the brim, decorate the front of the hat.

Garments: (a) The top of the sleeves of the pale green satin gown and the folded fichu of cream-coloured chiffon can be seen. (b) The gown is of black satin striped with coral. The frilled fichu is of cream-coloured organza and has a posy of coral-red and cream-coloured flowers pinned in the centre.

The outer wraps of the last thirty years of the century included the practical travelling cloak when needed and shaped mantelets with long, stole-like ends. A cape with arm-openings, called a pelisse, was in vogue with the transitional fashions between 1785 and 1895. Short, tight-fitting jackets called 'spencers', like men's similar jackets, were in vogue with the high-waisted dresses of the last four or five years of the epoch. Stockings were in most colours.

Footwear—Men: Men's shoes at the beginning of the 18th century kept the shape of those at the end of the 17th. The long, high vamp tapered to a slender squared-off toe and was tied with ribbons over the instep or fastened there with a small buckle or ornament. The heels were high or of moderate height and often coloured red. The tongues were high, and turned over at the top, hiding the fastening. Tongues grew broader, no longer being folded, and heels flat and wide in the 1720s. Vamps were high and large buckles worn. Tongues became gradually less conspicuous and by the '90s were not seen. Vamps were lower in the '60s and '70s.

By 1790 the buckle was very small or was not worn and the vamp low. In the final five or six years of the century men were wearing flat-soled black pumps as an alternative to boots. The men of the French street crowds in the Revolution wore wooden sabots or had bare feet. Riding boots ended below the knee. Top boots were only occasionally worn. Other late 18th or early 19th century boots are mentioned in Chapter XIV.

XIII.12. 1780s. Women's Headdress

Hair: (a) (1781.) The lightly powdered wig or hair is dressed in a pompadour (unseen) in front and swept up and back at the sides to the crown of the head, showing the ears. Horizontal ringlets are pinned low down at the back of the head. (b) (1794.) A short lock of the unpowdered hair comes forward on each temple. The hair at the sides of the head is puffed out a little and curled inward at the ends. A roll of hair is pinned into place on each side beneath this and continues round the back of the head. Two smooth tresses, probably knotted at the ends, hang down at the back of the neck. (c) (1795.) The hair is dressed in a tumble of curls across the top of the head and has a profusion of ringlets hanging down at the sides and back.

Headdress: (a) The beaver hat is tilted well forward, with the brim turned up at the back. It is trimmed with a garland of dark green artificial leaves and three curled plumes of a paler green are fastened at the back of the crown. (b) The hat of black velvet has a tall, diminishing crown and a narrow brim curving up at the sides and down at the back and front. A band of grey fabric with a silver buckle in front encircles the base of the crown. Two pale grey curled plumes are set upright behind the buckle. (c) The 'turban' is a band of white silk wound round the head, with its ends crossing in front above the forehead. Three brilliant red plumes are attached at the top with a gold and coral ornament.

Garments: (a) The riding jacket is of beaver-coloured cloth and the waistcoat of cream-coloured taffeta with silver buttons. The flat, round collar is of cream-coloured silk. (b) The riding dress is of vieux-rose faced-cloth. The waist-line is a little high, with a buckled belt of the same stuff as the dress. The long, rolled lapels cross over in front to a fastening at the waist. A scarf of pale grey chiffon is worn round the neck, with ends tucked inside the dress. (c) The high-waisted dress of white mousseline de soie has a wide belt of black velvet. The fichu is brought down in front to a low décolletage, where a posy of red flowers and green leaves is fastened. The puffed sleeves have long, close-fitting sleeves added to them.

Footwear—Women: Women's shoes at the beginning of the 18th century had the long vamps, slightly squared toes and ribbon ties or other fastening over the instep that were fashionable at the end of the 17th. A turned-over flap or tongue sometimes concealed a strap and buckle across the instep. Flat, made-up bows in the centre formed another trimming. Heels were shaped and could be high or only moderately raised. Clogs and pattens were worn to keep the feet out of the mud. Mules were a favourite form of footwear indoors, often trimmed along the top of the vamp with ruched ribbon or edging of some sort.

An unfolded tongue supported a buckle over the instep fairly early in the century and buckles became more usual, though bows and ties over the insteps continued into the '40s. Toes were pointed and heels low and shaped or of the high 'Louis' type. After 1750 toes could be more rounded, but were pointed again by the '70s. A fairly short vamp came into fashion, and heels were shaped but low. In the 1790s a fashion developed of binding the shoes on round the ankles and calves with criss-cross ribbons, but the simple shoes with small, low heels were generally worn with the high-waisted dresses that were now the mode until the last five or six years of the century brought in the vogue for flat slippers.

Materials, Colours and Ornament: Rich damasks and brocades, heavily patterned silks, taffetas, satin, velvet, quantities of lace and gold and silver galon characterized the dress of the first ten years or so of the epoch. With the establishment of the Rococo Period lighter and more delicate satin and taffetas, with gauze, muslin, fine lawn and silk in plain colours or exquisitely embroidered or patterned, pale brocades and linen and calico prints, often in Chinese designs, were at the height of popularity. A closely ribbed silk called 'lutestring' was used for women's dresses, silk, velvet or cloth for their outer wraps and for men's coats, while every gradation of wool and cotton could make up especially hard-wearing and serviceable clothes for either sex. Stripes were in fashion in the first quarter of the century as well as large or small flower patterns, also small checks for workaday dresses. Quilting for under-skirts, visible under panniered over-dresses, was especially in favour in the middle part of the century and was in use both before and afterwards. In the last quarter of the century, though all the materials mentioned remained in fashion, cloth was more widely used than other stuffs for men's coats and breeches to suit the 'countrified' styles that were adopted for town as well as country wear.

The bustled dress of the late '80s and '90s, preceding the high-waisted styles of the final years, brought importance to India gauze and every kind of muslin, with patterns of stripes, flower-sprigs or metal thread particularly favoured. These dresses were also often made in striped silk, as were men's coats and waistcoats and sometimes breeches in this period. The 'riding' dress was usually of cloth or velvet.

In this era of fine fabrics colours were at their most subtle and exotic. Bright or pastel silks as well as gold or silver thread were used to embroider in contrast clothes of other colours. Blue, from azure and slate to dark sapphire, lavender, violet, several varieties of soft rose and magenta, purple, red and wine-colour, yellow and green in every shade, white and black, browns, greys, parchment and dove colour were used. Men's clothes were as many-coloured as women's until the 1780s, although for country or utilitarian wear more sober tints were customary, as they were for women. The quieter colours were in the lead for the last twenty years or so of the century, but dark red and purple and the 'pink' of the hunting man were always in evidence.

In the first part of the Rococo Period, until about mid-century, women depended for decorative effect more on woven or printed patterns and on beauty of colour and fabric than on embroidered or applied decoration. Men had a taste for embroidery throughout the epoch until the 1780s. Coats and waistcoats, when not of figured or brocaded silk, were embroidered along the front edges and pocket-flaps. Waistcoats might be decorated all over with small motifs as well. An alternative to embroidery as a border was appliqué gold or silver braid or lace, also used on cuffs, pocket flaps and the brims of hats. Women's dresses in the second half of the century were similarly decorated, particularly the bodice-fronts or stomachers and the front edges of open over-skirts. Under-dresses could be embroidered all over, or exquisitely quilted. Many sleeve ruffles and fichus were of chiffon, lawn or muslin, but lace was also sometimes used for fichus, and for neck-edgings, sleeve ruffles, cravat-edges and in large motifs, usually circular, appliqués on the front edges of over-dresses and the hems of under-skirts. Artificial flowers were used as appliqué ornaments. Ribbon motifs in bows, edgings and involuted designs were also characteristic. Baskets of flowers, appliqués or embroidered, were linked by loops and bows of appliqué ribbon. This effulgence of decoration died out to a great extent with the plainer fashions of the late '80s and the '90s, but remained in the still hooped Court dress worn by some women on state occasions.

Jewellery and Accessories: Until 1780 or thereabouts men wore rings (not more than one or two) and jewelled sword-hilts, also the badge of an Order if they were entitled to it. Watches and fobs, often of fine quality, were not visible owing to the long coat and waist-coat, but were seen with the sloping-away or square-cut coat and waistcoat of the later years.

In the first half of the century women's use of jewellery showed a restraint in keeping with the fragile, flower- and lace-strewn dresses of the period. Necklaces were surprisingly few, considering the low-cut bodices and exposed throats and necks, and when worn were fine and delicate. Earrings, too, when worn, were small drops, not much in evidence. Rings, bracelets, pins and brooches followed suit, though diamonds, the most fashionable jewels at the time, could adorn the wig or powdered hair.

XIII.13. 1780s–90s. Headdress

Hair: (a) (1780s.) The man wears a lightly-powdered or naturally-coloured wig, with a single horizontally-rolled curl over each ear and a queue turned up on itself. (b) (1790s.) The hair is fluffed out at the sides with apparent negligence. It could be lightly powdered. (c) (1770s–'80s.) Short curls on the forehead and curled locks descending to the shoulders at the back are partly seen.

Headdress: (a) The 'round' hat is of black felt with a flexible brim, turned up at the edge all round, and a broad band finished with a buckle in front. (b) The hat, of black beaver, has a tall, diminishing crown and a curving brim. The band has a buckle in front. (c) The 'dormeuse' cap is of white muslin, with a double frill framing the face and a large, soft crown. A wide band of pink taffetas ribbon, edged with pink galon, is laid across the top, coming down on each side. Ribbons in a darker pink are set in front of this and tie at the back.

Garments: (a) The short-waisted 'spencer' of mole-grey cloth has a 'pouter-pigeon' front, sloping away towards the back. It has a large standing collar with revers of oyster-grey and is worn over a riding 'frock' of oyster-grey cloth partly visible at the base of the drawing. The cravat and shirt-frill are of white lawn. (b) The 'Garrick' overcoat is of pale fawn-coloured cloth, with a standing collar, revers of black velvet, and three capes over the shoulders. The plain cravat, of cream-coloured muslin, is tied in a bow in front. (c) A folded fichu of white muslin is crossed over on the bosom, tying (unseen) at the back of the waist. The dress is of pale pink silk with stripes in a deeper pink.

Men's jewellery remained inconspicuous all through the epoch. After 1750, however, with the growing ornateness in their dress, women's jewellery was more lavishly worn and less discreet, especially in the case of diamond hair ornaments, bracelets, necklets and shoe-buckles.

In the closing years, when the round dress with fichu and later the high-waisted gown with flowing skirts came into fashion, cameos, gold chains and beads and non-flexible bracelets set with enamel, cornelian and crystal took the place of earlier glittering jewels for ordinary wear, though these were worn on important occasions.

Men carried snuff-boxes, sometimes of gold or silver, possibly set with jewels, but often of papier mâché, lacquer, tortoiseshell, ebony or polished and inlaid wood.

Gloves were mainly for riding, travelling, driving and other practical pursuits and were not carried or worn in the ordinary way.

Swords were worn by men on all formal occasions in the first half of the century, hung on a baldrick or sword-belt over the shirt but under the waistcoat, with the scabbarded end protruding through a slit in the coat-pleats. They were light rapiers and the hilts were usually of silver, sometimes of gold, and ornamented or jewelled.

Walking sticks were long, with gold, silver, clouded amber or ivory heads. In the latter part of the century they were of shoulder height and carried by women as well as men.

Handkerchiefs for men and women were large, with deep lace edging. When carried by men as a decorative accessory, the central point of the handkerchief was often put between the second and third fingers and the rest allowed to drop from the palm of the hand.

Muffs were carried by men as well as by women in this century.

Parasols were used by women in the latter part of the century. Folding fans, on ivory, papier mâché or tortoiseshell sticks and made of silk or chicken-skin, exquisitely painted, were an important accessory. Women also had silver or gold châtelaines to wear with indoor dress and these were sometimes set with jewels.

The quizzing-glass, worn on a ribbon round the neck and held a little distance from the face, was in favour as a fashionable accessory for men in the final quarter and was still used in the opening years of the following century.

Ornamental aprons, varying in length, could be worn by women until the early '90s, but with the innovation of higher waists were worn only for practical purposes.

(*a*) Woman with Dutch Coiffure in 'Wrapping-gown', with Lace Collar
(*b*) English Officer. 1770s

XIII.14. Man in Early Form of Tricorne. About 1700

Hair: The natural hair or wig is unpowdered and lies in loose curls on the shoulders.

Headdress: The black felt tricorne hat has a narrow edging of gold galon. It has a pronounced downward point over the forehead and the sides flare outwards on either side of the shallow, rounded crown.

Garments: The coat is of pale sand-coloured cloth with facings of black satin. The loops fastening the gilt buttons on the turned back cuffs and the pockets, set low on the skirt, are of dull gold braid. The coat fits the figure but flares out over the hips. There are pleats at the sides and a pleated vent (unseen) at the back. The top edges of the waistcoat of biscuit-coloured grosgrain are turned back over the facings of the coat. The knee-breeches are of black velvet. The neck cloth and jabot are of cream-coloured lawn. The wrist-frills of the cream-coloured lawn shirt show below the coat sleeves.

Footwear: The shoes are of fawn-coloured reversed calf fastened over the insteps with a small gilt ornament. The heels are slightly shaped and of moderate height.

Accessories: A cream-coloured embroidered silk handkerchief is held in the right hand and a cane with a knob of clouded amber in the left.

XIII.15. Maidservant or Country Girl. 1711

Hair: The hair is worn in a fringe on the forehead and hangs to the shoulders in ringlets at the sides and back.

Headdress: The white muslin cap is a small fontange, with stiffened frills standing above the forehead and a frilled lappet at the back.

Garments: The over-dress of brownish maroon cotton patterned with buff-yellow flowers, has a narrowly fitting bodice and a skirt tucked up in panniers. The bodice has a square neckline edged with narrow white frilling and is open in front with a stomacher of tucked white lawn. The full sleeves are of white lawn and are gathered into a band and frill below the elbows. The under-skirt is of white cotton with narrow wavy stripes of dark green. A white apron is worn over it.

Footwear: The shoes of light brown reversed calf are tied over the insteps with brown ribbons and have long vamps and high, shaped heels.

Accessories: A glass jug with a silver lid is carried in the left hand.

XIII.16. Maidservant or Country Girl in Cross-over Bodice. 1720

Hair: The hair is taken back without a parting and brought forward a little at the sides. The chignon is at the base of the skull.

Headdress: The 'round-eared' cap of white cotton fits over the head and has lappets turned back from the face and pinned together at the top of the head.

Garments: The dress is of sage green cotton, patterned with horizontal stripes of light tan. It has a close-fitting bodice with a rounded waist-line and a cross-over fastening turned back with white linen. The loosely fitting three-quarter-length sleeves are turned back in the same way. The skirt is bell-shaped and ends just above the shoes. A large white cotton apron is tied on at the waist.

Footwear: The shoes are of black leather with slightly squared-off toes.

Accessories: A cleaning cloth is carried in the left hand.

XIII.17. Man in Wide-skirted Coat. 1725

Hair: The powdered wig is rolled back from the face on each side of a centre parting. The hair at the back of the head is worn smooth and uncurled.

Headdress: The ends of the wig are hidden by a black satin 'bag' tied with a large bow at the back of the neck. A black tricorne hat is held under the right arm.

Garments: The widely flared coat, ending just above the knees, is of olive green satin. It is collarless, with a neck-cloth of cream-coloured lawn. The large turned-back cuffs are ornamented with small silver buttons and have the seams left partly open. The flap pockets, with silver buttons, are set low on the skirt of the coat. The knee-breeches are of cream-coloured satin. They fit closely over the knees, and are fastened on the outside by four small buttons and a buckle. The stockings are of cream-coloured silk.

Footwear: The black leather shoes have flat red heels and long vamps, with short tongues and fastenings over the insteps, covered by silver buckles.

Accessories: A tall silver-headed cane is held in the left hand. A light sword is worn.

XIII.18. Country Girl or Maid-servant.
About 1728

Hair: The hair is taken back into a small coiffure, without a parting.

Headdress: The white linen or cotton cap fits the head at the back and is turned back over the forehead, this material forming lappets at the sides.

Garments: The dress of yellow cotton is worn over petticoats and has a pattern of small orange-coloured flowers with green leaves. It is laced in front with green ribbons over a white shift. The sleeves are turned back at the elbows, with the frills of the three-quarter-length chemise sleeves showing. A white lawn fichu is tucked into the front of the bodice. A white apron is worn.

Footwear: The plain buckled shoes of brown fabric with low heels have large tongues.

Accessories: The girl carries a basket of flowers.

XIII.19. Woman in Open Gown. 1720–30

Hair: The hair is drawn up all round, without a parting, into a small flat chignon on the top of the head.

Headdress: A flat cap, called a 'pinner', of écru lace is set on the top of the head.

Garments: The under-gown has a pointed, fitted bodice and a bell-shaped skirt. It is of striped satin in lilac and dark purple. The loose, flowing over-gown is of deep emerald green ribbed silk. Its oval décolletage shows the points of the shoulders and is fastened together at the bosom with a bow of purple satin but the gown is open all the way down from that point. The three-quarter-length sleeves are loosely turned back below the elbows, showing slightly puffed three-quarter-length chemise-sleeves of écru muslin with narrow frills.

Footwear: The slippers are of green silk fabric.

Accessories: A fan of pale green and lilac tinted silk, with an ebony handle, is carried in the right hand.

XIII.20. Girl in Printed Cotton Dress. 1738

Hair: The hair has a centre parting and is dressed close to the head, with a ringlet visible towards the back.

Headdress: The white muslin 'round-eared' cap fits over the back of the head and has an unstarched frill to frame the face. Over it is a shallow, wide-brimmed hat of natural Italian straw, with a band and bow of black ribbon round the crown and tied under the chin.

Garments: The dress is of blue-green cotton, printed with flower motifs in cream colour and yellow. The fitted bodice is laced with yellow ribbon over a white shift. The fichu of white lawn or muslin is fastened in front with a black satin bow. The sleeves have turned-back cuffs at the elbows showing the chemise-sleeves. The bell-shaped skirt is worn over petticoats. A white apron is tied on at the waist, beneath the edge of the bodice. The stockings are of white or grey cotton.

Footwear: The shoes are of black leather, with long vamps and silver buckles. The heels are partly shaped and are of moderate height.

Accessories: A black silk bag with drawstrings is held in the hands.

XIII.21. Man in Close-curled Wig. 1730s

Hair: The wig is dressed in rows of tightly curled hair arranged horizontally and has no parting. It is laid across the top of the forehead and comes down to the shoulders.

Headdress: The round hat of black felt, with a flexible brim, is held in the left hand.

Garments: The coat of dark sapphire blue corded silk fits the body and flares widely at the hips. It ends below the knees. Small black buttons are set close together down the open front. The waistcoat, a little shorter than the coat, is of pale grey silk, with small silver buttons. The 'boot' sleeves have the seams left partly open. The knee-breeches are of black satin and the stockings of black silk.

Footwear: The silver-buckled shoes are of black leather.

Accessories: A cane with a silver knob is carried.

XIII.22. Woman in Taffeta Stole. 1735

Hair: The natural hair is parted in the centre and taken up and back over a pad on each side. The remainder of the hair is hidden by the cap.

Headdress: The white muslin bonnet-shaped cap has a crown that covers the back of the head and a frill that frames the face and has a dip in the centre over the forehead. It is tied under the chin on the left side with heliotrope ribbon.

Garments: The gown is of black satin with a fitted and pointed bodice and a bell-shaped skirt touching the ground. The décolletage is low and topped with a narrow white frill. Two soft folds of white muslin are crossed over the chest above this. There is a short stomacher of black satin embroidered in silver. The sleeves are turned back at the elbows, showing the white lawn frilled three-quarter-length sleeves of the shift. A short ornamental apron of fine white embroidered muslin is put on beneath the edge of the bodice. A stole of lilac taffeta frilled with its own material is worn over the shoulders and hangs down over the gown.

Accessories: Mittens of black net are worn.

XIII.23. Elderly Man in Long Coat. 1740s

Hair: The powdered or half-powdered wig is untied and is dressed to be taken back from the forehead and to lie in thick locks on the shoulders.

Garments: The waistcoat and knee-breeches are of snuff-brown worsted bound with brown braid. The coat is of grey-blue cloth with large mother-of-pearl buttons. It is of calf-length, worn open and hanging loosely. The large button-holes at the opening of the coat and on the pockets and turned-back cuffs are bound in blue braid. The folded neck-cloth is of white lawn. Unstarched wrist-frills show below the sleeves. The stockings are grey.

Footwear: The black shoes have short tongues and silver buckles.

Accessories: A letter or document is held in the hands.

XIII.24. Man's Dress. About 1740

Hair: The powdered wig is taken back from the forehead and tied in a black silk 'bag' (unseen) at the back of the neck. Two horizontal curls are set at both sides, partly covering the ears.

Garments: The coat is of blue taffetas, embroidered in dull silver on both sides of the open front, on the wide turned-back sleeves and on the pockets. The skirts flare widely from the waist. There is no collar, but a black ribbon, called a 'solitaire', is fastened in the centre of the chest below the collar-bone and is attached to the wig-bag at the back. The neck-cloth and shirt-frill are of white lawn. The waistcoat is of pearl-coloured satin bordered with dull silver braid. The close-fitting breeches are of black velvet, and the cream-coloured silk stockings are rolled over them above the knees.

Shoes: The shoes are of black leather, with low heels, broad tongues and silver buckles.

Accessories: A large lace-bordered handkerchief is held between the fingers and thumb of the right hand, which also holds the cane. A sword is worn.

XIII.25. Maidservant and Child. 1745–50

Hair: (a) The hair is parted in the centre and arranged in waves. (b) The child's hair is taken back over a pad with ringlets at the sides, and on the shoulders.

Headdress: (a) The white muslin 'round-eared' cap is turned back, showing an embroidered edge. (b) A 'pompon' of artificial flowers in crimson, pink, orange and blue, with green leaves, is worn above the forehead.

Garments: (a) The grey ribbed silk dress has a fitted bodice with a rounded waist-line. The ends of the white lawn fichu hang down the front and are tied with black velvet ribbons sewn to the bodice. The sleeves are turned back, showing frilled chemise-sleeves of white lawn. The skirt is worn over a fan-shaped hoop and a white apron tied over it. (b) The child's dress of ivory silk is patterned with flower motifs encircled by garlands, matching the flowers in her hair. The décolletage is a slightly squared oval, frilled with écru net. The close-fitting bodice is pointed and the sleeves end in puffs of écru net and frilling. The skirt is worn over a miniature hoop or petticoats. An embroidered apron of écru lawn is worn.

Footwear: The maid's shoes are of grey fabric with a tie over the instep.

XIII.26. Woman in Quilted Petticoat.
About 1750

Hair: The hair is taken back from the forehead into a small chignon high at the back of the head. Curls are arranged horizontally over the ears and round the back of the head.

Headdress: The small perched cap is a combination of 'mob' and 'round-eared' styles. It is bound with a narrow black ribbon.

Garments: The gown is of pale blue silk. It has a front opening edged with the same cream-coloured frilling that trims the muslin fichu-collar. The two corners of the open skirt are turned under the side-folds and fastened at the back of the waist, forming draped panniers. The central point of the folds at the back is also turned under and secured. The sleeves are turned back at the elbows, with the cream-coloured frills of the chemise-sleeves visible. The under-skirt is of pale pink quilted satin, worn over a fan-shaped hoop.

Footwear: The shoes are of pale blue satin, with silver buckles and shaped heels.

Accessories. The girl has a pet bird perched on her left hand.

XIII.27. Woman in Wide Hoop. 1750

Hair: The hair is parted in the centre and drawn down at the sides. The flat chignon, unseen, is at the back of the head.

Headdress: A 'round-eared' cap of cream-coloured muslin lined with turquoise blue silk, covers the back of the head and has a narrow frill to frame the face. The hat of leghorn straw is trimmed with turquoise blue ribbon.

Garments: The gown is of lime-yellow taffeta. The narrowly fitted pointed bodice and sleeves ending above the elbows are made in one. Folds of cream-coloured chiffon are set inside the décolletage, joining in the front, where a bow of turquoise blue satin is attached. The open front of the bodice is filled in with a stomacher of ruched cream-coloured chiffon, and has a narrow turn-back of the lime yellow taffeta. Bands of turquoise blue satin edge the sleeves, which also have frills of cream-coloured chiffon.

Footwear: The shoes of turquoise silk fabric have long vamps, with silver buckles at the top, and moderate Louis heels.

XIII.28. Woman in Open Gown. 1758

Hair: The hair is drawn up into a small flat chignon at the top of the head.

Headdress: A 'pompon' of peach-pink flowers, with gilt leaves, is set on top of the small pompadour.

Garments: The gown is of peach-coloured grosgrain. The open bodice has a stomacher trimmed with bows of gold tissue. A 'ruff' of écru frilling, and peach-coloured satin ribbon encircles the neck. Folds of écru chiffon form a collar open to the waist. Bows of gold tissue are tied at the base of the sleeves, which have three deep ruffles of écru lace. The dress is worn over a wide oval hoop. The overskirt is long enough to lie on the ground and forms a short train. Its front opening is bordered by flower-motifs of écru chiffon, embellished with gold thread. The underskirt of écru chiffon over a peach silk foundation is in three deep flounces bordered with circular motifs and frills of écru lace embroidered with gold thread.

Footwear: The Court slippers are of gold brocade with Louis heels.

Jewellery and Accessories: Pearl and diamond drop earrings are worn. The fan has a red and gold papier mâché frame, covered in peach-coloured silk, with a painted scene on it.

XIII.29. Man's Dress. 1760

Hair: The powdered wig, or mixture of natural and false hair, is dressed close to the head, taken back without a parting, and has two moderate-sized horizontal ringlets on each side. Its short queue (unseen) is tied back with a black ribbon.

Headdress: The tricorne hat is of black felt.

Garments: The coat is of black velvet, lined in oyster grey satin. It flares moderately from the hips and ends at the top of the calves. The sleeves are plainly cut and have narrow turned-back cuffs. The pockets are set mid-way between the hips and the hem. The buttons are of black velvet, with loops of dull silver. The waistcoat is of oyster-grey grosgrain, embroidered in black. The knee-breeches are of black velvet. The neck-cloth, shirt-frill and wrist-frills are of white lawn and the stockings of oyster grey silk.

Footwear: The silver-buckled shoes are of black leather, with slightly squared toes and low heels.

Accessories: A silver-knobbed cane is carried.

XIII.30. Woman in Hooped Sacque Gown. 1760s

Hair: The powdered wig has a tall, wide pompadour, with a ringlet above each ear and horizontal ringlets arranged down the back of the head.

Headdress: A lunette-shaped ivory comb, ornamented with tiny crimson flowers, is set on the right of the head.

Garments: The dress is of bluish-white taffetas patterned with crimson roses and green leaves, on a background of sprays in silver thread and small crystal beads. The close-fitting bodice has box pleats at the back starting at the shoulders and descending to widen out from the waist and become part of the full skirt which is made up of more pleats stitched down for some distance. The skirt, worn over a wider oval hoop, touches the ground at the sides and back and is a fraction shorter in front. The neckline is square, and fairly close at the back of the neck. The sleeves are finished by narrow bands of black satin ribbon and three deep frills of écru chiffon.

Accessories: A black satin ribbon is worn round the neck and fastened in a double bow at the back. A fan of ivory and silk is carried in the right hand.

XIII.31. Labourer or Artisan. 1760–70

Hair: The hair hangs in an untidy fringe over the fore-head and is of 'bobbed' length at the sides and back.

Garments: The coat and breeches are of rough light brown woollen stuff and the waistcoat and stockings of grey-brown worsted. The neck-cloth is of cream-coloured cotton, matching the wrist-frills of the shirt.

Footwear: The shoes are of brown reversed calf, buckled over the insteps.

Accessories: An ash-stick with a handle at right-angles to it is carried in the right hand.

XIII.32. Country Girl or Maidservant. 1760s–'70s

Hair: The hair is taken back from the forehead, the remainder being hidden by the cap.

Headdress: The white muslin 'dormeuse' cap has a full, flat-topped crown, wider at the top than at the base, with a triple frill surrounding it. A triple neck-frill is attached to the back of the cap and fastens under the chin. The black ribbon band is tied in a bow in front.

Garments: The dress is of lilac pink cotton striped in maroon. Its fitted bodice, with a rounded waist-line and square décolletage, has a fold of white muslin across the front. The muslin fichu does not meet in the centre but has its ends fastened down under the arms. The sleeves are three-quarter length and turned back with a facing of white lawn caught by a small button. The puffed and banded sleeves of the shift are visible below these. The full skirt is held up at one point, showing an under-skirt of turquoise blue glazed cotton striped in yellow. A white apron is worn. The stockings are of white or pale-grey cotton.

Footwear: The buckled shoes are of fawn-grey reversed calf.

Accessories: A posy of flowers is pinned at the left side of the fichu.

XIII.33. Woman's Dress. About 1770

Hair: The hair, probably a mixture of real and artificial, is drawn up above the forehead over a pad and powdered white or grey. The chignon is tipped a little forward on the top. Two curls are placed behind each ear and round the back of the head and a loop of hair is coiled across the back of the neck.

Headdress: A wreath of pink flowers is twined round the chignon with a festoon coming down on each side and across the back of the head.

Garments: The bodice and square décolletage are edged by taffeta ruching, with a silk bow in the centre of the bosom. The over-dress of pearl-coloured satin is worn over an oval hoop and touches the ground, with the suggestion of a train at the back. Its opening is embroidered in several pale colours and silver thread. The pearl satin under-skirt has a deep flounce of the same type of embroidery. The sleeves end above the elbow with a band of ruching, a silk bow on the outside and three cream-coloured chiffon flounces.

Footwear: The shoes match the over-dress and have high, shaped heels and moderately pointed toes.

Jewellery: Diamond earrings, rings and bracelets are worn.

XIII.34. Woman in Open Gown. 1770

Hair: The powdered wig is dressed in a narrow 'pompadour', with ringlets set at an angle at the sides from the temples to the crown and meeting an upward sweep of hair from the back.

Headdress: The cap is made of rows of écru lace and tilted forward on the top of the wig. Its crown is covered by small peach-pink flowers, with a bow of black satin ribbon at the back, from which two lace streamers depend.

Garments: The dress, worn over a bell-shaped hoop, is of eggshell blue silk, patterned in tea roses and other flowers in peach-pink, cream and pale yellow, with pale green leaves. Narrow frills of écru net decorate the décolletage, fitted bodice and sleeves, which end in three wide frills of net. The under-skirt is of écru net over a matching silk foundation. It has two deep flounces topped with frilling. The open over-skirt is bordered by the patterned silk of the dress, crossed diagonally by bands of ruched frilling. The gown is worn over a bell-shaped hoop or petticoats and has a short train.

Jewellery and Accessories: Diamond drop earrings and a diamond ring are worn. A scarf of écru chiffon is tied on the bosom. The fan of 'chicken-skin' is painted in the tones of the dress, and has an ivory frame.

XIII.35. Woman in 'Bergère' Dress. 1777

Hair: The powdered wig is dressed in a high pompadour, with a horizontal ringlet above each ear and another below, joining a roll of hair at the back.

Headdress: A cap made up of frills of cream-coloured muslin is tilted forward above the forehead. A green velvet ribbon is tied round it and hangs in two streamers at the back.

Garments: The under-skirt is worn over an oval hoop and is of cream-coloured chiffon, with three flounces of cream-coloured lace and made on a foundation of prim-rose yellow silk. The over-dress of primrose yellow silk has a fichu of cream-coloured chiffon frilled at the edge and fastened in front beneath a green velvet bow. The sleeves end in frills of cream-coloured chiffon tied with green velvet. The over-skirt is arranged in panniers, edged with three rows of cream-coloured lace. The stockings are of cream-coloured silk.

Footwear: The shoes of green silk fabric have moderate Louis heels and yellow rosettes on the vamps.

Accessories: The yellow silk parasol has a white enamelled frame, an ivory knob, and cream-coloured silk fringe.

XIII.36. Woman in 'Polonaise' Gown. 1777

Hair: The powdered wig is dressed in a tall, narrow, pompadour with four ringlets placed horizontally at the sides of the head, and one vertically behind each ear. Ringlets cover the back of the head from the crown downward in two parallel lines of four each.

Headdress: Four violet-tinted plumes are set upright on the top of the head with a bow of black satin at the back.

Garments: The under-skirt is of violet watered silk, ornamented all round above the hem with festoons of black net. The draped-back, open over-gown is of pearl-grey satin, with double frilling of its own material round the edges of the drooping side and back panniers. The bodice of the over-gown is cut in one with the panniers that form its skirt. The waist-line is defined by a seam down the back and curved darts on either side of it, caught by silver buttons. Pearl-grey gauze ruching edges the oval neckline and the sleeves, which also have triple puffs of pearl grey gauze and frilling.

Footwear: The stockings are of pearl grey silk and the shoes of pearl-grey satin, with diamanté buckles and Louis heels.

Accessories: The white-enamelled cane has silver cords and tassels. A black velvet ribbon is tied round the neck.

XIII.37. Man with Quizzing Glass. 1770

Hair: The powdered wig is taken up unparted, in a backward slope to the top of the head where it is puffed out to cover the crown. It is supported by two horizontal rolls of hair, one above the other, round the back of the head. The short queue is tied with a black bow on a level with the back of the collar.

Headdress: A black satin tricorne is carried.

Garments: The coat of amber satin is embroidered in gold thread down the front edges, on the pockets, cuffs and the standing, turned-over collar. It is narrowly cut, fitting closely and sloping away from two buttons on the chest to narrow coat-tails ending at the back of the knees. The breeches are also of amber satin and the waistcoat of pale honey-coloured taffeta, embroidered in gold. The neckcloth, shirt-frill and wrist-frills are of cream-coloured lawn, matching the silk stockings.

Footwear: The flat-soled, silver buckled shoes are of black leather, without tongues.

Accessories: A silver-knobbed cane is carried in the left hand and a quizzing glass in the right, suspended from a black ribbon round the neck.

XIII.38. Maidservant. 1770

Hair: The hair is raised in a moderate pompadour, with a low chignon. Some ringlets show below the back of the cap.

Headdress: The 'dormeuse' cap of écru muslin has a high front, with a pleated frill all round and a tall crown with a flat top. A brown satin ribbon is tied round its base, with a bow at the back.

Garments: The striped under-petticoat of glazed cotton in cream-colour and café-au-lait ends just below the ankles. The petticoat, striped in brown and cream colour, has been bunched up on both sides. The open, sacque-backed over-dress is of mushroom-coloured poplin, bunched at the sides and back. The wide oval neckline, low at the back of the neck, has a frilled muslin collar. The sleeves end at the elbows with two rows of frilling and show the puffed and frilled chemise sleeves.

Footwear: The high-heeled shoes are of brown fabric, with high vamps and gilt buckles.

Accessories: The maid carries a tray with a coffee or chocolate pot and a cup and saucer on it.

XIII.39. Girl in Basqued Jacket. 1780s

Hair: The hair of this maid or country girl is allowed to tumble haphazardly round her face, with some ringlets hanging down on to the neck.

Headdress: The white muslin mob-cap is set high on the head and has a full, fairly high crown with a band of black ribbon tied in front.

Garments: The dress of mustard-yellow cotton printed in a small design of black has a close-fitting basqued jacket, separate from the skirt. A white muslin fichu is tucked in at the front fastening. The basque is longer at the back than the front and juts out over the back fullness of the skirt. The sleeves are made in one with the bodice and end below the elbows. A plain white apron is tied on under the basque. The stockings are of grey or white cotton.

Footwear: The shoes of black leather have moderate Louis heels and long vamps with silver buckles and short tongues.

XIII.40. Woman in Basqued Jacket. 1786

Hair: The unpowdered hair comes forward in short curled locks above the brow and is arranged in loose ringlets at the sides and back.

Headdress: The large mob-cap of white muslin has a full, soft crown and is edged by two deep frills. A band of dark green ribbon is tied in a bow in front.

Garments: The close-fitting separate jacket is of cream-coloured grosgrain striped in terracotta and pale green. It fastens in front and has a basque longer at the back than at the sides, protruding over the back fullness of the skirt. The three-quarter-length sleeves are frilled at the ends. A frilled fichu of écru-coloured muslin is arranged in full, puffed-up folds to give the fashionable pouter-pigeon look. The skirt is of cream-coloured satin, patterned with small terracotta flowers with green leaves.

Footwear: The shoes are of dark green silk.

Accessories: A dark green ribbon tied round the neck matches the stole of dark green velvet edged with dull gold lace.

XIII.41. Man's Dress, 1780s

Hair: The unpowdered wig, or combination of natural and false hair, is taken back smoothly from the forehead without a parting.

Headdress: A beaver hat is carried in the left hand.

Garments: The long, elegantly cut 'sloping away' coat is of dark mole-coloured velvet, with tails ending at the back of the knees. The stand-up collar is turned over and the lapels are short. The sleeves are close-fitting, with wrist-frills. The waistcoat is of pale mole-coloured corduroy, its short lapels turned back over those of the coat. The breeches are of pale oyster-coloured cloth. The neck-cloth and shirt-frill are of cream-coloured lawn.

Footwear: The boots of black leather have tops of light brown.

Accessories: Gloves of oyster-grey leather are carried.

XIII.42. Country Dweller. 1780s

Hair: The hair is taken back from the forehead over a roll and brought forward at the sides.

Headdress: The white muslin cap, a combination of 'mob' and 'dormeuse', has a tall, flat-topped crown and a triple-frilled brim that hangs down at the back but is raised to a central point well above the brow in front. The band of black taffeta ribbon is tied in a flat bow in front.

Garments: The gown is of pale grey cotton, patterned in decorative stripes and dots in blue, green and violet. It has a bell-shaped skirt, worn over petticoats, and a close-fitting over-bodice of white cambric which starts above the breasts and ends at the rounded waist-line. The jacket, worn beneath this, has a long basque at the sides and back, ending at the top of the thighs. The sleeves end below the elbow, where they have turned-back cuffs showing the puffed three-quarter-length sleeves of the white lawn shift. The white lawn fichu, frilled round the edge, is tucked into the over-bodice. A white apron is worn.

Footwear: The shoes are of black fabric.

Accessories: A posy of flowers is held in the hands.

XIII.43. Woman in Striped Silk Dress. 1789

Hair: The hair is taken back from the forehead and tied with a ribbon. A 'halo' of short ringlets is arranged behind this and ringlets of varying lengths hang at the sides and back.

Headdress: The ribbon tied round the head is of dark red velvet.

Garments: The dress of smoke-grey silk striped in dark red has a close-fitting bodice with a slightly high, rounded waist-line. The narrow sash of dark red velvet is tied at the back. The long, close-fitting sleeves end in small frills of oyster-grey chiffon, matching the round, frilled fichu. The full skirt is long enough to lie on the ground.

Footwear: The flat slippers are of black silk fabric.

Accessories: A red rose is pinned at the centre of the fichu and a round necklace of clear red amber beads is worn. The parasol has a cover of red silk and a malacca stem.

XIII.44. Woman in Open-fronted Gown. 1790

Hair: This is fringed in front. Ringlets are arranged round the sides and back of the head. Below these a swathe of smooth hair, curled at the ends, descends to the shoulder-blades, tied with a black ribbon. A loose ringlet lies on the left shoulder.

Headdress: The shallow crowned hat of natural straw, with a wide, curving brim, has a band of black satin ribbon bunched into loops in front.

Garments: The dress is of lime-green silk patterned with narrow black stripes and small cream-coloured dots. The bodice is open, from the centre of the décolletage to the rounded waist, in the form of an inverted triangle of cream-coloured silk. The matching under-skirt continues this line to the hem. The close-fitting sleeves end in cream-coloured chiffon frills, matching the knotted fichu. The over-skirt has back-fullness sloping downward and forming a short train.

Footwear: The black kid slippers have low vamps and almost flat heels.

Accessories: The tall white cane is tied with a black satin ribbon.

XIII.45. Maidservant. Late 1790s

Hair: The hair is cut short and worn nearly straight, showing a carelessly arranged fringe over the brow.

Headdress: A large high-fronted mob-cap of white muslin with lilac ribbons, fits over the back of the head.

Garments: The muslin gown has lilac-coloured dots on a white ground, and a rounded neckline without a collar. There are short puff sleeves and a rounded apron is attached at the high waist-line.

Footwear: The maid wears white cotton stockings and flat black slippers.

XIII.46. Man with Chapeau-bras. 1795

Hair: The hair is unpowdered, left fairly thick, and is long enough to touch the collar at the back. It is brushed back from the forehead and allowed to hang loosely at the sides and back.

Headdress: The black silk chapeau-bras is carried folded in the left hand.

Garments: The coat is of fine faced cloth in pale mushroom colour. The sleeves are close-fitting and have cream-coloured frills at the wrists. The shirt and cravat, which is tied in a bow in front, are of cream-coloured lawn. The waistcoat and knee breeches are of pale biscuit-coloured cloth. The stockings are of cream-coloured silk.

Footwear: The flat-soled shoes of black leather have vamps of ordinary length and silver buckles.

Accessories: A gold fob hangs from the hem of the waistcoat. An ebony cane is carried.

XIII.47. Woman in Flowered Bonnet. 1795

Hair: The hair is arranged in a fringe in front, with short, curled ringlets set back from it. Ringlets of varying lengths cover the back and sides of the head, with some descending to the shoulders.

Headdress: A band of cherry-pink ribbon surrounds the head between the fringe and the short ringlets. The bonnet of natural Italian straw is bound at the edges with cherry-coloured ribbon and has matching strings. White and cherry-pink flowers trim the front and a veil of cherry-pink gauze hangs over the shoulders.

Garments: The white muslin gown has a pattern of small cherry-red flowers. The neck and sleeve frills are ornamented with cherry-coloured ribbons which also form the narrow tied sash round the high waist-line and bind the skirt at the hem. The three-quarter-length sleeves are close-fitting.

Footwear: The flat-soled slippers are of cherry-red fabric.

Accessories: The mantelet of cherry-coloured net, edged with frilling, is turned back and shaped to form a cape over the shoulders.

XIV 19TH-CENTURY DRESS

Men's clothes were hardly concerned in the fashions of the so-called Classical Revival in France, since no classical influence appeared in their garments, apart from tunic, toga and sandals worn for a short time by some enthusiasts. Their hairdressing did, however, imitate Greek and Roman styles. Their high-waisted cut-away coats, tapering sleeves and close-fitting pantaloons followed the late 18th-century 'country gentleman' fashions.

Romantic elegance was developed in the narrow waist, the full-skirted coat, extra tall top hat and tapering trousers of the late '20s, '30s and '40s. These in turn gave way to the dull, practical clothes of the second half of the century, from the gradual changes of the '50s and '60s to the bulky overcoats, tight-fitting lounge suits, tweed and knickerbockers of the '70s and '80s, and, in the final decade, a certain return to elegance in greatly improved cut.

In women's dress the 'classical influence' appeared in extreme forms in France, where some women appeared in semi-transparent gauze or silk, exposing most of their bosoms and with skirts split to the thigh. Flesh-coloured tights and gilt boots increased the effect of fancy dress. After 1804, however, the newly created great ladies of Napoleon's Court achieved a classic beauty of line in their rich satins and glowing velvets and brocades and their modes were followed in wealthy circles in England. Early in this epoch women added narrow tubular drawers to the shift, corset and skirt that had made up feminine underwear for three hundred years.

The elaborate tight-waisted styles of the next phase, with their ballooning skirts showing feet and ankles in flat, beribboned slippers, and their vast puffed sleeves denoted a complete change, after a transitional period, from former fashions. By 1838 a modest simplicity had become the keynote. The round collars, plain sleeves and bell-shaped skirts paved the way, however, for the full crinoline in all its romantic splendour to enter the modes ten years later. Of the two bustle periods in the '70s and '80s, the first was pretty and picturesque, but the second had little to offer except fussiness of line and overloading of ornament. The graceful sweep of the 'tied-back' dress in the late '70s and early '80s brought greater attraction to women's clothes. The first rigid fashions of the '90s were dull and had little beauty, but gave place in due course to the flowing skirts and elegant puffed shoulders of the final five years.

Hair—Men: The 'classical' mode in hairdressing for men was followed in the first twenty years of the 19th century. Short at the back and brushed forward in curls or strands, it was sometimes parted at one side, but was more often worn without a parting. In the 1820s curls and waves could be thicker and a side parting was usual.

In the 1830s fashionable men allowed their hair to grow full at the sides and front and longer at the back than formerly. It was dressed elaborately and parted at one side or in the middle. Hair brushed forward from the crown was out of fashion by the early 1840s. During this decade a parting from the forehead to the nape of the neck, with the hair brushed outward and forward on either side of it, was fashionable and continued into the '60s or later.

In the '40s, '50s and '60s hair remained thick and rather long. In the '70s it was a little longer, though still arranged with some fullness at the sides and in front. A centre or side parting could be worn. By the 1880s men's hair was almost invariably cut close at the back and sides, except for some elderly men, artists, actors and musicians who preferred thicker hair.

Side-burns, short or long, but usually narrow and clipped fairly close, were fashionable in the early years of the 19th century. By 1814 they were sometimes grown low on the cheeks, with the sides of the cheekbones shaved, and this fashion increased, remaining for as long as whiskers were worn. In the late 1820s they frequently joined a fringe of beard round the chin. This style continued through the '30s, '40s and '50s and was still favoured by some elderly men in the last decades of the century. By 1850 whiskers were longer and fuller, and in the 1860s and '70s were large and thick, often drooping on each side of the chin in the 'Dundreary' mode. They were less fashionable in the 1880s and were seen chiefly on elderly men, still in the drooping or bushy style, in that decade and in the '90s.

Some men already wore moustaches by the beginning of the Regency (1811), following Continental military fashions spread by the Napoleonic Wars. The moustaches of that time were usually small and narrow. It was not until the late 1820s that they were generally worn, and now in some cases drooped to join the chin-beard or the whiskers. With the fashion for surrounding the chin with a fringe of beard, joined by the whiskers, the moustache might be omitted. This also applied to the wearing of large, low-growing whiskers. By mid-century the moustaches had increased in size, although the small and neat type was never out of fashion. They were now more frequently thick in the centre, with gradually tapering ends waxed in a straight or upturned direction. Very large moustaches, with the face otherwise clean-shaven, were a strong characteristic of men's fashions in the last twenty years of the epoch. There was also a fashion, from mid-century onwards, of joining a straggling, unkempt moustache to a beard of the same type.

A small 'Imperial' or a goatee beard could be worn from the 1830s onwards. Beards in the height of fashion were often large and full in the '60s and '70s and might still be worn thus for the remainder of the century. They could be trimmed to a point, spade-shaped, or left bushy and straggling.

Hair—Women: In the opening years of the century the chignon placed half-way up the back of the head or protruding at a fairly high point was fashionable. A centre parting was worn with smooth hair, but a mass of curls often overhung the forehead, festooned the back of the head over the chignon or in place of it, and clustered over the ears.

Fashion plates after 1805 show a greater degree of order in the hairdressing. The shape of the coiffure was more graceful and by the second decade was smaller and neater, with a tendency for the chignon or the cluster of curls to be placed nearer the top of the head and to be secured by some small decoration.

In 1820 the hair was parted in the centre or dressed in a fringe over the forehead, with curls massed over the temples and cheekbones and a chignon or cluster of curls near the crown of the head.

The wider coiffure developed after 1830 into eccentric forms and large proportions. Ringlets were wired out horizontally on either side of the head and a stiffened topknot or a built-up bunch of curls rose high above the centre of the head. Hair at the back was brushed smoothly upward to meet the topknot or alternatively was dressed in short curls or swathed across the back of the head and securely pinned. Straight hair returned to fashion and was wound into fashionable shapes on the same lines, with less width at the sides, and well pomaded.

By 1835 the smooth coiffure led the mode. The topknot was still high, but ringlets framed the face or were omitted altogether. Sometimes long plaits were wound across the head from side to side.

In the 1840s a chignon set low, high or half-way up, a centre parting and smoothly flattened hair with or without side ringlets, were the chief trends of fashion in hairdressing.

Similar styles prevailed at the beginning of the 1850s, but the hair was not brought down so low over the ears, and in some cases was puffed out at the sides.

In a style for evening the front hair was rolled back from the parting over narrow side-pads and the rest drawn back into the chignon. Pendant side-ringlets were not much worn after the early 1850s. In the later '50s a plait or padded coil across the top of the head,

XIV.1. 1805–11. Men. Six Figures

Hair: (a) (1811. A watchman.) The hair is hidden by the hood. (b) (1811. A water-carrier.) The hair is visible in short locks in front of his ears. (c) (1811. A Thames waterman.) The straggling hair is of moderate length. (d) (1805. A postman.) The hair is of medium length, brought forward in short locks showing beneath his hat in front and over his ears. (e) (1811. A fireman.) The short hair shows on his forehead under the rim of his helmet. (f) (1811. A plant-seller.) The hair is short and hardly seen under the hat.

Headdress: (a) The watchman's hood of dark grey felt has a small peak in front and a flap covering the back of the shoulders. (b) The water-carrier has a wide-brimmed hat of brown felt, with a rounded crown. (c) The waterman wears a round, flat-topped beaver hat with the brim turned up all round. (d) The postman's black felt hat resembles that of the waterman, with a slightly higher crown. (e) The fireman's helmet is of brass, with a leather flap at the back and leather straps for fastening under his chin. (f) The plant-seller wears a battered hat of

describing an arc that covered the ears, with a swathed chignon following the same line, gave a fashionable widened effect.

By 1860 a more elongated coiffure was in vogue. The hair in front was dressed in much the same way as formerly to begin with, but the chignon was large, spread into coils in various shapes and set low. Ringlets at the back sometimes took the place of the chignon.

During the first five years of the decade a vogue for a curled coiffure introduced rows of curls above the forehead and over the front of the head, dispensing with the parting. From 1865 the elaborate front dressing usually showed the ears completely, with hair dressed in short curls over the forehead and taken up at the sides, sometimes with a thick plait worn across the front of the head and brought down in a slanting line to meet the low chignon. For a time the chignon could be placed higher, in many instances exposing the back of the neck. Ringlets depending from it were still worn by some women.

By 1870 the hair was parted in the centre as a rule and drawn up from the temples to be dressed in swathes, coils and ringlets on the top of the head. It descended in similar forms at the back, sometimes on to the shoulders. Plaits were often used in circlet form on the crown or looped at the back of the head. Forehead curls or fringes frequently covered or replaced the centre parting. In the latter part of the decade this elaborate coiffure was modified and a simpler dressing, with a fringe and centre parting, and a low chignon, was evolved.

The hairdressing of the early 1880s followed this example with the chignon sometimes at midway or crown level. By 1885 arrangements of curls or fringe surmounted the forehead and the chignon could be worn on the top of the head.

In the conical coiffure of the early '90s the hair was drawn up tightly at the sides and back into a small knot of hair pinned on the top of the head. A curled or frizzed fringe was usually worn. A low chignon was still in vogue, and the Grecian knot provided a graceful line at a midway level. By the middle of the decade the hair in front could be dressed in a moderate pompadour with or without a small fringe and with the chignon usually on the top of the head.

Headdress—Men: The top hat was to be the most important item of men's headgear in the 19th century, until in the latter part of it other varieties became fashionable.

---

brown felt with a flexible brim and band and a small bow at the side.

Garments: (a) The watchman wears a long brown belted coat with a turned-down collar fastening at the throat and a double cape covering the shoulders. The plain sleeves have turned-back cuffs with buttons. (b) The water-carrier wears a short jacket and knee-breeches of light brown woollen stuff. The jacket has a narrow collar and lapels and is open in front. The waistcoat is of red woollen material. The shirt-collar is open with a green neck-cloth knotted in front. The stockings are of light brown yarn. (c) The waterman wears a short red jacket, with a widely flared skirt, full at the back. The collar turns down and has a white neck-cloth knotted in front. The breeches are blue and the stockings of grey yarn. (d) The postman's long close-fitting coat is scarlet and the knee-breeches blue. The coat sleeves are plain, with turned-back cuffs. The neck-cloth, shirt-frill and stockings are of white cotton. (e) The fireman wears an open blue jacket with a narrow collar and lapels. The sleeves are not turned back at the cuffs. The double-breasted waistcoat is of biscuit-coloured woollen stuff and the knee-breeches of fawn-coloured cloth with cords tied round them above the knees. A yellow neck-cloth is tied in a bow in front. The stockings are of light brown yarn. (f) The plant-seller wears a dark green, open jacket with a narrow collar and lapels. It is cut away at the waist and slopes backward into short coat-tails. The sleeves are plain without turnbacks. The waist-length single-breasted waistcoat is striped in red and white. The collarless shirt is of white cotton, with a red neck-cloth knotted in front. The grey breeches are unfastened at the knees. The apron is of white cotton and the stockings of grey yarn.

Footwear: (a) The watchman wears black boots, wrinkled over the ankles. (b) The water-carrier has flat-soled black shoes, with steel buckles. (c) The Thames waterman wears shoes like those of (b). (d) The postman's shoes resemble those of (b) and (c). (e) The fireman wears calf-length buff leather boots turned over at the tops. (f) The plant-seller's black leather shoes are almost covered by buff-coloured gaiters buttoned on the outside.

Accessories: (a) The watchman carries a staff and lantern and has a wooden rattle attached to his belt. (b) The water-carrier has two wooden buckets, bound with metal, hanging by chains from the wooden yoke over his shoulders. (c) The waterman carries a pole and wears a brass badge on a leather strap on his left arm. (d) The postman carries a large bell and a leather postbag bearing a crown and the initials G.R. (e) The fireman wears a brass badge on his left arm and carries a hatchet. (f) The plant-seller holds a potted plant in each hand.

XIV.2. 1814–17. Women. Three-quarter-length Figures

Hair: (a) (1814.) The hair is hidden by the bonnet. (b) (1817.) The curled fringe, and small ringlets on both sides of the face, can be seen under the hat. (c) (1814.) Only a lock of hair drawn forward on to the cheekbone is visible.

Headdress: (a) The natural straw bonnet is trimmed with an edging of eau-de-nil green silk, a small dark-green bow at the back and cream-coloured artificial roses with dark green leaves set on the top. (b) The hat of claret-coloured velvet has a brim turned up on the left side of the front and down at the right side towards the back. The crown is moderately tall and almost flat at the top. Ivory-white plumes decorate the right front and side. (c) The pseudo-classical 'helmet' is covered in gold tissue, with a band and chin-strap of gilt ribbon. Three terracotta-coloured plumes are set on the right side.

Garments: (a) The high-waisted gown, hardly seen, is of eau-de-nil silk muslin, with a small 'ruff' collar of cream-coloured lawn. The cloak of deeper green corded silk, embroidered in pale green, has oval épaulettes and is tied with a bow in front. From this point it slopes away, showing the front of the dress. (b) The 'military' riding dress of claret-coloured cloth is made on body-fitting lines all in one piece, except for the inset sleeves. It has an open standing collar, tied at the throat with gold ribbons. Below this it is left open, showing a chemisette of white silk trimmed with horizontal strips of gold braid. The opening is closed below the bosom by an upward point rising from the fitted waist and by borders of gold braid and gold galon surrounding the opening and continued round the sides and back, giving the effect of a short, close-fitting bolero. The 'military' sleeves have gold braid on the épaulettes and sleeve ends, where the seam is left open showing cream-coloured silk frills. (c) The gown of saffron-yellow satin piped in black is made in the 'princess' line seen in (b). Its open bodice is laced across, showing the front of a cream-coloured taffeta chemisette, with a standing frill-collar and low décolletage. The sleeve is pseudo-16th century, made in diminishing puffs to the wrist, with panes of cream-coloured taffetas and black piping.

Accessories: The girl in (c) carries a small beaded purse, made in an elongated shape with a slit wide enough to admit the fingers, and a gold ring to keep it closed.

It was originally made of 'beaver', felt or plush, first in fawn colour or black, with the surface a little roughened, but after 1820 or thereabouts with a smooth surface in most instances. Grey top hats were as fashionable as black in the 1830s and '40s, and from time to time during the remainder of the century. Examples of its variations in shape are to be found in the illustrations and described in the captions.

A country or riding hat with a hard crown of moderate height and a rolled brim was in use from 1800 onwards and was worn chiefly by tradesmen and farmers. It was made of felt in brown, black or fawn-colour. It became an item of high fashion in the 1870s, in the same colours or in grey, and was worn with sports clothes or with tweed ulsters in that decade and the two following.

The 'chapeau-bras' was fashionable until about 1805 with ordinary dress and worn or carried with evening dress until 1840.

A tweed shooting hat with a long front peak and strap under the chin was fashionable in the '40s.

In the first half of the century the round 'beaver' or felt hat was worn by countrymen and labourers. It was usually brown or fawn-coloured, but sometimes black. A version of it with a less flexible brim, in black, became established as a clerical hat. The round-brimmed tweed hat worn by anglers is also descended from it.

A tall-crowned bowler hat, in black or fawn-colour, came into fashion about mid-century. It had a low crown in the '60s and '70s, a high crown in the '80s and a moderate crown in the '90s. The brim was always rolled, rigid and curled up at the sides.

A 'sailor' hat in straw, with a moderate-sized round brim, worn on the back of the head, became favourite wear at the seaside and in the country in the '70s.

The rigid-brimmed straw hat, worn with a ribbon band, was one of the innovations of the '70s. Another was a bowler hat covered in tweed, to be worn with tweed suits or overcoats.

The small, close-fitting peaked cap became general wear with country clothes in the '70s, '80s and '90s.

A tweed hat with a small, down-turned brim was worn from the '70s to the '90s for angling. The crown was made of segments joined on top. The 'deerstalker' was made in the same way, but had a peak at back and front and ear-flaps which could be tied together on top in place of the down-turned brim.

A round pill-box cap, worn straight on the head, was worn in the '70s for tennis and for cycling in the '80s.

The felt hat with rolled brim and dented crown, known later as the Homburg, fedora or trilby, was an advanced style, seldom seen, in the late '70s and came into general fashion in the '80s and '90s for wear with tweed or knickerbocker suits or tweed overcoats.

Headdress—Women: In the opening years of the century hats with wide, commodious crowns and rounded brims turned back or shading the face a little, were set back on the head. Caps and bonnets, also set back, were drawn to a point at the top of their full crowns and had small decorations of flowers, feathers and ribbon attached there. Turbans might be set back or worn level on the head and boat-shaped bonnets, worn level, were tied on with ribbons or gauze scarves. Coal-scuttle shapes hid the face in profile. Helmet-shaped bonnets and caps were intended to follow the ideal of the Classical Revival. In the second decade bonnets were the chief item of headdress. Many had tall, cylindrical crowns and large brims, some of which were curved attractively to frame the face.

In the early 1820s hats were the most fashionable headdress. They had moderately wide brims, many with 'mushroom' crowns, and were often tied with ribbons under the chin. Caps were less often worn indoors, but the hair was decorated with flowers, ribbon and jewelled chains in the evening. Wide turbans of draped silk, ornamented with feathers and jewels, were fashionable by 1825 and were worn well into the 1830s.

By 1827 very large-brimmed hats were worn straight or tilted on the head and covered with plumes, large ribbon bows and flowers. They had tall, narrow crowns to accommodate the topknot of hair.

By 1836 plumed and beflowered bonnets, with large oval brims and tall crowns were fashionable.

In 1840, with the more modest new modes established, the size of the bonnet-brim decreased and its shape was deeper from front to back, sometimes hiding the face entirely in profile. Caps and evening decorations of flowers and ribbon were set back on the head and had festoons of lace, ribbon or flowers at the sides to give width. Turbans were also set back in halo fashion.

By the later '50s the bonnet was small, set well back on the head, with a shallow brim. Decorations for the hair were concentrated at the sides and back of the head, sometimes

XIV.3. 1807–37. Men. Eight Figures

Hair: (a) (1807.) The hair is almost hidden by the hat, but side whiskers can be seen. (b) (1805. An admiral.) The lightly powdered hair is puffed out at the sides. (c) (1818.) The man in nankeen breeches wears side-burns. The hair is cut short. (d) (1812. A general.) The hair is covered by the hat, but the side-burns are visible. (e) (1825.) The side-whiskers and some hair on the right side can be seen. (f) (1837.) The thick, wavy hair is parted on the left side and brought forward in a curled lock over the forehead. The remainder is arranged in waves and curls at the sides and back. (g) (1833.) The straight hair is cut short at the back and has a lock in front of each ear. (h) (1831.) The hair has a short parting over the right side of the brow and is arranged in waves and curls above the ears, with a 'quiff' over the forehead. The hair at the back (unseen) is cut short.

Headdress: (a) The black top hat has a curling brim and a large, moderately tall crown widening at the top. (b) The admiral wears a black cocked hat with an edging of gold braid and a jewelled cockade on the left side of the front. (c) The black top hat has a narrow brim dipping at front and back and a large, fairly tall crown widening near the top. (d) The general's black uniform hat has the brim turned up sharply on the right side of the head and curving forward to a point over the centre of the forehead and to a corresponding point at the back (unseen). The tall crown, of the same height as the turned-up brim on the right, is exposed on the left, where the brim is flat and narrow. The brim and crown are ornamented in gold braid. (e) The black top hat has a narrow brim dipping at the front and back, with a tall, shaped crown, tapering a little in the middle and widening at the top. (f) The man carries a folded black chapeau-bras. (g) The black top hat has a narrow brim dipping at front and back, with a tall 'stove-pipe' crown.

Garments: (a) The knee-length redingote of brown frieze fits closely to the body, flaring a little in the skirt. It has a rolled, standing collar, moderate-sized lapels and plain sleeves shaped slightly at the wrists. The partly seen under-waistcoat has horizontal stripes of green and white. Over it is a shorter single-breasted waistcoat of pale buff cloth. The close-fitting breeches are of biscuit-coloured whipcord. The frilled shirt and neck-cloth tied in a bow in front are of white linen. The points of the starched collar come up on to the cheeks. (b) The admiral wears a 'sloping-away' coat of dark blue cloth. It is shaped to the figure at the waist and has facings of white satin, ornamented with three gold buttons on each side, continuing upwards to the sides of the standing collar. The coat-tails end above the back of the knees. Large gold épaulettes are worn and the sleeve-ends have two single and one double band of gold braid. The single-breasted waistcoat of white ribbed silk, with a gilet of white lawn, ends in points below the waist. A narrow upright white frill is tucked into it below the black silk neck-cloth. The knee breeches are of white cloth and the stockings of white silk. (c) The coat is of sapphire blue cloth, cut away at the waist, with long, narrow tails. The sleeves are puffed at the shoulders and taper towards the wrists. The collar and lapels are rolled, standing out over the chest and neck. The waistcoat of striped red and white silk shows below the coat. Its lapels

are stiffened and stand out at right-angles to the chest. The large, starched shirt-frill stands out beyond them. The high white neck-cloth shows the points of the collar coming up on to the cheeks. The loosely fitting trousers of buff-yellow nankeen end above the ankles. (d) The general wears a fitted scarlet tunic, cut away at the waist and sloping into wide coat-tails. Rows of gold buttons decorate the chest, and gold épaulettes are worn. The plain sleeves have cuffs of black cloth edged with gold braid. The high, standing collar has a narrow 'V' in front, showing the black silk neck-cloth. The breeches are of white cloth or buckskin and end (unseen) at the calf. (e) The redingote of grey-green cloth is fitted to the body but full in the skirts and has a large rolled collar and a shoulder cape. The sleeves taper from the gathered shoulders (unseen) to the wrists. The coat is fastened in front by buttons from chest to hip-level. The white lawn neck-cloth is tied in front. The trousers of striped maroon and grey velvet are strapped under the insteps. (f) The open evening dress coat is of lavender faced-cloth cut away at the waist. The large collar and lapels, faced with matching satin, are rolled so that they throw the chest into prominence. The sleeves taper to the wrists from puffed shoulders (unseen). The frilled shirt and the neck-cloth are of white lawn. The plain bands of the shirt-sleeves show at the wrists. The waistcoat is of ivory satin, sprigged with lavender-coloured flowers. The ivory-white trousers fit the legs closely and are strapped under the insteps. The cloak is of black velvet, lined with ivory satin. It has a wide collar, and a tasselled cord for fastening it. (g) The redingote is of brown woollen stuff. It is fitted to the hips, but the long skirts widen towards the hem and have fullness at the back. The sleeves are puffed at the shoulders and taper to the wrists. The large rolled collar is of astrakhan. (h) The double-breasted riding coat is of royal blue cloth. It is cut away at the waist and has two rows of gilt buttons decorating the chest. The sleeves are puffed at the shoulders, tapering to the wrists. The collar stands up at the back of the neck and widens towards its ends, which form a horizontal line across the top of the chest. The white linen neck-cloth is tied in front. The trousers of pale grey whipcord are bell-bottomed.

Footwear: (a) The black hessian boots end a little below the knee. (b) The black leather shoes have flat heels and silver buckles. (c) The black leather pumps have small bows of black ribbon in front. (d) The black hessian boots are bordered with gold braid, cut in two points in front. (e) The black leather shoes or bootees are almost hidden by the strap-under trousers. (f) The slippers of black kid are cut down at the insteps showing part of the white silk stockings. (g) The pumps of black leather have black ribbon bows and are partly covered by the strap-under pantaloons. (h) The shoes or bootees of black leather have squared-off toes.

Accessories: (a) A walking stick and gloves are carried. (b) The sword is attached by straps to a belt beneath the waistcoat. (c) The slender black cane has a silver top. (d) The sword is attached by straps to the belt round the waist. (e) A walking stick is carried. (h) A riding crop is held in the left hand.

XIV.3. 1807–37. Men. Eight Figures

XIV.4. 1805–52. Women's Outdoor Dress

connected by an ornamental band across the top. Caps often had side-lappets of lace or ribbon.

In the '60s bonnets were still small, and many were provided with a flap of material at the back or alternatively with streamers or a veil to cover the back hair. With the crown sloping downward from front to back, they were known as 'spoon' bonnets. During this decade the low-crowned straw hat, with a wide brim dipping at front and back, already seen on children in the late 1850s, was in fashion. In the middle '60s a small, perched hat, rather like a miniature bowler, with a short plume curving forward from the centre front, came into fashion, and from about 1860 the pill-box or pork-pie hat, perched forward on the forehead, often with the chignon put into a coarse net or caul. The hat 'à la Reine', with a low, rounded crown and the narrow brim dipping fore and aft, was another feature of the middle of the decade and had a flower decoration in front or a plume fastened there and curving back over the brim.

In the '70s hats were small, not meant to fit the head and perched forward over the brow. Veils and streamers often supplied a downward line at the back. Bonnets consisted of a collection of ribbons, flowers and sometimes feathers, mounted on a foundation, perched in the same way and tied with ribbons under the chin. They might also have streamers or veils at the back. Caps were at first no more than a small ornament of lace, perched at the

---

XIV.4. 1805–52. Women's Outdoor Dress

Hair: (a) The hair is curled in a fringe over the forehead and arranged in short curls round the face. (b) The curled fringe can be seen. The chignon, pinned high at the back of the head, is unseen. (c) The hair is parted in the centre and puffed out at the sides, with an unseen chignon on the top. (d) The hair is parted in the centre with coils over the ears. (f) The short ringlets at the side and a little of the low chignon can be seen.

Headdress: (a) (1805.) The hat of dark green velvet, trimmed with pink plumes, has an upturned brim. (b) (1817.) The bonnet is covered in corn-yellow satin, the brim bordered in dark red velvet and a narrow cream-coloured frill. The band, strings and large rosette on the front of the crown are of dark red velvet. The crown is tall and wider at the top than at the base. (c) (1827.) The hat of fawn-coloured velvet has a diminishing crown and a large curving brim. It is worn at an angle and tied under the chin with brown and orange ribbons. The same ribbons trim the crown and brim. (d) (1838.) The turban is of twined purple and rose-coloured satin, with fringed ends descending on to the left shoulder. (e) (1845.) The bonnet, seen from the back, is covered in slate-blue silk, with ruching to match round the edge of the brim and a small blue silk frill at the back of the neck. Black velvet ribbons trim the crown, with a pink flower added. (f) (1852.) The flat-topped hat of sherry-coloured velvet has a brim curving down at the front and back and up at the sides. Pale turquoise blue plumes decorate the crown and sherry-coloured ribbons tie under the chin.

Garments: (a) The open high-waisted coat is of dark green velvet, with white facings on the standing collar and lapels. It ends at the ankles, the skirt increasing slightly in width towards the hem. The close-fitting sleeves have shaped 'goblet' cuffs. The dress is of pale pink satin, embroidered on the lower part of the skirt in green. The transparent over-tunic is of écru net, edged with lace. Its bodice is outlined by edgings of pale pink satin. (b) The high-waisted coat of corn-yellow satin fastens down the front. It is decorated on the sleeves, front and hem by oval and chevron-shaped puffs of its own material. The skirt widens towards the hem. The belt is of twisted yellow satin, fastened by circular gilt link-buttons. The collar stands up and has a standing frill of cream-coloured lawn inside it. (c) The coat of orange-tan cloth is pinched in at the waist but widens towards the hem. The upper sleeves are made in large puffs, giving a wide shoulder-line, and are attached to close-fitting lower sleeves. The belt of brown fabric is fastened in front by a gilt buckle. The wide, flat collar is of brown fur, which borders the front and hem of the coat. (d) The gown is of rose-pink gauze over a silk foundation, with a rouleau of gauze edging the skirt. The 'burnous' cloak is of purple velvet, with a quilted rose-pink satin lining turned back to form a collar fastened by silver link-buttons. The folds of the cloak are lifted up on the left arm showing some of the lining. The right arm comes through an arm-opening in the side of the cloak. (e) The shawl is of slate-blue cashmere with an edging of black embroidery and fringe. The hem of the crinoline skirt of heliotrope silk, edged with black velvet, is visible. (f) The fitted, sherry-brown velvet coat has a short basque and is fastened down the front, where it is decorated at intervals by flowers of turquoise blue velvet. It has a moderate bell-shaped skirt and three-quarter-length sleeves turned back below the elbows, showing the full under-sleeves of turquoise silk, sewn into bands at the wrists. The flat, round collar is of turquoise silk, edged with a narrow frill.

Footwear: (a) The flat slippers are of black kid. (b) The flat slippers are of yellow kid, with small bows in front. (c) The flat-soled slippers are of brown kid, cut low at the insteps.

Jewellery and Accessories: (a) A long, narrow stole of white fur and a necklace of crystal beads are worn. The gloves are of white kid. (b) The gloves are of yellow kid and the bag of dark red velvet with a gilt frame. (c) The muff is of brown fur. (d) The fan is of pink silk and ivory. (e) The gloves are of grey kid or silk and the parasol of heliotrope silk. (f) The gloves are of cream-coloured kid and the frilled parasol of turquoise silk.

XIV.5. 1820–75. Maidservants

front of the coiffure, and evening hair ornaments were attached in the same position. In the late 70s women often wore a small mob cap at home or in the evening.

In the '80s hats and bonnets were usually worn squarely on the head, but a curving brim or drooping feather was sometimes seen. Hats with brims were perched, but small rounded hats of the early '80s tied on like bonnets with upturned brims were given a backward tilt. A bonnet with a halo-shaped brim and a similar hat, upturned in front, both set back on the head, were worn about 1887.

In the 1890s the 'mannish' mode resulted in women's adoption of the hard-brimmed straw hat, the tight-fitting peaked cap like a schoolboy's, the deerstalker hat and miniature versions of the bowler and the Homburg. Hats with flat or curving brims were worn level on the head or slightly tilted and were trimmed with flowers, feathers and ribbon. Small flowered toques were in fashion. All headgear in this decade was perched up.

Garments—Men: By the beginning of the 19th century the vogue for the tailed coat, square-cut or sloping away from the waist, had been established as the mainstay of masculine fashion. The collar in both types was high at the back, and was rolled over, with lapels. From about 1804 until 1840 it was permissible to cut collar and revers in a long curve, resembling that of a rolled collar, but straight-cut edges were equally fashionable. The line from collar to shoulder was narrow and often drooping, the waist-line a little above normal when square-cut and considerably above it when sloped away. The tails of both were squared off and ended just above the back of the knees. The square-cut coat was adopted as formal evening-dress. The waistcoat, fastened throughout, ended in a straight hem at a slightly high waist-level. It was made of cloth or silk lighter in colour than the coats and could be striped.

XIV.5. 1820–75. Maidservants

Hair: (a) (1820.) Short curls over the forehead and at the sides can be seen under the cap. (b) (1830.) The hair is parted in the centre and puffed out at the sides. The chignon near the top of the head is hidden under the cap. (c) (1841.) The hair is parted in the centre and smoothed down on each side. The chignon at the back is hidden by the cap. (d) (1853.) The hair is drawn to the sides from the centre parting. The cap hides the small chignon half-way up the back of the head. (e) (1865.) The hair is taken over a circular pad and rolled back all round. (f) (1875.) The centre-parted hair is lifted at the sides above the ears and drawn back tightly to a bun at the back.

Headdress: (a) The mob-cap has a narrow black ribbon tied in a bow in front. (b) The starched and frilled white muslin cap is tied on by black satin ribbons under the chin. The large full crown is gathered into a band and covers the chignon near the top of the head. A black ribbon is tied on the left of the front. (c) The plain white linen cap is turned back in front and has a short frill at the back of the neck. (d) The white muslin cap is a frilled strip placed across the top of the head. It has a muslin rosette on either side. (e) The cap is contrived from a circle of white muslin gathered into a double row of frills. It is set on the back of the head and is tied by drawstrings at the back. (f) The small mob-cap is set high on the head.

Garments: (a) The high-waisted dress is of white muslin. The starched white collar stands up a little on the shoulders. The puffed sleeves are joined to long, close-fitting lower sleeves. The frilled white muslin apron has a frilled bib and is tied on at the high waist-line. (b) The black silk dress has a fitted bodice, and a full circular skirt. The large balloon sleeves form a wide, downward-sloping line on the shoulders and taper towards the wrists. The flat collar and deep cuffs are of white embroidered muslin. The muslin apron tied on at the waist has embroidery at the hem. (c) The dress is of blue and white checked cotton, and has a fitted bodice and a bell-shaped skirt with some fullness at the back. the plain white linen collar fastens at the throat and the long, plain sleeves end in white linen cuffs. A white apron without a bib is tied on at the waist. (d) The pink and white printed cotton dress has sleeves rolled up above the elbows and is fastened down the front of the fitted bodice. The round, flat white collar fastens at the throat. The full skirt, ending above the ankles, has bands round it at two points to prevent it from billowing out. A white apron without a bib is worn. (e) The black silk gown has a full skirt, worn over a crinoline and touching the ground. The high neck has a narrow white frill and the full sleeves end in white muslin cuffs. A frilled white muslin apron without a bib is worn. (f) The dress of grey alpaca has a fitted bodice, fastening down the front, and a plain skirt, not very full. The high collar and the cuffs are of plain white linen. The white cotton apron has no bib and is frilled at the hem.

Footwear: (a) The flat slippers are of black kid. (b) The flat black kid slippers have narrow crossed bands over the insteps. (c) The flat-soled black slippers are of black kid. (d) The flat shoes are of black leather. (f) The black leather shoes have 'baby Louis' heels.

Accessories: (a) The maid carries a brass warming-pan with a handle of polished wood. (b) The bedroom candlestick is of silver. (c) The maid carries a small bowl. (d) The broom is made up of feathers bound to a wooden rod. (f) The maid carries a porcelain table-lamp with a brass lamp-fitting and a globe of opaque white glass with floral decoration.

A high, starched white collar with points framing the cheeks was supported by a broad, tightly wrapped cravat, usually white in the early years.

The shirt-frill was still worn, but in many cases had become a plain, buttoned fastening edged with its own material. The cuffs of the shirt, now plain bands or narrow goffered frills, were rarely visible except in Court dress.

Sleeves were at first plain and close-fitting, but after 1804 were puffed at the shoulder, and tapered to plain, close-fitting or goblet-shaped cuffs.

Knee breeches and silk stockings were still worn, especially at Court or with other formal dress, close-fitting pantaloons ending just below the calf or a little above the ankle were worn until about 1825.

A third type of coat, known as a redingote and originally worn as a greatcoat, was of calf-length and single-breasted, with a small collar and revers, close-fitting, tapering sleeves and only moderate fullness in the skirt. The version of it known as the 'Polish' coat had a fur collar and frogged fastenings.

Another greatcoat was the voluminous 'Garrick', first seen in the 1780s, made with two or more shoulder-capes and with internal draw-strings and strap-and-button fastenings to increase or decrease its girth at will. It ended well down the calves, sometimes descending almost to the heels after 1804. It was fastened down the front and had a collar which could be turned up at the back and fastened at the base of the throat. Its sleeves were wider than those of other coats.

The short jacket known as the spencer, first seen about 1795, was worn early in the century over the ordinary coat. It ended at its high waist, and had long sleeves of the same shape as those of the coat or short, puffed sleeves ending half-way down the upper arms. It formed an additional garment until about 1815.

Between 1804 and 1815 the waist of the sloping-away coat was lowered, the cut of the body of the coat made more generous and the slope-away less abrupt, with fairly broad coat-tails, squared at the ends, which could be almost of calf-length or end at or above the knees.

The square-cut coat was usually made double-breasted, with the option of buttoning back the two sides if it were to be worn open, though single-breasted examples were known. In this case the cut-away at the waist was slight and the coat-tails therefore broader. From about 1804 to 1820 the length and size of coat-tails varied greatly and the size of collars and revers almost as much.

Many men now wore a narrow scarf wrapped round the neck and crossed over in front in place of the cravat, particularly in the country or for travelling.

The redingote had developed by 1820 into an elegant coat, with a rolled collar high at the back and fastening on the chest, puff-shouldered, tapering sleeves and a closely fitted waist. The chest was padded and the body was at first made in one with the bell-shaped skirt. When worn as a greatcoat it often had a shoulder cape, but was now frequently worn as the only coat. The garment ended as a rule at the knees or calves. It could be fastened at the front by buttons or 'frogs'.

By 1820 waistcoats might have long, narrow, roll-collars instead of lapels.

Narrow 'peg-top' trousers with fullness at the waist and a strap under the instep, became very fashionable in the 1820s, as did loose Nankeen trousers, braced high and showing the ankles. The front fastening was now in general fashion.

The semicircular cloak was in use for evening or formal occasions, made in velvet or fine cloth, lined with satin, and also for travelling, in more practical materials. It was often very large, reaching the heels, or could end at calf or knee level. It could be collarless or have a small upstanding collar or a short, broad collar lying flat, with a chain or cords as a fastening across the chest. Other examples had long roll collars. The last two were often made of astrakhan or other short fur.

Many lapels and rolled collars ended at the waist in a single-breasted fastening, between 1825 and 1835. The waistline was lowered again at this time, defining waist and hips. Waistcoats were longer to follow suit.

An unusual form of the square-cut coat in fashion in 1831 and worn chiefly for riding, has been illustrated and described among the captions.

The redingote had the skirt attached at the waist by the 1830s. Pleats from the back of the waist gave considerable fullness. By 1837 it could be double-breasted and the revers could be buttoned over the chest and meet a rolled, front-fastening collar. Frogs or a double row of buttons could trim the breast.

Puffed shoulders were still worn in 1830, but by 1836 or thereabouts were more plainly set in. In general the sloping shoulder-line remained.

Collars and high cravats with a bow in front were often ready-made, with a buckle and strap to fasten them. By 1837 a large, coloured silk cravat could be worn which covered the collar and shirt-front entirely.

By 1836 the bodies of men's coats and waistcoats were padded in the chest. This fashion continued into the 1840s and '50s.

Waistcoats could be very ornate, of embroidered silk or brocade in pale colours.

Peg-topped trousers continued in fashion until the early '40s. Wider trousers covering a good deal of the shoes were strapped like the others to keep them in place. Pantaloons were worn with evening dress until about 1837.

In the 1840s the skirts of the coat could curve in a wasp-like shape at the back from waist to hem. The rolled collar, high at the back, had given way to a turned-over collar meeting broad lapels and fastening at the waist or small lapels fastening high on the chest. The sloping shoulder had the tapering sleeve set in without gathers.

Coats were frequently worn open, showing ornate, pale-coloured waistcoats. These ended at the waist in the early 1840s, fastened about half-way down the chest, and were shaped, like the coat, by padding. For evening wear, with a black tail-coat, the waistcoat could be black, cream-coloured or white, showing the frilled white evening shirt above its medium-high fastening. Towards the end of the decade the waistcoat for day wear was longer, covering the hips, with pointed corners at the base of the front fastening.

Wide cravats for wear in the daytime were of dark-coloured silks, either wound high to show the frilled or starched shirt-front or arranged to cover it almost entirely. A high, narrow, turned-over white collar was sometimes just visible above the folds of the large cravat. Narrower cravats were wound round the neck showing more of the collar, with narrowed ends tied in a bow in front. A white cravat of this type was worn by this time with evening dress.

Loosely hanging greatcoats ending just above or below the knees came into fashion about 1850. They had sleeves wider than usual, made in one with the garment and could be single- or double-breasted. Many were lined with quilted silk or satin. They usually fastened high, with a turned-down collar of medium width and short, broad revers, and could be fastened with frogging or rows of buttons.

In 1850 the redingote, worn as the only coat, had only a short flare below the pinched, hip-level waistline, but by the middle '50s coat skirts were narrower and ended a little above the knees. With the more loosely fitted waist now in fashion the development of the frock coat can be discerned.

Cravats were still occasionally seen wrapped round the neck, with narrowed ends tied in a bow, but ties of moderate width, often of satin, were tied in the same way and showed a good deal of the collar. The bow was usually made-up and the material stiffened.

The 'dicky', worn as a substitute for a plain starched shirt-front, was rivalled about the middle of the century by an inset shirt-front which was also starched and glazed.

Trousers were well-tailored to encase the legs, of moderate width and could still be strapped under the insteps. The trouser ends were wide enough to cover part of the insteps and the backs of the shoes. A sloping-away coat, with a longer waistline than formerly, was seen at formal functions during the 1850s. The shoulders of some coats were broader than they had been, but still sloped.

The collar with open points covering the jaws remained in use until the early '50s. An upstanding circular stiff collar now came into fashion, worn with a narrow tie and made-up bow or with an Ascot tie and tiepin. A narrow, white, turned-over collar was also in favour, also a wide, soft tie passed through a ring instead of being knotted.

Trousers tended at the end of the 1850s to be fuller in the legs, tapering a little towards the ankles. They could be striped or checked or made of rougher material than the coat. It was unusual now for them to be strapped under the foot.

The semicircular cloak, when worn for travelling, could have one front corner thrown over the opposite shoulder.

XIV.6. 19th Century. Women's Indoor Caps

Hair: (a) (1800–10.) The hair is in short curls over the forehead and is pinned up at the back in a cluster of curls. (b) (1810.) Only short curls on the forehead and temples can be seen. (c) (1810–20.) Short curls on the forehead and coming forward at the sides can be seen. (d) (1832.) The hair is parted at an angle a little to the left of centre. It is arranged in horizontal rows of curls, not quite symmetrically. (e) (1845.) The hair is parted in the centre and brought down smoothly on the temples, where narrow ringlets hang down at the sides. The chignon, hidden by the cap, is fairly high at the back of the head. (f) (1850.) The hair is brought down smoothly from a centre parting, turned over at the sides and taken back to form part of the chignon with the hair at the back. (g) (1855.) The coiffure is similar to that of (e), but is brought down lower at the sides and looped back into a lower chignon. (h) (1860.) The hair is rolled up and back from the forehead and temples leaving the ears partly exposed. A thick plait is laid across the top of the head behind the roll and is fastened at the back of the neck under the low chignon. (i) (1865.) The pad over which the hair is rolled back comes further forward than in (h) and the chignon is higher, making an elongated shape in profile. (j) (1870.) The hair in front is swept up from a centre parting to be fastened on the top of the head and to descend at the back, mingled with the back hair, in rolls and twists. (k) (1880.) There is a short fringe over the forehead. The rest of the hair is taken up tightly and wound in a bun on the top of the head. (l) (1890.) The hair is arranged in the same way as in (k), but in this case without the fringe.

Headdress: (a) The cap is a bandeau of white muslin, wider in the centre than at the ends and frilled at the edges, laid over the head and fastened under the chin by a pink ribbon, with small pink rosettes on each side and bands of the same ribbon attached to them tied in a bow on the top of the head. (b) The cap is a hood of white linen, covering the head and neck, with a short tail or elongated point at the back. A frill is added across the forehead. It was chiefly worn by maidservants. (c) This white muslin cap has a double frill framing the face with a bandeau of plain muslin behind it and behind that a larger double frill. The back (unseen) is of plain muslin. A daffodil-yellow ribbon encircles the bandeau and ties under the chin. (d) This cap is a mass of lace frills giving the wide outline favoured in the early 1830s. A broad taffeta ribbon in large

In the 1860s coats were only slightly fitted at the waist. Frock-coats had developed from the redingote, which was almost outdated, and some of these ended below the knees. Others finished about two-thirds of the way down the thighs. They had narrow collars and lapels and fastened high on the chest, but were often left open. They could be single- or double-breasted. The square-cut coat was now worn solely as evening dress. Shorter coats were the close-fitting jackets, with matching trousers, which introduced the lounge suit. They had high, small lapels which were worn fastened as a general rule. A box-like single- or double-breasted casual jacket, ending at mid-thigh, was a feature of the mode. It was bordered all round with braid or narrow strips of fur. Sleeves were set in plainly and narrowed a little between elbow and wrist, where they showed the edge of the starched cuffs. The inset bosom of the shirt was still starched.

Waistcoats could be made to match the coat and trousers or could be of lighter cloth, often checked or tartan material, satin, taffetas, embroidered silk or brocade in cream, greys and dove-colours, with small stripes or patterns, and occasionally made in brilliant colours when of silk. They ended a little below the waist with a straight hem and could fasten high or half-way down the chest. The evening waistcoat could be black or white and was made of fine cloth or grosgrain. It had long, curved revers and a low fastening.

Collars were round and upstanding, almost meeting in front, or low and turned down, often lying a little away from the neck.

Narrow bow ties, ties wider than those of today, but knotted in the present fashion, or the broad, soft ties passed through a ring could be worn with either type of collar. The turned-down collar could be worn, rather incongruously, with the frock-coat, and the high, circular collar with the casual jacket. An Ascot tie could be worn with the latter type of collar.

Trousers were rather baggy and shapeless for much of the decade, narrowing a little towards the ankles from a point at about mid-calf.

Overcoats ended just below the knee or at calf-length and were straight-cut and moderately loose-fitting. They had high-fastening lapels meeting a curved collar and plain sleeves.

The use of hopsack, frieze, homespun, checked and striped material and tweed increased as the latter half of the century advanced and never went out of fashion.

---

checks of cherry red on pale blue slants over the right side of the brow, with ringlets pinned over it, and is bunched in loops towards the right with two artificial roses attached on the left. Another rose is set lower down at the left side. (e) This cap is of white muslin, with an elongated back to accommodate the chignon and a wide lappet of embroidered muslin laid across the head in front and descending to the shoulders at the sides. Two more lappets also touching the shoulders are attached on either side towards the back. (f) The cap of écru muslin fits the back of the head and has an undulating frill in front making a frame for the face. Large double bows of turquoise-blue picot-edged taffeta ribbon are set on each side, with streamers coming down on to the shoulders. (g) A wide pale green satin ribbon is laid across the head, with its ends, cut in points, touching the shoulders. A flat bow of the ribbon is tied on the top and artificial roses in tea-rose colours decorate both sides. (h) The round cap of cream-coloured muslin, frilled round the edge, is set back on the head, with a flat bow and streamers of black velvet ribbon at the back. (i) The cap of ruched ivory silk covers the top of the head, with frilled lappets at the sides. Silk flowers in mauve and cyclamen pink trim the front and sides, with purple satin ribbons tied in a bow at the back, above the chignon. (j) The cap of cream-coloured dotted muslin is perched forward over the brow. It has a double frill and two small brown satin bows. Two frilled streamers of the muslin hang at the back. (k) The white muslin mob-cap is perched on the top of the head. It has a narrow black satin ribbon round it tied in front, and a deep frill. (l) The

cap is made up of rows of écru net, gathered in the centre to make a circular shape. It is worn on the top of the head and is surmounted by a flat black velvet bow.

Garments: (a) The oval, frilled neckline of the high-waisted white muslin gown can be seen. (b) The top of the grey cotton gown and the chemisette of white muslin, with a high neck-frill are visible from the back. (c) The neck-frill of the pale yellow muslin dress fits closely round the base of the neck. (d) The off-shoulder neckline of an evening gown of cherry-red taffeta can be seen. (e) The flat, round collar of white embroidery fastens at the throat. (f) A narrow neck-frill fits round the base of the neck. (g) The flat, round collar of écru muslin fastens at the throat and has a short shoulder-cape. (h) The plain collar, fastening at the throat, is of white lawn. The gown is of biscuit-coloured silk, with vertical stripes of dark red and red buttons. (i) The violet silk gown has a chemisette of ivory net, with a frill and purple ribbon round the neck, also edging the square neckline. (j) The round collar of écru lawn is fastened at the throat. The gown is of 'feuille morte' satin with horizontal cream-coloured stripes. (k) The dress of slate-blue silk, with a frill descending to a point in front, has a chemisette of white silk with a frill and a black velvet ribbon round the neck. (l) The gown of dark grey ribbed silk fastens in front and has a high collar with a narrow white frilled edging.

Jewellery: (g) and (j) have small brooches to fasten their collars. (l) has a large gold brooch set with small stones and a gold chain and locket.

The frock-coat could be worn with checked or widely striped trousers, especially when made in grey. The sloping-away coat fitted the figure closely and was worn with striped or matching trousers. A more casual, sporting version of it was worn with checked or rough-surfaced trousers or with matching knickerbockers and gaiters. It had a cartridge belt put on round the waist for shooting parties. The tails varied in length, in some instances ending near the top of the thighs and in others reaching a point about half-way down. They were rounded off at the ends. In the sports coat they were often little more than a vent at the back of the coat. The lounge suit developed on lines recognizable to our eyes, with a short jacket, rounded or square at the corners, and plain sleeves. Lapels were short and the jacket fastened only at the top button. The 'boxy' jacket now had a small upstanding collar, fastened above the lapels. It could be single- or double-breasted, and was usually made of tweed or other informal woollen stuff. The evening dress square-cut coat had rather short, squared-off tails.

The last representation of the redingote was seen in the double-breasted 'surtout' ending at mid-thigh, of the early '70s. An open wing collar was now worn, with an ordinary knotted tie or an Ascot tie. The Ascot tie could also be worn with a striped, close-fitting turned-down collar and with a sports suit and knickerbockers. This collar remained in fashion. The upstanding 'jampot' collar was now often very high, with a wide opening in front in the height of fashion. It was worn with evening dress with the white bow tie but usually with an Ascot tie in ordinary dress. The low, turned-down collar could also be worn with evening dress and a white bow tie.

Trousers fitted the legs loosely, but narrowed a little at the calf and widened towards the hem, covering the backs of the shoes and a little of the insteps.

Men wore white for tennis, boating and cricket. Striped blazers for boating, cricket, tennis and seaside wear came into fashion in this decade. An alternative outfit for tennis in the late '70s and early '80s consisted of a long-sleeved white jersey and white knickerbockers ending at the calf, worn with thick stockings and flat shoes.

The existing fashions continued through the 1880s with some additions but few changes. A double-breasted lounge suit was fashionable for wear at the seaside.

Trousers lost their outward flare just above the foot and were moderately loose-fitting with little variation in the width all the way down the legs. They still covered the backs of the shoes and came forward a little over the insteps.

The morning coat developed from the sloping-away coat in the 1890s, though it was fastened by three buttons and so was not quite as it is known today. The chief addition to men's fashions in this decade was the Norfolk suit, a development of the knickerbocker suit. It was belted and had large pockets, without flaps, on the hips. Box-pleats, of about the same width as the belt, ran down each side of the chest and back to the hem of the jacket. The knickerbockers had only moderate fullness at the knees. Overcoats ended just below the knees as a rule, but tweed 'Ulsters' could be much longer. They fastened high, were loose-fitting and sometimes had fur collars. With the addition of a waist-length cape, they were known as Inverness capes.

Few other alterations can be noted in the '90s, except a general improvement in tailoring. The turned-down collar was worn with informal dress, with a knotted or bow tie. The 'jampot' collar, now joined in front, might be worn with either of these ties and with Norfolk or other country suits. The wing collar, however, was the most popular during the '90s and was worn with everything, becoming the accepted wear with evening dress.

Garments—Women: Most of the dresses of 1800–5 were high-waisted. In others the bodice was shaped to the figure and ended only a little higher than the normal waistline, often with a small basque at the back.

Many skirts were long and full in the first three years of the century, and trailed on the ground at the back. About 1803 they grew less bulky and trains were shorter and less voluminous. Skirts for walking in some instances cleared the ground.

Over-dresses and over-skirts were a feature of the period, made and draped in various ways but generally shorter in the front than at the back. Some were draped diagonally, over the dress, in an attempt at the 'classical' line.

Décolleté necklines could be round, square or heart-shaped or could be draped and caught by jewelled ornaments on the shoulders and in the centre of the bosom. They could have an upstanding frill or a ruched edging, a narrow border of fur or a guimpe inside the bodice gathered into a band or tightened by a draw-string.

High collars encircling the neck could have a frilled or furred edge, could open in front like the collared partlet of the 16th century or have a round, turned-down collar. An example of the high collar is put on separately, fastens at the back and has a pointed yoke at back and front meeting the high waistline.

XIV.7. 1860–70. Women's Headdress

Hair: (a) (1860.) The hair in front is rolled back over a pad. The remainder is hidden by the bonnet. (b) (1866.) The hair curves back from the forehead above the ears and is arranged in two ringlets pinned behind them and a small, low chignon. (c) (1870.) The hair is swept up over a pad from a centre parting. Two horizontal ringlets are pinned one below the other on the crown of the head. The rest of the hair hangs at the back in loose ringlets.

Headdress: (a) The 'spoon' bonnet is covered in pale blue silk, with a narrow white net frill in front and black velvet piping and scalloped edging behind it. Pink roses are pinned under the front of the brim, which slopes away to a small circular shape at the back edged with black velvet. A deep frill of pale blue silk, with double scalloped edging, hangs at the back. A flat bow of pale blue ribbon is set on the top, with ends coming down at the sides and tying under the chin. (b) The hat of moss-green velvet has a narrow brim, dipping at the front and back and curving up at the sides. A long, curled, coral-pink ostrich plume curves over the hat from front to back. (c) The small hat of natural straw is tipped well forward over the front of the coiffure. A narrow band of brown satin ribbon and a wreath of pale yellow flowers encircle the small, shallow crown. Brown satin ribbons come from under the brim and are tied under the ringlets at the back of the neck.

Garments: (a) The pelisse of pale blue cloth has a collar and epaulettes of black velvet. (b) The dress of coral-pink silk has double stripes of moss green and a close, round neckline bound in dark green velvet, with a neck-frill. The epaulettes, of the striped silk, are edged with dark green velvet, which also edges the front fastening of the bodice. (c) The dress is of maize-coloured silk, the square neckline edged with matching ruching and filled in with a chemisette in cream-coloured net.

Jewellery: (c) wears a short gold chain and small locket.

Sleeves could be short and moderately puffed, long and close-fitting, extending over the hand or finished by frills, or they could consist of two short swathes joined over the upper arm, or a flounce that extended only a little below the shoulder. An interesting sleeve has a double puff ending just above the elbow, and another, worn very early in the century, is close-fitting to the elbow or just below it, with a plain edge or narrow frills.

Short 'spencer' jackets, with long tight sleeves, were fashionable from 1800 to 1810, and had a military note when trimmed with braid. A shaped wrap (mantelet) with long scarf-ends in front, wider where it curved across the back, could be worn indoors or out.

High-waisted coats with upstanding collars, long, close sleeves and a straight, practically unflared skirt to the ankle or instep were worn as outer wraps, also semicircular capes, sometimes fastened on one shoulder, leaving one arm exposed. Both these garments were usually trimmed with narrow borders of fur or marabou. By 1805, three-quarter length coats, still of straight and narrow shapes and with high collars, were made of cloth or velvet for warmth or of flimsy stuff in summer.

By 1810 skirts were narrower and some were shorter, often well above the ankle. A new line in some dresses from about 1810 to 1820, contrived the dress all in one piece, darted in to cling to the figure from bust to hips and widening only a little from thigh to hem. About 1810 puffs were added to the shoulders of some long, close sleeves, and by 1815 a boat-shaped neckline had appeared. The skirts of high-waisted coats were wider to cover the now wider skirt of the dress.

By 1815 frills and femininity were increasing in favour and little trace of the classical model remained. Waists were still high, but the shaping of the figure by the stays constricted the rib-cage and waist. The top of the skirt could be narrow and close-fitting and in some cases was darted so that it gave a corseted effect from below the bust to the hips. The skirt gradually widened to fairly full flares and ended at or above the ankles. It was circular in shape with a certain amount of extra fullness at the back. Trains were rare.

Upstanding or standing-falling ruffs adorned high necklines and guimpes, and wide cape collars edged with frills, marabou or fur were also worn.

By 1820 the skirt had begun to flare more widely. Hemlines had dropped and now only showed the shoes and occasionally the ankles. Frills, flowers, looped or fluttering ribbons, lace, gauze, ruched trimmings and every kind of ultra-feminine ornament decorated gowns on necklines, sleeves, bodices and deep borders above the hems.

Between 1820 and 1825 the waistline was lowered.

1825 saw the end of the very high waist. The tightly fitting, almost unwrinkled bodice now ended at or a fraction above the normal waist-line. Narrow belts, out of favour for some years, were worn again. The rib-cage appeared almost non-existent, the waist was closely corseted and a narrow sloping line below it only gradually swelled out into the circular skirt. The hemline had dropped and the edge of the dress almost touched the floor. There was still moderate fullness from the back of the waist to the hem.

The boat-shaped neckline, low or high in front, predominated, with alternatives such as a neckband encircling the base of the throat with a round lace or embroidery collar, or wide frills worn round the neck like a ruff.

A 'leg o' mutton' sleeve, wide at the top and tapering to the wrist, now largely took the place of the plainer long sleeve and widened the shoulder-line. Frilled shoulder capes of stiffened lawn, lace, embroidery or taffetas and full bishop sleeves of gauze or muslin, held out at the shoulders by puffed sleeves beneath, enhanced this effect.

By 1830 the fashions had developed the styles always connected with the Romantic Movement in France. The width of the shoulder-line was now below the shoulder itself, swelling out into huge puffed sleeves, often capped by shoulder-frills or capes. Belts were often wider than they had been and usually fastened in front with a buckle. The waist-line was normal. Tight-fitting sleeves from elbows to wrists were frequently attached to puffed sleeves.

The circular skirt was very full and held out by flounced and starched petticoats. Between 1830 and 1835 it could end just above the shoes or show the ankles.

Outer wraps or pelisses had cape-like collars that followed sloping lines from the neck to the tops of the huge cape sleeves. They had close-fitting bodices with tight belts and large full skirts. Added shoulder-capes formed the sleeves. Wide stoles, long scarves and large silk or cashmere shawls were also worn.

By 1837 simpler and more modest styles had prevailed. The bodice was fitted to the figure and a bell-shaped skirt now touched the ground or just cleared it. Round, turned-down collars or frilled guimpes encircled the necks of many day gowns. A modified version of the boat-shaped line, extending to the shoulders and edged by narrow frills, could be worn for day or evening. In evening dress deep berthas or other edgings kept the sleeve-line low, exposing the shoulders in some instances.

Most sleeves were plain and close-fitting, set in below the shoulders and ending in close-fitting cuffs of the same stuff as the dress or of lawn or embroidered muslin, or alternatively one or two small puffs. Others had a moderate puff below the elbow, ending in a turned-back cuff and a close-fitting lower sleeve covering part of the forearm and the wrist. Miniature sleeve-capes, attached below the shoulders, decorated some plain sleeves. Other sleeves depending from these capes were made in a series of small puffs to the wrist. Most evening dresses had tiny, short puffed sleeves, sometimes covered by the bertha. Others had short, loose sleeves ending above the elbows and edged with ruching and frills.

The bodice could end in a rounded line or a point in front.

It was the custom in the decade 1837–47 to wear shoulder-capes, diamond-shaped wraps edged with lace or fur (with a point hanging at back and front and an opening for the head in the centre, but fastened down the front rather than put over the head), mantelets (the shaped wrap with scarf-like ends) and other cape-like coverings as alternatives to the usual shawls and scarves. Pelisses, full-skirted but often of three-quarter length, sometimes with a deep shoulder-cape covering much of the body, were also worn out of doors. Mantles without over-capes had long, close sleeves and round collars fastening at the neck. They could be made all in one, fitted to the figure, or with the skirt put on at the waist. Large shawls could be made into shaped wraps with a point hanging down at the back, one over each arm and the fourth formed into a collar. Wraps were made of merino, cashmere, silk, satin and velvet, according to their useful or ornamental purpose.

Before the end of the '40s, sleeves were set in a little higher and by 1850 were at the normal level. The bell-sleeve took on a wider opening at this date and some three-quarter length sleeves, with wide, frilled or lace-edged openings were shown. Between 1845 and 1850 the skirt grew longer, usually touching the ground or sweeping it a little, though some ball dresses still just cleared the floor.

Three-quarter length jackets fitted loosely to the figure and often bordered with fur, with wide, loose sleeve-openings were in fashion by 1847 and continued through the '50s. Shorter, fitted jackets of silk, velvet and lace or of the same stuff as the dress, took the place of some of the shoulder capes and casual wraps formerly worn. The basques of these jackets could be short or could cover the hips.

The guimpe often extended to the waist with an open bodice. It was in the early '50s that the crinoline, a bell-shaped petticoat stiffened from waist to hem by horizontally placed bands of steel or whalebone, took the place of some of the many petticoats hitherto worn.

The long, close sleeve was unusual after 1850. The loose three-quarter length sleeve with frills appearing from beneath the opening or with a bishop sleeve underneath were popular fashions and some were very wide.

The crinoline was larger by the later 1850s and the skirt had now almost reached the greatest circumference it was to achieve during the crinoline period. Women now wore full drawers with lace or embroidery frills below the knees. These were fashionable for a further fifty years.

Skirts in tiers or a series of flounces were especially fashionable during the 1850s. Long basques and double skirts, the upper one ending at about calf-length, were also in the mode. An effect of an over-dress open from the waist, with a central panel representing the under-dress, was another item of fashion.

The pelisse or the walking-dress made all in one, with long darts to define the bust, waist and hips, was in fashion by 1850, and the same line was used for other day and evening dresses. Large shawls, folded double, with a point depending at the back, formed an all-enveloping wrap for wearing out of doors.

By 1857 very loose, tent-like coats and capes, of full or three-quarter length, with flat, round collars tied by broad ribbons in front, had come into fashion and became very voluminous during the '60s. Some were fitted to the figure in front, but were full and loose at the back. Others were fitted back and front with protuberant fullness at the back to accommodate the backward extension of the crinoline. Short, loose jackets were also worn.

In the 1860s the bodice had downward pointing lines from the shoulder to the centre of the waist and curved lines from shoulder to shoulder, deepening over the bosom, with low décolletage for evening. Plain bodices for daytime wear fastened down the front and were finished with a round collar and a bow or brooch at the base of the neck.

XIV.8. 1865–95. Women's Outdoor Dress

Hair: (a) (1865.) The hair is parted in the centre and brought down smoothly on each side. (b) (1875.) The hair is rolled above the forehead from a centre parting. Two small coils are pinned above the temples and above the ears at the sides. A coiled chignon is worn low at the back of the neck. (c) (1885.) The hair is taken up above the forehead and ears to a knot (unseen) on the top of the head.

(d) (1895.) The hair is dressed in a pompadour (unseen) in front and swept up at the back to a knot on the top of the head.

Headdress: (a) The small dark green velvet bonnet fits the back of the head and is tied by green ribbons under the chin. A long white ostrich plume droops over the left side. (b) The hat of bronze velvet has a

Sleeves early in the 1860s were again set in a little below the shoulder. There was a return to long, plain sleeves with or without turned-back cuffs. By the end of the 1860s wide and full sleeves were less often seen, the bell sleeve with bishop sleeve beneath being of moderate size and very short sleeves, often hidden by the shoulder drapery, being fashionable with evening dress.

Length as well as fullness at the back of the skirt was very fashionable in the first half of the '60s but the circular fullness at front and sides remained.

By 1866 the great size of the skirt had begun to diminish. The fullness of long coats or wraps was now increased further at the back, the front being loose or fitted to the body. Hooded cloaks in silk, satin or velvet had become fashionable as evening wraps. The fitted, three-quarter length coat continued in fashion.

In 1870 the first fashions of the bustle period were shown in a slightly short-waisted bodice joined to an over-skirt open in front, or with a draped-up front, and bunched up at the back. An under-skirt touching the ground in front formed a train at the back.

The bodice had a short point in front or a rounded base. Sashes or belts might be worn. With a draped front to the over-dress, the bodice was often made in one piece with it, and the waist defined by darts.

'V'-shaped décolletage, generally edged by upstanding frills, could be close to the neck or moderately low. Some day dresses with close, round necklines that reached the base of the throat had a narrow, plain collar attached to an upstanding neckband, often with a small cascade of frills in front, or alternatively a round, frilled collar. Evening dresses had round or squared décolletage or alternatively the frilled or swathed top of the bodice exposed the shoulders, with a low, curved line at front and back.

Wide sleeves for daytime wear were fashionable again between 1870 and '75, of full or three-quarter length. They were now put in at the normal level again.

Short jackets designed with a basque to flare out over the bustle and mantles shaped from folded shawls were the usual outer wraps. The heavy, lined skirts of the dresses must in themselves have given a good deal of protection from the weather.

By 1875 a long 'cuirass' bodice, fitted to the figure and covering the hips, was coming into fashion. The bustle became smaller and took on a downward-sloping line. The skirt was much narrower, with fullness drawn to the back, where many different arrangements of 'waterfall' drapery descended over the long train of the under-skirt.

The front of the over-dress was usually drawn upward and back in an 'apron' shape and its folds caught together below the bustle to join the 'waterfall', but variations in the lines of this drapery occurred. In some instances the front of the draped-back over-dress ended only

---

small crown edged with light brown fur, which forms the brim. A cluster of brownish-pink curled plumes trims it in front. It curves up at the sides and down at front and back. (c) The high-perched 'bowler' hat is of black felt and has a tall crown and narrow brim. (d) The hat is covered in black satin and has a cluster of lilac-coloured flowers in front. The brim is level in front, turning up a little at the edge, and is turned up at the back, where it is decorated by a bow of lilac ribbon.

Garments: (a) The coat is of dark green velvet, fitted to the body but full in the skirt particularly at the back, to accommodate the crinoline. It is three-quarter-length and has a deep border, collar and cuffs of white fur. The dress, of which part of the skirt can be seen, is of pale green grosgrain, with vertical stripes of picot-edged magenta ribbed silk. It is worn over a large crinoline with considerable fullness at the back. (b) The coat of bronze velvet is edged all round with a border of light brown fur. The body of the coat is fitted to the body, the lower part shaped to fit over the downward-sloping bustle and longer at the back than in front. The sleeves are loose-fitting and wide at the wrists. The dress of

brownish-pink satin is seen from below the bustle at the sides and back. The skirt has two deep tied-back swathes of bronze velvet, edged with pleats of the satin, in front, finished at the sides by bronze velvet bows. Two matching swathes, sloping downward, decorate the lower part of the skirt and tie back the three large puffs of the satin which form the back of the skirt with another bronze velvet bow. (c) The ulster is of dark grey and green checked woollen stuff. It fits the body to the waist, where it juts out at the back over a large bustle. It is bordered down the front with grey fur, with matching collar and cuffs. (d) The shoulder-cape is of sable fur. The coat of lilac cloth fits snugly at the waist. The skirt is shorter in front than at the back, where it flows out to lie on the ground. The sleeves are close-fitting. Part of the skirt of the black satin dress can be seen.

Footwear: (c) wears bootees with fairly high heels. These are hardly seen.

Accessories: All four figures carry muffs matching the fur on their coats.

a few inches above the hem. A substitute for the cuirass was an over-dress closely moulded to the body and extending to the knees or calves in the same narrow form.

Necklines from 1875 to 1880 were much the same as in the previous five years.

Most sleeves were plain and long, usually close-fitting, occasionally widening a little at the wrists and finished with narrow frills. Some were of three-quarter length, edged with frills or with turned-back cuffs. Some informal evening dresses had these sleeves, but in general they were almost sleeveless as before.

Three-quarter length coats, fitted to the figure and generally longer at the back than in front, with round collars fastening at the neck, were in fashion as outer wraps. Others had hems of even length all round, and were made with lapels and button fastenings.

XIV.9. 1871–84. Women's Headdress

Hair: (a) (1871.) The hair is arranged with three parallel vertically-placed ringlets over the centre of the forehead, with the hair on the temples swept up to the top of the head and fastened there, leaving the ears exposed. The hair fastened at the top and that at the back of the head are combined to form a cascade of coils descending over the back of the neck. (b) (Late '70s, early '80s.) The hair is worn in a fringe in front and is taken back into a small, low chignon. (c) (1884.) The hair is taken up tightly, away from the forehead and ears, into a small, severe knot (unseen) on the top of the head.

Headdress: The small bonnet of black velvet fits over the crown of the head. A large rosette and loops of rose-coloured taffeta ribbon decorate the front. Streamers of the same ribbon come from beneath the loops to tie under the chin and two streamers hang down at the back. (b) The natural straw bonnet fits over the back of the head and has an upturned brim. It has a brown velvet bow at the top with

ends hanging over the back surmounted by yellow and peach-coloured artificial roses. Brown ribbons are tied under the chin. (c) The black felt hat has a tall, diminishing, forward-leaning crown and a brim turned up sharply on the left, and curving round the back to turn down on the right. It is trimmed with stiff puce-coloured ribbon in two swathes and ends set upright in the turn-up of the brim.

Garments: (a) The black satin gown has a high collar with a small turn-over, open in front, of ivory satin and deep rose-coloured ruching edging the draped cape-collar. (b) The dress is of amber silk crêpe, open in the front of the bodice, with upstanding écru frilling and a chemisette of écru silk decorated with gilt buttons. This has a high 'V'-shaped neck-opening, trimmed with upstanding écru frilling and a brown ribbon tied in front. (c) The dress of pale grey cloth has small checks of puce colour. The high collar of pale grey silk matches the facings and has a narrow neck-frill.

In 1878–9 the cloth or tweed dress for travelling or country wear had appeared and was often made as a long over-dress or coat, fitted to the figure, with a pleated skirt, not necessarily matching, beneath, and with no back drapery. This was in any case reduced in day dresses, though in many formal and evening gowns the 'waterfall' or flounces continued in fashion.

The round, close-fitting high collar, which was to have such a lengthy vogue, came into fashion during the '80s. Some evening dresses took on a deep 'V'-shaped décolletage, trimmed with swathes of various designs and sometimes filled in horizontally by a 'modesty-vest' across the bosom.

In 1883 there were signs that the full bustle was returning and by 1884 it was at the height of fashion and grew to enormous size in the following four years. This brought to an end the very long 'cuirass' bodice and the waistline now just covered the top of the hips. The bustle jutted out suddenly under the back of the dress. The over-dress was draped back over it in various ways, with a fashion in 1887–8 for wide turned-back side panels, heavily ornamented, and the usual bunched effect at the back. The plainer dress of cloth or tweed and the full-length tweed coat simply hung over the bustle, with some concentration of pleats or folds at the back and was trimmed with buttons, braid or frogged fastenings. Cape sleeves were a feature of these coats.

Evening dress trains were attached at the back of the waist, over the bustle, and were not part of the skirt itself.

'Aesthetic' dress flourished in artistic circles in the early 1880s and continued with modifications into the 1900s. In the '80s its chief features were that it discarded the bustle, the long, clinging skirt flowing from low flares on to the ground, and that there was some attempt at medievalism in the sleeves.

In 1887–9 sleeves were slightly raised at the shoulders and the bustle was rather smaller.

In 1890 the gathered shoulder was higher and larger with the sleeve tapering to the wrist. Some sleeves between 1893–7 were made with a full upper part, dwindling only from below the elbow. Many evening dresses were sleeveless, with decorative straps holding up the shaped top of the bodice. Others had a minute flounce or a small swathe of material under each arm, caught up to the shoulder-join of the dress, which was often ornamented with an upstanding decoration of flowers, sequins, feathers or ribbons. Very short plain sleeves covering the top of the upper arm and short, puffed sleeves both with added 'wings' of material standing up above the shoulders, were also worn.

Skirts of evening dresses retained the bustle effect in 1890, in many cases, but many were made in a narrower shape, with only an indication of back fullness. Advance fashions were made with the round, flaring skirt, usually with godets extending at the back into a train, which was to become a general fashion by 1895.

The severely cut coat and skirt, of cloth or tweed, with short or hip-covering jacket, fitted to the figure, had become a firm fashion in 1895. The jacket had lapels like a man's and was often worn with a waistcoat over a shirt-blouse with mannish collar and cuffs and a man's tie. The skirt was long and flared and sometimes of a different material from the jacket.

Softer and more feminine versions of the coat and skirt were made of velvet, silk or supple cloth, and could have large puffed upper sleeves and short, flared basques to the jackets.

Bodices of dresses or blouses in 1895 showed a trim, normally placed waistline, sometimes basqued and often accentuated by a softly draped but well-boned sash belt. They could be pointed in front only or at back and front. The bodice sometimes had a cross-over effect, tied at the waist. Sleeves were at their widest and largest in the upper part in 1896. By 1897 the fashion had reverted to puffed and gathered shoulders and sleeves tapering to the wrists.

The high neckline was still in vogue for daytime wear, often with a large bow at front or back.

Large puffed sleeves or stiffened, wing-like frills could be worn with evening dress soon after the opening of this decade. Décolletage was low and could be rounded, heart-shaped or square.

The outer wraps of the 1890s generally followed the lines of the dresses, hanging over the diminished bustle and flowing over the flared skirts. Hip-length, basqued cloth or fur jackets and three-quarter length coats of cloth or fur remained in fashion. They frequently had a small upstanding circular or petal-shaped collar and a short shoulder-cape as well, of fur or with fur edging. Those that wrapped over had turned-back lapels. Exceptions to the fitted coats were the loose, hip-length jackets and the full-sleeved evening coats, hanging loosely from the shoulders and flowing on to the ground, which appeared in the early 1890s. Loose capes were also worn, full-length or ending at the waist or hips, almost always with an upstanding collar and often a small added shoulder-cape. Ulsters with long capes attached were in fashion for travelling, bad weather or country wear.

Footwear—Men: At the opening of the 19th century men's shoes were flat, the thin sole made all in one, sometimes with a shallow heel. They had low fronts and could be plain or with ribbon bows or flat, moderate-sized buckles. These shoes were in fashion, with modifications, until about 1830 and became the pumps worn with evening dress throughout the epoch, varied by laced shoes from the '60s. Front-laced shoes had appeared by 1860 and patent leather a little earlier.

Riding boots for general wear, even in town, were in vogue early in the century. These were of black leather with a deep top of brown or buff, fitting the calf and ending near its top or a little higher, just below the knee. They were pulled on and wrinkled about the ankles, with the foot well-fitting. They had thin soles and a wide, low heel. They went out of everyday fashion in the early 1820s, but became part of hunting dress and are still worn for this purpose. 'Hessian' boots, ending near the top of the calf or rather lower and with the front at the top a little higher than the back, were worn about the same time and on into the 1820s for riding and sometimes for ordinary occasions. They resembled military boots and often had a gilt tassel in the centre front. They could be made with the flat, wide heel or with the 'military' heel. Other boots, of black buckskin, ended at the calf. Leather bootees, sometimes with uppers of fabric, came into fashion about 1818, and by 1880 could have long vamps, squared-off toes and raised 'military' heels. Their tops were hidden by the trousers. They were worn until the 1880s with little change except the introduction of elastic side-gussets about 1847. They were the chief item of footwear for about thirty years. Boots for sport, country walking and cycling were worn in the '70s, '80s and '90s. They

---

XIV.10. 1845–91. Men. Six Figures

Hair: (a) (1845.) The hair is parted from front to back and brushed towards the front, leaving the ears exposed. A narrow fringe of beard continues the line of the side-whiskers, but the upper lip is clean-shaven. (b) (1865.) The hair is thick, but fairly short at the back. Whiskers are worn on the jaws, but the upper lip and the point of the chin are clean-shaven. (c) (1890s.) The hair is hidden by the hat. A large moustache is worn. (d) (1899.) The hair is cut short and brushed back above the ears. Most of it is hidden by the cap. (e) (1891.) The short hair is almost hidden by the hat. The moustache droops a little. (f) (1891.) The hair is parted on the left and forms a moderate quiff on the right. It is combed downward at the sides above the ears and is cut short at the back.

Headdress: (a) The tall black top hat, held in the right hand, widens a little towards the crown. (b) The round brimmed hat of black felt has a shallow crown. (c) The Homburg hat of buff-coloured felt has a dented crown and a narrow brim curling up at the sides. (d) The cloth cap of green and grey checks is small in circumference and has a short peak. (e) The deerstalker hat is of brown and fawn checks with a peak fore and aft and ear-flaps tied together on the top of the head.

Garments: (a) The 'sloping away' coat of black cloth has short oval coat-tails ending above the knees. The collar has a deep turnover and stands up at the back of the neck. The sleeves taper from the shoulders to the shaped wrists, where they come well down on to the hands, with the seams left open a few inches. The strapped-under trousers are of blue-grey cloth. (b) The loosely fitting casual jacket is of slate-blue woollen stuff, bordered at the hem, sleeve-ends and down the front by narrow edging of dark grey fur. This also trims the pockets and forms

the low, flat collar. A turned-down collar and blue knotted tie can be seen within this. The grey and blue checked trousers come down over the boots. (c) The shooting jacket is of brown and buff-coloured checked tweed. The knickerbockers are of brown whipcord. The stockings are of grey-brown wool with a diamond pattern in brown. (d) The Norfolk suit is of grey-green worsted. It has short lapels and is buttoned down the front, with a belt of its own stuff at the waist. There are flat pleats on either side of the front and pockets at the sides. The knickerbockers end below the knee. The stockings are of grey wool. (e) The ulster is of oatmeal-coloured tweed, lightly checked in fawn colours. It ends at the calves and has a deep cape ending at waist-level. The coat is double-breasted, with the skirt buttoned across the body in the same manner. The cape is buttoned down the front and has a tri-angular buttoned patch to secure the fastening at the throat. The trousers are of large grey and fawn checks. (f) The evening dress suit is cut much as today, but with coat-tails ending at the knees. The waistcoat is white and the 'boiled' shirt is fastened with one stud. A wing collar and white evening tie are worn. The socks are of black silk.

Footwear: (a) The bootees of black leather have flat heels and moderately pointed toes. (b) The boots are of black leather with flat heels. (c) The gaiters are of cream-coloured cloth, buttoning on the out-side. The boots are of brown leather. (d) The laced boots of brown leather end above the ankle. (e) The brown shoes or boots have moderately pointed toes. (f) Black leather pumps are worn.

Accessories: (b) The man carries grey leather gloves. (c) The man carries a shot-gun and has a game pouch slung from right shoulder to left hip on a leather strap. (d) A golf club is carried.

XIV.10. 1845–91. Men. Six Figures

were laced up the front and had broad heels and thick soles. They were made of black or brown leather and ended above the ankle or a little way up the calf. Leather gaiters, ending below the knees, were often worn with them over thick woollen stockings. In the '70s these gaiters might be of cloth. Shorter cloth gaiters, side-buttoning and ending at the base of the calf, in white or pale buff-colour, and worn with knickerbockers, were introduced in the 1880s. Cloth-topped bootees buttoning at the sides, were seen with knickerbocker suits as well as with town clothes from the '70s onwards.

Footwear—Women: Women's flat, dancing-sandal type of shoes at the opening of the century, made of soft fabric or of kid or satin in black, pale colours and white, remained in fashion until the 1840s. A very shallow suggestion of a heel was sometimes added. In the opening years women who followed the extreme fashion of the Classical Revival often wore classical sandals on bare feet and bound them on by means of coloured ribbons round their ankles, in the same way that the ordinary flat shoes were sometimes tied on. Open-work or embroidered fronts could ornament these shoes. Bootees of the same general shape fastened with tiny buttons down the centre front after 1815.

The pointed toes worn at the beginning of the century became more rounded after 1820. In the late 1820s some shoes were made only with soles and heels, like sandals, and tied on with ribbons. Flat slippers continued to be worn in the '30s, '40s and '50s.

After 1840 small heels, still very low, were added. Elastic side-gussets to bootees were introduced about 1847. When not gusseted, bootees were laced on the inside of the instep. By the mid-'60s, heels could be a little higher. Bronze slippers were an addition to the white and coloured shoes of satin or kid.

At the end of the decade small 'military' or 'Louis' heels were in evidence on women's footwear. Boots for outdoor wear laced up the front or buttoned at the side. Footwear of these types continued through the '70s and '80s. Brocaded and beaded slippers were worn at this time.

In the 1890s women's shoes had long pointed toes and, for ordinary wear, 'baby Louis' heels. They could have straps or be of a 'court' shape with a small tongue and buckle. For day wear they were usually of black kid or other supple leather, with bronze house-slippers still in fashion. The vamps of leather shoes could be beaded. Evening shoes were of satin, brocade or bronze kid. If coloured, they usually matched or toned with the dress. Boots lacing up the front with moderately stout soles and heels were worn for country walking and for cycling with tweed coats and skirts or cycling knickerbockers, though many women did not yet wear special country dress. An alternative was to wear front-lacing walking shoes with cloth gaiters.

Materials, Colours and Ornament

Materials: In the early 1800s woollen fabrics were gaining favour after the preponderance of silk worn during the 18th century. Fine quality cloth for men's coats and some women's dresses, for breeches and waistcoats and for cloaks was used, with cashmere and other woollens and wool stockinette for close-fitting pantaloons. Silk jersey was also used for these, and men's breeches could be made of satin or velvet. Silk was used for women's dresses and capes and men's waistcoats. The so-called 'moleskin' breeches were of velvety-looking stuff in pale neutral colours.

The simple feminine fashions of the opening years maintained the popularity of cotton, cambric and muslin. Silk gauze was used for stoles and scarves and semi-transparent dresses.

These materials suited the crisp, frilled garments that superseded those of stark simplicity. Silk, satin, grosgrain, velvet and brocade were also worn in England, although on formal occasions gauze and muslin, often embroidered in gold or silver thread, were seen at the same time as richer stuffs. In France, after 1804, when Napoleon was trying to encourage the silk industry, a wealth of beautiful materials adorned his Court and all important events. Dotted and striped weaves were fashionable.

The trousers worn by men from about 1820 and gradually increasing in favour were made of twill, thick corded cotton, good quality woollen stuffs, corduroy, 'moleskin' and the cotton known as 'Nankeen'.

Grosgrain and taffetas had a special vogue in women's dresses with the huge puffed sleeves and full, off-the-ground skirts of the late 1820s and the '30s, and kept their place in the fashion for the remainder of the century.

People wearing more utilitarian clothes were dressed in the hardier woollens and less delicate cottons, linen, gingham and printed cambric. A silk gown could be a prized possession, kept for holiday occasions.

Fur was used for trimmings and edgings and marabou was popular.

The 1830s saw a revival of deep embroidered flounces. Lace was also used for these and for shawls, veils, collars and sleeves. A particularly heavy satin, comparable to the 'slipper' satin of today, and 'watered' silk were favoured materials in the '50s and '60s. The entire range of stuffs that would hang well over a crinoline or make boned bodices sit smoothly was available and in fashion, but 'stretchy' or clinging materials were not adaptable to the mode. Gauze, net and tarlatan were well suited to the styles.

The 1840s and '50s also saw a development in the use of plaid and checked weaves which remained in fashion throughout the epoch. Gingham was much in use for morning and children's dresses.

With the waning of crinoline fashions and the adoption of the bustle in the 1870s and '80s, heavier and less pliable materials began to take an important part in the making of clothes. Bombazine, alpaca, serge and cotton poplin were among these and were used for plainer dresses. All rich silken stuffs, particularly satin and velvet, were in use and silk poplin and grenadine (silk and wool mixed) were other stuffs in frequent wear. Striped and shot silks were more modish than flowered stuffs, though these were used again for summer dresses of the late 70s. Cloth and woollen stuff in great variety was worn.

In the last ten years of the period additions to the choice of stuffs were a supple silk velvet known as 'panne', nun's veiling (a thin woollen material), dresses of machine-made lace, though real lace was used as often as possible for trimming, and serge for men's suits and women's coats and skirts.

Fur was used for capes in the final quarter of the century and for jackets in the last ten or fifteen years, with fur lavishly used for edgings, collars and facings. For the greater part of the century straw, silk, satin, velvet and some taffetas were used for bonnets and hats. Felt was used in the late '60s and tweed and cloth in the final quarter.

Colours: In men's clothes at the beginning of the 19th century colour was by no means lacking in coats and waistcoats. Plum-red, dark green, cinnamon and a brilliant or duller blue were used, while varying shades of buff, grey, grey-green and brown maintained the trend towards more sober colour. Black was worn, often with black pantaloons, though these were more usually in lighter neutral shades or in cream-colour, as were knee-breeches. Waistcoats were usually lighter than coats and could be striped, dotted or checked in colours. Buffs and browns were in favour, the coat darker than the waistcoat and pantaloons or breeches.

Many women's dresses were in white or pale colours while the very simple mode prevailed and throughout the later fashions when frills, embroidery and crisp sprigged muslins and cottons were in vogue. Deeper and more brilliant shades, in particular cherry red, violet, royal blue, yellow and crimson, also black trimmed with vivid colours, obtained from the early '20s until the late 1830s and were used with thinner and paler stuffs as contrast in sashes, stoles, ribbons, edgings, embroidery, appliqué and all-over sprigs, dots or stripes of patterning.

The same colours as before were seen in men's fashion of the 1820s and early '30s, with the more sober tints growing in favour, except that tail coats in the evening might be of light colours such as yellow, light blue, royal blue and light tan.

With the elaborate and exotic gowns of the late 1820s and first part of the '30s light silks and gauzy materials took on rather more definite hues such as cerulean blue and deep rose, deep yellow, cinnamon, cherry red, leaf green and violet. Lavender grey, pale blue, pale biscuit and pink, pearl-colour and white were also worn in light stuffs. Contrasts such as black with crimson, olive green with sky blue, and turquoise with yellow were used.

With the change in fashion to plainer and more modest modes in 1837, dove-grey, lavender, lilac, soft green, a greyish blue and pale fawn-colour, also shot silks in various hues, were favourites for silks and other light stuffs. For dresses in heavier materials, slate-blue, dark green, shades of brown and grey, subdued checks and stripes and black were chosen.

In the '50s, when the large crinoline was in vogue, the invention of aniline dyes allowed startling shades of magenta, green, red, purple and a brilliant blue to be used. The tendency, apart from these specially produced tints, was to wear deep, solid colours including the ordinary maroons and reds, plum-colour, sapphire blue, purple, bottle-green and bright green, also strong plaids and checks. Pastel colours and white were still used, especially for young girls, and black and brown were elegant in the prevailing mode. Lace

XIV.11. 1880s–90s. Women. Three Figures

Hair: (a) (1880s.) The maidservant's hair is taken up above the ears to a chignon (unseen) at the top of the head and has a curled fringe over the forehead. (b) The hair is arranged close to the head, taken up above the ears to a chignon (unseen) on top of the head. There is a short curled fringe in front. (c) The hair of (c) is done in the same way as that of (a) and (b).

Headdress: (a) A small mob-cap of white muslin is perched on the top of the head. (b) the toque of black satin is ornamented with a bow and a violet-coloured curled plume set on the left side. (c) The parlour-maid's white muslin cap has double, starched frills, one over the forehead and the other standing upright above it, and long streamers at the back. It is bound with a black ribbon, tying at the back.

Garments: (a) The parlour-maid's dress is of black serge with a fitted bodice, fastening down the front and long plain sleeves. The collar and cuffs are of starched white linen. The black over-skirt is turned up over a bustle and matches the under-skirt. A white lawn apron, with embroidered edging, is tied on round the waist and has a bib pinned in place on the bosom. (b) The gown is of Parma violet-coloured watered silk, with a close-fitting bodice crossing over to the left of the waist. The shoulders have large double shoulder-frills and the sleeves are puffed at the top and diminish to the wrists. The flared skirt touches the ground and has outstanding frills of its own stuff over the hips. The high-collared chemisette is of cream-coloured chiffon, with a bow at the back of the neck. (c) The parlour-maid's dress is of black poplin, with a gored skirt and diminishing sleeves puffed at the top. The white linen collar and cuffs are glazed and starched. The long white muslin apron has a frill of its own stuff all round. This is repeated on the outside edge of the wide shoulder-straps holding up the bib (unseen) and crossing over at the back.

Footwear: (a), (b) and (c) wear thin-soled black kid shoes.

Accessories: (a) Carries a wine-glass on a salver. (b) A folding fan and a parasol of violet silk, with an insertion of cream-coloured lace are carried. The gloves are of white kid.

was used to cover taffetas or satin evening dresses in pale or brilliant colours and was important as trimming throughout the crinoline period.

Men continued to wear light trousers and waistcoats in cream or pastel colours, during the '40s, but by the 1850s coloured coats were no longer worn and black, grey or dark blue were usual, with brown, drab and grey-green as alternatives. By the 1860s suits of coat, trousers and waistcoat to match were seen. These were of dull and often dark tones, but ties could still have light or vivid colour and men still favoured light and patterned trousers, and light-coloured waistcoats and greatcoats.

In the '70s black or grey frock coats with light-coloured checked or striped trousers, plaid trousers with dark jackets, and plaids and tweeds used for capes, knickerbocker suits and tweed suits gave some relief from the mode for sombre ensembles. Men wore white for tennis, boating and cricket.

Colours for women were much the same in the '70s and '80s as those in the late '50s and the '60s.

In the 1890s men continued with similar fashions in the same colours, except that plaids, stripes and checks were as a rule considerably quieter. Since tailoring was improved, the general effect was smarter and more sophisticated.

Colours worn by women were bright but more subtle and delicately varied than they had been since the beginning of the crinoline period. Flowing lines and the absence of the large bustle gave dignity and effectiveness to the clear tints, shot silks, unobtrusive dots, stripes and checks, Indian and Chinese silks, shining satins and écru-tinted lace. The finely woven cloth and suiting used were especially satisfying to the eye.

Ornament: The ornamentation of men's clothes was restricted during the whole of this epoch. Buttons during the first quarter of the century might be of gold, silver, brass, mother-of-pearl or steel. Waistcoats were embroidered in colours or gold thread, but the use of this was restrained and in the second half of the century decoration upon the waistcoat was usually woven into the material and buttons were discreet: e.g. a cream-coloured heavy silk waistcoat with very small pearly buttons and a dull gold thread woven into the stuff or another in subdued red or blue brocade or moiré. These were for special occasions.

On women's dresses in the opening years classical motifs, such as the Greek key pattern, conventionalized flowers, berries and leaves and geometrical formations were used to decorate the necklines, sleeve and tunic borders, hemlines and waists. After Napoleon's campaign in Egypt an Egyptian and near-Oriental influence came into this type of ornament. At no time, however, were classical motifs the only patterns used. Frills, lace and ruching were worn by many women from the inception of the classical mode. Appliqué ribbon and motifs cut from contrasting stuff, silk bows, borders of ornamental buttons, narrow fur edging, gathers and small sprigged all-over designs recalling the 18th century were seen at the same time as borders of acanthus leaves or 'dog's tooth' patterning.

Trimming became more lavish with the waning of the attempt at classical styles. By 1815 few edges remained unadorned and ornament was particularly evident on the high-waisted bodices, sleeves and hem, where a deep border of decoration of some sort was almost invariable. Large appliqué flowers in garlands, clusters, or joined by undulating stems and leaves, lace flowers and bands of padded and ruched silk were notable features.

In the 1820s the same kinds of decoration were still fashionable and it was not unusual for the skirt to be quite differently decorated from the bodice and sleeves.

After the change of fashion at the end of the 1820s the vogue for large appliqué flower decoration increased, while other forms of ornament were adapted to the new styles. Fur was used to make shoulder-capes for coats and 'walking' dresses and deep borders at the hems. Lace and embroidered net overdresses had large and definite patterns. Over-all designs were rather larger than they had been and the diamond-shaped repetition was marked by criss-cross formation.

With the change to less exotic fashions in the late 1830s, lasting through the '40s, lace, embroidery and borders of appliqué velvet in outstanding designs were favourite trimmings. Narrow bands of satin or velvet, three or four deep, bordered the bell-shaped skirts. Fur edgings were put on velvet capes and mantles. Puffed and ruched silk, satin or velvet, used as piping, could also edge dresses and outer wraps.

Dresses in the 1850s were often flounced or tiered or were ornamented with broad bands of trimming which suggested this effect. One example of this type has two wide bands of velvet, bordered with thick fringe, on the skirt.

In the 1860s and '70s fringe, pleated frills, lace, ruching, piping, embroidery, bands of velvet, satin, taffetas or padded silk, beads and still, occasionally, appliqué flowers, were used with special effect to mark the important lines of the fashions in dresses as well as for mere decoration. With the large crinoline, the first type of bustle and the 'waterfall' or 'tied back' line, this had considerable importance.

In the '80s, with the later type of bustle, and the '90s, with wide, flowing skirts developing from the restrained lines at the opening of the decade, trimming in general, with exceptions, fulfilled its decorative purpose rather than one of special emphasis, although to our eyes it may seem over-lavish.

Jewellery and Accessories: Men's jewellery was limited and inconspicuous in the 19th century. A ring or a fob in the first half of the epoch, perhaps with a gold watch attached to the latter, were the most that they would wear. Shirt and coat buttons might be of gold or silver and the former might be set with mother-of-pearl, coral, crystal, amethyst or cornelian.

In the second half, a gold watch-chain might be worn and the shirt studs might again be of precious metal, sometimes by this time set with pearls or diamonds. Gold cuff-links were worn and tie-pins set with jewels.

Quizzing-glass and cane were favourite accessories at the beginning of the period and throughout the century the cane, with a knob of silver or ivory, was frequently carried. Men's gloves were of pale colours, yellow, grey, lavender, lilac or cream-colour, with white for evenings. Umbrellas carried by men late in the century were usually unwieldy objects with hooked handles.

Women wore large jewelled brooches in the first quarter to secure plumes or turbans or decorate the dress, and necklaces copied from classical models. These were often set with precious stones, though the diminished gleam of semi-precious stones was popular with the fashions of the day.

Bangles and segmented bracelets showing Greek, Roman or Egyptian influence were introduced in the early years and remained in vogue, not necessarily with classical motifs, all through the century. They were usually of gold or silver and might be set with cameos, cornelian, coral or more valuable jewels.

Jewelled pins and combs for the hair, diadems, long drop earrings and rings for the fingers were owned by most women of position. For young girls, a locket on a ribbon or a string of coral or seed pearls was considered suitable. Bead necklaces that hung down over the bosom were fashionable at first. Early in the century the fashion of having bracelets, necklace and earrings to match gained a firm hold and never died out.

Lockets were popular and long chains bearing gold watches were in fashion from the 1830s.

Throughout the crinoline and bustle periods the liking for cameos, crystal, coral, amethyst, turquoise, onyx, cornelian and amber was an important characteristic and such items in heavy settings were widely worn, as well as magnificent rubies, pearls, diamonds and emeralds by those wealthy enough to own them. The circular or oval shape of the classical necklace, and some other designs of the early years, remained after the innovation of the more close-fitting type of necklace or ribbon neck-band in the late '70s, and both outlasted the century.

Accessories used by women in the first quarter of the epoch included small parasols, one type often held, when closed, by the ferrule; reticules of the 'Dorothy bag' type and in shapes like a modern handbag, usually made of tapestry or embroidered or jewelled satin and set on a frame; fans, both folding and rigid and gloves of silk or kid.

In the ensuing twenty years, fans were usually folding, reticules of the 'Dorothy bag' types, and gloves short or three-quarter length and made of silk or kid. Silk mittens were worn.

Folding fans were small and could be of soft feathers as well as the usual silk, 'chicken-

XIV.12. 1892 and 1897. Women

Hair: (a) (1897.) There is a short curled fringe on the forehead. A little of the pompadour and the puffed-out hair on the left side can be seen. (b) (1892.) A thick, curled fringe is brought forward on to the forehead with short locks over the temples. The remainder of the hair is drawn up into a high chignon at the back of the head leaving the ears exposed.

Headdress: (a) The hat of black velvet is slanted upward on the left side. It has a flat crown bordered with grey fur and a narrow undulating brim on the left side only. Two bunches of artificial violets surmount the brim.

Garments: (a) The coat of black velvet is fitted to the figure and flows out below the hips into a wide circular skirt with a short train (unseen). The sleeves are puffed and gathered at the shoulders and taper towards the wrists. The collar is high and frames the face with its wide, undulating shape, bordered with grey fur. A lace jabot is worn at the throat and the fastening of the coat is made in zig-zag fashion and bordered with fur. (b) The evening gown of cream-coloured satin has a cross-over bodice and large puffed sleeves. The big, stiffened collar of cream satin is edged with lace. It stands up with a winged effect over the shoulders, dipping at the back, and follows the cross-over line of the bodice in front. The sash is of black satin, tied at the back. The skirt (unseen) just reaches the ground in front and forms a train at the back.

Jewellery and Accessories: (a) A bunch of artificial violets with their leaves is pinned on the left side of the chest. (b) A necklace of pearls is worn and a folding fan carried in the left hand. The gloves are of white kid, ending above the elbows.

skin' or paper. Gloves were as a rule short. Small umbrellas or parasols could still be carried upside down by the ferrule whether the handles were long or short.

Handbags or reticules were not in evidence after mid-century, women relying on pockets under or in the seams of their skirts for carrying purse and handkerchief.

The small adjustable sunshade known as a 'carriage' parasol was known from the first years of the century. In the two final decades, long-stemmed umbrellas and parasols were carried by women. Folding fans were an important accessory at dances. Gloves might be long or short.

XIV.13. Woman in 'Spencer' Jacket. 1800

Hair: The hair is arranged in a tumble of short curls round the face and at the back of the neck.

Headdress: The bonnet is covered in apple-green silk, with piping of darker green silk which also forms the strings tied under the chin on the left side. Two pale yellow plumes are fastened on the crown of the bonnet.

Garments: The gown of pale yellow muslin is visible from waist to hem and is long enough to trail a little on the ground. The short spencer is of apple-green taffeta. It is high-waisted, and has a crossover, frilled bodice. The frilled basque is longer at the back than at the front. The sleeves are long and close-fitting, with wrist-frills.

Footwear: The flat-soled slippers are of green fabric.

Jewellery and Accessories: The gold chain worn round the neck has gold beads and clear green drops attached to it. A small parasol of green taffeta with a cane handle is carried in the manner of the time, upside down, in the left hand. A large muff of white fur is held in the right. The gloves are of white silk.

XIV.14. Man's Dress. 1804

Hair: The hair is rather long at the back and sides, and is brought forward in a fringe in front.

Headdress: The chapeau-bras of black silk has tiny gilt tassels at the corners. It is worn in the fashion favoured in France, across the head instead of fore-and-aft as was more usual in England.

Garments: The coat of darkish blue cloth is cut away in front and has narrow coat-tails ending at the calf. It is single-breasted, with wide lapels. The rolled collar stands up, turned over, at the back of the neck. The single-breasted waistcoat, with long, rolled lapels, is of cream-coloured grosgrain. The wide neck-cloth of white lawn is tied in a bow in front by narrow ends. The shirt frill and wrist-ruffles are of white lawn. The sleeves taper from the shoulders to the wrists, where they have 'goblet' cuffs with the seams left open. The pantaloons are of cream-coloured stretching material, ending just below the calf. The stockings are of cream-coloured silk.

Footwear: The flat slippers are of black kid.

Jewellery and Accessories: A gold fob is worn at the waist and a light, short cane is carried.

XIV.15. Woman in Trained Evening Gown. 1804

Hair: The hair is arranged in a thick fringe over the forehead, ringlets of varying lengths hanging at the sides and back of the head and a chignon at the level of the crown.

Headdress: A wreath of silver leaves is set above the fringe and two white ostrich plumes curl over the top of the head.

Garments: The low-bosomed, high-waisted gown is of white and silver gauze with decoration of silver thread and brilliants round and above the hem. The short open sleeves, in the classical mode, are joined below the shoulder by silver ornaments. The train is of purple velvet, attached at the bosom by an ornament of brilliants and diamonds set in silver and by an open, high-waisted bodice of its own material, showing only as narrow strips on either side of the breasts in front, but covering the top of the back (unseen).

Footwear: The slippers of silver fabric are cut to look like sandals with a silver ornament in the centre front. They have flat soles and shallow flat heels.

Jewellery and Accessories: Large hoop earrings of silver are worn. The elbow-length gloves are of white kid. The circular folding fan of white gauze edged with silver lace, has a pointed silver handle.

XIV.16. Man's Dress. 1807

Hair: The hair is unparted, cut short at the back and brought forward from the crown to form a curled fringe.

Headdress: The beaver hat has a curling brim and a large crown of moderate height.

Garments: The squarely cut-away coat of black cloth has a double-breasted front and long lapels. The collar stands up and is turned over at the back of the neck. The narrow coat-tails end at the back of the knees. The sleeves are close-fitting, with plain cuffs. The points of the wing collar come up on to the cheeks. The neck-cloth is of white lawn, tied by its narrow ends in a bow in front. The shirt-frill is of white lawn, fastened with pearl buttons. The breeches are of biscuit-coloured cloth or whipcord, fastened by buttons on the outside of the legs, below the knees and are tucked into the boot-tops. Vertical pocket openings are set on either side of the front below the waist.

Footwear: The boots are of black leather, with tan-coloured leather tops and short loops on the inside for pulling them on.

Jewellery and Accessories: A gold fob is worn at the waist. A malacca cane is carried.

XIV.17. Woman in Evening Dress. About 1810

Hair: The hair is done in 'classical' style, with a curled fringe in front and ringlets behind it. A mass of curls is pinned up at the back to form a chignon.

Headdress: A bandeau of parchment-coloured silk is fastened over the top of the head.

Garments: The high-waisted gown is of parchment-coloured silk striped in maroon. The short sleeves are caught up in a drapery to the shoulders. The bodice has a narrow edging to the oval décolletage of black velvet and maroon silk and a matching belt. The skirt, which forms a small train at the back, has a similar border.

Footwear: The flat slippers are of black satin.

Jewellery and Accessories: A necklace of gold and garnets and long white kid gloves are worn. The fan is parchment-coloured, with black sticks.

XIV.18. Woman in Evening Dress. 1812

Hair: The hair is parted in the centre, with a lock curled forward on either side of the forehead and the remainder taken up above the ears and from the back, to be piled in curls (unseen) on the top of the head.

Headdress: A garland of coral-pink flowers set in two rows, one above the other, is worn high on the head.

Garments: The high-waisted satin gown, with low décolletage bordered with narrow net frilling, is of pearl-coloured satin, with a matching train attached at the back of the shoulders. It has a narrow belt of gold ribbon and the base of the skirt, which widens towards the hem, is decorated with garlands of gilt leaves and coral-pink flowers.

Footwear: The flat-soled slippers are of gold tissue.

Jewellery and Accessories: The long gloves are of white kid or silk and the stole of gold gauze. The gold chain worn round the neck has pearl drops attached. Pearl earrings are worn.

XIV.19. Girl in Ball Dress. 1815

Hair: The hair is arranged in a fringe on the forehead and drawn up behind the ears into a bunch of curls on the top.

Headdress: A garland of pink and white convolvulus flowers and green leaves surrounds the top-knot of hair.

Garments: The short-waisted dress is of lilac-pink satin. The skirt, increasing in width towards the hem, ends above the ankles. The top and base of the bodice, and of the short sleeves, made in one with it, are bound in satin ribbon of the convolvulus pink. A band of this is round the hem and another some way above it. Between the two bands, wreath-like motifs of the deep pink ribbon are attached at intervals. In the centre of each is a posy of three convolvulus flowers and their leaves. The stockings are of pink silk.

Footwear: The pink slippers have flat soles and ribbons to tie them on round the ankles.

Jewellery and Accessories: The bag is of pink velvet, with a draw-string at the top and a tassel at its base, and the fan is decorated in colours to tone with the dress. The long gloves are of white kid or silk. The neck-chain has a gold heart-shaped locket attached to it. The earrings are gold, set with pearls.

XIV.20. Woman's 'Morning' Dress. 1821

Hair: The hair is parted in the centre, with two ringlets on each side of the face.

Headdress: The white muslin cap has a full, tall crown (unseen), with starched double frills in front and blue velvet bows, with streamers, attached behind them.

Garments: The white muslin gown has an open bodice, joined at the waist, with the front filled in by three rows of white embroidered muslin. A starched 'ruff' collar of white muslin is tied in front with white satin ribbons, matching the belt of the gown. The sleeves are puffed at the shoulders and joined to long, close-fitting lower sleeves. Diamond-shaped motifs of embroidered muslin decorate each shoulder and form pointed cuffs over the hands. The skirt is close-fitting over the hips but widens out towards the base, where it is trimmed with three rows of embroidered muslin.

Footwear: The slippers of white silk fabric have embroidery on the toes.

Accessories: The woman carries a saucer of crumbs for feeding the birds.

XIV.21. Woman in Feathered Turban. 1825

Hair: The hair is parted in the centre and arranged at the sides in ringlets. The chignon (unseen) is near the top of the head.

Headdress: The turban is of satin striped in cocoa brown and tawny pink. It has a full soft crown, sewn into a band to fit the head. Five tawny-pink plumes are set on the top, some curling over the crown.

Garments: The dress is of cocoa-brown gauze over a tawny-pink silk foundation. The short, puffed sleeves are frilled and decorated with lines of gold galon. The oval neckline is edged with a gauze frill, with an added downward point in the centre. Lines of gold galon curve downward from the shoulders, converging to a point at the waist. The rounded waist-line has a belt of cocoa-brown satin with a gold buckle. Five rows of gold galon in upward and downward points ornament the skirt and are edged with gauze frills. The circular skirt ends just off the ground.

Footwear: The flat-soled slippers are of cocoa-brown satin.

Jewellery and Accessories: The necklace is of gold beads and the gloves of pale biscuit-coloured kid. A scarf of tawny-pink silk gauze is draped over the right arm and held in the left hand.

XIV.22. Woman in Riding Dress. 1833

Hair: The hair is parted a little to the left of centre and arranged in horizontal ringlets on both sides. The chignon (unseen) is on the top of the head.

Headdress: The hat of black velvet has a sweeping brim, curved up on the right and down on the left. The tall, narrow crown is trimmed with a brilliant green ribbon and two green plumes.

Garments: The riding dress is of black velvet, decorated on the front of the bodice and the front panel of the skirt with horizontal tucks or piping. The remainder of the full skirt trails on the ground so that the train (unseen) can be thrown over the arm. The sleeves are close-fitting at the shoulders with tucks or piping at the top and assume a balloon shape to a point below the elbow, where they are joined to close-fitting lower sleeves. The collar and turned-back cuffs are of white lawn and embroidery.

Footwear: Bootees of white leather with black toe-caps are worn.

Accessories: A riding-crop is carried. The gloves are of white leather.

XIV.23. Girl in Ball-dress. 1833

Hair: This is parted in the centre with a short lock curled inward on each side. Horizontally placed ringlets are piled on both sides of the head, and the remainder swept up at the back to form two large curls at the top.

Headdress: The top-knot of curls is tied with black velvet ribbon. Posies of flowers toning with those on the dress are attached on both sides.

Garments: The gown of honey-coloured satin has a rounded waist-line and an oval off-shoulder décolletage, edged with écru frilling. Two bands of cerulaean-blue ribbon converge from the shoulders in the front of the bodice. The short, puffed sleeves are in two parts, joined to create a shoulder-widening effect. The lower part is of honey-coloured chiffon and the upper part is covered with écru lace, which continues on the bodice, edging the bands of blue ribbon. Écru lace decorates the base of the full circular skirt, which ends above the ankles. Above this are bands and bows of blue ribbon, and swathes and bunches of flowers in pale shades of pink, violet, blue and yellow. The stockings are of honey-coloured silk.

Footwear: The flat-soled slippers are of honey-coloured satin.

Jewellery and Accessories: A jewelled bracelet and gold drop earrings are worn. The gloves are of white silk.

XIV.24. Man's Dress. 1834

Hair: The hair is fairly long and thick with a lock showing in front of the ear and the ends at the back touching the high neck-cloth. A small moustache and narrow whiskers with a fringe of beard are worn.

Headdress: The black top hat has a curled brim and a tall crown.

Garments: The body of the open black cloth coat is cutaway, with a rolled collar and sleeves tapering to the frilled wrists from slightly raised shoulders. The coat-tails are attached at the sides and back of the waist and have fullness in their back folds. The neck-cloth is of white lawn. The trousers are of lavender-grey cloth with grey braid down the outer seams. They fit closely, cover the vamps of the bootees and have straps under the insteps.

Footwear: The black leather bootees have high, shaped heels.

Accessories: A slim malacca cane is carried.

XIV.25. Woman in Outdoor Dress. About 1836

Hair: This is parted in the centre, puffed out over the ears and dressed in a chignon (unseen) near the top of the head.

Headdress: The brown velvet bonnet has a large oval brim, and is trimmed with a spray of pink and blue flowers, with green leaves and three blue ostrich plumes. The cylindrical crown, unseen, is nearly upright and the strings are of blue ribbon.

Garments: The gown has a full circular skirt and is of pale blue taffetas patterned with large pink flowers and green leaves in the centre of cinnamon-brown squares. The sleeves are balloon-shaped, with close-fitting cuffs. The pelisse of cinnamon-brown faced cloth, with a full circular skirt, has a tight-fitting bodice, fastening down the front. The buckled belt is of blue and brown striped velvet. The sleeves are formed of large shoulder-capes. The brown velvet collar has another over it of pale blue embroidered silk, bordered with brown velvet.

Footwear: The shoes are of brown velvet.

Accessories: The buttoned gloves are of pale cinnamon kid.

XIV.26. Woman in Bell-shaped Skirt. About 1841

Hair: The front tresses of the centre-parted hair are taken back and fastened at the nape of the neck. The remainder is smoothed down over the ears and wound with the hair already fastened at the back into a low chignon.

Garments: The gown is of blue and cream-coloured striped silk, the stripes converging at the waist of the front-fastening bodice. The skirt is bell-shaped and the sleeves plain, with narrow cuffs of cream-coloured silk. The flat, round embroidered collar is of the same stuff, frilled at the edges.

Footwear: The shoes are of black kid.

Accessories: A gold brooch is worn at the fastening of the collar and a book carried in the right hand.

XIV.27. Man's Dress. 1842

Hair: The thick, wavy hair is parted on the right side. The moustache droops to meet the fringe of beard and whiskers.

Headdress: The black top hat has a fairly tall crown.

Garments: The redingote of plum-coloured cloth has a rolled collar and long, wide lapels extending to the waist. This is fitted to the figure and the skirts of the coat are full, with fullness towards the back. The cream-coloured taffetas waistcoat is single-breasted, fastened with small pearl buttons and ends at the waist. The peg-top trousers are of pinkish-grey cloth and are strapped under the insteps. The round, stiff white collar is open in front, showing the top of the wide, black satin cravat, which is arranged in overlapping folds covering the shirt-front. The sleeves taper to the wrists and show plain white linen bands at the ends of the shirt-sleeves.

Footwear: The black leather bootees, worn under the trousers, have slightly shaped heels and squared-off toes.

Accessories: The gloves are of grey kid. An ebony cane is carried.

XIV.28. Woman in Bonnet and Shoulder-wrap. About 1845

Hair: The hair is parted in the centre and smoothed down, with ringlets at the sides.

Headdress: The small bonnet is covered in pale green silk and has a pleated lining. The brim is piped with black satin, which also forms the strings and the bow near the back of the bonnet. A wreath of lilac-coloured flowers and green leaves trims the shallow crown.

Garments: The gown of green cashmere has a bell-shaped skirt, decorated on its lower part and on the bodice with bands of checked woollen fabric in black, lilac and green on a cream-coloured ground. The oval décolletage is filled in with a chemisette and neck-frill of cream-coloured muslin. Inner sleeves of the same stuff show at the wrists. The frilled shoulder-wrap of lilac taffetas has long, stole-like ends.

Footwear: Shoes of black kid are worn.

Accessories: The gloves are of cream-coloured silk, with black stitching. A small umbrella of green silk is held upside down by a ring attached to the ferrule.

XIV.29. Man's Outdoor Dress. 1850s

Hair: The hair is parted on the left side (unseen) and is taken back in a wave above the ears on both sides. It is thick and rather long at the back. Whiskers fringe the jaws, but no moustache is worn.

Headdress: The top hat is of greyish fawn hatter's plush, with a 'stove-pipe' crown and a brim dipping a little at front and back.

Garments: The short, loose, light fawn-coloured overcoat has sleeves made in one with the body and buttoned straps at the ends of the sleeves, which can be fastened round the wrists for warmth. It is worn open, showing an open jacket of brown frieze which ends below the top of the thighs. The waistcoat of biscuit-coloured cloth is double-breasted, with rolled lapels and a cross-over fastening. The low wing collar and the shirt-front are stiff, the latter being fastened by studs. A narrow bow-tie of blue silk is worn. The narrow trousers are of greyish-brown frieze.

Footwear: Bootees with elastic sides are worn under the trousers.

Accessories: The man carries a walking-stick with a silver knob.

XIV.30. Woman in Evening Gown. Mid-1850s

Hair: The hair is parted in the centre and taken back, showing the lobes of the ears, into a chignon half-way up the back of the head.

Headdress: A festoon of rose-pink flowers is pinned on in front of the chignon (unseen) and hangs over the right side of the head towards the back.

Garments: The pale blue silk gown is worn over a crinoline, its circular skirt just touching the floor all round. It is in three tiers or flounces, the edges cut in rounded points and edged with rose-coloured net. The short, plain puffed sleeves are almost covered by an off-the-shoulders bertha collar of the same stuff as the gown, edged with rose-coloured net.

Jewellery and Accessories: Matching bracelets of diamonds and pink topaz are worn on the wrists. The short, buttoned gloves are of white kid. A formal posy of pink and blue flowers, set in a holder with a stem and a wide, circular silver paper frill is carried in the right hand.

XIV.31. Man's Dress. 1850s

Hair: The thick, wavy hair is parted on the left side. A moustache and a fringe of whiskers below the cheek-bones are worn.

Headdress: The brim of the black top hat curls up a little at the sides and the crown is fairly tall.

Garments: The jacket is of dark grey hopsack. It fits closely at the waist, but the skirts are flared, ending at the top of the thighs. The shoulders slope downwards, but appear broad because the tops of the sleeves are slightly puffed. These diminish toward the wrists, where the shaped sleeve-endings show white linen wrist-bands. The wide collar stands up at the back of the neck and has short, wide lapels. The shirt has a plain band of white linen down the front with studs at intervals. The high black satin cravat is fastened by a narrow bow in front. The trousers are of checked woollen material in grey and fawn.

Footwear: Black leather bootees with high heels are worn beneath the trousers.

Accessories: A malacca cane is held in the right hand. The gloves are of buff-yellow leather, with black stitching.

XIV.32. Girl in Porkpie Hat. About 1858

Hair: This is parted in the centre and looped back over the ears to join the hair from the back of the head in a low plaited or coiled chignon.

Headdress: The 'porkpie' hat, a little like a Glengarry, has a soft crown of bottle green velvet and a band of checked woollen stuff in green, black and brick red on a cream-coloured ground. A brick-red feather stands up on the left side.

Garments: The bolero jacket is of bottle-green velvet, bordered all round with ermine, which also edges the loosely fitting sleeves, widening towards the wrists. The buttoned blouse is of cream-coloured silk and has a flat round collar, with a neckband of black velvet and 'bishop' sleeves. The under-skirt matches the band on the cap. It is worn over a short, wide crinoline and ends well above the ankles. The draped-up over-skirt of brick-red wool is buttoned on at the waist. The stockings are of cream-coloured cashmere, with horizontal green stripes.

Footwear: The bootees of black kid have elastic sides and end above the ankles. They have shaped 'military' heels.

Accessories: The girl carries an ermine muff.

XIV.33. Woman in Wide-brimmed Hat. 1860

Hair: The hair is brought down in smooth swathes from a centre parting to cover the ears and looped back to join the hair from the back of the head in a low, coiled chignon.

Headdress: The hat of 'burnt' straw has a wide brim dipping in front and at the back. The shallow crown is trimmed with a band of folded black satin, with a rosette in front and two streamers hanging below the brim at the back, where the band gives the appearance of disappearing beneath it.

Garments: The gown is of 'vieux rose' cashmere fitted to the body and flowing out over a crinoline. It is left open to the waist, and is worn over a white muslin blouse with a frilled, flat collar and 'bishop' sleeves. The bell sleeves of the dress widen near the wrists. Undulating bands of black satin, frilled with pleated taffetas matching the dress, are festooned over the sleeves and skirt.

Footwear: The shoes are of black kid.

Jewellery and Accessories: An onyx and silver brooch is worn at the collar fastening. The woman holds the lead of her pug-dog and has a lump of sugar to give him.

XIV.34. Woman in Ball-dress. 1859

Hair: The hair in front is drawn back from a centre parting and fastened at the back of the neck. The hair at the sides is brought down loosely, covering the ears, and taken back to be wound into a low chignon with the hair already fastened there and the hair from the back of the head.

Headdress: A festoon of cream-coloured velvet flowers with orange centres and green velvet leaves, is fastened at the left side of the head and hangs down on to the shoulder.

Garments: The gown of cream-coloured satin has a full circular skirt, touching the floor, worn over a wide crinoline. The off-shoulder décolletage is boat-shaped, and the top of the bodice draped. The short, puffed sleeves are joined to 'épaulettes' edged with silver cord. A festoon of flowers matching those of the headdress is fastened with silver cord across the bodice, from shoulder to shoulder. Arrangements of flowers, ruching and silver cord decorate the lower part of the skirt.

Accessories: Bands of green velvet ornamented with cream-coloured flowers, are worn on the wrists.

XIV.35. Man in Frock Coat. 1865

Hair: The hair is shaped to the head at the back and is rather thick. A moustache is worn, with whiskers covering the jaws, but leaving the chin clean-shaven.

Headdress: The black top hat is shaped much in the fashion of today, but with a lower crown.

Garments: The frock-coat of black cloth is worn open. The single-breasted waistcoat is of black and white checked material. The round, starched collar fits the neck closely. The cravat is of black satin. The trousers are of grey flecked stuff, with narrow stripes of darker grey.

Footwear: The black bootees have slightly pointed toes and raised heels.

Jewellery and Accessories: The man holds a large gold watch in his left hand and carries a walking-stick. His gloves are of pale grey kid.

XIV.36. Woman in Crinoline Gown. About 1865

Hair: The coiffure is made up of curls over the forehead and temples, waves across the back and ringlets of varying lengths, some touching the shoulders.

Headdress: A band of jet beads, with crimson flowers and black satin leaves attached, encircles the head. Crimson flowers are pinned behind the ears. A black satin bow is tied at the back of the neck.

Garments: The parchment-coloured satin bodice has a matching swathe of chiffon draped across the bosom and two similar swathes, caught with crimson flower ornaments, on the shoulders. The skirt is full all round and formed into a train at the back. It is decorated with swathed chiffon caught with flower ornaments larger than those on the shoulders.

Footwear: The flat-soled slippers are of ivory satin.

Jewellery and Accessories: Long drop earrings and black satin bracelets with pearl drops and borders of pearl beads are worn. The bouquet of pink and crimson flowers is in a frilled paper holder with the stems covered in silver foil.

XIV.37. Woman in Bustle Dress. About 1870

Hair: The hair in front is arranged in a loop on either side of the centre parting. The hair at the sides is taken upward and pinned on the top of the head. Part of the hair at the back is wound into a low, coiled chignon. The remainder is swept up and dressed in two rolls coming forward, curled under, on the top of the head.

Garments: The trained over-dress is of bronze and blue shot taffetas, worn over a bustle. The bodice is slightly high-waisted, with a downward point in front and a small basque at the back. The oval collar is made up of strips of the shot taffetas, arranged in joined diagonals, edged with motifs of dull gold net which in turn are bordered with blue pleated ninon. The open over-skirt is bordered with decoration matching that of the collar. This also ornaments the loosely fitting sleeves, widening towards the wrists, and the under-skirt of pale blue ninon.

Footwear: The slippers are of bronze kid.

Jewellery and Accessories: Gold drop earrings set with turquoise and a matching ring are worn. A cup and saucer are held in the left hand.

XIV.38. Man's Suit. 1871

Hair: The hair is parted on the left side and brought across the forehead in a quiff that turns upward on the right. The sides and back are short and are brushed outward a little above the ears.

Headdress: The low-crowned black bowler hat has a brim curving up slightly at the sides.

Garments: The jacket and trousers are of matching grey worsted. The shoulders are narrow, the lapels short and only the top button of the coat is fastened. The waistcoat is of a lighter grey. The trousers are rather loose-fitting and shapeless. The collar is starched, turned over and open in front to show the knotted tie.

Footwear: The blunt-toed laced boots are of black leather.

Accessories: A walking-stick is carried in the right hand.

XIV.39. Woman's Dress. About 1875

Hair: The hair has a fringe in front and a chignon worn low, with its coils extending a little way up the back of the head.

Garments: The gown of black velvet has a hip-length fitted bodice fastening in front with silver buttons and ending in a deep point. Double rows of black velvet pleats edge its base. Two rows of the pleating placed end to end and bound in the centre by a band of velvet, decorate the under-skirt and edge the close-fitting three-quarter-length sleeves. The high collar has an opening in front and a narrow white neck-frill. The overskirt is lifted to the hips in apron fashion at the sides, the rest of the drapery being first bunched at the back over the sloping bustle and then dropped to form a train.

Footwear: The slippers are of black velvet.

Jewellery and Accessories: A folding fan is carried in the right hand. Pearl drop earrings and a pearl and silver brooch are worn.

XIV.40. Woman with Japanese Fan. 1880

Hair: The hair has a deep fringe coming from a parting across the head. This is hidden by a roll of hair pinned transversely over it. The remainder is dressed in a coiled chignon on the crown of the head.

Garments: The 'cuirass' bodice is of pale caramel-coloured cashmere ending in waistcoat-like points piped in brown velvet. The buttons of the front fastening are of brown velvet, which also edges the top and base of the standing collar. This has a small upright frill of cream-coloured silk and is covered in silk matching that of the draped over-skirt. The sleeves are long and close-fitting, with cuffs and wrist-frills to match the collar. The over-skirt is of cream-coloured silk, striped in brown, orange-tan and black. It has a pleated edging of cream silk and is draped back into a cascade of brown velvet loops at the back. The pleated under-skirt, seen below the drapery, is of brown velvet.

Footwear: The slippers are of brown velvet.

Accessories: The silk fan, stretched on a narrow black frame, with a black papier mâché stick, has a Japanese scene painted on it.

XIV.41. Woman in Evening Dress. 1881

Hair: This is curled in a fringe on the forehead, starting from a parting across the head. The remainder is dressed in a low chignon.

Headdress: An ornament of deep pink flowers and dark green velvet is set behind and below the left ear.

Garments: The dress is of shell-pink satin and ninon, with a 'cuirass' bodice of satin open in front to show rows of small tucks in shell-pink ninon. A swathe of ninon with matching fringe crosses the bosom diagonally from the left shoulder, passing under the right arm and leaving the right shoulder exposed. Dark green fringed velvet bows and pink flowers decorate the shoulders. Larger bows and loops of dark green velvet, with pink flowers, are attached at the right hip and left side holding in place a swathe of fringed ninon wound round the body in a downward diagonal from right to left. The skirt is of pleated ninon, held in by two narrow satin bands. The satin train, edged with ninon pleats, swirls round the hem and spreads on the floor.

Footwear: The slippers (unseen) are of shell-pink satin.

Jewellery and Accessories: Linked bracelets of gold and brilliants are worn over the white kid gloves, which end above the elbow. The pink silk fan has ivory sticks.

XIV.42. Man's Suit. 1885

Hair: The hair is cut short and brushed back over the ears. A moustache is worn.

Headdress: The fawn-coloured bowler hat has a low crown and a small brim curving up at the sides and down at front and back.

Garments: The suit is of brown, tan and fawn checked tweed. The jacket fits fairly closely and the lapels are short. The waistcoat is of buff-coloured cloth and is cut straight across at its base, which is a little below the waist. The stiff collar is turned over and a large tie of dark red silk is worn. The trousers are without a crease and come well down over the shoes.

Footwear: The brown laced boots have slightly pointed toes.

Accessories: A walking stick with a crooked handle is carried in the right hand.

XIV.43. Woman's Dress. 1885

Hair: The hair is drawn closely back from the front of the head and up from the back into a small chignon (unseen) on the top of the head.

Headdress: The bonnet of black satin, dipping at the sides, is perched high, and tipped forward. The curved brim is edged with pleated absinthe-green silk. Flowers of 'old gold' satin trim the front.

Garments: The black satin jacket is decorated with gilt beads and has a basque cut in petal shapes, which also edge the three-quarter-length sleeves. The narrow standing collar is tied with black satin ribbons at the throat. The over-skirt of 'old gold' satin is draped over the front of the under-skirt, caught at the hips, and then draped over the bustle and allowed to hang down at the back. The under-skirt is of satin in narrow stripes of absinthe green and black.

Footwear: the black kid shoes would have small ornaments in front and low, shaped heels.

Accessories: The gloves of pale biscuit-coloured kid end half-way up the forearms. A rolled umbrella with a tall stem is carried.

XIV.44. Woman's Walking Dress. 1887

Hair: The hair is parted across the head and brushed forward in a curled fringe. A roll of hair brought up from the sides is pinned across the head at the parting. The top-knot, unseen, is placed behind it.

Headdress: The bonnet of grape-purple velvet has a cylindrical crown and a tall oval brim with rose-pink ostrich feathers showing over the top, and a matching satin bow in the front. Rose-pink silk strings are tied under the chin.

Garments: The over-dress matches the bonnet, fastens down the front, and has a high, close neck-band. There is lavish embroidery in rose-pink and green on the bodice, the three-quarter-length sleeves and the sides of the skirt. This is made in apron form, draped up at the hips and taken back to be looped and draped over a bustle. The under-skirt is of rose-pink pleated silk.

Footwear: Bootees of kid to tone with the dress, with high, shaped heels and buttons at the sides, are worn.

Accessories: The three-quarter-length gloves of pale grey kid have frilled edges. A slim, rolled umbrella is carried.

XIV.45. Woman's Dress. 1890

Hair: The hair is pulled back from the forehead and above the ears and wound in a tight bun on the top of the head (unseen).

Headdress: The grey felt hat has a black band and imitates a man's Homburg, but is smaller and perched higher on the head. An ornament of black and grey feathers is pinned on the front.

Garments: The tailored jacket is of black cloth, with long lapels and sleeves puffed and gathered at the top. The waistcoat is of pale grey satin, with a pattern of dark red dots. The man's wing collar and dark red knotted tie are worn with a stiff shirt front. The flared skirt is of grey tweed, with two narrow bands of black braid near the hem. It just clears the ground but was considered a serviceable length for walking. This type of costume was typical of the 'New Woman'.

Footwear: The 'sensible' laced walking shoes are of black leather with low heels.

Accessories: A rolled black umbrella and a lorgnette are carried. The gloves are of grey kid with black stitching.

XIV.46. Woman's Dress. 1897

Hair: The hair is drawn up above the ears and at the back into a chignon on the top of the head (unseen).

Headdress: The hat is of black velvet, with a stiffened, diminishing crown and a brim turned up on the left side and down on the right. A large satin bow in a shade to tone with the coat and skirt decorates the front and large black curled plumes are set behind it.

Garments: The coat and skirt are of dark blue-green cloth. The fitted jacket has a cross-over fastening at the waist, and ends in a short, curved basque. There are short lapels, a small open upstanding collar and a high-collared chemisette with a three-tiered jabot of cream net. A black ribbon is tied round the neck with a bow in front. The sleeves are puffed and gathered at the shoulders and taper to the wrists, where there are frills of cream-coloured net. The skirt reaches the ground in front and forms a train at the back.

Footwear: The shoes are of black kid.

Jewellery and Accessories: Pearl drop earrings are worn. The gloves are of oyster-grey kid and the parasol or umbrella matches them.

XIV.47. Man in Frock Coat. 1899

Hair: The hair is cut short and brushed back over the ears. The parting, in the centre or to one side, is hidden by the hat.

Headdress: The black top hat is a little lower in the crown than those worn in the next century.

Garments: The frock-coat of black cloth has comparatively long lapels, faced with black silk. The double-breasted fastenings are left open. The high, starched collar has a centre fastening. The shirt front is also starched. The waistcoat is of pale grey cloth. The wide knotted tie is of grey silk. The black-and-grey striped trousers have no crease, though this was already worn by some men.

Footwear: The laced boots are of black leather.

Accessories: The gloves are of pale grey leather. A walking-stick is carried in the right hand.

XV 20TH-CENTURY DRESS
(1900–1914)

The short period covered by this chapter offers strongly contrasting styles of dress, the soft draperies and flowing skirts of the early years giving place to the tapering silhouette and clinging draperies introduced towards the end. The two trends of fashion themselves show some contrasts between severely practical and exotically flamboyant costume.

The period saw the end of the frock-coat and the further development of the lounge and morning suits, the popularity of the tea-gown and the motoring outfit, the decline of the mannish mode for women and later of the briefly worn hobble skirt.

With the 1914–18 war many more changes were to occur; and in the spirit of the period from 1900 to 1914 we find the last expressions of carefree, unthinking enjoyment of a life which was soon to disappear for ever.

Hair—Men: The centre parting, with the hair brushed back, or flattened down in a curve on each side of the parting, was the most usual in the first five years. After that a side parting ending in small quiffs was equally in fashion. The fashion for brushing the hair straight back without a parting arose in 1910 and the centre parting was seen less often. Most men had their hair neatly trimmed at back and sides. Elderly men sometimes wore their hair rather thick at the back.

Beards were worn by some older men and moustaches included the small 'toothbrush', the walrus type, the waxed moustache, the 'military' sort turned up at the ends and the long straggling variety, but a large number of men were clean-shaven. Side-whiskers of the 'mutton-chop' kind were still worn by some elderly professional and business men, farmers and tradesmen.

Hair—Women: A softer, wider pompadour than the small, neat version of it that had already appeared was gaining ground in 1900. The hair in the front of the head might be evenly raised over the forehead or arranged in puffs and waves to make an attractive setting for the face. A loose upward sweep at the back, with a high chignon was thought preferable to a severely upswept line. The chignon could be placed on the top of the head, sometimes very near the front, at medium height or low on the neck. An alternative to the pompadour was a centre parting, with wide side-puffs. The front fringe was worn from time to time. Occasionally a parting a little to one side was worn.

By 1903–4 a large figure-of-eight twist often formed the back of the coiffure. Upswept sides with a dip in the middle made a variation in the pompadour. By 1906 a more closely upswept line at the back was attempted, though not always maintained, with the high chignon.

In 1907–8 the pompadour was still worn, but the centre parting with puffs at the sides and a low or medium-high chignon had become a favourite way of dressing the hair, which lasted with modifications until 1914 and after. Combs were worn to keep the side-pieces in place and by 1909 a band of ribbon was often worn across the head. Another coiffure involved drawing the hair back unparted into a wide comb worn across the head instead of a ribbon. The hair over the forehead could be slightly raised by this method and retained some

XV.1. 1901–6. Women. Three-quarter-length Figures

Hair: (a) (1904.) The hair is puffed and waved in a high pompadour with a forward dip over the centre of the forehead. The line continues unbroken to the large, low chignon. (b) (1901.) The front hair is drawn back to the top of the head in a moderate pompadour. Moderate side-puffs over the temples leave the ears exposed. The hair at the back is puffed and drawn loosely up to the top of the head where it is pinned under the pompadour, with no chignon. (c) (1906.) The hair is parted in the centre and brought down over the forehead to the temples, where it is turned back and pinned on the top of the head. It is then drawn loosely down over the back of the head, joining the remainder of the hair in a low chignon.

Garments: (a) The dress is of pale amethyst silk. It has a close, round neckline and a deeply bloused bodice. Vertical tucks decorate the bodice and the tops of the sleeves, which are made in one with the bodice. The sleeves are full in the lower part and sewn into bands at the wrists. The skirt fits neatly at the waist and hips but flows out (unseen) into a flared skirt forming a short train. (b) The evening gown is of apricot satin, giving prominence, rather low, to the bosom and tightly fitted at the waist. The low décolletage is off the shoulders, with narrow brown velvet shoulder straps. The long, close-fitting sleeves of coffee-coloured lace which are attached below the shoulders are edged with brown velvet. A large ornament of coffee-coloured lace is worn at the front of the bosom and another towards the left side of the brown velvet waist-belt. Velvet flowers in flame colour and yellow are worn on the bodice. The skirt is broad over the hips and is full, long and trained. (c) The dress is of corn-flower blue ninon over a silk foundation in fuchsia pink. The bodice is full over the bosom but not bloused. The wide neckline comes to a downward point in the centre of the front. It has a 'bertha' collar of the blue ninon. The chemisette of ivory lace is attached to the top of the 'bertha'. The full sleeves end in bands and frills below the elbow and are lined with fuchsia-coloured silk. The lower sleeves are close-fitting and match the lace of the chemisette. The skirt flows out gradually from the waist into a long, widely flared skirt (unseen).

of the shape of the pompadour, while the side-pieces were held by combs. A style initiated about 1909 was made up of a mass of waves and curls covering the head, with a centre or side parting, or none, bound with a ribbon that crossed the top of the head and passed under the bunched curls at the back. It was still in vogue in 1911 and a version of it, with the hair dressed more flatly at the front and sides and the band further forward, was worn until 1914.

All these styles were dependent on the use of pads, wire frames, combs, slides and of course hairpins. With a growing preference for easier hairdressing, the coiffure grew smaller and less complicated. Plaits wound round the head were worn from 1908 onwards, with waves in front of the 'coronet' of plaits and sometimes from about 1913 a small chignon at the back.

The invention of Marcel waving in 1907 made the use of tongs at home and of curling pins and papers less necessary.

By 1912 the hair was brought down to cover the ears completely and much of the forehead as well. The chignon could be low or could jut out in a 'bun' at medium height, elongating the coiffure. An alternative was a large Grecian knot.

In 1913–14 hairdressing continued the elongated look. A chignon worn at medium height at the back of the head was built out as far as possible, often with a swathe of hair twined round it to enhance the effect. An oval coiffure was achieved by taking a broad swathe from each side of the head closely round the back and pinning it with ends turned in above the ear on the opposite side, the hair from the front being taken smoothly up and back to the crown, folded in on itself and pinned there.

Headdress—Men: At the opening of the 20th century the soft felt hat, with the alternative of a cloth or tweed cap, was worn by men in the country or for travelling. The straw boater and the wide-brimmed panama, the latter often unbecomingly turned up in front, were also worn in the country and at the seaside.

The top hat was worn a great deal in London and was considered correct wear for the majority of smart gatherings. Bowler hats with lower crowns than in the previous century and felt hats with rolled brims were also worn with the smarter lounge suits now in vogue and could be seen at formal garden parties and on other fashionable outdoor occasions.

The opera hat, like a top hat but with a matt instead of a shiny surface and a collapsible crown, was worn or carried with evening dress.

By 1913 bowlers and felt hats were superseding the top hat, though this was still worn with morning suits and the now disappearing frock-coat. The hard flat-crowned felt hat favoured by farmers and many tradesmen and the tweed hat of the angler with brim turned down were in use during this period.

Headdress—Women: Women's hats varied greatly both in design and the angles at which they were worn. As many examples as possible have been illustrated.

Hats were perched high on the head in the first eight to nine years. Bandeaux were put inside the rim of the crown to lift the hat so that it did not fit closely or come down on the forehead and the majority of hats made of fabric were contrived on foundations of buckram or wire, or both.

Flowered bonnets and toques appear from the beginning of the period. Although the bonnet was soon to be relegated to the costume of older women, some young married women still wore them for a year or two.

Hats with brims could be put on straight or tilted forward or back or to one side. Brims could be contrived to curve at all angles or could lie flat. They could be large or small and trimmings of ribbon, flowers and feathers were profuse.

Chiffon, tulle or net were among the materials used at this time and many hats were composed entirely of some fragile stuff over a silk lining and buckram foundation.

The straw boater and a version of the man's felt hat were widely worn in the early years by women with plainer dresses, coats and skirts and tweed coats. Tweed caps were also worn for cycling, golf and walking. For motoring, the flat, wide circular cap was varied about 1907 by a version in which the crown was segmented and had a button in the centre beneath which the long motoring veil was attached.

Flowers could be worn in the hair until about 1910 and scarves of tulle, chiffon, lace or net were thrown over the head out of doors when evening dress was worn. Veils put on over the face and the front of the hat, fastened at the back and twisted into a little knot under the chin, were very fashionable. After 1908–9 hats were lower on the head, but because of the large crowns which now came into fashion in toques and mushroom-shaped hats the bandeau inside was still a necessity.

Neo-Georgian imitations of men's hats under the Directoire were worn between 1910 and 1912, and hat brims reached a tremendous size in 1911.

Simpler hats of felt or straw, trimmed only with a ribbon, were worn with practical dress

XV.2. 1900–5. Women

Hair: (a) (1900.) The hair is rolled back over a semi-circular pad, forming a moderate pompadour. A low chignon is worn at the back of the neck. (b) (Early 1900s.) The hair of the country woman is parted in the centre and smoothed down at the sides. The rest is hidden by the sunbonnet, but would be in a bun or coil at the back of the head. (c) (1905.) The hair is taken up from a centre parting in puffs at the sides, showing the lobes of the ears. The chignon is low at the back of the neck.

Headdress: (a) The hat of black paille has a wide, slightly curving brim turned up in front. Loops of turquoise blue ribbon show over the brim with a small plume of the same colour. (b) The sunbonnet is of white linen. Its brim frames the face in undulating curves. Tucks ornament the sides of the bonnet and the back is flat, with a deep flap of linen attached there. Untied strings hang over the bosom of the dress. (c) The crescent-shaped hat of grey surah silk is set high on the head and has no separately shaped crown. Two small, curled Parma-violet plumes are set on the top. The grey circular veil has a small frill at the top to attach it to the brim of the hat and hangs down all round.

Garments: (a) The dress is of turquoise blue mousseline de soie, with long plain sleeves ending at the wrists in triple frills (unseen). The bodice throws the bosom into prominence and the black silk belt has a point in the front of the waist. Triple shoulder frills of the same stuff as the dress have a narrow black edging. The chemisette is of cream-coloured lace. (b) The cotton dress has pink dots on a white ground. The bodice fits closely but the skirt is fairly full and ends (unseen) clear of the ground. The sleeves are plain and are rolled back on the forearms. A white apron is worn. (c) The dress is of grey and violet patterned silk voile. The bloused look is apparent. The high-collared chemisette is of cream-coloured net. The loose, open coat is of grey shantung silk.

and at the seaside, but it was still permissible to wear huge, over-trimmed hats in the country and for travelling.

By 1913–14 smaller hats, covering the head without being raised from it and following much simpler lines, with very little trimming, had become fashionable. They followed the elongated or rounded line of the hairdressing of these years.

Ribbon bands and wide bandeaux of velvet or satin, often beaded, were worn half-way back on the head and fastened under the chignon in 1910–12 and from 1912 to 1913 round the forehead or just above it. Aigrettes were worn in 1912 and 1913–14.

Garments—Men: The frock-coat was still worn by professional men such as doctors and lawyers and some business men. The morning suit was worn for many formal and semi-formal social occasions, but the lounge suit was increasing in favour.

The lapels of the morning coat were still high and the first of the three fastenings was therefore buttoned high up, but by 1906 the lapels were longer and the coat had one link fastening at waist-level. Until after 1914 the morning coat was usually edged all round with narrow braid. The tails ended behind the knees or a little higher.

The short-tailed sloping-away coat introduced in the 1870s, resembling the morning coat in some ways, was worn throughout the period. It was made in tweed and checked woollen stuff to wear with riding breeches, knickerbockers or flannel trousers, and in black for city workers to wear with striped trousers or in material matching the trousers and waistcoat so that the ensemble could be worn as a suit.

The coat of the lounge suit had the same short lapels and fastenings as other coats at first. By 1904 it had longer lapels and was looser in fit, fastened only at the waist. The length of the jacket altered with the vagaries of fashion and individual preferences. The corners could be square or rounded off.

Double-breasted 'reefer' jackets could be worn until about 1906.

Other jackets and blazers for sporting activities followed the lines of the jacket of the lounge suit, with the exception of the Norfolk suit, whose jacket kept its tight-fitting shape and always fastened high up. Tweed or checked jackets with a half belt at the back, made rather in the Norfolk style, and ordinary tweed jackets were also worn with knickerbockers. Plus-fours were in fashion from 1912 to 1913 onwards.

Men's formal evening dress had altered very little from the fashion at the end of the last century. Dinner jackets, worn for informal evenings only, had appeared by 1905, but were frowned on at first as being too casual in appearance.

Stiff collars and cuffs were obligatory with all town suits and were worn in the country and at the seaside until after 1910. They were made separately from the shirts and always starched. Coloured shirts, in inconspicuous stripes, came into fashion about 1910, and were worn with starched collars to match or of white linen. Boiled shirts were usually worn with dinner jackets as well as with tails, although some unconventional younger men experimented with soft pleated or frilled shirts.

Ties were of various kinds; Ascots with wing-collars and bow or knotted ties with turn-over collars; Ascots, bow or knotted ties with 'jam-pot' collars. White ties were worn with 'tails' and black with dinner jackets as today. Stripes, dots or plain subdued colours were used for knotted and bow ties.

Waistcoats of lounge suits usually matched the coat and trousers, but with the morning suit and the frock-coat pale-coloured waistcoats might be worn. These were made of gros-grain, silk piqué, small-patterned brocade or fine facecloth in pearl colour, cream or pale grey. White piqué waistcoats were worn with 'tails' and black grosgrain with dinner jackets.

Trousers were of medium width and covered the tops of the shoes in morning suits, evening dress and, at first, lounge suits and flannel trousers. Turn-ups to the trousers of lounge suits and flannel trousers had begun to appear by 1903 and in 1906 a short-lived fashion of bracing them high to show the ankles and even the tops of the spats was followed by some younger men. The crease down the front of the leg, already apparent in the middle '90s, gradually came into general fashion in the first years of this century.

Outer garments included loose, three-quarter-length overcoats of cloth or tweed, and others, for wearing in town and with evening dress, slightly shaped to the figure and made of black cloth. In the first five years or so long 'ulsters', with or without capes and made in tweed or checked stuff, were an essential for travelling and bad weather, but the development of the raincoat and the less weighty overcoat made the wearing of ulsters less frequent. Motorists had 'dustcoats', sometimes nearly to the ankles, of heavy natural-coloured linen.

Garments—Women: The erect figure of the 1890s, with the neatly defined bust, slim waist and narrow hips, the skirt springing out into flares a little below them, was altered to a more opulent line soon after the beginning of the 20th century. A slightly forward-leaning posture, with more emphasis on the curves of bust and hips, produced the fashionable new outlines, which was shown off especially well by the 'princess' type of dress moulded to the figure from the shoulders downwards and flowing out into a flared skirt.

A change in the lines of corsetry in 1902, pushing the natural form into a series of artificially contrived curves, provided a good foundation for the deeply bloused fashions which were at their height from 1903 to 1905.

Blouses and bodices made as separate garments from their skirts had tapes at the back of the waist which were brought round to the front, tied, and fastened to the inside of the waistband of the skirt. Hooks and eyes kept skirt and bodice together at the back.

By 1905 the outline was less exaggerated, though the pouched fashion in bodices lasted into 1907.

Skirts were fitted over the wide hips of the new stays, and flowed out from their godets towards the hem; the godets at the back were extended to form a train in many evening and afternoon gowns before 1908, on separate skirts and on some coats and skirts. More practical skirts were made on an almost circular plan, with little extension at the back and with the godets stitched down to some distance below the knee, creating a trumpet-shaped effect. Others were made on deep 'yokes' ending above the knees with flares depending from a band or from gathers at the base of the yoke. Silk skirts, to be worn with a 'dressy' blouse, were often accordion-pleated. Skirts made in three or four tiers or flounces were worn about 1905–6. Dresses and skirts worn for active pursuits cleared the ground and frequently had deep inverted or box pleats. The former were stitched down to about knee level and the latter were released rather higher, generally below the hips. Tennis was played in skirts of white linen or piqué, with a collar-and-tie blouse.

The coat-and-skirt was popular and was made of cloth, suiting, linen, 'holland' and heavy tussore silk, and of tweed for cycling, golfing, walking and for country wear generally. The coat could fit the figure to the waist and have a short basque, or it could be made as a bolero or as a short double-breasted 'box' jacket. Another figure-fitting type fastened at the waist and sloped away from it into a long, wasp-like tail. During the first eight years of the epoch a coat-and-skirt could have a three-quarter-length coat, loose or fitted to the figure. A mannish jacket, rather long, was worn with a matching or odd tweed skirt.

The tea-gown was fashionable during the reign of Edward VII and in altered forms persisted until the 1920s. In the first decade of the century it hung loosely from a yoke at the shoulders, the train formed by the back length and the loose front fastened in the centre all the way down. It was made of many different stuffs, from cashmere and velvet to lace and chiffon and was lined with silk, satin or taffetas.

The motoring outfit was another feature of this decade. Its main items were a long, loose 'dustcoat' (also worn on other occasions, particularly for travelling), a veil tied over the hat, and goggles to protect the wearer from glare and dust.

The neckline was almost invariably high, though a few, during the first eight years of the century, were cut to end at the base of the neck or in a moderate 'V'. Some dresses had upstanding neck-bands of their own material or of satin or silk in a matching colour. Many had a 'chemisette' of lace, net or embroidery, with a high, close-fitting, boned collar, put on under the dress as a separate garment, or stitched inside it. The gown in this case usually had a wide round, oval or 'V'-shaped neck-opening, with some form of narrow edging, or alternatively a cross-over bodice. A deep lace yoke with a high collar often formed the top of the dress, covering the chest and descending to the shoulder-blades at the back. The yoke could end in a square, rounded, heart-shaped or undulating line just above the bust, and extended to the points of the shoulders. Between 1903 and 1905, deep flounces and 'Berthas' hung from the shoulders, finishing wide yokes or collars.

The blouse with stiff collar and tie was worn for outdoor pursuits and by some women as practical morning dress. In 1900 the collar was often of the rigid 'jam-pot' variety, with no turn-over, but during this year the stiff turned-over collar became more usual. The tie could be knotted like a man's, but a bow tie (frequently ready-made) could be worn instead. Schoolgirls wore ties with cotton or flannel blouses.

A vogue for winding a length of soft tulle round the neck and tying it in a bow in front, at the side or at the back, was seen from time to time prior to 1909. 'Jabot' frills were a frequent adornment at the base of the throat and a so-called stock, a band of dark silk stuff, was worn round the neck, tied or knotted in front. Blouses were made on the same lines as complete dresses, and could have high-collared yokes or chemisettes. With the coat and skirt a chemisette was often worn instead of a blouse.

Evening décolletage was both low and wide. Dresses showing the shoulders sometimes had shoulder-straps with long sprays of flowers. Some evening dresses had two or three flounces as sleeves with small puffed sleeves, unseen, beneath them. With the bloused

XV.3. 1900–7. Women. Six Figures

Hair: (a) (1907.) The side-puffs can be seen under the cap. (b) (1901.) The hair is parted in the centre and brought down loosely to cover the ears, then turned over and taken up with the hair from the back into a chignon on the top of the head. (c) (1907), (d) (1904) and (e) (1903.) The side puffs of the hair are all that can be seen. (f) (1907.) Large side puffs are taken up over pads and pinned near the top of the head.

Headdress: (a) The motoring cap has a wide, flat, circular crown and a small peak in front, attached to the band (unseen) at the base of the cap. It is of blue felt and has a matching button in the centre of the crown to which the motoring veil of blue chiffon is attached. This is tied under the chin. (c) The wide-brimmed black velvet hat is covered all over the top with downward-pointing white feathers, which cover part of the brim as well. (d) The high-perched, styles of 1903–5 and later large, soft folds and looped arrangements of tulle, lace and chiffon surrounded the exposed shoulders. Deep flounces and 'Berthas' were also fashionable, worn below the shoulders in the evening. Fichus for evening wear could be seen from time to time, worn at the edge of the shoulders, with a deep flounce.

The puffed shoulders of the '90s disappeared for the time being after the turn of the century. Many sleeves of the early 1900s were long and plain and some had cuffs shaped to extend over the hand in points or a goblet-shaped form. Others were full to the elbow, ending there in a frill or attached to a narrow, close-fitting lower part continuing to the wrist. These were worn until 1903 and returned to fashion later. In 1901 a narrow type of bell-shaped sleeve, ending a little way above the wrist, had a modified 'bishop' sleeve beneath it, gathered into a band at the wrist-opening. This lasted through the next six years, becoming wider and fuller below the elbow with the fashion for pouched bodices, when the shoulder-line drooped and interest was concentrated on the lower half of the sleeve. Others worn at this time included a bishop sleeve from shoulder to wrist with or without one or two bands to hold in the narrow upper part and considerable fullness below the elbow, increasing above the wrist; a close sleeve to the elbow or below it, with a lower part in 'bishop' shape attached; and a sleeve full to the middle of the forearm with a long, close-fitting wrist-band, still worn in 1906–7.

In 1904 three-quarter-length sleeves were popular and remained so for some years to come. A sleeve narrow at the top, widening into a large puff over the elbow and ending in a close-fitting band at the middle of the forearm was an important feature; so was a loose sleeve gradually widening to the elbow, with frills of increasing graduated fullness attached. This could be decorated above the frills by a band of ribbon tied in a bow. Very wide, full-length sleeves with deep flounces at the opening were also worn.

Neatly fitted bodices with darts above the waist, still giving prominence to the bosom, were in fashion by 1906, and there was a return to the gathered shoulder, so that long diminishing sleeves came back into favour for a time.

---

flat-crowned toque of coffee-brown silk fabric has a cascade of small café-au-lait feathers, drooping over the left side. (e) The hard straw hat, worn for tennis or cycling, has a black band, a narrow brim and a flat, shallow crown. (f) The parlourmaid's cap is a rosette of starched white lawn frills, tipped forward with two streamers which hang down at the back below the shoulder-blades.

Garments: (a) The open, loosely fitting motoring coat is of heavy natural linen. The lapels are short and there are three button fastenings. The sleeves are raised and gathered at the shoulders, and have turned-back cuffs. The long, dark blue serge coat and flared, matching skirt worn beneath the dust-coat are partly seen. The white cambric blouse (hardly seen) has a high collar. (b) The evening gown is of rose-du-barry satin, clinging to the figure and flowing out into a wide circular skirt. The décolletage is low, with triple shoulder straps of the satin. Three bands of the satin also outline the bust. A silk rose matching the dress is worn in the centre of the bosom. (c) The coat of black velvet slopes away from a fastening at the waist showing part of the flared skirt of the grey silk dress. The large white fur stole, open to show the white chemisette at the neck, is probably attached to the coat as a collar, hanging loose from the waist-fastening. The sleeves are made in one with the garment and are wide at the ends. (d) The fitted jacket, with a deep basque, is of fur toning with the feathers on the hat. The collar stands high and crosses over at the fastening. The sleeves are slightly broadened at the shoulders and widen towards their ends.

The circular skirt of a practical length is of coffee-brown cloth with a moderate flare, and has pleats stitched down as far as the knees. (e) The blouse is of starched white cambric worn with a man's starched double collar and a coloured knotted tie. The sleeves are gathered at the shoulders, with the upper parts in large puffs and the lower parts close-fitting to the wrists. The skirt is of white piqué, with inverted pleats at the sides of the front, and two similar pleats at the back (unseen). It has a moderate flare and partly shows the shoes. A white stiffened belt is round the waist, fastened with a buckle. (f) The parlourmaid's black dress has a close round neck-line and plain sleeves with starched white cuffs. It is worn with a starched white double collar. The skirt is flared and shows part of the shoes. The voluminous white apron covers most of the dress and has a deep frill crossing the bottom and standing out beyond the shoulders. It ties in a large bow at the back of the waist, with ends hanging down (unseen).

Footwear: (a) The plain, laced walking shoes are of black leather with moderate 'sensible' heels. (d) The shoes are of brown kid, laced for walking and with low partly shaped heels. (e) The laced tennis shoes are of white canvas and have flat heels. (f) The parlourmaid has black leather shoes, with straps and buttons over the insteps, and low heels. Only the toes of the shoes are actually visible.

Accessories: (a) Goggles are worn to protect the eyes. They have thick, clumsy frames and are fastened round the back of the head by a band of fabric or elastic. The gloves are of leather to tone with the coat. A rolled black umbrella is carried. (c) The white fur muff matches the stole-collar. (d) The gloves tone with the fur of the jacket. A rolled umbrella of brown silk is carried. (c) The girl carries a tennis racquet. (f) The parlourmaid carries a small silver salver.

The long outer wraps had godets in the skirts until 1908, so that they followed the lines of the dresses they covered. They had full sleeves, gathered into a band or frill at the wrist or ending in a wide opening, and upstanding roll collars which could be turned back or large, flat collars in a square or rounded shape, fastened at the throat. Many were inter-lined for warmth as long fur coats were not much worn at this time. Wide stoles of rich and heavy fur, fur jackets, muffs and fur capes were used instead. Loose raincoats were by this time in general use.

By 1907–8 plainer sleeves, plainly set in at the shoulder, were fashionable. They could be of full- or three-quarter-length or could end at the elbow. Short, more elaborate sleeves, ending at the upper arm, cut in one with the dress, were a feature of evening dress, which no longer exposed the shoulders. Ruffles or frills sometimes ended the sleeves of formal gowns.

XV.4. 1903–9. Six Figures

Hair: (a) (1903.) The hair is cut short and is hardly seen under the hat. (b) (1904.) The hair is hidden by the cap and goggles (c) (1909.) The side-puffs of the woman's hair can be seen under the toque. The little boy's short hair is hardly seen. (d) (1907.) The coster girl's hair is cut in a thick fringe in front and parted across the head behind the ears, the hair at the back being wound into a loose, low chignon. The hair at the sides is dressed in a large curl or roll over each ear. (e) (1908.) The child's nurse has hair dressed very much as in (c). (f) (1906.) The policeman's short hair is almost hidden by his helmet. He wears a walrus moustache.

Headdress: (a) The straw hat has a shallow crown with a black band. (b) The motoring cap of brown cloth has a full, soft crown. A peak protrudes from the band that fits the head. A second band of brown leather is worn round the base of the crown. (c) The large round toque is of pale blue tulle with a matching feather on the right side. The little boy wears a sailor hat of natural straw, with black binding and a black band. This has the name of a warship on the front in gilt lettering and ends hanging down at the back. (d) The coster girl's large black velvet hat is trimmed with curled plumes of various colours, some hanging over the edge of the brim. (e) The nurse's bonnet of navy blue straw is set back on the head with the brim turned back. A flat bow of navy blue ribbon is attached in the front, matching the strings that are tied under the chin. The little girl's white muslin bonnet has three large frills standing up to frame the face. It is lined with pink silk and has matching ribbons tied under the chin. (f) The policeman's dark blue helmet has a tall crown, with a flat metal ornament on the top, and a narrow turned-down brim.

Garments: (a) The man's suit is of cream-coloured flannel, worn for boating, tennis or at the seaside. The jacket has short lapels, narrowly cut shoulders and buttons fastening it down the front. The trousers are narrow, with a crease and turn-ups and are short enough to show the socks. The starched white collar fastens in front and is worn with a blue and white bow-tie. The socks have a diamond pattern in blue and white. (b) The man's loosely fitting motoring coat ends above the ankles. The collar stands up and the sleeves are shaped, with some fullness below the elbows. The trousers of green and brown checked tweed come well down over the boots. (c) The woman's coat and skirt are of mushroom-coloured cloth. The jacket ends below the knees and has long, narrow lapels. The skirt is just clear of the ground and slightly flared. The blouse of pale blue silk has a high collared chemisette of cream-coloured net. The boy wears a sailor suit with a white cotton blouse and dark blue serge knickers ending just above the knee-caps. The collar of the blouse is dark blue, with three white stripes bordering the sides and back. A narrow black silk scarf is passed under it round the neck and knotted in front. His stockings are of black cashmere. (d) The coster girl's coat is of blue-green cloth. It fits closely to the hips, where it evolves a moderate bell-shape, ending below the knees. The sleeves are puffed and gathered at the shoulders and taper towards the wrists. A scarf of white cotton stuff with red dots is wound round the neck and tied in a large bow in front. The brown serge skirt has a deep flounce round the hem. (e) The nursemaid's coat and skirt are of navy blue serge. It is plainly cut, with the jacket ending at the top of the thighs. The skirt resembles that of (c). The starched white collar and the front of the blue and white striped blouse can be seen at the neck. The little girl's loose, full frock is of white muslin over a pink silk foundation. Four frills trim the bottom of the skirt. The narrow collar-band is hidden by the bonnet strings. A wide frill hides the short yoke. The sleeves end in frills at the wrists, and the stockings are of white silk. (f) The policeman's navy blue tunic is double-breasted and ends below the knees. It has a close-fitting upstanding collar with his number on it in metal lettering, and fastens on the right side of the chest with silver buttons with a corresponding row of these decorating the left side. The sleeves are plain and there is a band of blue and white striped fabric round the left arm a little above the wrist. The black leather belt is buckled in front. The narrow trousers come down over the boots.

Footwear: (a) The man wears white canvas laced shoes. (b) The motorist has laced boots of brown leather. (c) The woman wears laced black leather walking shoes with low heels. The boy has blunt-toed black leather laced shoes. (d) The coster girl wears black leather buttoned boots with flat heels. (e) The nursemaid wears laced walking shoes of black leather with low heels. The little girl's slippers are of white kid. (f) The policeman has laced boots of black leather.

Accessories: (a) The man carries a light walking-stick. (b) The man wears motoring goggles. (c) The woman wears a long sable stole. The boy wears a whistle on a white cord (unseen). (e) The nursemaid has white cotton gloves. The little girl's gloves are of white silk. (f) The policeman has a black japanned lantern attached to the left side of the front of his belt.

XV.4. 1903–9. Six Figures

Many skirts were still long and moderately flared in 1908, but some dresses were now made on straight lines and some higher waists were seen. The straight skirt usually just touched the ground and its train, where it had one, was narrow. Skirts for active pursuits were still pleated and flowed out towards the hem, which was now more often above the shoes and sometimes showed the ankles. A collarless, close-fitting neckline ending at the base of the throat became fashionable by 1909 and a high, closely fitted waistline was established, but normal waistlines continued at the same time. A close-fitting over-tunic was often added to the dress. It was longer at the back than the front as a rule and ended some inches above the hem of the dress.

In 1910–12 the hobble skirt, of ankle or instep length, close-fitting to the calf and bound there so that its very slight flare was of no help in walking, came into fashion, but was by no means universally adopted; the lower neckline, in rounded or 'V'-shape, sometimes with a plain or frilled turn-down collar, began to rival the high, close-fitting collar; and a new 'sheath' corset, very long with slenderized hips, was generally adopted. The frilly, gored petticoats were replaced by more straight-cut underslips, usually of silk.

In 1912 the 'bound' hobble skirt, which had been found dangerous, gave place to one almost as restricting, but sometimes ornamented with buttons which could be left unfastened to the calf. A short underslip was worn, with 'Directoire' knickers, close-fitting and banded at the knees.

A temporary fashion for a 'harem' skirt in which a form of Turkish trousers showed under a long over-tunic was ridiculed out of existence. More high waists were seen and all skirts tapered to some extent towards the hem.

Necklines were lower at this time, sometimes filled in with a 'modesty vest'. Some crossover bodices were seen and square necklines were in favour. Long kimono-sleeved coats, narrowing towards the hem, with wide roll collars wrapping over to a low fastening, were worn as outer wraps.

A mixture of styles was to be noted in 1913–14. The so-called 'Medici' collar, standing up at the back of the neck, was introduced by stiffened frills in 1913. High waists were still as much a part of the fashion as the normal waistline. A vogue for loose, almost shapeless dresses and coats and skirts, with the 'waist' very low on the hips in the case of coats and jackets and a little below normal in dresses and with a fairly broad, loose belt in both cases, foreshadowed the later loosely-fitting styles. Sometimes a coat or jacket had only a half-belt across the back.

At the same time elegant and sophisticated evening and afternoon dresses had draped skirts, with a wrap-over effect in front which divided just above the ankles and was swept towards the back in a short 'fishtail' train. Another skirt tapered from the 'peg-top' drapery below the hips to the usual 'hobble' hem.

The 'lampshade' style in the skirts of evening and some afternoon dresses was in vogue. This was part of an over-dress and was cut in an elliptical shape with wider circumference at the bottom than at the top and the back longer than the front. The lower edge was wired to stand out if it was intended to hang in folds. It was put on at the waist and usually ended half way down the thighs.

Footwear—Men: Men's footwear followed the shape of the foot and had well-shaped toes, neither very pointed nor over-rounded. Many wore boots that just covered the anklebones. If made entirely of polished leather they were laced, but those with 'uppers' of black kid or pale grey cloth from the base of the toes were buttoned on the outer side. Brown shoes or laced boots could be worn with Norfolk or knickerbocker suits. White canvas or buckskin shoes were worn for yachting, boating and at the seaside, with the alternatives of brown canvas with leather toe-caps, soles and heels or of Plimsolls for wear on the beach.

Black lace-up shoes, pumps or slip-on shoes with small elastic gussets at the sides were worn with evening dress.

Brown or tan leather gaiters were worn with knickerbocker suits as well as for riding, and top boots for hunting and riding. The 'Continental' gaiters of the 1890s, covering the top of the shoe and reaching a short way up the calf, were worn very frequently until 1902 and less often until 1914, but by that time shoes were more usual with knickerbockers and were invariably worn with plus-fours.

XV.5. 1904–7. Women's Headdress

Hair: (a) (1904–6.) The hair is puffed at the sides above the ears and is dressed in a pompadour (unseen) in front. It is drawn up from the back and wound into a chignon at the top of the head. (b) (1906.) The hair is arranged in puffs to form a pompadour over the forehead and temples. A part of the low chignon can be seen on the right of the neck. (c) (1907.) The hair is dressed in large puffed waves to a higher level on the left, where the brim of the hat turns up, than on the right.

Headdress: (a) The hat is covered in ice-blue satin. It is perched high and tipped forward and to one side. The up-turned brim diminishes at the back. The veil of ice-blue tulle covers the front of the hat and the face and is knotted at the back of the brim. (b) The shell-shaped hat of black satin is set on the back of the head and curves high over the front. At the back (unseen) it retains the shell-like shape, curving down to its base with no separately moulded crown. The brim is lined with shell-pink silk, with matching artificial roses set across it just above the hair. (c) The hat is perched high and is of natural straw with an undulating brim curving up on the left at its widest part. It is edged with narrow black

velvet. Large pale green satin bows trim the front above the brim, with one set towards the back on the left of the upturned side.

Garments: (a) The dress is of ice-blue glacé silk, with a bloused bodice and upstanding frilled collar ending in a 'V' shape just below the top of the breastbone. The bodice is trimmed with frills, ruching and narrow sapphire blue piping. The top of the loose, flowing upper sleeve can be seen. (b) The dress is of oyster grey lace over a foundation of shell-pink double ninon. An insertion of tucked shell-pink ninon crosses the bloused bodice just above the bosom. The high collar is of oyster grey lace and the feather boa of the same colour. (c) The dress is of pale green tussore silk. It has a rounded neckline and a bloused bodice with a wide collar covering the shoulders and ending in points edged with black silk.

Jewellery and Accessories: (a) A band of ice-blue tulle is worn round the neck and tied at the back. (b) Pearl stud earrings are worn. (c) A narrow black ribbon encircles the neck and is tied at the back.

Socks were usually black or grey, though from time to time after 1910 a vogue for 'loud' socks appeared among younger men. Thick woollen stockings, often with coloured patterns at the top, were worn with knickerbockers.

Footwear—Women: Women's footwear for daytime in the first fourteen years of the century was usually black, but sometimes brown. They wore laced walking boots, court shoes with tongues, buckles or bows, or boots with tops of kid or cloth in grey or pale buff out of doors. Stouter boots were worn in the country, for sport or long walks and by women with a preference for practical clothing. Otherwise walking shoes or even court shoes could be worn. Low-heeled white canvas or buckskin shoes were worn for yachting, boating and at the seaside.

Indoors, slippers with a strap across the instep, pumps or court shoes, sometimes beaded in front, were usual. Toes were long, soles thin and heels of 'baby Louis' shape. Some

XV.6. 1910–12. Women. Three Figures.

Hair: (a) (1911.) The hair is parted on one side with downward puffs on the right side of the forehead and over each ear. (b) (1910.) The hair is dressed in waves and curls over the forehead and covering the ears. Similar curls are piled over the back of the head behind the head-band. (c) (1912–13.) The hair covers the ears, puffed out a little, and curves downward over the forehead.

Headdress: (a) The large hat of black paille has a curving brim and grey-blue plumes curling over it. (b) A band of green satin ribbon is fastened over the top of the head. (c) The soft-crowned hat of brown velvet has a narrow upturned brim and a flame-coloured silk rose on the left front of the crown.

Garments: (a) The yoke and sleeves of the dress are of mist-blue lace. The neckline is close-fitting, and the sleeves end below the elbows with narrow bands, matching the mist-blue satin of which the dress is made. This has a close-fitting 'princess' line and a narrow skirt, showing the shoes. (b) The dress is of cream-coloured silk, with an overskirt folding over in front and a little longer on the left than on the right. The neckline is squared, and the bodice and skirt plainly cut. The elbow-length sleeves have puffs and frills of cream-coloured chiffon. The embroidery ornamenting the bodice-sleeves and the hems of both over-skirt and under-skirt are of pale yellow, pale green and heliotrope silk. (c) The three-quarter-length coat of brown velours has a rolled collar and cuffs of light brown fur. It is full at the top, growing narrow towards the hem, and has full 'Magyar' sleeves. Part of the bodice and narrow, draped skirt of the brown velvet dress can be seen. A cream-coloured silk frill edges the cross-over bodice. The stockings are of pale brown silk.

Footwear: (a) The court shoes are of grey suède. (b) The court shoes are of cream-coloured satin. (c) The court shoes are of brown suède.

Jewellery and Accessories: (a) The parasol is of grey silk, with pleated frills at the edges, and the handbag of grey suède, with long white kid gloves. (b) A small gold locket on a gold chain is worn and a folding fan is carried. (c) The gloves are of biscuit-coloured kid and the handbag of brown suède.

shorter, rounded toes came in about 1913–14, and from 1912 to 1913 some shoes were tied on with crossed ribbons ending at the calf. These had eyelet holes for inserting the ribbons.

For evening, shoes were of satin dyed to match the dress, or, from about 1908, of bronze kid, which was often beaded. They were of court shape, with pointed toes and generally with 'baby Louis' heels, though some were higher.

Galoshes were worn in wet weather. Bedroom slippers were of the same court shape as shoes for day or evening, or flat-soled, without added heels.

Women's stockings were generally black, of cashmere, cotton or silk, but brown stockings were of course worn with brown shoes or boots and white with white shoes. Silk stockings in colours to match the dress were worn in the evening. Openwork stockings were a feature of this time for evening dress.

Materials, Colours and Ornament: All woollen materials such as serge, tweed, hopsack, broadcloth, faced-cloth and suiting were in use. Checks and rough tweeds were popular for men's knickerbocker and country suits and the three-quarter-length capes worn by some women for travelling and in the country. Tweed for women's coats and skirts and 'Ulster' coats was usually of smoother surface and inconspicuous patterning.

Cashmere, nun's veiling, delaine and, after 1912 or thereabouts, wool georgette, were thinner woollen stuffs used for women's dresses.

Many different kinds of muslin and lawn, plain, flower-printed or embroidered, voile, linen, piqué and organdie were in fashion. Piqué and linen were used for tennis skirts and heavy linen for coats and skirts and 'dustcoats'.

Washable silks such as thick, natural-coloured shantung and surah were in great demand for women's coats and skirts. Men's 'tropical' suits, made of such materials, were very occasionally worn in England.

Coloured shantung was also used for women's dresses. Satin, velvet (including the soft, silky 'panne'), taffetas, glacé silk, chiffon, net, foulard, brocade and watered silk were among the fashionable materials. After 1912 silk georgette and the 'grained' satin known as charmeuse were introduced. Flower-printed chiffon and ninon were used for evening and summer dresses.

Lace, real or machine-made, was used for dresses, blouses, edgings, insertions, sleeves, over-dresses and lined summer coats.

The foundations and linings used for the last two items were of satin, jap silk, taffetas, moiré or glacé silk.

Colours for men's suits and overcoats and for the majority of women's coats and skirts and outer wraps for daytime were neutral and subdued, and both sexes used suitings with stripes or small checks, but women sometimes wore such colours as deep red or purple, rust-colour, sapphire blue or soft green. With the vogue for pastel colours, in the first nine years of the century, women's coats and coats and skirts could also be in these tints.

Lilac, 'heliotrope' or mauve, and light shades of pink, yellow, blue and green, pale rose madder and terracotta, white, cream, parchment-colour and fawn, a light brown known as 'feuille morte', generally made in satin, sand-colour, grey and oyster or pearl-colour were among the delicate hues employed for dresses until 1909. Blouses were generally in neutral shades but could be coloured.

These colours did not disappear in the remaining five years of the time now being considered, but the influence of the great French dressmakers, who favoured stronger, more Oriental tints, introduced more deep and brilliant colour. Black and brown were used a great deal as contrast for collars, cuffs, belts and accessories. Black dresses, coats and coats and skirts were at the height of elegance.

Embroidery, appliqué and handwork generally in the first years of the century were exquisitely done and lavishly used. Minute tucks, narrow ribbon or ruching gathered on in the outline of a pattern, tiny beads applied in the same way, lace insertion and edging and the use of miniature buttons with finely-worked loops or buttonholes were all characteristic of the first eight or nine years of the century. Chemises, drawers and petticoats were made in lawn and cambric, lace-edged and embroidered in many ways, broderie anglaise being very popular, but silk underwear in pale colours, also embroidered or edged with lace, was beginning to enter the fashion. In the last five years, from 1909 to 1914, ornament was inclined to be bolder in design, and much use was made of beading, sequins, fringe and other trimming in the dress of older women.

Jewellery and Accessories: Men wore small jewelled tiepins, shirt studs and links set with enamel or such stones as agate or onyx, and occasionally pearls in evening studs. Watch-chains had not given place to wrist-watches in the early part of the century, but they were in fashion among younger men by 1912.

Brooches were worn by women at the base of the throat, often in the jabot or fall of lace put on as a finish to the high, boned collar. They were also worn on the corsage of afternoon and evening dresses, sometimes to hold flowers in place. They were of medium size and delicate design, not too conspicuous.

For the very well-to-do, the 'dog-collar' necklace, of pearls or other precious stones, was worn for formal evening occasions. Other necklaces were 'lavallières', groups of small jewelled ornaments designed to be set in a row on the front of a thin gold chain, the ornaments resting just below the collar-bones; gold chains of the same length supporting lockets or pendants; longer chains holding pendants which hung a little below the waist or held a watch or a tiny purse of gold or silver mesh to be tucked into the belt. Beads were not usual, but short necklaces of coral, amber, turquoise, crystal and other semi-precious stones could be worn.

The combs and slides so necessary to the piled-up coiffures were often jewelled and generally made of tortoiseshell.

Earrings were studs or drops, not conspicuous, and not worn by young girls.

Rings held precious stones in delicate settings, but again were neither large nor ostentatious.

'Curb' bracelets of thick gold links, rolled like twisted cord, with small padlocks, were very much in fashion, also gold bangles, sometimes set with jewels, and chain bracelets of gold or silver with small 'charms' attached.

Miniature pencils, notebooks, scent bottles, smelling-salt bottles and cases for needles, scissors and cotton, all very tiny, were put together on silver rings or chains to be worn at the waist until after the change in the fashion was established by 1910.

Gloves were almost invariably worn out of doors by women, but men sometimes carried theirs. Women's long kid gloves were often unbuttoned and slipped back over the hands but not entirely removed at afternoon tea. They were also worn by women with evening dress for dancing, though in many illustrations of the period they are seen without their gloves. Men kept their white gloves on for dancing. Silk gloves, long or short, in white or pale colours were worn with summer dresses.

The cigarette case became a usual accessory for men at this time, but women did not carry cigarettes and seldom smoked them.

Folding fans were carried in the evening, but became less fashionable after 1911–12 and were hardly seen by 1914 except that some older women still carried them.

Purses were sometimes worn in a pocket under the dress, attached by webbing straps round the waist, in the opening years of the century.

Gauze or chiffon scarves were worn round the shoulders with women's evening dress.

From 1907 onwards large silver or gold mesh purses or beaded handbags could be carried and after 1909–10 handbags of leather, tapestry or silk became an ordinary part of women's equipment, though there were many who still only carried a purse.

Umbrellas were covered in silk, generally in black, dark grey or navy blue for women, black for men, and had long, thin ferrules. Parasols could be very ornate, their pale-coloured silk covers having lace insertion, tulle frills or fringe to trim them, or made of natural-coloured shantung with a green lining as a protection from the sun. These had bamboo sticks, straight or hooked, but more decorative parasols had tops or handles of ivory, flowered porcelain or silver.

Real or artificial flowers were worn on the bodice of the dress in the evening and real ones on the lapel of the coat or coat and skirt or tucked into the belt of afternoon dresses until about 1910.

Muffs were carried in winter, of average size in the first five years of the period, but larger after this and very large from 1912 to 1914. Small neck-pieces of fur were seen, but long, wide fur stoles were most frequently worn.

Long feather boas were very fashionable until about 1912. Until 1910 shorter boas of chiffon or tulle were also worn, just long enough to lie on the chest, with long tassels or ribbons hanging down in front.

XV.7. Woman's Dress. 1905

Hair: The hair is drawn up from the forehead into a pompadour and pinned at the crown of the head. The hair at the back is drawn up not too tightly to the same point, where all the ends are wound into a chignon.

Garments: The dress is of mignonette green crêpe silk. The bodice, seen from the back, has a wide collar coming down to a point between the shoulder-blades. The high-collared chemisette of cream-coloured net has a frill at the top and is finished at the back by a small matching bow of satin ribbon. The upper sleeves are made in large puffs, and finished by draped bands just above the elbows. Close-fitting lower sleeves are attached, ending in wrist-frills of cream net. There is a wide waist-belt of the same stuff as the dress, coming to a deep point in front and a shorter point at the back. The collar is edged with embroidery of white flowers with yellow centres and dark green leaves and has a frilled border of the same silk as the dress. This ornament is repeated in two rows above the hem of the flared, flowing skirt.

Jewellery: Gold earrings set with beryls are worn.

XV.8. Woman in Coat and Skirt. 1911

Hair: This is parted in the centre (unseen) with puffs at the sides.

Headdress: The dark blue velvet hat is worn well down on the head and has a rounded crown showing above the upturned brim. A pale grey ostrich plume curves over the right side of the brim, with another at the back.

Garments: The coat and skirt are of dark blue silk. The coat has a high waist-line, fits closely over the hips and is longer at the back than in front. It has a cross-over fastening, with one button set above the waist-line. There are wide triangular revers but no collar. The plain three-quarter-length sleeves have wrist-frills of ivory net. The net chemisette has a high frilled collar. The skirt is plain and straight. The stockings are of black silk.

Footwear: The black suède court shoes have pointed toes and low, shaped heels.

Accessories: The long gloves are of pale grey suède and the silver-framed handbag of blue tapestry decorated with white flowers. A black silk umbrella is carried.

XV.9. Country Woman. 1912

Hair: The hair in front is parted in the centre, smoothed down on the temples, then turned over and puffed out a little at the sides. It is taken back, almost covering the ears, and wound into a bun at a half-way level with the hair covering the back of the head.

Garments: The dress of striped blue and white cotton is plainly cut, with a round flat collar and front-fastening bodice. The sleeves end at the elbow and the skirt ends just above the shoes. A white cotton apron, with a bib and shoulder-straps, also a narrow frill round the hem, almost covers the dress. The stockings are of black cashmere or cotton.

Footwear: The shoes are of black leather, with flat heels and laced-up fronts.

Accessories: A large kitchen bowl is held in the hands.

XV.10. Man's Suit. 1913

Hair: The hair is brushed back without a parting and is short at the back.

Garments: The lounge suit is of blue-grey flecked tweed. The jacket and waistcoat are longer than those of today. The double collar is starched and worn with a white shirt and blue knotted tie. The trousers are creased and end in turn-ups well above the shoes.

Footwear: The laced shoes are of black leather.

Accessories: The man carries a lighted cigarette.

XV.11. Girl in Blouse and Skirt. 1913

Hair: The hair is parted in the centre and taken back into a chignon which is in two rolls, one above the other. Curled locks are arranged on the forehead and one over each ear.

Garments: The blouse of pale mauve crêpe de Chine has a wide, rounded neckline edged with a frill of its own stuff. The long full sleeves are caught in by a narrow band of the mauve crêpe de Chine on the upper arms and deeper bands, with wrist-frills, form the cuffs. The skirt of black cloth fits closely at the hips and widens gradually to a moderate flare at the hem.

Footwear: The stockings are of grey silk and the court shoes of black suède have buckles in front and shaped heels of moderate height.

Accessories: The girl carries a gardening trug with cut flowers in it in her left hand and a pair of sécateurs in the right.

XV.12. Man's Morning Suit. 1913

Hair: The hair is brushed back from the forehead and cut short at the back.

Headdress: The grey top hat is much like those of today.

Garments: The black morning coat is fastened by one button above the waist and slopes away to coat-tails ending at the back of the knees. The wing collar is worn with a large black satin cravat. The waistcoat is of pale grey cloth. The black-and-grey striped trousers have a crease and come well down over the shoes.

Footwear: The black patent leather boots have grey cloth tops, buttoned at the sides.

Jewellery and Accessories: The gloves are of pale grey suède. A pearl pin is worn in the centre of the cravat. A walking-stick is carried in the left hand.

XV.13. Woman's Formal Dress. 1914

Hair: The hair, almost hidden by the hat, is drawn back and put up in 'beehive' style.

Headdress: The hat of black satin has a rounded crown, and a brim turned up at the back, where it stands above the level of the crown and slopes down to a forward peak over the right eyebrow. Two curled, ivory ostrich plumes are set high at the back.

Garments: The gown is of aquamarine 'charmeuse' satin. The cross-over bodice has a cape effect and is tucked into the wide belt of the same stuff as the dress. The cross-over décolletage is bordered with bands of sable-coloured fur which also trim the ends of the close-fitting three-quarter-length sleeves. The skirt is draped round the body from the waist and is open on the left side to a point above the ankle. The end of the drapery at the back forms a small train. A wide band of the fur is draped diagonally round the skirt. The silk stockings match the dress.

Footwear: The satin shoes match the dress and have paste ornaments on the fronts, long, pointed toes and 'baby' Louis heels.

Accessories: Pearl and diamond drop earrings and white kid gloves are worn. A sable muff and a silver mesh bag are carried.

XV.14. Woman's Evening Gown. 1914

Hair: The hair is parted on the right and brought across the head in undulating waves. The ears are covered by waves at the sides. There is no separate chignon, but the hair from the top and sides is wound in a long, vertical roll (unseen) down the back of the head, pinned on the right.

Headdress: A band of gold ribbon is fastened round the head, and a pale yellow aigrette attached over the right side of the forehead.

Garments: The sheath gown of pale yellow satin ends in a short train. The over-tunic of yellow georgette has a draped bodice edged at the oval neckline and on the shoulders with yellow marabou. This also borders the flared hem, which is wired to stand out and is longer at the back than at the front. The narrow belt is of gold fabric.

Footwear: The evening slippers are of yellow satin.

Jewellery and Accessories: A necklace of small gold beads and long white kid gloves are worn. The 'Dorothy' bag is of yellow silk, trimmed with gilt beads and a gilt tassel.

AUTHORITIES CONSULTED

BOOKS ON COSTUME

Le Costume chez les Peuples Anciens et Modernes. F. Hottenroth.
Iranische Felsreliefs. Friedrich Sarre and Ernst Herzfeld.
A History of Costume. Kohler and von Sichart.
Kostumkunder für Sammler. Hans Mutzel.
Bekleidungskunst und Mode. Max von Boehn.
Le Costume—Antiquité—Moyen-Age. Jacques Ruppert.
Costumes of the Greeks and Romans. Thomas Hope.
History of British Costume. J. R. Planché.
Costume in England. F. W. Fairholt.
Costume through the Ages. James Laver.
Costume of the Western World (The Tudors to Louis XIII). James Laver.
Fashion. James Laver.
17th and 18th Century Dress. James Laver.
19th Century Costume. James Laver.
The Fashionable Lady in the 19th Century. C. H. Gibbs-Smith.
The Art of English Costume. C. Willett Cunnington.
The Perfect Lady. C. Willett Cunnington.
Englishwomen's Dress in the 19th Century. C. Willett Cunnington.
Handbook of English Costume in the XVIth Century. C. W. and P. Cunnington.
Handbook of English Costume in the XVIIth Century. C. W. and P. Cunnington.
Handbook of English Costume in the XVIIIth Century. C. W. and P. Cunnington.
Costume in Pictures. Phillis Cunnington.
The Woman in Fashion. Doris Langley Moore.
Costume and Fashion, vols. I, II, III and IV. Herbert Norris.
British Costume during nineteen Centuries. Mrs Charles Ashdown.
A History of Fashion. Douglas Gorsline.
Ancient Assyrian, Babylonian and Persian Dress. Mary Houston.
Ancient Greek, Roman and Byzantine Dress. Mary Houston.
Mediaeval Costume in England and France. Mary Houston.
Dress Design for Artists and Dressmakers. Talbot Hughes.
The Cut of Men's Clothes, 1680–1900. Nora Waugh.
Women's and Children's Garment Design. W. H. Hulme.
Historic Costume for the Stage. Lucy Barton.
English Fashion. Alison Settle.

BOOKS ON ART

New Kingdom Art. Cyril Aldred.
Roman and Etruscan Painting. Arturo Stenico.
Pompeii and Herculaneum. Marcel Brion.
Larousse Encyclopaedia of Byzantine and Mediaeval Art. René Huyghe.
Byzantine Art. David Talbot Rice.
The Art of the Byzantine Era. David Talbot Rice.
Romanesque Painting. Juan Ainaud.
Larousse Encyclopaedia of Renaissance and Baroque Art. René Huyghe.
Renaissance Painting. Franco Russoli.
The Horizon Book of the Renaissance. J. H. Plumb.
Les Crayons Français du XVIème Siècle. Leonard Hazan.
Masterpieces of the Tate and National Galleries.
National Gallery Illustrations (Continental Schools).
Art Treasures of the World. Paul Hamlyn.
The Masters Series.
'Discovering Art' Series. Editor: Hugh Elwes.
Seventeenth Century Painting. Raymond Cogniat.
Eighteenth Century Painting. Vassily Photiades.
Hogarth. Anthony Bertram.
French Engraving of the 18th Century. Editor: Archibald Younger.
Thomas Rowlandson. 'The Studio'.
A Microcosm of London. T. Rowlandson and A. C. Pugin.

OTHER ILLUSTRATED WORKS

The Egyptians. J. Gardner Wilkinson.
The Temple Dictionary of the Bible. W. Ewing and J. E. H. Thomson.
The Bible as History. Werner Keller.
Ur of the Chaldees. Leonard Woolley.
Dictionary of Classical Antiquities. Oskar Seyffert.
Dictionary of Classical Antiquities. Anthony Rich.
Dictionary of Classical Antiquities. William Smith.
Women in Antiquity. Charles Seltmann.
England under the Regency. John Ashton.
The Dawn of the 19th Century in England. John Ashton.
Volumes of Punch, 1878, 1889–1907.
St Nicholas Magazine, 1884, 1896, 1910–11.
'The Stage' Year Book, 1912–13.
Illustrated English Social History. G. M. Trevelyan.

MUSEUMS AND ART GALLERIES VISITED

The British Museum.
The Victoria and Albert Museum.
The London Museum.
Sir John Soane's Museum.
The Wallace Collection.
The National Gallery.
The National Portrait Gallery.
The Tate Gallery.